D1256762

AMERICAN EDUCATION

Its Men,

Ideas,

and

Institutions

Advisory Editor

Lawrence A. Cremin
Frederick A. P. Barnard Professor of Education
Teachers College, Columbia University

AMERICAN EDUCATION: *Its Men, Ideas, and Institutions* presents selected works of thought and scholarship that have long been out of print or otherwise unavailable. Inevitably, such works will include particular ideas and doctrines that have been outmoded or superseded by more recent research. Nevertheless, all retain their place in the literature, having influenced educational thought and practice in their own time and having provided the basis for subsequent scholarship.

THE HISTORY OF
BROWN UNIVERSITY

1764–1914

BY

WALTER C. BRONSON, Litt.D.

ARNO PRESS & THE NEW YORK TIMES

*New York * 1971*

WILLIAM MADISON RANDALL LIBRARY UNC AT WILMINGTON

Reprint Edition 1971 by Arno Press Inc.

Reprinted from a copy in
  The Wesleyan University Library

American Education:
  Its Men, Ideas, and Institutions - Series II
ISBN for complete set: 0-405-03600-0
See last pages of this volume for titles

Manufactured in the United States of America

Library of Congress Cataloging in Publication Data

Bronson, Walter Cochrane, 1862-1928.
    The history of Brown University, 1764-1914.
    (American education: its men, ideas, and
institutions. Series II)
    Bibliography: p.
    1. Brown University--History. I. Title.
II. Series.
LD638.B7 1971   378.745'2   75-165708
ISBN 0-405-03697-3

LD638
.B7
1971

137805

THE HISTORY OF
BROWN UNIVERSITY

THE HISTORY OF
BROWN UNIVERSITY

1764–1914

BY

WALTER C. BRONSON, Litt.D.

PROFESSOR OF ENGLISH LITERATURE

PROVIDENCE

PUBLISHED BY THE UNIVERSITY

1914

COPYRIGHT, 1914, BY BROWN UNIVERSITY

D. B. UPDIKE, THE MERRYMOUNT PRESS, BOSTON

PREFACE

THIS history of Brown University is intended chiefly for its graduates, and some of the contents will have little interest for other readers. The effort has been to portray the university in all its aspects—not merely as a gallery of academic worthies, or an educational experiment station, or a stage where men now grave and reverend disported themselves in thoughtless youth, or an athletic and social club, but as all these and more. Even to graduates, therefore, some parts of the narrative will appeal less strongly than others; but it seemed more essential to give a just account of the university as a whole than to rivet the attention of every reader on every page.

The book is based almost entirely on original sources, a list of which will be found in the Appendix. In quotations from these the spelling, capitalization, punctuation, etc., have been reproduced as accurately as possible: this method helps the reader to get the flavor of times past, and is peculiarly worth while in the history of an educational institution because it illustrates the use of English by Corporation, Faculty, and students.

It is a pleasure to record my thanks for aid received from graduates and friends of the university. Professor William MacDonald, the Rev. Dr. Henry M. King, and Professor Walter G. Everett, of the Committee on the Academic Celebration, read the manuscript and made helpful criticisms. Mr. Corne-

[v]

lius S. Sweetland, treasurer of Brown University, gave certain information in advance of the publication of his report for the last fiscal year. Professor Harry L. Koopman, librarian of the university, Mr. George P. Winship, librarian of the John Carter Brown Library, Mr. Frederick T. Guild, university registrar, Mrs. Louise P. Bates, university archivist, and Mr. Howard M. Chapin, librarian of the Rhode Island Historical Society, afforded every facility for consulting the documents in their keeping. The librarians of the Rhode Island State Library, the Newport Historical Society, Princeton University, the University of Pennsylvania, the College of Charleston, and Crozer Theological Seminary, the secretaries of the Corporations of Princeton University and Columbia University, and Professor Weldon T. Myers, of the University of Virginia, rendered aid in various ways. The Rev. Arthur W. Smith, until recently librarian of the New England Baptist Library in Boston, generously put at my disposal the results of his own researches into the early history of the university. Mr. Franklin B. Dexter, librarian of Yale University, furnished a transcript of the letter printed on page 14, which settles a long disputed question about Ezra Stiles's plan for a college in Rhode Island. Mrs. Sarah K. Birckhead, of New York, contributed a transcript of the important letter printed on page 23. Mr. Theodore F. Green, of Providence, allowed me to examine his large collection of leaflets, pamphlets, and books connected with the history of the university. Mr.

Henry R. Chace, of Providence, presented a set of his maps of Providence in 1770. Mr. George Henderson, of Philadelphia, gave me the use of unpublished letters by President Manning and Morgan Edwards to his ancestor, the Rev. Dr. Samuel Jones. Mr. H. T. Cook, of Greenville, South Carolina, sent copies of letters by Presidents Manning and Maxcy to Southern clergymen. The late Rev. James C. Seagrave, '45, the Rev. Henry I. Coe, '46, President James B. Angell, '49, Mr. Alexander J. Robert, '49, the Hon. Richard Olney, '56, and the Rev. Dr. Henry S. Burrage, '61, supplied reminiscences of their undergraduate days. Several of my colleagues on the Faculty aided me: Professors John H. Appleton and William C. Poland, by their intimate knowledge of the university through many years; Professors Nathaniel F. Davis, Albert G. Harkness, Walter G. Everett, Francis G. Allinson, and Raymond C. Archibald, by statements relating to the history of their departments; Professor Edmund B. Delabarre, by information about the history of athletics at Brown; and Professor Albert K. Potter, by suggestions about matter and style. The editors of *Memories of Brown* and *The Brown Alumni Monthly* freely opened their pages for pillage. My greatest obligation is to my wife, who revised the whole manuscript with minutest care, prepared the copy for the printer, gave invaluable aid in proof-reading, and made the index.

W. C. B.

Cuttyhunk, Massachusetts
September 12, 1914

This volume has been written to commemorate the celebration of the one hundred and fiftieth anniversary of the founding of Brown University, and is published under the general supervision of the Committee in charge of the Celebration. The Committee, however, assume no responsibility for the statements of the text. The author is alone responsible both for facts and for expressions of opinion

CONTENTS

[ix]

CONTENTS

THE HISTORY OF
BROWN UNIVERSITY

CHAPTER I

THE FOUNDING

THE BAPTISTS AND THE COLLEGE : RHODE ISLAND AND THE
COLLEGE : THE STRUGGLE OVER THE CHARTER : COMPARISON
WITH OTHER COLLEGE CHARTERS

ONE hundred and fifty years ago Brown University was
founded by the Baptists of America, in the colony of
Rhode Island and Providence Plantations. For a century
and a half, while political, economic, and social conditions
in the New World have undergone many and sometimes
turbulent changes, it has continued its quiet work of educating American youth for private and public life. The
university has grown with the growth of the country. The
numbers of its Faculty and students have greatly increased,
its buildings and all its material resources have multiplied,
its courses of study have widened and deepened, its methods have changed with changing conditions; but through
all it has in the main held fast to the ideal expressed in these
words of its charter : "Institutions for liberal Education are
highly beneficial to Society, by forming the rising Generation to Virtue Knowledge & useful Literature & thus preserving in the Community a Succession of Men duly qualify'd for discharging the Offices of Life with usefulness
& reputation. . . . Into this Liberal & Catholic Institution
shall never be admitted any Religious Tests but on the Contrary all the Members hereof shall for ever enjoy full free
Absolute and uninterrupted Liberty of Conscience."

As a result of faithful work done in this spirit, Brown
University, like its sister institutions, has from the first been
a powerful influence for good in church and state and home,
both in its own community and in distant parts. It has

[1]

supplied the denomination which founded it with leaders; it has sent missionaries to the far East and the far West; it has given to the nation and the world jurists, statesmen, and diplomats; it has graduated a few men to win fame in literature and art, and many to become eminent in education, theology, medicine, law, and business; and it has enriched the private lives of thousands who in turn have been centers of higher life for thousands more.

The history of such an institution is inspiring, but it is for the most part unpretentious, addressing the mind and not the eye. The record must therefore be written quietly if it is to be written truly, and it should be read in the same spirit. From time to time, indeed, we shall be in touch with stirring events in the life of the state and the nation; but these pages must be filled chiefly with other things: the material growth of the college, the development of the curriculum, the personality of members of the Corporation and Faculty, the intellectual and social life of the students; in brief, all the academic influences that go to the shaping of men and their preparation for right living.

It was not an accident that Brown University was founded when and where it was, and under the leadership of the Baptists.

In the seventh decade of the eighteenth century the tide of life in the English colonies of America was running strong and steadily rising higher. Forest and field had been subdued to the uses of man. Danger from the Indians, except along the frontier, was a thing of the past. The recent French and Indian War had freed the colonists from fear of their northern neighbors and made them realize their strength. Their numbers had increased to nearly three millions; and while the population was still mostly agricultural, many towns and a few cities had grown up and become centers of thought and action. Agriculture was profitable; manufactures were yet in their infancy, but commerce was extending on land and sea; the wealth of the country was considerable, and was well distributed. In short, a century and a half had settled a hardy transplanted stock deep into the soil; its roots were spreading, its sap was rising, and new shoots were springing forth in ever increasing numbers. The great result of this expanding energy was to be the political independence of the country: but in a land where education had always been highly esteemed, it was inevitable that the growing life should show itself partly in the founding of colleges; and at this period it was equally certain that the new colleges would be established chiefly by religious denominations and largely with a view to educating young men for the ministry. In the first hundred years of English colonization three colleges had been founded in America —Harvard College in 1636, William and Mary College in 1693, Yale College in 1701. During four decades of the eighteenth century no fewer than twelve colleges were established, including the College of New Jersey (now Princeton University) in 1746, King's College (now Columbia University) in 1754, the University of Pennsylvania in 1755, Rutgers College in 1766, Dartmouth College in 1769, and the College of Charleston in 1785. Midway in this period of college-planting came Brown University, in 1764.

Most of these institutions were controlled by religious bodies: Harvard and Yale by the Congregationalists; the College of New Jersey by the Presbyterians; the University of Pennsylvania, King's College, and William and Mary College by the Episcopalians; Rutgers College by the Reformed Dutch Church. It was natural that the Baptists also should desire a college of their own. It does not appear, however, as has often been alleged, that their need was urgent because of religious tests at the existing colleges or disabilities attaching to Baptist students. At Harvard no religious tests for students had ever been countenanced; and some of the Hollis scholarships, in accordance with a provision of the donor, an English Baptist, were given by preference to Baptist students. At Yale the temper was more severe, yet President Clap could say in print in 1766, "Persons of all Denominations of Protestants are allowed the Advantage of an Education here, and no Inquiry has been made, at their Admission or afterwards, about their particular Sentiments in Religion." The charter of King's College forbade the authorities to make any laws which should "exclude any Person of any religious Denomination whatever, from equal Liberty and Advantage of Education, or from any of the Degrees, Liberties, Privileges, Benefits, or Immunities of the said College, on Account of his particular Tenets in Matters of Religion." In the University of Pennsylvania no religious tests were allowed. The second charter of the College of New Jersey, granted in 1748, stipulated that the laws of the college should not exclude "any Person of any religious Denomination, whatsoever from free and equal Liberty and Advantage of Education, or from any of the Liberties Privileges or Immunities of the said College on Account of his or their being of a religious profession different from the said Trustees of the said College." It is clear, therefore, that Baptist students could obtain a good education without being made by college authorities to suffer for their creed.

Why, then, should a religious body so small and poor as were the Baptists undertake to found a college? It may be replied that prejudice against an unpopular sect doubtless made itself felt in college halls, in spite of charters and rules, and rendered the life of Baptist students uncomfortable. But even if this be granted, it does not furnish a sufficient motive. That must be sought deeper, in the condition of the Baptist denomination at this time.

During the first hundred years of its existence in the New World the denomination spread slowly, but over a considerable area. Beginning with churches in Providence and Newport before the middle of the seventeenth century, it soon took root in Boston and other parts of Massachusetts (including what is now Maine), had planted churches in Pennsylvania, New Jersey, and South Carolina by 1700, and early in the next century gained foothold in Connecticut, New York, Delaware, Virginia, and North Carolina. In the sectarian warfare then raging the Baptists thus had a long firing-line, but it was very thin. In 1740 there were but twenty-one Baptist churches in all New England, eleven of them in Rhode Island; the other strongest centers were Pennsylvania and New Jersey, which had about a dozen churches, made up in part of Baptist immigrants from Wales. Then came the Great Awakening of 1740. The Baptists held rather aloof from it. They shared, nevertheless, in the general quickening; and in subsequent years they gained considerable numbers by the accession of entire churches of the so-called "New Lights," who in consequence of the revival had separated from the more conservative Congregationalists. The denomination now entered upon a period of rapid growth, although its numbers were for many years relatively small. In 1768 the Baptist churches in New England numbered sixty-nine, more than treble the number in 1740; and by 1790 they had increased fourfold, numbering two hundred and sixty-six and having a membership of more than seventeen thousand; while in all North America their membership was sixty-five thousand.

[5]

When a Baptist college was first talked of, in 1762, the denomination was still in the earlier stages of this remarkable growth. Dr. Ezra Stiles, a Congregationalist clergyman, estimated in 1760 that the total Baptist population in New England was twenty-two thousand, which number would be considerably increased by adding the Baptists in the Middle and Southern States. At most, however, they were one of the smaller sects; but their leaders evidently felt thus early the thrill of a larger life and had some sense of a great future. This feeling was strongest in the Middle States, where the Baptist churches had a fair degree of union through the Philadelphia Association, which in 1762 embraced twenty-nine churches in Pennsylvania, New Jersey, New York, Maryland, Delaware, and Virginia. Among these leaders a great need had begun to make itself felt, the need of an educated ministry. The mass of the Baptist laymen were poor and ignorant, and most of the pastors had little learning. Backus, the historian of the Baptists, writing to an English friend in 1765 or 1766, said: "One grand objection made use of against Believer's Baptism, has been that none but ignorant and illiterate men have embraced the Baptist sentiments. And there was so much color for it as this, namely, that ten years ago there were but two Baptist ministers in all New England who had what is called a liberal education; and they were not clear in the doctrines of grace." Again, writing in defence of the Baptists in 1768, he said: "Several who have formerly sent their sons to college have been disappointed, as the clergy have found means to draw them over to their party; which has discouraged others from sending their sons. And the Baptists in general have been so much abused, by those who boast of their *Learning*, that it is not strange if many were prejudiced against such men." These conditions must be changed if the Baptist denomination was to work out its destiny under God; and to get an educated ministry the Baptists must have schools and colleges of their own: first, because Baptist youth, living for four years in a college atmosphere strongly charged with influences hostile to their faith, might cease to be Baptists or at least become lukewarm; and, secondly, because many Baptists were indifferent or even averse to higher education, and could best be won over by means of institutions controlled by their own sect.

In the records of the Philadelphia Association is this entry for October 5, 1756: "Concluded to Raise a sum of Money towards the encouragement of a Latin Grammar School for the promotion of learning amongst us under the care of Brother Isaac Eaton and the inspection of our brethren Abel Morgan, Isaac Stelle, Abel Griffith, and Peter Peterson Vanhorn." Thus was founded the first Baptist academy. It was opened in Hopewell, New Jersey, where Mr. Eaton was pastor, and ran very successfully for eleven years. Among its pupils were James Manning, first President of Brown University; Samuel Jones, who gave the college charter its final form, and who was invited to be the second president; Hezekiah Smith and Samuel Stillman, eloquent Baptist preachers; Isaac Skillman, member of the Boston Committee on Grievances in pre-Revolutionary days; and David Howell, the first professor in Brown University.

The success of Hopewell Academy paved the way for a greater enterprise, the establishment of a Baptist college. Among some papers left by Howell is one containing this statement: "Many of the Churches being supplied with able Pastors from Mr Eatons Academy & thus being convinced by experience of the great usefullness of human

Literature to more thoroughly furnish the Man of God for the most important work of the gospel ministry the hands of the Philadelphian Association were strengthend & their Hearts encouraged to extend their designs of promoting literature in the Society by erecting on some suitable part of this Continent a College or University which should be principally under the Direction & Government of the Baptists." There is no record in the minutes of the association of any formal action looking to the founding of a college; but the tradition is that the matter was discussed at the annual meeting in October, 1762, and some plan of procedure agreed upon. Backus, in his second volume, published in 1784, says: "The Philadelphia Association obtained such an acquaintance with our affairs, as to bring them to an apprehension that it was practicable and expedient to erect a college in the Colony of Rhode-Island, under the chief direction of the Baptists; wherein education might be promoted, and superior learning obtained, free of any sectarian religious tests. And Mr. James Manning, who took his first degree in New-Jersey college in September, 1762, was esteemed a suitable leader in this important work." The historian does not say in what year the association arrived at this "apprehension." But the Rev. Morgan Edwards, who was moderator of the association in 1762, and according to tradition "the first mover" in the project, made a more explicit statement; in his *Materials for a History of the Baptists in Rhode Island*, he said, speaking of the college: "The first mover for it in 1762 was laughed at as a projector of a thing impracticable. Nay, many of the Baptists themselves discouraged the design (prophesying evil to the churches in case it should take place) from an unhappy prejudice against learning; and threatened (not only nonconcurrence but) opposition. Nevertheless a young

Jersey-man (who is now at the head of the institution) went to Rhode-island government and made the design known."

Nearly a year elapsed, however, between the meeting of the association and Manning's visit to Rhode Island. It was not until July, 1763, when his vessel touched at Newport on the way to Halifax, Nova Scotia, that the future president "made the design known." The reasons for the delay and for the final choice of this colony as the site of the college are given in the Howell paper already quoted, which goes on to say: "At first Some of the Southern Colonies seemed to bid fairest to answer their purpose there not being so many Colleges in those Colonies as the northerly but the [several words illegible] northerly Colonies having been visited by some of the Association who informed them of the great increase of the Baptist Societies of late in those parts & that Rhode Island Government had no publick School or College in it & was originally settled by persons of the Baptist persuasion & a greater part of the Government remaining so still: there was no longer any doubt but that was the most suitable place to carry the design into execution." Edwards emphasizes the legal aspect of the case, saying, "The reason of his attempt in this province was (as has been observed), That legislature is here chiefly in the hands of Baptists, and therefore the likeliest place to have a baptist college established by law."

In accordance with the clear evidence of contemporary documents, stress has thus far been laid upon the part which Baptists of the Middle States played in founding the college. But Brown University is neither an exotic nor a denominational preserve; it has always been in a true sense what it was first called, "Rhode Island College," owing its legal existence to the colonial legislature, built up largely by the wealth and culture of the colony and state, and in return giving much of its energy to educating the sons and daughters of the community in which it is placed. We shall see how well prepared that community was to receive and to carry forward the Baptists' plan for a new college.

When the young graduate of New Jersey College set foot on Rhode Island soil in the summer of 1763, he came to a region already rich, for a new world, in human interest and the elements of higher civilization. A century and a quarter had passed since Roger Williams, fleeing from the "unco guid," had paddled down the Seekonk to the site of Providence, and William Coddington and John Clarke had founded Newport. During that time there had been many a tempest in the little teapot of Rhode Island and Providence Plantations. The afflicted and the eccentric from various quarters, Antinomians, Quakers, "Seekers," and Anabaptists of all stripes, had lived here together in tumultuous amity, attacking one another's heresies but steadily respecting everybody's right to preach heresy without restraint from the civil power. At Portsmouth had resided for a time that extreme individualist Samuel Gorton —in comparison with whom Roger Williams was a conservative—and Anne Hutchinson, that "new woman" born out of due time. A little later many Quakers, scourged out of Boston, found safety in Newport and other parts of the colony; from which, however, they went forth again and again to face "the enemies of the Lord" in Massachusetts. The founder of the Quakers had himself been in Newport in 1762, and Roger Williams rowed down from Providence to refute his errors in the bloodless warfare of debate; Fox had departed, but his associates fought for him the battle of the Lord in the Quaker meeting-house. Yet the principle of "soul liberty" had done more even than the presence of these strong characters to make the colony famous and its soil almost sacred. "For the first time in human history," writes the historian Richman, "State had wholly been dissociated from Church in a commonwealth not utopian but real."

To this age of small beginnings and great principles there had succeeded, in the half-century before Manning's arrival, a period of growing prosperity in material things; and this wealth had brought, especially to Newport, a considerable degree of culture.

The wealth of Newport came from the sea. She and her neighbor towns built staunch little craft and sent them forth, some to capture rich prizes from the enemies of Great Britain, others to carry on profitable trade. Vessels laden with New England rum set sail for the coast of Guinea, exchanged their cargo for slaves, sold them at Barbadoes, and brought home molasses from which to make more rum. In addition to this traffic over the "triangular course," there was a certain amount of general commerce with the Mediterranean countries and the Levant. The great Newport merchants, the sea lords of their day, were of various nations, thus giving the little seaport town a cosmopolitan air. In addition to the Wantons, the Browns, the Hazards, the Whipples, and others of Rhode Island stock, says Richman, "the Redwoods were there from Antigua, the De Courcys from Ireland, the Grants and Edward Scott (grand-uncle of Sir Walter) from Scotland, and the Bretts from Germany," besides Huguenots from the Carolinas, and Jews from Spain and Portugal. These sea-traders were characterized by largeness of view and generous tastes. They built themselves spacious dwelling-houses and country villas, furnished with comfort and some degree of elegance, and surrounded by gardens. The social amenities among them and their families were cultivated by clubs of various sorts and by teas, balls, and occasional plays. Love of good literature showed itself in the growth of private libraries and in the opening of the famous Redwood Library in 1750. Education in Rhode Island as a whole was backward; but Newport had a schoolhouse by 1685, and in 1710 granted permission for keeping a Latin school in a part of it. A printing-press was set up in 1727 by James Franklin, who five years later began to publish the *Gazette*, the first newspaper in Rhode Island.

While these and other elements of culture in "the Golden Age of Newport" were due primarily to wealth and leisure and to the temper of the leading men, the finer spirit of the community had been quickened by the sojourn within it of a distinguished visitor from England. In 1729 Dean Berkeley came to Newport on his way to found a college in the Bermudas, and there awaited the arrival of the endowment promised him by the English prime minister. He waited nearly three years, and went away at last empty handed; but he left behind him a rich legacy of lofty thought and generous culture. The accomplished European gentleman and divine, the friend of Addison, Steele, Swift, and Pope, the brilliant idealistic philosopher, entered sympathetically into the life of the colonial town. He built a country house near the sea, and composed there some of the most charming of his philosophic dialogues; he preached occasionally in the Episcopal church; and he became the friend of all the leading men. They were not unworthy of his friendship, including in their number William Wanton, governor, Daniel Updike, attorney-general and student of history, William Ellery, father of a signer of the Declaration of Independence, Samuel Johnson, afterward president of King's College, and Henry Collins, patron of art, who has been called the Lorenzo de'Medici of Newport. It was during Berkeley's stay, and very likely at his instance, that these and other men with him formed the Philosophical Society, the "precursor of the Redwood Library."

After Berkeley went away the ideals which he represented were continued down to the time of the Revolution by a group of talented men. Among them were several painters: Smibert, who had come with the dean, Feke, King, and Alexander, the reputed teacher of Gilbert Stuart. Richard Munday and Peter Harrison were skillful architects: the latter, trained under Vanbrugh, built the Redwood Library, the City Hall, and the impressive Jewish synagogue (dedicated a few months after Manning's visit); the former designed Newport Trinity Church and the colony capitol. Redwood and Collins were munificent patrons of art. Science was well represented by Dr. Thomas Brett, a graduate of the University of Leyden, and Dr. William Hunter. Among the clergymen were scholars of ability; and one of them, Ezra Stiles, subsequently became president of Yale College. The Redwood Library and the excellent private libraries in Newport and Narragansett — containing such works as *The Faerie Queene*, *Samson Agonistes*, Jonson's plays, Molière's plays, Pope's *Homer*, and the writings of Addison, Steele, and Swift, at a time when Harvard had none of them — contributed much to the general culture of the southern part of the colony.

It was, then, no illiterate or narrow-minded community that James Manning entered in the summer of 1763 with the project of establishing a college. The Baptists of the Philadelphia Association had chosen perhaps even better than they knew. The soil was well prepared for the planting of an institution of liberal culture; and the wonder is not that the gentlemen to whom he presented the plan welcomed it at once, but rather that such a project had not already been realized. That Ezra Stiles had been planning a college for Rhode Island is clearly proved by the following extracts from a letter written to him on January 20, 1762, by Chauncy Whittelsey, pastor of the First Church in New Haven: "The week before last I sent you the Copy of Yale College Charter. . . . Should you make any Progress in the Affair of a Colledge, I should be glad to hear of it; I heartily wish you Success therein. . . . Your Governmt. have as good a right to a Seminary of Learning as any other, and had you a Colledge of your own, Learning would undoubtedly be in Credit and prevail among you, much more than it otherwise will." The Newport friends of Dr. Stiles probably shared his purpose. At any rate, the relation between the culture of Newport and the founding of the college is strikingly shown by the fact that of the first petitioners for a charter, numbering sixty-two, twenty-one were shareholders in the Redwood Library.

So immediate was the indorsement of Manning's plan that a charter was framed and laid before the General Assembly at its August session in Newport in 1763; but action on it was postponed. A somewhat different charter was presented at sessions in October, 1763, and January, 1764, and was finally granted at the session in East Greenwich on March 2 and 3, 1764; it was signed and sealed by the governor and secretary on October 24, 1765. Such are the bare facts; but among the chief movers in the affair a famous struggle took place between the first drafting and the final granting of the charter.

James Manning himself, quoted by Morgan Edwards in his *Materials for a History of the Baptists in Rhode Island*, compiled in 1771, gives the following account of the whole matter:

In the month of July 1763 we arrived to Newport, and made a motion to several gentlemen of the baptist denomination (whereof col. Gardner the deputy governor was one) relative to a seminary of polite literature subject to the government of the Baptists. The motion was properly attended to, which brought together about 15 gentlemen of the same denomination at the deputy's house, who requested that I would draw a sketch of the design against the day following. That day came; and the said gentlemen, with other Baptists, met in the same place when a rough draught was produced and read. The tenor of which was that the institution was to be a baptist one; but that as many of other denominations should be taken in as was consistent with the said design. Accordingly the honourable Josias Lyndon and col. Job Bennet were appointed to draw a charter to be laid before the next general assembly with a petition that they would pass it into a law. But the said gentlemen pleading unskilfulness touching an affair of the kind requested that their trusty friend, Rev. Ezra (now Dr.) Styles might be solicited to assist them. This was opposed by me as unwilling to give the Dr. trouble about an affair of other people; but they urged that his love of learning, and catholicism, would induce him readily to give his assistance. Accordingly their proposal was consented to, and his assistance obtained; or rather the draughting of the charter was left entirely to him, after being told that the Baptists were to have the lead in the institution and the government thereof forever; and that no more of other denominations were to be admitted than would be consistent with that. The charter was drawn; and a time and place appointed for the parties concerned to meet and hear it read. But the vessel in which I was to sail for Halifax going off that day prevented my being present with them long enough to see whether the original design was secured. And as the corporation was made to consist of two branches, trustees and fellows; and those branches to sit and act by distinct and separate powers it was not easy to determine by a tra[n]sient hearing what those powers might be. The trustees were presumed to be the principal branch of authority; and as 19 out of 35 were to be baptists, the baptists were satisfied without sufficient examination into the authority vested in the fellowship (which afterwards appeared to be the soul of the institution while the trusteeship was only the body), and placing an entire confidence in Dr Styles, they agreed to join in a petition to the assembly to have the charter confirmed by authority. The pe[ti]tion was prefered and cheerfully received by the assembly, and the charter read; after which a vote was called for and urged by some to pass it into a law. But this was opposed by others, particularly by Daniel Jenckes Esq. member for Providence, alledging that the assembly required more time to examine whether it was agreeable to the design of the first movers for it; and therfore prayed the house to have the perusal of it while they adjourned for dinner. This was granted with some opposition; then he asked the governor (who was a baptist), Whom they intended to invest with the governing power in said institution? The governor answered, The baptists by all means. Then Mr Jenckes showed him, that the charter was so artfully constructed as to throw the power into the fellows' hands whereof 8 out of 12 were presbyterians (usually called Congregationalists) and that the other four might be of the same denomination for ought that appeared in the charter to the contrary. Convinced of this, governor Lyndon immediately had an interview with Dr. Styles (the presbyterian minister of Newport) and demanded, Why he had perverted the design of the charter? the answer was, *I gave you timely warning to take care of yourselves, for that we had done so with regard to our society;* and finally observed, the [=that] *he* was not the rogue. When the assembly was convened again, the said Jenckes moved that the affair might be put off to the next session, adding, That the motion for a college originated with the Baptists and was intended for their use, but that the charter in question was not at all calculated to answer their purpose; and since the committee (entrusted by the Baptists) professed that they were misled, not to say imposed upon, that it was necessary the Baptists in other parts of the colony should be consulted previous to its passing into a law, especially as few (if any of them except himself) had seen it; and prayd yt [=that] he might have a copy for the said purpose, —which he promised to return. All which were granted. When the charter came to be narrowly inspected it was found to be by no means answerable to the design of the agitators and the instructions given the committee. Consequently application was made to the philadelphia association (where the thing took its rise) to have their mind on the subject, who immediately sent two gentlemen[1]

---

[1] The Rev. Samuel Jones was the only one sent, but Mr. R. S. Jones voluntarily came with him.

hither to join with the Baptists of this colony in making what alterations and amendments that were to them specified before their departure. When they arrived Dr. Ayeres of Newport was added to the committee; and they happily draughted the present charter, and lodged it, with a new petition, in proper hands. The most material alterations were, Appointing the same number of baptists in the fellowship that had been appointed (of presbyterians) by Dr. Styles; settling the presidency in the baptist society; adding 5 baptists to the trustees, and putting more episcopalians than presbyterians in the corporation.

Daniel Jenckes is next quoted by Edwards, presenting a fuller narrative of proceedings in the legislature:

While I attended the business of the assembly (held Aug. 1763) capt. William Rogers came to the council chamber & presented me with a paper with a design I should sign it, adding, That as it was a petition for a baptist college he knew I would not refuse. Business not permiting me to attend to him immediatly I requested he would leave with me the pe[ti]tion and charter; mean while the serjeant made proclamation requiring the members to take their seats; in my seat I began to read the papers, but had not done before the petition and charter were called for, which I gave to the serjeant and he to the speaker at the board. The petition being read a motion was made to receive it and grant the charter. After some time I stood up to oppose proceeding immediately on the petition, giving my reason in words to this effect, *I understood that the college in question was sought for by the baptists; and that it was to be under their government and direction, with admition only of few of other religious denominations to share with them therein, that they might appear as catholic as could be, consistent with their main design; but on the contrary I perceived by glancing over the charter, while I sat in my place just now, that the main power of government and direction is vested in twelve fellows, and that 8 out of the 12 are to be presbyterians; and that the other may or may not be of the same denomination; but of necessity none of them is to be a baptist. If so, there is treachery some where, and a designn of grossly imposing on the honest people who first moved for the institution; I therefore desire that the matter may lie by till the after noon.* This was granted. In the after noon the matter was resumed with a seeming resolution in some to push it through at all events; but I had influence enough to stop proceeding then also. That evning and next morning I made it my business to see governor Lyndon and col. Bennet and to inform them of the construction of the charter. They could not believe me for the confidence they had in Dr. Styles honour and integrity, untill seeing convinced them. What reflections followed may be better concealed than published. However we all agreed to post[p]one passing the charter into a law; and did effect our purpose for that session, not withstanding the attempts of Mr Ellery and others of the presbyterians to the contrary. Before the breaking up of the assembly the house at my request directed the speaker to deliver the charter to me after I had made a promise it should be forth coming at the next meeting of the assembly. I took the charter to Providence and showed it to many who came to my house: others borrowed it to peruse at home. Mean while the messengers from the Philadelphia association arrived in Newport which occasioned the committee of Newport to send to me for the charter. I asked for it of Dr Ephraim Bowen who had borrowed it last. The Dr. said he lent it to Samuel Nightingal Esq.; search was made for it there, but it could not be found; neither do I know to this day what became of it. When the next general assembly met (last Wednesday in Oct. 1763) the second charter was presented; which was much faulted and opposed by the gentry who concerned themselves so warmly about the other. And one in particular demanded yt [=that] the first charter, which had been entrusted with me, might be produceed. Then I related (as above) that it was lost; and the manner how it was lost; but the party, instead of believing this very rudely suggested that I had secreted the charter, and in the face of the court, charged me with a breach of trust; which brought on very disagreeable altercations and bickerings, — till at last I was necessitated to say, *that if there had been any foul doing it was among them of their own denomination at Providence.* Their clamors continued; and we gave way to them that session for peace sake. Meanwhile Dr Bowen, who is a man of strict honour and integrity, used all means to recover the former charter, posting an advertisement in the most public place in town, and making diligent enquiry; but to no purpose. At the next assembly (which met in Feb. 1764) the new charter was again brought on the carpet; and the same clamour against it, and unjust reproaches against me were repeated, It was said, that the new charter was not like the old, and was constructed to deprive the presbyterians of the benefit of the institution. To which it was replied, *That it was agreeable to the design of the first undertakers; & if calculated to deprive the presbyterians of the power they wanted it was no more than what they themselves had attempted to do to the Baptists.* After much and warm debate the question was put, and carried in favour of the new charter by a great majority.

The most obvious interpretation of these contemporary statements is that Dr. Stiles played a trick upon the Baptists, or allowed some one else to play it, abusing the trust they had in him to thwart their purpose. This was the view of Edwards, who says, "Thus the baptists narrowly escaped being jockied out of their college by a set of men in whom they reposed entire confidence." Such an explanation is simple and intelligible, but there is an insuperable objection to it—the character of the Rev. Ezra Stiles. All else that we know of him makes it incredible that he should have been thus false, not merely to the Baptists, but to his personal friends in Newport, who, as Manning says, placed "entire confidence" in him. Mr. Stiles, then thirty-six years of age, a graduate of Yale and for six years a tutor there, had been settled in the pastorate of the Second Congregational Church in Newport since 1755. He was librarian of the Redwood Library, a student of Hebrew, Arabic, and astronomy, and a man of very liberal spirit, as is shown by his warm friendship with the Newport rabbi, Dr. Touro, and by his inviting Baptist ministers (including Mr. Edwards himself) to preach in his pulpit. The University of Edinburgh recognized his character and ability by giving him the degree of D.D. in 1765; and in 1777 Yale College called him to the presidency, an office which he filled with great ability until his death in 1795. It is incredible that

a Christian scholar of high character and unblemished reputation should in this instance have stooped to trickery that
would shame an unprincipled politician. President Manning apparently did not think so meanly of Stiles, for he
remained his friend, as is shown by the following entry
in Stiles's diary for November 26, 1773 : "Last Evening
President Manning visited me and stayed from a little before Nine to within about a quarter of Twelve, discoursing
on sundry Things — he brought a Copy of a Diploma,
which he was sending to London to be cut on copper plate."
The friends of the college, chiefly Baptists, did not lose
faith in him, for they tried to make him one of the original
fellows; neither did the Corporation, a majority of whom
were Baptists, for in 1765 they elected him a fellow, an
honor which he again declined. Furthermore, Governor
Lyndon and Colonel Bennet were still on good terms with
him in later years, as various entries in his diary show.
Finally, the words of Stiles himself give the impression
that in this matter he acted openly and with a good conscience. Instead of acknowledging that he employed under-
hand means, he asserts that there was an agreement as to
the charter, and reproaches the Baptists for having abandoned a liberal plan for a narrower one. "In an interleaved
Almanac for 1763, . . . is this entry, in Dr. Stiles's hand,"
says the editor of his diary: " 'Sept. 20. The Baptists desert
their Junction with the Congregationalists, and engross all
the Power in the proposed Rh. Isl. College to themselves,
after they had agreed to share the Ballances with us.' "
Again, according to his editor, this note, signed by Dr.
Stiles, is attached to a copy of *The Providence Gazette* for
April 28, 1764, which contains the newly granted charter :
"This charter draughted by Mr. William Ellery, Junr.
and myself before the Baptists deserted the Congregation-

alists.'' Finally, in a letter dated August 26, 1768, he writes: ''We had lately a catholic plan for a College in Rhode Island, but it turned out Supremacy & Monopoly in the hands of the Baptists, whose Influence in our Assembly was such that they obtained a most ample Charter to their purpose. . . . However I heartily wish the College prosperity, as it is the only Means of introducing Learning among our protestant Brethren the Baptists, I mean among their Ministers.''

These do not sound like the words of a trickster caught in his trickery; they seem rather those of a broad-minded man disappointed and somewhat indignant that a liberal plan once assented to had been abandoned. We may grant that his plan of dividing the power about equally between Baptists and Congregationalists was not wise, and would not have carried out the wishes of the majority of the Baptists; but must we not believe that he was perfectly frank and honest in his method of promoting it? The charter was not to go direct to the legislature from his hands: it was to be read to a company of intelligent men especially assembled to hear it. How could he hope to deceive them, if he had wished to do so? How could he anticipate that the main provisions of his charter would fail to become perfectly clear during this first reading and discussion? President Manning thought that there was a misunderstanding due to the intricacy of the document. He himself, being called away early, could not examine it then, and probably never did so later, since it was soon lost. The ground for misunderstanding lay, he thought, in the division of power between the trustees and the fellows, the Newport Baptists assuming that the former were ''the principal branch of authority,'' whereas the latter really proved to be ''the soul of the institution.'' Yet Mr. Jenckes grasped the facts by merely "glancing over the charter" while he sat in his place in the Assembly. How could the original movers, among whom were cultivated men of trained minds, have been either deceived or blinded, unless by their own heedlessness or indifference? They heard the charter and approved it, and petitioned for its granting. There is no charge that it was altered before it reached the legislature. There it was that objections began, started by one who was not present at the Newport conference. In the face of all later accusations stands the fact that those who asked Dr. Stiles to write the draft heard and accepted it; and it is wholly improbable that he could or would have imposed upon them. Neither could he or would he have allowed his friend William Ellery to do it in his name, as some have said: that would have been equally impossible, and doubly improbable, implying weakness as well as treachery in a man incapable of either.

Furthermore, a careful examination of the charter that he drew (of which copies have survived) fails to reveal any imposition. According to President Manning, Dr. Stiles was told "that the Baptists were to have the lead in the institution and the government thereof forever; and that no more of other denominations were to be admitted than would be consistent with that." His instructions were, it will be observed, very general. In the charter which he framed nineteen of the thirty-five trustees were to be Baptists, seven Congregationalists or Presbyterians, five Friends, four Episcopalians. Of the twelve fellows eight were to be Congregationalists or Presbyterians, and the rest of any denominations. The trustees were to elect the president (who might be of any Protestant denomination), after consultation with the fellows. The fellows (of whom the president was one) were to confer degrees, nominate all officers except the

president, enact the laws, and have control of the instruction and immediate government; but the confirmation of
every nomination and enactment was to rest with the trustees. This division of power between the two branches
was not very unequal, and, in spite of Manning's impression, what advantage there was belonged to the trustees.
Indeed, the only unfettered power of the fellows was that
of granting degrees; and the one unfettered power of the
trustees, that of electing the president (after "consultation"
with the fellows), far outweighed in its consequences the
fellows' independent power, for any man worthy of election to the presidency would profoundly affect the whole
policy and character of the college. In all but the purely
academic matter of granting degrees the trustees had the
ultimate power, in the form of a veto, besides possessing
absolute control in the election of the head of the whole
institution.[1] Surely the document does not bear out Man-

---

[1] That the Congregationalists understood the charter's provisions in this way,
and believed them to answer the condition "that the Baptists were to have
the lead in the institution and the government thereof forever," is a view
independently reached. When it had already been stated and explained, as
above, it received confirmation from a copy of a letter, apparently by William Ellery, found among the papers of the late Dr. David King, former
president of the Newport Historical Society; the letter was written at the
request of Dr. Stiles in reply to certain objections "respecting the Charter
for a College in this Colony," and is in part as follows: "The design of the
College which was first started here, originated among the Baptist Denomination. They opened it to some Congregationalists, of whom I was one,
and requested us to join them in this laudable Undertaking. In consequence
hereof a Meeting was held, and the following Articles proposed and finally
agreed to, as the immutable Basis of the Constitution, First, that the Corporation shall consist of two distinct Branches by the name of Trustees &
Fellows. 2d. That in the former the Baptists and in the latter, the Congregationalists should forever have the Majority's specified in the Charter. 3d.
That the Election of President should always be in the Trustees and that
they should have the Negative and Controul upon all the Nomination of Officers and upon the Laws proposed by the Fellows and in short that they
should have a disallowance on every Proposal of every Kind made to them

ning's statement that the fellowship was "the soul of the institution" and the trusteeship "only the body." The truth may be expressed by saying that the fellows were the intellect and the trustees the will; but, even so, the will was to elect the president, who would presumably be the most powerful intellectual as well as volitional force. That the intellect should have been placed under the control of the Congregationalists is not hard to explain: they were the most intellectual and best educated religious body in New England, and could most easily furnish men qualified to be fellows of a college. Even in this provision it is more than credible that Dr. Stiles thought he was doing the best thing for the projected institution—and that without "jockeying" the Baptists out of their college.

The facts, taken all together, seem to warrant the following view: The leading Baptists in Newport, true to the liberal atmosphere of the place, under the immediate influence of Dr. Stiles, agreed to the charter which he presented at their request, thinking that, while it granted the Congregational body more power than the Philadelphia Baptists had perhaps anticipated, it preserved the main point of giving the Baptists ultimate control, and would at the same time win more general support from the best educated men in the colony and neighboring colonies. This liberal charter was presented to the Assembly by many petitioners of various denominations;[1] but being held up by a Providence Baptist who had not been present at the original conference, and who, although a most respected citi-

by the other Branch. . . . These articles were virtually agreed to as the Foundation of the Charter which was draughted, conformably thereto, and as the Cement of our Coalition."

[1] Of 44 whose religious affiliations have been ascertained by the Rev. A. W. Smith, 20 were Baptists, 11 Congregationalists, 4 Quakers, and 9 Episcopalians.

zen, was more narrowly sectarian and perhaps somewhat influenced by the bitter rivalry between Providence and Newport, the document became the center of a heated debate that stirred up sectarian prejudice on both sides. The final result was a charter which, although still very liberal, was more strongly Baptist than the first draft had been.

This view is plainly not altogether consistent with the narratives by President Manning and Mr. Jenckes. But these narratives — as has already been implied — are themselves not altogether consistent with the facts of the case as a whole. Both bear marks of sectarian bias, natural enough at a period when feeling between Baptists and Congregationalists was running high, but not favorable to a just statement or interpretation of facts. Manning's account of the contest appears on its face to be wholly second-hand; it is quite unlikely that he was in Newport at the time, having recently sailed for Nova Scotia. Mr. Jenckes narrates transactions in which he was a prime agent, but apparently he was writing eight years after the event, when he might easily have over-colored some details. What he says about the indignation of Governor Lyndon and Colonel Bennet at Dr. Stiles's supposed trick is particularly hard to reconcile with their subsequent friendship with Stiles and the esteem of other Baptist leaders for him. But even if they thought at first that he had deceived them, it does not follow that their opinion was justified; it merely shows that the charter which he had put into their hands to read was not what they, through blindness or heedlessness, thought it was. It is noteworthy that Mr. Jenckes's own narrative does not ascribe to Dr. Stiles the remark about his having given timely warning and not being the rogue. But even if credence be given it, the case against Stiles is rather weaker than stronger: the giving of timely warning acquits him of intentional deceit; and therefore "rogue" cannot be a confession of trickery by himself or another, but only an adoption — perhaps semi-jocose — of the accuser's point of view. The utmost that can be safely inferred from the narratives of Manning and Jenckes, in modification of the conclusion already reached, is that the Newport Baptists assented to the first form of the charter, not because they were liberal minded, but because they were too stupid or too careless to understand its provisions when it was in their hands — a view which seems scarcely reasonable. There is abundant proof, however, that when the sectarian fight began, the Baptists in Newport vigorously took sides for the charter in its later form, for of the 221 petitioners for it, 148 were residents of Newport; of the 62 petitioners for the first form, 25 also petitioned for the second, and 22 of these lived in Newport.

Finally, it may be added that the narratives of Manning and Jenckes did not escape contemporary criticism by one who was himself a Baptist, though not a church member, David Howell, the first professor in the college. In an unpublished letter to Backus (now in the New England Baptist Library, Boston), dated April 13, 1775, he says, commenting on the manuscript of the second volume of Backus's history of the Baptists: "I think what is taken from Mr Edwards's Book about the Quarrel in geting the Charter ought to be buried in oblivion if ever we wish to engage the Presbyterians in the Interest of the College & it it [= is] nothing to our honor or advantage but rather disgracefull to Mr Manning, and altogether respects the Conduct Surmises Suspicions, &c. of Individuals whom it is not our Interest to offend for nothing. . . . I would by no means have Mr Mannings & Jenckes injudicious ill-natured reflections in your History." While it is true that

Howell's criticism is concerned chiefly with the imprudence of publishing such statements then, there is also a plain implication that they are far from being impartial and reliable accounts.

Leaving the sectarian contest behind, we find the charter that was granted for the new Rhode Island college an academic document so worthy of admiration that it compels gratitude to the man who drew it. With the exception of the changes in denominational representation, this final charter, under which Brown University has lived and thrived for a century and a half, is almost wholly the work of Ezra Stiles, aided, as he said, by William Ellery; although it should never be forgotten that Manning in his "rough draught" laid the foundation for liberal representation of "other denominations." Mr. Ellery, a practicing lawyer, later a signer of the Declaration of Independence, probably supervised the instrument chiefly on the legal side. The large outlines and most of the phraseology are undoubtedly due to Dr. Stiles, who was exceptionally fitted for the work by reason of his law studies, his experience as a tutor in Yale, and his broad scholarship. It is hardly possible, however, that even a man so well qualified could have produced so long, so detailed, and so wise a document in the short time that seems to have elapsed between the application to him and Manning's departure from Newport. As he actually had been planning a college, it is likely that he had already given thought to the charter, and had perhaps made a written draft of it; his friends Lyndon and Bennet may even have known this when they suggested calling upon him for aid.

A man with so wide a knowledge and so keen an interest in education must have been familiar with the charters of the leading American colleges of his time; and it is easy to see that in shaping his charter he was influenced by existing documents. In phrasing there is little similarity, except in the conventional legal terms. The preamble, with its broad view of the scope and purpose of collegiate education, has a few points of likeness to the charters of Yale and New Jersey College. The Yale charter of 1701 speaks of the rearing of "a succession of Learned & Orthodox men" as the main purpose of the college. Dr. Stiles had in mind "a Succession of Men duly qualify'd for discharging the Offices of Life with usefulness & reputation"—language which seems to owe something to Milton's famous sentence, "I call therefore a complete and generous education that which fits a man to perform justly, skilfully, and magnanimously all the offices, both private and public, of peace and war." The Yale charter, however, also has a phrase about fitting youth "for Publick employment both in Church & Civil State." The clause in the New Jersey College charter of 1748, "wherein Youth may be instructed in the learned Languages, and in the liberal Arts and Sciences," appears in the Brown charter almost unchanged except for the significant insertion of "Vernacular" before "Learned Languages."[1] But on the whole the language in the preamble, and in the noble paragraph barring religious tests, is not derived from any other source, and has a vigor and largeness seldom found in legal documents of this class.

The main outlines of the charter have more in common with other college charters than has usually been recognized. The division of the Corporation into two bodies, fellows and trustees, may have been suggested by the Harvard charter of 1650, with its fellows and overseers, or perhaps by the bicameral legislatures of colonial America. The legal powers of the Corporation, the mode of electing presidents,

---

[1] For a discussion of the clause, "The Public teaching shall in general Respect the Sciences," see page 497.

fellows, trustees, professors, and other officers, the provisions about discipline, instruction, granting of degrees, etc.,
are much like those in the charters of the other American colleges. The exemption of "the Estates Persons and
Families of the President and Professors," and "the Persons of the Tutors and Students" from "all Taxes, serving
on Juries and Menial Services," is taken, with a few verbal
changes, from the Yale charter of 1745. The chief differences are in the provisions regarding denominational control and religious tests. But even in these things the Rhode
Island charter does not, as many have thought, stand in
complete isolation.

The facts about religious tests for students in other colleges have been stated in another connection. No college
charter in the country required students to subscribe to any
religious creed as a condition of becoming members of the
institution. Some charters, as those of Harvard and Yale,
were silent on the point. Others, as those of New Jersey
College and King's College, expressly forbade such tests.
The Brown charter, therefore, in its ringing declaration that
"into this Liberal & Catholic Institution shall never be
admitted any Religious Tests," but that "Youths of all
Religious Denominations shall and may be freely admitted
to the Equal Advantages Emoluments & Honors of the College," was not establishing a precedent, but only supporting a practice already established.

The case is somewhat different as regards religious instruction. At Yale, although the charter did not require that
any particular creed be taught, the president and fellows
in 1753 passed a resolution of fidelity to the order of the
founders that "the Students should be established in the
Principles of Religion, and grounded in polemical Divinity,
according to the *Assembly's Catechism*, . . . and that special

Care should be taken, in the Education of Students, not to suffer them to be instructed in any different Principles or Doctrines." The laws forbade students to attend religious meetings other than Congregational without permission of the president; but "the Sons of those, who profess themselves to be Episcopalians," says President Clap, in his history of the college in 1766, had "Liberty to go out on the Lord's-Day, and at other Times, to attend on the Mode of Worship in which they were educated, as often as will not be an Infraction on the general Rules of Order in the College." All students were required to take a course in divinity, which was taught by a professor of strict orthodoxy. At Harvard all juniors and seniors were required to attend the lectures on divinity; and the professor of divinity was obliged before election to satisfy the Corporation of his orthodoxy. At King's College, the University of Pennsylvania, and the College of New Jersey, there seems to have been no sectarian instruction in the class-room. The liberal spirit which prevailed in the last-named institution is well expressed in the following words of President Witherspoon in 1772: "It has been and shall be our care to use every means in our power to make them [i.e., the students] good men and good scholars; and if this be the case, I shall hear of their future character and usefulness with unfeigned satisfaction, under every name by which a real Protestant can be distinguished." It is thus apparent that no greater freedom was established at Brown than actually prevailed in a few other colleges; but the Brown charter alone, in its provision that "Sectarian differences of opinions, shall not make any Part of the Public and Classical Instruction," grounded that freedom in the fundamental law of the institution.

Brown University's charter was also more liberal than others in rejecting religious tests for members of the Faculty and providing definitely for broad representation on the governing board. At Harvard, in 1738, the high-Calvinistic members of the board of overseers who attempted to examine into the theology of a candidate for the professorship of mathematics and natural philosophy were defeated; but in the following year the overseers refused to approve the election of a tutor until satisfied of his orthodoxy, because he had to conduct religious services and give religious instruction. These tests were not required by the charter, nor forbidden by it; nor did the charter specify the religious denominations of the president, fellows, and overseers, except that "the teaching Elders of the six next adjoining towns" should be among the overseers, but as a matter of fact the power was in the hands of the Congregationalists. The Yale charter made no express provision for denominational control of the governing board or the Faculty; yet here, too, because of political and ecclesiastical conditions, the Congregationalists were in power. The president and fellows were all Congregational clergymen; and the president was elected by the fellows, who were self-perpetuating. Furthermore, at a meeting of the president and fellows in 1753, it was voted, "That every Person who shall hereafter be chosen a President, Fellow, Professor of Divinity, or Tutor, in this College, shall before he enters upon the Execution of his Office, publickly give his Consent to the said *Catechism* and *Confession of Faith*," *i.e.*, the *Westminster Assembly's Catechism* and an abridgment of the *Westminster Confession;* and this rule was strictly administered for many years, receiving some modification in 1778, at Dr. Stiles's instance, when he became president.

In several other colleges, however, the conditions were more liberal. The charter of King's College specified that the president should be a member of the Church of England, and the governing board included the Archbishop of Canterbury (empowered to act by proxy) and the rector of Trinity Church; but the senior minister of the Reformed Protestant Dutch Church, the ministers of the Ancient Lutheran Church, of the French Church, and of the Presbyterian Congregation, in the city of New York, the lieutenant-governor, the judges of the supreme court, and other civil officers, were *ex officio* members of the board, besides twenty-four leading men of the city. The University of Pennsylvania was characterized by the same union of Episcopal control with a liberal spirit. The second charter of New Jersey College, granted in 1748, imposed no denominational restrictions in the choice of president or trustees. Eleven of the original trustees under this charter were laymen, and twelve were Presbyterian ministers; among the laymen were members of the Presbyterian, Episcopal, and Quaker denominations.

The charter of Brown University admitted no *ex officio* representatives of the civil power to its governing board; but in this respect it was not alone. It was like the charter of King's College in providing for the representation of denominations other than the dominant one, but exceeded that in the relative strength allowed them. It differed from the Harvard, Yale, and New Jersey College charters in explicitly recognizing denominations and openly securing the control to one; but in effect it was much broader than the charter of Yale, in which only one denomination had power, and also broader than that of Harvard, in which the power was divided between one denomination and certain civil officers, most of whom were of the same religious body. The charter of New Jersey College allowed all the power to be concentrated in one denomination, although others actually shared it; the Brown charter compelled a partition of power, and on a more ample scale. The representatives of the various denominations were to be chosen by the Corporation, not by the denominations themselves, and might be either clergymen or laymen. The outstanding fact is that the instrument governing Brown University recognized more broadly and fundamentally than any other the principle of denominational coöperation. In so doing it was true to the best traditions of the Baptist denomination and of the colony; and it was also wise after the manner of this world, by thus securing broader support than an institution controlled wholly by one sect could have won.

CHAPTER II

PRESIDENT MANNING'S ADMINISTRATION

THE struggle over the charter being ended, the organization of the college proceeded with reasonable speed. On the first Wednesday in September, 1764, the first meeting of the Corporation was held at Newport, when twenty-four of those named in the charter as original incorporators took the oath of office. They were a distinguished company, including some of the best known men of the colony. The most eminent among them was Stephen Hopkins, several times governor, afterwards chief justice of the superior court, a delegate to the Continental Congress, and a signer of the Declaration of Independence; in November, 1764, he put forth his famous pamphlet, "The Rights of Colonies Examined," one of the ablest remonstrances against the Stamp Act. Samuel Ward was Hopkins's rival for the governorship during the years 1758 to 1768, being three times victorious; he was governor in 1765, and signed the college charter, which for some reason had not been signed by Hopkins in the year it was granted; he also was a delegate to the Continental Congress. Joseph Wanton and Josias Lyndon later served as governors. James Honyman was attorney-general and king's advocate for the court of vice-admiralty for the colony. Job Bennet was a judge of the superior court. Joshua Babcock, a judge of the superior court of judicature, in 1775 became major-general of the Rhode Island militia. Daniel Jenckes was for many years a member of the General Assembly, and chief justice of a court of common pleas. Nicholas Brown was a prominent Providence merchant, father of the Nicholas Brown from whom the college later took its name. Edward Upham, a Harvard graduate, was pastor of the First Baptist Church, Newport. Jeremiah Condy, also a graduate of Harvard, was a Baptist minister in Boston. Thomas Eyres was a graduate of Yale and an eminent physician in Newport.

Governor Hopkins was chosen chancellor; John Tillinghast, treasurer; and Dr. Eyres, secretary.[1] The first need was to provide funds for the new institution; accordingly a subscription-form was adopted, and sixty-nine persons living in different parts of the country (among them Benjamin Franklin) were authorized to receive subscriptions. Before adjourning, the Corporation appointed a committee, as was often done thereafter, to transact necessary business between meetings. No officers of instruction were elected at this first session of the governing board; that would hardly have been prudent in the absence of funds and students.

The second meeting of the Corporation was held in Newport on the first Wednesday in September, 1765; twenty-five members were present, and much important business was done. The following entries on the records have peculiar interest: "A Seal for the College was ordered to be procured immediately by the Reverend Samuel Stillman with this Device; Busts of the King and Queen in Profile, Face to Face. Underneath George III. Charlotte. Round the Border, The Seal of the College in the Colony of Rhode Island and Providence Plantations in America."[2] "Revd:

---

[1] From the beginning the fellows and the trustees sat and voted together, as appears from minutes by "M. B." of a Corporation meeting on November 14, 1769: "Mr: Henry Ward . . . urged it should be done in seperate departments by the trustees & fellows agreably to charter, but it being answered that upon that principal it never had been legally fixed, nor no other business done from the first Authentic as the corporation had always acted as one body, it was therefore given up."

[2] See page 520 for an imprint of this seal.

James Manning was appointed President of the College, Professor of Languages and other Branches of Learning with full Power to act in those Capacities at Warren or elsewhere.'' It was high time to have a president and faculty, for already a student body existed. On the day before, William Rogers, a Newport lad of fourteen years, had matriculated in Rhode Island College; and for more than nine months he was the only student.

The Rev. James Manning was a remarkable man, and peculiarly fitted to be the first president of the college. He was born October 22, 1738, in Piscataway, New Jersey, originally a part of the Elizabethtown grant. His parents, of the farming class, were descended from early settlers in the region. After two years in Hopewell Academy, he entered New Jersey College in 1758, and four years later graduated second in a class of twenty-one. In 1763 he was ordained as a Baptist minister; and in April, 1764, he settled in the town of Warren, Rhode Island, some ten miles from Providence, where he opened a Latin school and became the first pastor of a Baptist church, organized in November, 1764, an offshoot from the venerable church in Swansea. When the Baptists of the Middle States, in planning for a college, chose Manning as leader in the enterprise, it is probable that they were influenced in part by his person as well as by his scholarship and character. In later life weighing upwards of three hundred pounds, he must even at twenty-four have had an impressive presence. ''In his Youth,'' wrote Howell, ''he was remarkable for his Dexterity in athletic Exercises, for the Symmetry of his Body, and Gracefulness of his Person.'' It is clear that he found favor upon his first entry into the cultivated Newport circle, stranger as he was; and he seems to have had no rival for the presidency.

The college was now launched, but for several years its progress was slow. A "Matriculation Roll," in Manning's hand, shows that in 1766 five new students were enrolled; in 1767, four; in 1768, eight; and in 1769, eleven. Of the twenty-nine enrolled from the beginning only eleven lived in Rhode Island, two of them coming from Newport and four from Providence; the other eighteen lived in Connecticut, Massachusetts, New York, New Jersey, and Pennsylvania. The second student, Richard Stites, who entered June 20, 1766, was the President's brother-in-law. The students of both Latin school and college met in the Warren parsonage, which was built in 1765–67 partly for their use, as appears from the following item in *The Newport Mercury* for September 28 to October 5, 1767:

SCHEME OF A LOTTERY, Granted by the General Assembly of the Colony of *Rhode-Island*, &c. for raising £.150 Lawful Money,[1] to be applied towards finishing the Parsonage House belonging to the Baptist Church in *Warren*, and rendering it commodious for the Reception of the Pupils, who are, or shall be, placed there for a liberal Education. . . . It is hoped that the extraordinary Expence of that infant Society, in building a new Meeting-House, and Parsonage House, as far as the Building is advanced, together with the immediate Necessity of Room for the Pupils under the Care of the Rev. Mr. *Manning*, and the great Encouragement for the Adventurers, there being but little better than two Blanks to a Prize, will induce those who wish well to the Design, speedily to purchase the Tickets.

Further evidence is afforded by a bill, dated April 18, 1768, for work done on "the Parsnig house," including "the Colleg Chamber."

The growing number of pupils made an assistant teacher necessary; and in the records of the Corporation's meeting at Newport in September, 1767, is the entry, "The

---

[1] A pound in "lawful money" was worth $3.33⅓.

Reverend President Manning's Conduct for the Year past, and his engaging Mr. David Howell a Tutor of the College is approved of.'' The next year Mr. Howell was formally elected tutor at a ''Salary of Seventy two Pounds Lawful Money,'' and was ''authorized to collect the Tuition Money as it became due as part of his Salary ''; in 1769 he was appointed professor of natural philosophy. Mr. Howell was born in Morristown, New Jersey, in 1747; he graduated from the College of New Jersey in 1766, and soon after came to Warren at President Manning's suggestion. His connection with the college was long and various. He was professor of law from 1790 to 1824, but gave no instruction. In 1773, while holding a professorship, he was elected a fellow, and retained the position until his death, in 1824. He was secretary of the Corporation from 1780 to 1806, and president *ad interim* in 1791–92. He also received high honors in civil life, being a member of Congress under the Confederation, associate justice of the supreme court of Rhode Island, attorney-general, United States district judge, and by appointment of President Washington one of the commissioners, under the Jay treaty of 1794, to determine the true St. Croix River as a part of our northern boundary. The college was fortunate in the intellectual caliber of its first tutor and professor.

The expenses of the institution were as yet small, the tutor receiving but $240 a year, and the president having no salary at all. But continuance and future growth would be impossible without an endowment. A beginning had been made by the Corporation itself, at the meeting in 1765, when $1992 was subscribed by the members present. At a meeting on November 20, 1766, the Rev. Morgan Edwards was ''requested & duely authoriz'd to go to Europe & solicit Benefactions for this Institution.'' Mr. Edwards spent about a year and a half in Great Britain, returning in the latter part of 1768, and collected £888 10^s 2^d sterling (or about $4300), of which nearly one-fourth came from Ireland, where he had first been a pastor. His subscription book, still in the archives of the university, is of singular interest. Here may be seen the signatures of famous men —Benjamin Franklin, Thomas Penn, Rev. Dr. Stennet, and others, — who gave sums ranging from £10 to £20; and on the same time-stained pages the names of obscure men and women—Benjamin Boon, Sarah Burdock, John Fury, Susanna Ferguson, and others—who out of their poverty gave their one shilling or two shillings sixpence, to aid the cause of education in a distant college from which they could never expect to receive any personal benefit. It is worthy of note, too, that three Presbyterian churches in Belfast and one in Ballymony contributed over £30 to "this Liberal & Catholic Institution." An extract from Edwards's letter to Manning, dated London, April 26, 1768, will give some idea of the difficulty of his task and also of his ardent and vigorous nature:

There have been no less than six cases of charity pushed about town this winter. . . . The unwearied beneficence of the city of London is amasing! Your news papers, and letters from your government, published in other papers, have hurt me much—You boast of the many yards of cloth you manufacture &c. This raises the indignation of the merchants and manufacturers—I have been not only denyed by hundreds, but also absused on that score—My patience, my feet, and my assurance are much impaired—I took a cold in November, which stuck to me all winter, owing to my trampoosing the streets in all weathers.

In 1769 and 1770 the Rev. Hezekiah Smith was sent on a similar mission through the Southern States, and collected sums amounting to about $1700.

Meanwhile, in the face of all difficulties, the work of instruction went forward, and in the autumn of 1769 a class of seven was ready for graduation. At the meeting of the Corporation held in Warren on Wednesday, September 6, it was voted, "That the Meeting-House in Warren be fitted up at the charge of the Corporation, in the best manner the shortness of time will admit, for the reception of the people Tomorrow, the day of Commencement." The meeting-house was the new Baptist church, a plain wooden building, sixty-one feet by forty-four, with a hip-roof and a tower, and furnished with galleries. Here was held the first Commencement of Rhode Island College; and in spite of crude surroundings the occasion was a dignified and memorable one. So far had interest spread in the Baptist denomination that tradition says a company of Baptist preachers from Georgia rode over a month on horseback to be there. The events of the day were thus described in *The Newport Mercury* of September 11, 1769:

On Thursday the 7th Instant was celebrated, at Warren, the first Commencement in the College of this Colony, when the following young Gentlemen commenced Bachelors in the Arts; viz. JOSEPH BELTON, JOSEPH EATON, WILLIAM ROGERS, RICHARD STITES, CHARLES THOMPSON, JAMES MITCHEL VARNUM, and WILLIAM WILLIAMS.

About 10 o'Clock A.M. the Gentlemen concerned in conducting the Affairs of the College, together with the Candidates, went in Procession to the Meeting-House.

After they had taken their Seats, and the Audience were composed, the President introduced the Business of the Day with Prayer; then followed a salutatory Oration in Latin, pronounced with much Spirit, by Mr. STITES; which procured him great Applause from the learned Part of the Assembly. He spoke upon the Advantages of Liberty and Learning, and their mutual Dependence upon each other, concluding with proper Salutations to the Chancellor of the College, and to the Governor of the Colony, &c. particularly expressing the

Gratitude of all the Friends of the College to the Rev. MORGAN ED-
WARDS, who has encountered many Difficulties in going to Europe
to collect Donations for the Institution, and lately returned.

To which succeeded a forensic Dispute in English, on the following Thesis, viz. "*The Americans, in their present Circumstances,
cannot, consistent with good Policy, affect to become an independent
State.*" Mr. VARNUM ingeniously defended it by cogent Arguments,
handsomely dressed, though he was subtilely, but delicately, opposed
by Mr. WILLIAMS; both of whom spoke with much Emphasis and
Propriety.

As a Conclusion to the Exercises of the Forenoon, the Audience
were agreeably entertained with an Oration on *Benevolence*, by Mr.
ROGERS; in which, among many other pertinent Observations, he
particularly noticed how greatly that infant Seminary stands in Need
of the salutary Effects of that truly christian Virtue.

At 3 o'Clock, P. M. the Audience being again convened, a syllogistic Dispute was introduced on this Thesis, "*Materia cogitare non
potest.*" Mr. WILLIAMS the Respondent, Messieurs BELTON, EATON,
ROGERS and VARNUM, the Opponents: In the course of which Dispute the principal Arguments on both Sides were produced, towards
settling that critical Point.

After which the Degree of Bachelor of Arts was conferred on the
Candidates.

Then the following Gentlemen, (graduated in other Colleges) at
their own Request, received the honorary Degree of Master in the
Arts, viz. Rev. EDWARD UPHAM, Rev. MORGAN EDWARDS, Rev.
SAMUEL STILLMAN, Rev. HEZEKIAH SMITH, Rev. SAMUEL JONES,
Rev. JOHN DAVIS, Hon. JOSEPH WANTON, jun. Esq; Mr. ROBERT
STRETTLE JONES, Mr. JABEZ BOWEN, Mr. DAVID HOWELL the Pro-
fessor of Philosophy in said College.

The following Gentlemen, being well recommended to the Fac-
ulty for literary Merit, had conferred on them the honorary Degree
of Master in the Arts, viz. Rev. ABEL MORGAN, Rev. OLIVER HART,
Rev. DAVID THOMAS, Mr. JOHN STITES, Rev. JAMES BRYSON, Rev.
JAMES EDWARDS, Rev. WILLIAM BOULTON, Rev. JOHN RYLAND, Rev.
WILLIAM CLARK, Rev. JOSHUA TOULMIN, Rev. CALEB EVANS.

A concise, pertinent and solemn Charge was then given to the
Bachelors, by the President, concluding with his last paternal Bene-

diction; which naturally introduced the valedictory Orator, Mr. THOMPSON; who, after some Remarks on the Excellencies of the oratorial Art, and Expressions of Gratitude to the Patrons and Officers of the College, together with a Valediction to them and all present, took a most affectionate Leave of his Classmates.—The Scene was tender—the Subject felt—and the Audience affected.

The President concluded the Exercises with Prayer.

The whole was conducted with a Propriety and Solemnity suitable to the Occasion: The Audience (consisting of most of the principal Gentlemen and Ladies of this Colony, and many from the neighbouring Governments) tho' large and crouded, behaved with the utmost Decorum.

In the Evening the Rev'd. MORGAN EDWARDS, by particular Request, preached a Sermon, peculiarly addressed to the Graduates and Students, from Philippians iii, 8. "*Yea doubtless, and I count all Things but Loss, for the Excellency of the Knowledge of Christ Jesus my Lord:*" In which, (after high Encomiums on the liberal Arts and Sciences) the superior Excellence of the *Knowledge of Christ*, or the *Christian Science*, was clearly and fully illustrated in several striking examples, and Similes; One of which follows: "When the Sun is "below the Horizon, the Stars excel in Glory; but when his Orb irra- "diates our Hemisphere, their Glory dwindles, fades away, and dis- "appears."

The President and all the Candidates were dressed in American Manufactures.

Finally, be it observed, That this Class are the first Sons of that College which has existed only four Years; during all which Time it laboured under great Disadvantages, notwithstanding the warm Patronage and Encouragement of many worthy Gentlemen of Fortune and Benevolence: But it is hoped, from the Disposition which many discovered on that Day, and other favourable Circumstances, that these Disadvantages will soon be happily removed.

The close sympathy of the college with the political feeling of the time is shown not only by the fact that "the President and all the Candidates" wore clothes of American manufacture (as the graduating class at Harvard had done the year before), in protest against the unjust trade

laws of Great Britain, but still more by the discussion of
American independence, which was the principal feature
of the morning. This debate breathed the same spirit that
had stubbornly resisted the Stamp Act and was soon to burst
out in the Boston Tea Party and the burning of the Gaspee. Varnum, the "respondent," or speaker in the affirm-
ative, although he opposed the attempt to set up an independent state, yet condemned unsparingly the course of
the British government. "Had British America," he said,
"been left to the peaceful enjoyment of those privileges,
which it could boast of in former reigns, the most romantic
genius, in its wildest excursions, had not dreamt of independence. But the late alarming attacks of the parent state
upon American freedom, . . . has, with justice, roused the
advocates of American liberty to the most vigorous exertions, in defence of our rights." Williams, the "oppo-
nent," was yet bolder: "Let not the menaces of a British
Parliament, in the least affright, nor their fair promises deceive you, into any base compliances. *Latet anguis in herba.*
Their evident design is to make us slaves. They are wrest-
ing our money from us without our consent. Do not be
charmed by the fascinating sounds, Parent-State, Mother-
Country, Indulgent-Parent, &c. . . . Their menaces might
terrify and Subjugate Servile timid Asiatics, who peaceably prostrate their necks to be trampled on by every bold
usurper. But my auditors, you have not so learned the principles of liberty. . . . My point is gained; your counte-
nances indicate the patriotic feelings of your breasts, and
with one voice you declare, that AMERICA SHALL BE FREE."

On this Commencement Day, 1769, the Corporation attempted to settle upon a permanent home for the college.
A meeting was held at seven in the morning, and a committee that had been appointed the year before reported in

favor of Bristol County, in which Warren is situated; the Corporation accepted the report, and appointed a new committee to select and buy a site, put up a building, and solicit subscriptions. This vigorous action, aided no doubt by the success of the first Commencement, woke up the colony, and a very pretty fight ensued. Almost immediately a voice was heard from the County of Kent, across the bay, where a subscription for endowing the college had been opened, asking that a special meeting of the Corporation be called to reconsider the vote in favor of Bristol County.

This meeting was held in the court-house at Newport during three days, November 14–16, and lively days they proved, for Newport and Providence had now entered the lists. It is not known what arguments were advanced on behalf of Warren; but the Baptist church there voted on November 13 that "the Baptis meeting House in sd Town be and is: for the Use of the Corporation & President at commencement times: . . . Provided the College Edifice be founded & Built in the County of Bristol," and that "the Parsonage House . . . be for the use of the President: So Long as he the President be our Minister." The committee from East Greenwich, in the County of Kent, urged its pleasant site and central location, which would secure the support of the whole colony; they also argued that Providence was too large, "As Institutions of this kind have been found by Experience not to prosper in popular Towns," whereas East Greenwich was "Large enough to accomodate the Students effectually, . . . There being likewise a post office in the Town," besides a Quaker and a Baptist meeting-house, and a Separatist church only three miles away, "upon a Good road free from ferries." The memorial from Newport has not been preserved, but an article in *The Newport Mercury* of November 20 doubtless reproduces some

[44]

of the main points. The writer speaks of "the Number of Inhabitants in Newport, the Reputation of the Island for Health and Pleasantness, the easy Communication we have with all Parts of this Government, and with the Western and Southern Colonies, and the Cheapness with which Pupils may be boarded," and also of the scholarly Redwood Library, "the Use of which may be allowed the Pupils under the discreet Care of the President and Tutors." The memorial from Providence, signed by John Cole, Moses Brown, and Hayward Smith, is a long document. The chief reasons it adduces in favor of locating the college in Providence are these: a large sum of money has been subscribed, nearly $9000; the situation is central, and communication easy; living is cheap; there are four schoolhouses, a public library, and good libraries for the study of law and medicine; there are "two printing offices which will much cont[r]ibute to the emolument of the college, the[re] being a weekly collection of the interesting inteligence published which will not only assist in enlarging the mind of the youth but give them early opportunity of displaying their genius in all useful or speculative subject"; and, finally, professors and students of various faiths will readily attend college in Providence, where there are "places of public worship of all the various denominations of Christians in America."

The Corporation, besieged in this fashion, on the second day rescinded the vote in favor of Bristol County. On the third day it passed the following vote:

Resolved. — That the place for erecting the College Edifice be now fixed. — But that nevertheless the Committee who shall be appointed to carry on the Building do not proceed to procure any other Materials for the same, excepting such as may be easily transported to any other place, should another hereafter be thought better, untill further Orders from this Corporation; if such Orders be given before the first day of January next.—And that in case any Subscription be raised in the County of Newport, or any other County, equal or Superior to any now offered; or that shall then be offered, and the Corporation be called in consequence thereof, that then the Vote for fixing the Edifice shall not be esteemed binding; but so that the Corporation may fix the Edifice in another place in case they shall think proper.—Voted—That the College-Edifice be at Providence.

Here, evidently, was not an ending of the struggle, but rather a skillful incentive to fight longer and put up larger stakes. The contest was now practically narrowed to Providence and Newport, and each side worked actively to increase its subscriptions. At first the former was in the lead; but about the middle of January there appeared in the Providence and Newport newspapers a call for a meeting of the Corporation at Warren on February 7, because "the County of *Newport* hath raised a larger Sum than any that hath yet been offered to the Corporation of the College in this Colony." The call was signed by three of the fellows; President Manning refused to join in it, holding, with the others who favored Providence, that the time for reconsidering the vote had expired on January 1. Failing in their attempt to prevent the calling of a meeting, the Browns and other leaders of the Providence party made one final effort to strengthen their side. A handbill was spread through the town, containing this notice:

Providence, Monday, February 5, 1770. THE Inhabitants of this Town and County are desired to meet at the Court-House THIS AFTERNOON, at Two o'Clock, to hear and consider of some effectual Plan for establishing the COLLEGE here. As this is a Matter of the greatest Consequence, and the Corporation is to meet on WEDNESDAY next, a general Attendance is earnestly requested.

A large number attended the meeting; Stephen Hopkins presided; and a committee consisting of Moses Brown and several other prominent citizens was appointed to take charge of the subscriptions and present them to the Corporation.

Two days later the various forces moved to Warren, and the final contest began. The attendance was large for a special meeting, seven fellows and twenty-eight trustees being present, besides the representatives of the rival counties. It was now generally understood that the choice lay between Newport and Providence; but East Greenwich, hoping that she might still be made happy in case of a deadlock, presented a memorial, signed by James M. Varnum, of the class just graduated, Nathanael Greene, Jr., soon to be famous as the greatest general of the war next to Washington, and two others. The memorialists argue again "that a Considerable Degree of Retirement is very Requisite in Order to acquire any Great Proficiency in literary Pursuits," and inquire, "Is there Sufficient Retirement in Newport or Providence?" On the other hand they are sure that there is more than sufficient politics in either place, for "It is likewise well known that Newport & Providence have ever been the Capital Sources of Party in this Colony, And Consequently the Institution must Annually be Subject to the Attacks of one party or the other if placed in either." The Providence faction presented a memorial protesting that the time-limit for reconsidering the vote had expired when the meeting was called, and that even then Newport had not raised so large a sum as Providence. There is no record of what was said in behalf of Newport or Warren.

The battle raged for two days, from 10 a.m. Wednesday till 10 p.m. Thursday, according to President Manning in a letter of February 12; and he adds, "The matter was debated with great Spirit, & before a Crouded Audience." The maneuvering between the two leading contestants is vividly described in a statement by Moses Brown dated the day after adjournment; the latter part of it is here quoted, partly as a picture of the methods of men in colonial days:

At length Henry Ward took me out towards the door and declared there was all they had and that they had no Orders to go any higher & proposed if we would not lodge any further subscriptions they would lay down their papers & proceed to Trial accordingly, we agreed Wm: Ellery then lodged the papers before held and would not deliver to any body, being one bond for 150£ L. Money & one other for £300, when we came to foot our sums, we had about £226 more then their's, ours being £4175. Here upon they delayed by many evasions proceeding to business and insisted for adjournment, to dinner, after which the meeting met and after waiting ¾ an hour Samuel Ward, Doct. Babcock H. Ward &c. came in and presented a security for their unconditional Subscription which they said was £508: 14 and a Bond for 500£ more. All this time no subscriptions was produced they alledging they had left them at home and none was finally produced. By this last bond they exceeded our subscriptions land and all about £385. Whereupon it was thought advisable to lodge the last subscription we had to be made use of upon this occasion amounting to £226 not caring to Trust the Vote they so much ahead aspecially as they insisted that our unconditional subscriptions ought not to tell any thing, whereby they would be about 1235£ over us, this reduced it so that reckoning the whole of their sum and the whole of ours they were 158£ more than we. We presented a calculation in the arguments of the amount of the building if at Newport more than Providence, amounting to £574 L. M. which we insisted should be added to ours which leaves a ballance in our favour of £415.

These tactics won the day, the Corporation finally voting:

Whereas the Corporation have fully heard Committees from the Counties of Newport, Kent and Bristol upon their application for a repeal of the Vote of this Corporation on the Sixteenth day of November last past for locateing the College Edifice in the Town of Providence, & maturely considered the several Sums offered, and all the Arguments used by all the parties concerned, and thereupon the Vote being put, Recede, or Not, It passed in the Negative, Twenty-one Votes to Fourteen: It is therefore Resolved that the said Edifice be built in the Town of Providence, and there be continued forever.

Contemporary financial statements are widely at variance, President Manning and Chancellor Hopkins both saying that Newport's subscription did not exceed that of Providence, while a writer in *The Newport Mercury* of February 12, 1770, who attended the meeting, says it was £600 or £700 larger. But the figures given by Moses Brown, who was in the thick of the fight, agree in their totals with the sums entered on the Corporation records, and make it clear that Providence raised less money than her rival. Why, then, was she given the prize? The Corporation were perhaps affected by her association with the founder of the colony, by the zeal she had shown in promptly raising so large an unconditional subscription, and by the business energy which was already so conspicuous among her leading men. A stronger motive still was undoubtedly the religious atmosphere of the place, where the Baptists were more influential than in Newport. Manning, in the letter quoted above, says it is reported that the eight ministers at the meeting "were all for Providence," although three lived in Newport, and he adds significantly, "I believe the Baptist Society in General are not displeased at ye Determination."

Leading men in Newport, however, were greatly dissatisfied with the result. Manning's letter further says: "You asked me in your last whether it had not raised a Party in the Govt. I answer no. but it warmed up ye old one something considerable." Some of this warmth broke out in a communication to *The Newport Mercury* of February 12, which accused Providence men of having "for 20 years past, . . . on every occasion, manifested the most inveterate malice against this town and island," charged the Providence party in the Corporation meeting with bribery and corruption, and called the President "a wolf in sheep's clothing." A more dangerous consequence of this political, commercial, and perhaps denominational rivalry was an attempt to secure a charter for another college. Dr. Stiles records in his diary on February 23, 1770, "Mr Ellery came to discourse about the Charter of another College, on the plan of equal Liberty to Congregationalists, Baptists, Episcopalians, Quakers." On April 5 he notes, "There is now depending before the Gen. Assembly of Rhode Isld a petition for a Charter for a College here in Newport, since the first Rh. Isl'd College is fixed at Providence." The charter passed the lower house, but in the upper house it was referred to the next session. The situation was alarming. Rhode Island individualism seemed about to beget colleges as freely as churches. A special meeting of the Corporation was therefore held at Warren, and a committee was appointed to draft a remonstrance to the Assembly against granting another college charter. A very able document was drawn up and approved, and a committee of influential men presented it to the legislature. Nothing more was heard of the rival charter.

Newport, then as now, had many natural advantages as the site of a college; and at that time it also had superiority in numbers, library facilities, and general culture. But the seeds of a larger growth were already stirring in Providence soil, and Time at least has justified the choice of the academic Fathers.

The Providence of that day was a town of some four thousand inhabitants, containing about four hundred houses, most of which stood near the water's edge on the east side of the river, or rose along the hill to Benefit Street. Great Bridge, eighteen feet wide, with a draw, connected the east side with Weybosset Point, to the north and west of which lay Great Salt Cove, while to the south ran the Providence River, then much wider than now, and fringed with wharves. At the extremity of the Point stood a few houses, reaching to the intersection of Weybosset Street and the newly named Westminster Street. On the former were some sixty-five houses; on the latter only six. On the south side of Weybosset Street, not far from where it joins Westminster Street again, stood Elder Snow's "New Light" Congregationalist meeting-house, on the site of the present "Round-Top" church. On the east side of the river were four meeting-houses — the Baptist, Episcopalian, Friends', and Congregationalist, — and the principal shops and public buildings. The narrow streets, with their swinging shop-signs, must have had some of the picturesqueness which we now associate with Old World towns. The newspapers of the time abound in advertisements of things for sale "next Door to the Sign of Shakespear's Head," "at the Sign of the Black Boy," "opposite the Golden Eagle," "at the Sign of the Elephant," etc.; of especial interest to the modern reader is the announcement, on July 30, 1763, of a "new Shop called the Sultan, at the Sign of Mustapha, . . . at the Corner near the East End of Weybosset Great Bridge," for this was probably the famous Turk's Head, later moved to the west end of the bridge. Old World customs, too, still survived. The whipping-post stood near the bridge, and was not a mere civic ornament. There was still imprisonment for debt. Slavery was accepted as a matter of course by the majority, in spite of the protests of the Quakers and a few others. The *Gazette* of May 5, 1764, has this business-like notice: "To be sold for no Fault, and very cheap for Cash; A Likely strong healthy Negro Girl, about 14 Years of Age. — Inquire of the Printer." Obadiah Brown, uncle of the four Brown brothers, at his death in 1762 left five slaves valued at £5400. John Brown, for twenty-one years treasurer of the college, engaged in the slave trade; and Stephen Hopkins, the first chancellor, was a slave-owner.

The beginnings of intellectual culture existed. No free school system had yet been established, but there were several private schools, and the children of the well-to-do were frequently sent away to famous "seminaries" elsewhere. There were some good private libraries, distinguished for solidity rather than size; and a public subscription library, founded in 1753, contained in 1768 more than nine hundred works, the use of which was offered to the students when the college came to Providence. Books were sold at Jenckes's book-shop and elsewhere; those advertised testify to religious rather than to literary tastes, although such works as *The Spectator* and *Pamela* occasionally appear in the lists. *The Providence Gazette*, started by William Goddard in 1762 and taken over in 1768 by John Carter, a pupil of Benjamin Franklin, was one of the best of the colonial newspapers. Even before the coming of the college the town was not wholly destitute of lectures on learned subjects, for the *Gazette* of March 3, 1764, announced a series of lectures on "that instructive and entertaining Branch of natural Philosophy, call'd Electricity" : the first lecture was to prove "that our Bodies contain enough of it, at all Times, to set an House on Fire" ; and the lecturer promised to show that "the endeavouring to guard against Lightning" was not "chargeable with Presumption, nor inconsistent with any of the Principles of natural or revealed Religion."

The energies of the citizens, however, were directed chiefly to commerce on land and sea. By the middle of the

century the situation of Providence at the head of navigation had won it the trade of northern Rhode Island and adjacent parts of Massachusetts, whence products were sent
to be exchanged for goods imported from abroad. The river
even above Weybosset Point was then deep enough to float
ocean-going vessels; and barks lying off what is now Steeple
Street, and at other wharves along the water-front, took on
cargoes of lumber, horses, candles, and rum, set sail for the
West Indies or London, and returned laden with slaves,
sugar, molasses, and European wares of all sorts. Priva-
teering during the French and Indian War had also been
a great source of wealth. At the period when Rhode Island
College was founded, two great families, the Hopkinses and
the Browns, were leaders in these commercial enterprises,
and both were closely connected with the early fortunes of
the college. William Hopkins was a famous merchant; his
brother Esek, after years of service in command of merchant vessels, became commander-in-chief of the first
American fleet; and the third brother was Stephen, the first
chancellor. The four sons of James Brown — Nicholas, Joseph, John, and Moses — were all eminent merchants; "by
1760," says Richman, "the family were operating no less
than eighty-four sloops, schooners, and brigantines." They
were all men of broad outlook, and were deeply interested
in the college.

Into this community the president, the professor, and the
students of Rhode Island College came in May, 1770. "On
Dr. Manning's taking up his abode here," says John Howland in his reminiscences, "he lived in the old house of
Benjamin Bowen, which stood on the lot at the foot of Bowen
street. . . . Mr. Howell was unmarried, and boarded. The
students boarded in private families, at one dollar and a
quarter per week. There they studied, and at certain hours

met in one of the chambers of the old brick school house, with the officers, for recitation." The schoolhouse is still standing, near the lower end of Meeting Street; the college exercises were held in the upper story. The change from rural Warren to a bustling town seemed likely, at first, to fulfill the forebodings of the memorialists in East Greenwich, if we may judge by the following passage from a letter written on July 9 by Theodore Foster, a member of the senior class:

The greatest Degree of Steadiness and firmness of Mind is very requisite in a Town no larger than this, to cause one as steadily to persue his Studies as in a Place no larger than Warren. One used to Noise and the Hurry of a Tradeing Town would not be much desturbed thereat, but for my own Part I must confess, the jolts of Waggons, the Ratlings of Coaches, the crying of Meat for the Market, the Hollowing of Negros and the ten thousand jinggles and Noises, that continually Surround us in every Part almost of the Town, Confuse my thinking and leave me absorpt in a Maze of eddying Fancy, which frequently overwhelmes me in the profound Depths of Nonsense even while engaged in the Study of Moral Philosophy which teaches the proper regulations of the Passions.

Meanwhile the committees of the Corporation had been energetically at work to rescue the perturbed students by lifting their abode as soon as possible "above the smoke and stir of this dim spot" into the "regions calm of mild and serene air" on College Hill. On February 17, only nine days after the meeting at Warren adjourned, the Building Committee, headed by Stephen Hopkins, John Jenckes, and John Brown, published a notice in *The Providence Gazette* urging subscribers to arrange at once to furnish timber and other materials, "as said Building will begin as soon as may be in the Spring." No time was lost indeed, for Solomon Drowne, a freshman, recorded in his diary on March 26, "This day the Committee for settling the spot for the College, met at the New-Brick School House, when it was determined it should be set on ye Hill opposite Mr. John Jenkes; up the Presbyterian Lane.'' The next day he wrote, ''This day they began to dig the Cellar for the College.'' The site chosen embraced about eight acres. The southern half, which was sold to the college by John and Moses Brown for $330, had formed a part of the original home lots of their ancestor, Chad Brown, and of George Rickard, who bought them from the Indians. The northern half cost the college $400; one-third of this had originally belonged to Chad Brown, and the rest to Daniel Abbott, one of the first settlers. The grounds were only three hundred feet wide, and did not include the land on which Hope College and Rhode Island Hall now stand. Presbyterian Lane (now College Street) was so named because it ran by the Presbyterian, or Congregational, church on Benefit Street, where the court-house now is. The site of the college was described by Morgan Edwards, in 1771, as ''commanding a prospect of the town of Providence below, of the Narraganset bay and the islands and of an extensive country, variegated with hills and dales, woods, and plains.'' ''Surely,'' he adds, ''this spot was made for a seat of the Muses!''

Here was soon rising the building known since 1823 as University Hall, but before that called merely '' the College Edifice.'' It was modeled on Nassau Hall at the College of New Jersey, although somewhat smaller and plainer. The Corporation built for the future, raising a structure not only noble in its proportions and massive simplicity, but for the time even magnificent in its dimensions. Manning describes the ''Edifice,'' with pardonable pride, as ''an elegant brick Building, 4 Stories high, 150 by 46 feet besides a Projection on each side of 33 by 10 feet.'' An enemy had therefore some basis for his sneer, in *The Boston Gazette* of July

27, 1772, that the Corporation had built "a College near as large as Babel; sufficient to contain ten Times the Number of Students that ever have, or ever will, oblige the Tutors of that popular University with Opportunity of educating, or instructing them."

Credit for the rapid yet thorough execution of the work belongs chiefly to the firm of Nicholas Brown and Company, consisting of the four Brown brothers, who volunteered to take entire charge of erecting the college building and the president's house. Their final account, presented to the Corporation in September, 1771, shows their minute care in performing this labor of love, which they pushed forward with characteristic energy and skill. On May 19, 1770, *The Providence Gazette* published the following news item: "Monday last [May 14] the first Foundation Stone of the COLLEGE about to be erected here was laid by Mr. JOHN BROWN, of this Place, Merchant, in Presence of a Number of Gentlemen, Friends to the Institution.—About twenty Workmen have since been employed on the Foundation, which Number will be increased, and the Building be compleated with all possible Dispatch." There is a tradition that Mr. Brown treated the crowd liberally to punch; and the accounts show that what was begun at the corner-stone was continued, almost in arithmetical progression, as the structure rose:

June 28	To 1 Gall, W I, Rum when Laying the Fi[r]st Floor	3^s 6^d	...
Augt 8	To 2 Galls. W I. Rum 7^s. 2 lbs Sugar 1^s. when Laying the 2d floor.........	8^s	...
Augt 25	To 4 Galls. W I, Rum (very good & old) a 3^s 9^d is ....15^s 1 lb Sugar $7\frac{1}{2}^d$. when raising 3d floor.......................$7\frac{1}{2}^d$	15^s $7\frac{1}{2}^d$	...

Sepr 14　To 4 Gallons W I Rum a 3ˢ 6ᵈ......　14ˢ　...

　　　　　to 1 lb Sugar 7ᵈ. when raising 4th Floor　7ᵈ　...

Octob 9　To 7¾ Gallons Old W I　...

　　　　　Rum a 3ˢ 6ᵈ............. £1 7ˢ 1½ᵈ　...

　　　　　2 lbs Sugar 1ˢ 2½ᵈ, when

　　　　　raising 5th floor ....1ˢ 2½ᵈ £1 8ˢ 4ᵈ　...

Octob 13　To 3 Gallons W I, Rum when raising

　　　　　the Roof a 3ˢ 6ᵈ ....　10ˢ 6ᵈ

The above items, in addition to revealing the habits of our forefathers, show how rapidly the walls went up, although made of brick and very solidly built. The speed was due partly to the disturbances following the Boston Massacre of March 5, which made it easy to secure plenty of skilled workmen from the neighboring city. The interior finishing went more slowly; Stiles records in his diary that on November 18, 1771, he "went to view the College where five or six lower Rooms are finishg off: they have about twenty Students, tho' none yet living in the College Edifice." The two lower stories were ready for use in the winter of 1771–72; the upper two were not finished on the inside until after the Revolution—the third in 1785, the fourth in 1788. The accounts show that up to March 11, 1771, the expense had been £2844 5ˢ 3¼ᵈ, or about $9480, including the cost of the president's house, the frame of which was raised on August 21, 1770; it was a plain two-and-a-half story house, set a little to the northwest of the college building. How much the interior finishing of the two buildings cost is not known. Money to "defray the Expence of Slateing the College Edifice" was still lacking in September, 1772, as a vote of the Corporation shows.

Now, at last, the affairs of the college and its officers began to have a settled air. President Manning had left his pastorate in Warren, rather abruptly and not without hard feeling on the part of the church; but in 1771 he became pastor of the Baptist church in Providence, at a salary of £50; as president his salary was now £100, besides his house; and he still had a Latin school, which in 1772 was removed to the college halls.[1] A deed now in the university archives shows that in 1771 he bought for $464 about seven acres of land adjoining the college grounds on the east, which he doubtless cultivated very successfully, for the biographical sketch of him by Howland says that "as a practical farmer and husbandman, he had but few equals." Professor Howell received a salary of £72, which was increased to £90 in 1773, and to £100 a year later, to commence "upon his removal from his present dwelling to the neighbourhood of the College Edifice." In 1774 a third teacher was appointed — John Dorrance, of the class of 1774, who acted as tutor and librarian, being the first graduate of Rhode Island College to give instruction in it.

The number of students steadily increased, rising from twenty-one in 1770 to forty-one in 1775, according to a list preserved among the Howell papers.[2] The income from their

---

[1] The school continued to prosper until the Revolution. After the war it was opened again in the college building; but in 1785 it was removed to the schoolhouse on Meeting Street, and lost its connection with the college for some years. In 1794 the Corporation voted, "That the President use his influence and endeavour to establish a grammar school in this Town as an appendage to this College," and the school was accordingly resumed. In 1810 the college built for the school a brick building costing $1452, at the head of College Street. The Corporation records show that in 1823 the school was still under the direction of the college. Just when this supervision ceased is not clear, but in 1852 a committee was appointed to sell the building and lease the lot; both land and building, however, remained the property of the college, which rented the latter for many years to principals of a private school still called the University Grammar School. In 1900 the building was torn down to make room for the Administration Building.

[2] According to Stiles's diary of June 24, 1773, there were 180 students at Harvard in 1773; at Yale there were 170 or 180 in 1777, according to the

tuition formed a considerable part of the college funds, and the total amount of it, at $12 a year per student, increased from £72 12ˢ in 1769 to £138 12ˢ in 1775; room rent at $5 yearly brought in something more. Yet the entire income was of course meager, and plans for enlarging the endowment were often under consideration. "Our whole College Fund consists of about £900 Sterl:," wrote Manning to an English friend on February 21, 1772, "being the whole Sum collected abroad: For no Money collected without the Colony is made use of in the Building: but solely applied to endowing it, with the strictest regard to the Donor's Intentions. the interest of which Sum is quite insufficient to provide for Tuition as two of us are now employed, and we stand in need of further help. May we not expect some further Assistance from our Friends in Engla[n]d?" On May 19 he asks of another English friend, "Wd: a well concerted scheme of a Lottery to raise a 1000, or 2[000]£ Sterl: meet wt: Encouragmt: by ye Sale of Tickets in England." The reply was: "We have our fill of these cursed gambling Lotteries in London every Year they are big with ten thousand Evils. Let the Devils Children have them all to themselves: Let us not touch or taste." At the Corporation meeting in September, 1772, a committee was appointed "to consider who may be a proper Person to Solicit Donations in Europe, and if the Revd. President should be thought most suitable for that purpose; then to Consider by whoom the place of President may be supplied during his Absence." In 1773 and 1774 honorary degrees were showered liberally on English clergymen of various churches, and on other persons more or less distinguished, in the hope of arousing their interest in the young institution.

diary of September 27, 1777, which also says that New Jersey College "used to have," *i.e.*, before the war, "70 or 80; Dartmo[uth] 60 or 70."

One of those recommended for the honor was suggestively described as "an old rich Man & learned that can leave £100 to ye Coll." But political events soon cut off all hope of aid from the mother country by any means.

The first five Commencements in Providence were held in Mr. Snow's meeting-house, the largest in town. Commencement before the Revolution was not the general and rather turbulent holiday which it was to become later, but the contemporary notices show that it attracted large crowds and excited much interest. The following description of the first Commencement in Providence is taken from the *Gazette* of September 1–8:

The Parties concerned met at the Court-House about Ten o'Clock, from whence they proceeded to the Reverend JOSEPH SNOW's Meeting-House, in the following Order; First, the Grammar Scholars, then the under Classes, the Candidates for Degrees, the Bachelors, the Trustees of the College, the Fellows, the Chancellor and Governor of the Colony, and lastly the President. When they were seated, the President introduced the Business of the Day by Prayer; then followed the *salutatory Oration*, in Latin, by Mr. DENNIS—and a *forensic Dispute;* with which ended the Exercises of the Forenoon. Those of the Afternoon began with an intermediate Oration on *Catholicism*, pronounced by Mr. FOSTER; then followed a *syllogistic Disputation*, in Latin, wherein Mr. FOSTER was Respondent, and Messieurs NASH, READ and DENNIS, Opponents. . . . The Business of the Day being concluded, and before the Assembly broke up, a Piece from *Homer* was pronounced by Master BILLY EDWARDS [son of Morgan Edwards], one of the Grammar School Boys, not nine Years old. This, as well as the other Performances, gained Applause from a polite and crowded Audience, and afforded Pleasure to the Friends of the Institution.

In spite of the politeness of the audiences at these early Commencements there seems to have been some disorder, at least that of a pushing crowd. On the day after this Commencement the Corporation expressed its thanks for the use of the church, and also voted to "repair all damages that were occasioned by the Throng." A similar vote was passed in 1773. From the accounts of Nicholas Brown and Company are taken the following items: June 2, 1772, "for hinges broke at Commencement," 3 shillings; "for mending Pews broke Commt Day," 1773, 8 shillings; "for Mending Windows broke in Mr. Snows Meeting House at Commencements 1773 & 74," 15 shillings.

The esteem in which the honors of a public Commencement were held by the undergraduates in these early years is amusingly shown by the following document:

Providence Febry 19th:: 1773 The remonstrance of the Senior Class of Rhode Island College, to the respectable, the PRESIDENT and PROFESSOR of the Same. Worthy Sirs, 'T is impossible we Should remain Calm and unconcerned at the present alarming Aspect of our affairs. Forgive us therefor if we express a Little Generous Warmth at the Indignity we have had sufficient Reason to fear will be offered us. Aroused by the too just Apprehension of the Ignominy and Disgrace that must unavoidably pursue us in future Life from the Deprivation of a public Commencement and collegial Honours, we are reduced to the disagreeable Necessity of addressing you in this manner. . . . The principal Objection is this, That we are not Orators. Now our Opinion of an Orator is Something similar to Longinus's of a poet, "That a Man must be born Such." . . . Since, then, it cannot be expected that a mere College Education without the previous Endowments of bounteous Nature can form the Orator, how Can it appear just or reasonable to any that for this Cause we should be deemed unfit to receive our Degrees in an honourable Manner. Another and far more reasonable Objection, prehaps, is, That we have not applied ourselves to our Studies with all that Dilligence and Assiduity we ought to have done. We Confess there are some Arts and Sciences for the Studying of which we had not a suitable turn of Mind and therfore could not apply ourselves attentively to them. . . . If we are Lacking in point of mental Faculties who is to be blamed? If what little Proficiency we have made in Literature joined with what through indefatigable Industry and unremitting Ardour we may make between this and Examination, will not entitle us to a Degree, we despair of ever having the Honour to be ranked among the Sons of this Seminary. . . . We shall add no more; but remain with all due Deference and Esteem, your dutiful Pupils.

Thus early in the history of the college did the students take the Faculty firmly in hand. The logic of the remonstrants was irresistible; the Commencement exercises were held as usual and without perceptible ebb in eloquence, for the *Gazette* remarked that "the young Gentlemen performed their respective Parts with great Propriety, which justly procured them the universal Applause of a judicious and candid Audience."

The Commencement of 1774 was especially glorious, for, says the *Gazette*, "the Honourable Governor of the Colony, escorted by the Company of Cadets, under the command of Col. NIGHTINGALE, preceded the usual Procession." The governor was Joseph Wanton, who wore full court dress. Howland's recollections of him at Commencements are vivid: "The governor's wig, which had been made in England, was of the pattern and size of that of the Speaker of the House of Commons, and so large that the shallow crowned hat could not be placed on his head without disturbing the curls. He therefore placed it under his left arm, and held his umbrella in his right hand. . . . The white wig of President Manning was of the largest dimensions usually worn in this country." Even the governor and his wig, however, could not rob the cadets of their share of glory on this occasion; the *Gazette* says they "made an elegant and truly military Appearance, and both in the Procession and Manoeuvres, which they performed on the College Green, procured universal Approbation, and convinced the Spectators, that Americans are no less capable of military Discipline than Europeans." The next year, on account of the outbreak of war, the public exercises of Commencement were omitted, at the suggestion of the seniors themselves.

In 1776 Commencement was held for the first time in the new Baptist church, now so familiar to all graduates of Brown University. This noble example of colonial church architecture was completed in 1775, at a cost of nearly $21,000. The building is much larger than was needed for the ordinary services of the church, and was erected, in accordance with the vote of the society on February 11, 1774, both "for the publick Worship of Almighty GOD; and also for holding Commencement in." Here the Commencements, with two exceptions,[1] have been held ever since, and the sons of the college have repaid in gratitude and veneration the generosity of the builders.

The Commencement of 1776 was the last until after the Revolution. The clouds of war had been gathering thicker and darker over the whole country, and in the events leading up to the outbreak of hostilities Rhode Island had taken a prominent part. In 1772 the king's schooner Gaspee, of eight guns, which had been prowling up and down Narragansett Bay to enforce the hated Sugar Act, was surprised by a party led by John Brown and burned to the water's edge. Two years later the colony was among the first to choose delegates to the Continental Congress, sending the old-time political foes, Stephen Hopkins and Samuel Ward. On March 2, 1775, in accordance with the recommendation of Congress against the purchase or use of East India tea, the people of Providence gathered in the Market Place and burned three hundred pounds of tea, along with Lord North's speech and copies of Tory newspapers, while the

[1] In 1804 and 1832 the First Congregational Church was used: in 1804 at the request of the seniors, who wished to "have the benifit of the Organ"; in 1832 because the First Baptist Meeting-House was undergoing repairs.

church bells tolled. When news of the battle of Lexington reached Rhode Island, the little commonwealth rose in open rebellion. The General Assembly created an "army of observation" of fifteen hundred men. It also instructed the colony's delegates in Congress to "use their whole influence" toward the formation "at the continental expense of an American fleet"; and when the fleet was put in commission in the following spring, a Rhode Islander, Esek Hopkins, was appointed commander. "Ere this," says Richman, "Rhode Island had discarded nearly every badge of colonialism. It had issued bills of credit for local defense; had established a local postal system; had erected fortifications; had confiscated the estates of wealthy loyalists of Newport and Narragansett; had even at length deposed Governor Wanton and chosen Nicholas Cooke—a Providence man—governor in his stead. Only one thing remained to be done to make explicit the independence which by these acts had been implied, and that was to pass a declaration formally absolving the people of Rhode Island from their allegiance to the British crown. Such a declaration was passed on May 4, just two months before the signing of the great Declaration at Philadelphia."

In such times, and in such a center of rebellion, the college could not remain unaffected or impassive. The Commencement programs on the whole reflect the agitation of the period less than might have been expected; probably the youthful orators were somewhat restrained by the Faculty. Yet in spite of the predominance of such themes as "Solitude," "Agriculture, and the Pleasures of a Country Life," "Female Education," "The Incomparable Advantages of Religion," "Politeness," and "Theatrical Exhibitions corrupt the Morals of Mankind," there appear on the program from time to time topics of a more stirring nature.

In 1770 the English dispute was on the thesis, "Standing Armies in a Time of Peace are detrimental to States." In 1771 the "Necessity of perpetuating the Union betwixt Great Britain and her Colonies" was made the subject of a dialogue, and was followed by an oration on "The Advantages of Peace." In 1773, the year of the Boston Tea Party, Theodore Foster, afterwards United States Senator from Rhode Island, spoke on "The Discovery, progressive Settlement, present State, and future Greatness, of the American Colonies." In 1774 Samuel Ward, soon to be lieutenant-colonel of the first Rhode Island regiment, took "Patriotism" as the subject for his master's oration; and the theme of the valedictorian in the year of the Declaration of Independence was "Liberty, with some Anecdotes from the present Times." The class of 1775, as we have seen, denied themselves the pleasure of a public Commencement, being, as they said in their petition to the Faculty and Corporation on June 8, "deeply affected with the Distresses of our oppressed Country, which now most unjustly feels the baneful Effects of arbitrary Power." President Manning and Professor Howell, in granting the petition, speak in a strain of ardent patriotism which proves that the officers as well as the students of Rhode Island College were worthy of its name: "And though the Din of Arms, and the Horrors of a civil War, should invade our hitherto peaceful Habitations; yet even these are preferable to a mean and base Submission to arbitrary Power, and lawless Rapine. Institutions of Learning will doubtless partake in the common Calamities of our Country, as Arms have ever proved unfriendly to the more refined and liberal Arts and Sciences; yet we are resolved to continue College Orders here as usual, excepting that the ensuing Commencement, by the Advice of such of the Corporation as could be con-

veniently consulted, will not be public." The Corporation
at the annual meeting in 1776 showed their spirit by hon-
oring thus the man who had been put in command of the
forces of the state: "IN consideration of the great Abilities,
literary merit and the many eminent services performed by
MAJOR GENERAL GREENE to this State in particular, and the
Continent in general — VOTED, that the Honorary Degree
of Master in the Arts be conferred upon him."

The foreboding in the Faculty's reply to the seniors was
soon realized. The battle of Bunker Hill and the plunge of
the whole country into war made the closing of the college
only a matter of time. The next year conditions grew rapidly worse for academic life in Rhode Island. In April the
American fleet under Hopkins was worsted in a fight with
a British man-of-war off Point Judith; and the enemy's
vessels patrolled the bay, greatly interfering with trade. In
September the situation was so threatening that the Corporation, at the time of the annual meeting, waited upon the
General Assembly in a body and successfully petitioned
them "to continue the College Funds in the Colony Treasury, notwithstanding their Act of March 4th: last." By this
prudent policy the small but precious funds of the college
safely weathered the storm. At about the same time the college library was removed to the country for safe keeping.
On November 13, 1776, President Manning wrote to an
English friend: "May you newer be alarmed, as we have
been, with the horrid roar of Artilery, and the hostile
Flames, destroying your Neighbours Habitations! These
I have repeatedly seen and heard, sitting in my House &
lying in my Bed. . . . You will not think strange that the
Colleges have suffered greatly, by this tremendous Convul-
sion: though, I believe, we have not suffered more than
our Neighbours." Less than a month later, on December 7,

seven ships of the line and four frigates, commanded by Sir Peter Parker, with seventy transports carrying six thousand British and Hessian troops, sailed into Newport harbor. "The royal Army landed on Rhode Island," wrote Manning in a letter after the war, "& took possession of the same: This brought their Camp in plain View from the College with the naked Eye; upon which the Country flew to Arms & marched for Providence, there, unprovided with Barracks they marched into the College & dispossesed the Students, about 40 in Number." On December 14 Manning published the following notice in *The Providence Gazette*:

THIS is to inform all the Students, that their Attendance on College Orders is hereby dispensed with, until the End of the next Spring Vacation; and that they are at Liberty to return Home, or prosecute their Studies elsewhere, as they think proper: And that those who pay as particular Attention to their Studies as these confused Times will admit, shall then be considered in the same Light and Standing as if they had given the usual Attendance here.

On May 17, 1777, he published another notice:

AS the Term of Vacation in the COLLEGE at Providence is now expired, the Students are hereby informed, that, in the present State of public Affairs, the Prosecution of Studies here is utterly impracticable, especially while this continues a garrisoned Town: It is recommended therefore to them, to prosecute their Studies elsewhere, for the present, to the best Advantage in their Power. The senior Class are desired to meet at the College, to pass their Examination, and receive their Degrees, at the usual Time, being the Second Day of September next, unless the College should be called together sooner.

In accordance with these announcements the Corporation met on September 3, 1777, and granted seven bachelor's degrees and four master's degrees. A meeting held the following day was adjourned to "next Wednesday Week." The week proved to be a long one, lasting until May 5, 1780.

The story of the interval, so far as exercises at the college are concerned, is told briefly in the following entry on the Corporation records: "As the College Edefice was taken for Barracks and an Hospital for the American Army, and continued to be so occupied by them & the Troops of France from December 7th: 1776 until June 1782, the course of Education in the College, and the regular meetings of the Corporation, were in a great measure interrupted during that period."[1]

During the war twenty-three of the sixty-seven graduates of the college between the years 1769 and 1782 engaged in active service on the American side, some as soldiers, others as chaplains, surgeons, and members of military committees. None of the officers of instruction, however, took active part in the war. Professor Howell and Tutor Dorrance both studied law, the former resigning his professorship in 1779. President Manning's pastorate of the Baptist church absorbed much of his energy, the more so because of increasing destitution and distress among his parishioners as the war went on. But there is evidence that he found time for other good works. Howland, in a biographical sketch of Manning, tells how he obtained from General Sullivan, at the last moment, a reprieve for three soldiers condemned by court-martial, and, by hard riding, arrived in time to prevent their execution. Early in the year 1779 he gave proof of his powers as a persuasive diplomat in an important mission for the commonwealth. By this time the destitution in Rhode Island was very great. "Two thousand persons," says the historian Arnold, "driven

[1] In the claim for damages presented by the Corporation to the United States Government after the Revolution it is stated that the American troops used it for barracks and hospital from December 10, 1776, to April 20, 1780, and that the French troops used it for a hospital from June 26, 1780, to May 27, 1782.

from Rhode-island were scattered about, homeless and pen-
niless, through the State, but chiefly in Providence, dependent upon public or private charity.'' The case was the more
desperate because several of the neighboring states had laws
forbidding the exportation of food stuffs. The service that
Manning did in this crisis is best told in the words of
Howland:

The Governour and Council of War of this State, wishing to give
their language of remonstrance, a power of impression which paper
could not be made to convey, commissioned Doctor Manning to
repair to Connecticut and represent personally to the government of
that State our peculiar situation, and to confer with, and propose to
them, a different mode of procedure. The Doctor in this embassy
obtained all that he desired, the restrictions were removed, and in
addition to this, on his representation of the circumstances of the
refugees from the Islands, contributions, in money or provisions,
were made in nearly all the parishes in the interiour of Connecticut,
and forwarded for their relief.

It should be added that Deputy-Governor Bowen was also
a commissioner. The following letter to Moses Brown com-
pletes the story:

Providence March 25th: 1779

Respected friend

The Distress of the Poor in this Town for want of Bread is so great
that unless some speedy Provision can be made I fear many must suffer
extremely, if not perish. Upon looking into the Matter I can see but
one way to prevent it; and that is that those who have any more than
for a present Supply for their Families should lend it to Capt Peleg
Clarke, to be immediately distributed, & to repay it on the Arrival of
the Grain from Connecticut, which the depths of the Roads prevent
being brought, till better Weather — Clarke says he will do this, as
soon as in his Power: But all agree that unless 20 Bushels can be got,
such a Distribution will be impracticable, so great is the Number in
distress. I have got ready five Bushels of Indian Corn, & Arthur Fenner 2 Bushels of Rye: and if you can do any thing in this Way shd.
be glad you would communicate it to Capt Clarke as soon as may be.

It would be best to have the whole ground, and distributed at the Market House. I know I need use no Arguments, but only recite the facts to a benevolent Mind.

I am &c

James Manning

On April 29, 1779, President and Mrs. Manning left Providence on a journey by horse and carriage to the Middle States. They were gone five months; and the President's journal[1] contains much interesting information about bad roads, "tremendous mountains," the crops, distinguished men, and the political and military situation. They visited relatives in New York and New Jersey, and reached Philadelphia on July 2. The return itinerary included West Point, where Manning dined at General Greene's quarters, and met Washington, the French ambassador, and Baron von Steuben.

In the midst of these varied experiences President Manning did not forget the college nor lose heart over its prospects. In a letter of November 17, 1778, to the Rev. Thomas Ustick, of the class of 1771, he says, after urging him to consider settling in Pomfret, Connecticut: "It would be a good place for a Latin school, a nursery for the College, which I wish you immediately to engage in, and endeavor to influence as many as you can of our people to educate their children. . . . I have written and am about writing to all our ministers capable of teaching Latin, to immediately engage in the business. I hope, from present appearances, that college orders may be again revived next spring." It was not, however, until the spring of 1780 that even an attempt could be made to resume instruction at the college. By a notice in *The Providence Gazette* of April 29, the chancellor, the president, and two fellows called a meeting of the

[1] Published in Guild's *Brown University and Manning*.

[70]

Corporation for May 5 "at the College-Hall"; the call is dated April 28, only eight days after the troops left the building. At this meeting, say the records, "President Manning presented a proposal for reviving the College containing the terms on which he would begin to instruct the youth who might apply for Education, which was approved; and, he was accordingly ordered to begin." His salary was fixed at £60. In the archives is the following notice, signed by Manning and dated April 13, 1780, or a week before the troops vacated the college building; it was published in the *Gazette* of April 29:

NOTICE is hereby given, that on the 10th of May next the College in this Town will be opened, to receive the Youth who desire to prosecute their Studies under my Direction: And that a Grammar School will be opened, at the same Time and Place. The Terms of Tuition, and Boarding, may be known by applying to the Subscriber; who will pay particular Attention as well to the Morals as Instruction of those committed to his Care.

This courageous beginning amidst the ruin left by war was destined to a speedy interruption. On the fifth of the next month Governor Greene wrote to Manning the following note, which cannot look more somber now, on its paper browned by age, than it did to the President when it came fresh into his hands that day:

Sir,

Doctor Craick, who is directed by General Washington to apply to this State to be furnished with some Convenient Building for a Hospital for the Reception of the French Invalids, has represented to the Council of War that the College Edifice is the most convenient in Every Respect for the purpose. I am desired by the Council to acquaint you with this matter & request your attendance to give them information of the Use, which is now made of said Edifice.

According to Backus, the building was seized on Sunday, June 25, "while Dr. Manning was gone to preach in town."

For nearly two years the college was again homeless. But the stout-hearted President was not discouraged, nor utterly thwarted. In September, 1780, a meeting of the Corporation, attended by four fellows and four trustees, met at his house and reëlected Stephen Hopkins as chancellor and John Brown as treasurer, and elected David Howell secretary. They transacted no other business—indeed, what could they have done? But it is probable that they informally sanctioned Manning's purpose to continue the work of instruction as best he might. It is certain that he did continue it, perhaps in his own house, for two years later four candidates for the bachelor's degree are spoken of, in the Corporation records, as "having pursued their Studies under President Manning."

Some time before this, however, the college building had been restored to the uses for which it was designed, the last of the French invalids having been removed on May 27, 1782. But it was in a dreadful condition. Manning, in an unpublished letter of June 17, 1782, says, "The Corporation have ordered the augean Stable cleansed. . . . It is left in a most horrid dirty, Shattered Situation." The first draft of an undated petition to the General Assembly, in Manning's hand, praying that the building may be restored to the college, contains the following graphic details: "Great Injury hath been done to every Part of it since taken out of the Hands of the Corporation; Especially by two bui[l]dings adjoining it one an House of Office at the North End, with a Vault 15 Feet deep under it, having broken down the Wall of the College to facilitate the Passage of the Invalids from the Edifice into it; from which Addition, the intolerable Stench renders all the northern Part uninhabitable; and the other an Horse Stable bui[l]t from the East Projection to ye North End by which the House is greatly weakened many of the

Windows are also taken entirely out of the House, & others so broken as well as the Slate on the Roof that the Storms continually beat into it.''

The followed undated letters, hitherto unpublished, set before us in realistic vividness the distressful state of things, during the occupation of the building by the French troops at least, and the helplessness of its would-be guardians. The urgency of the situation and the haste with which the notes were interchanged are shown by the fact that both are written on a single sheet, the first on one side and the reply on the back.

Gentn

I just now am informed, through a french Soldier, that speaks English, that they are about knocking down the Closets in the College, to sell the Boards; and that they are going to sell all the College Windows, at the Vandue to Morrow, & say that they put them all in, and of Course they belong to the King — These Orders, he says come from the Commissary at Boston — There is not one of the French now here, who was at the Repairing the College — I think Mr Joseph Brown, ast. [= assisted by?] David Martin took an Acct: of the Situation of the Building, after the Council Voted it away — I am inclined to think this Information true from the Noise of Hammers there for some Days past; & from some of the Windows being taken out — I would have seen you both if I had not been lame — The sale begins at ten OClock to-morrow, it will be necessary to see to this early —   Yours,

Wednesday Evg. 10 OClocke
Messrs Jos: & Nicho. Brown   Jas. Manning

Sr

I can only advise your sending an account of the within addressed to such of the Corporation as are in this town as early as you can in the morning Requesting a meeting of them at your Howse or if you choose at my Howse Tho it may be best upon the spott & if they will generally come together I beleve if nothing ells can be done they may be prevented from selling the windows

[73]

you will appoint the time & p[l]ace & be sure to notify all the members in town   yours

Jos Brown

N Brown

The following Gentlemen, Members of the Corporation, agreeable to the above Advice, are earnestly requested to meet at my House this Morng at 9 OClock,

Thursday Morng   J. Manning

6 OClocke

[*Fifteen names follow.*]

It was natural that the Corporation should determine to get compensation for the use of and injury to the college property through so long a time. They set about it early, and kept at it for years, until, at the end of the century, the slow machinery of government ground out partial justice. At a meeting of seven members of the Corporation on May 31, 1782, four days after the building was vacated by the French, a committee was appointed to make a careful estimate of the damage; and their report shows that doors, hinges, locks, window frames, etc., were gone from every room on the first and second floors, and that serious damage had been done to the walls and roof. On the basis of this report, made June 12, 1782, the following bill, splendidly engrossed in a bold hand, was presented to the central government:

The United States of America To Rhode Island College Dr. To the use of the College Edifice of 150 Feet Long & 4 Storeys high from 10 Decemr: 1776, to 20 Aprl: 1780: for Barracks & an Hospital for the American Troops. @ £ 120. pr: Ann: 3 yrs. 4 mo: and 10 days £403–6–8. To the use of the College from 26 June 1780 To May 27. 1782. for a Hospital for the Troops of his Most Christian Majesty, 1 Year & 11 Months, @ £120. pr Ann. £230. To damage . . . £675–17. Total £1309–3–8.

This bill was presented in 1782, and persistent attempts were made to get a settlement. On December 13, 1792, an additional charge of £991 0ˢ 6ᵈ for simple interest was calmly added, making a total of £2300 4ˢ 2ᵈ, or about $7667. On May 27, 1800, as the manuscript accounts of Nicholas Brown, treasurer, show, the sum of $2779.13 was received by the college for the use of and damage to the building by the American troops.

CHAPTER III

PRESIDENT MANNING'S ADMINISTRATION

[CONTINUED]

FINANCIAL DIFFICULTIES AFTER THE REVOLUTION : GROWTH OF THE
COLLEGE : COMMENCEMENTS : PERSONALITY AND WORK OF MANNING :
CURRICULUM : SCHOLARSHIP AND SUCCESS OF THE EARLY GRADUATES

THE final evacuation of the college building by the
soldiers in 1782 left the way open for a complete resumption of all college activities, but the difficulties were
very great and required energetic action. The President in a
notice dated August 16, 1782, and published in *The Providence Gazette* of August 31, asked for a full attendance
at the coming meeting of the Corporation : "The present
deplorable Situation of the College loudly calls for every
possible Assistance from all its Friends, but more especially
for that of the Corporation." In response to this call, fifteen trustees and six fellows met at the college on September 4 and 5. They granted the bachelor's degree to seven
candidates, four who had been studying under President
Manning, and three who had been juniors in college at the
time of its breaking up. They voted to ask the legislature
to approve of sundry minor changes in the charter necessitated by the severance of the colonies from Great Britain.
The vigorous and judicious measures by which they met
the immediate needs of the situation and planned for the
future are best shown by a few entries from the records :

The Chancellor, the President & Henry Ward Esqr: were appointed a committee to break the old Seal of the College, which contains the Busts of the present King and Queen of Great Britain; and
to agree upon a new Seal with suitable devices, to be made of Silver, and to report their proceedings thereon to this Corporation.[1]

[1] For an imprint of the second seal, see page 520.

RESOLVED that the President & Govr: Bowen be a Committee to arrange all the College papers, which are now loose & in a scattered condition; and to get the same as soon as possible recorded in the book containing the College records.

RESOLVED that the College Library, which, owing to the public confusions, has for several years been in the country, after being compared & examined by the Catalogue, be immediately brought, with care into Town, that the books may be made use of by the Students, as formerly. — President Manning & John Jenckes Esqr: are requested to see this order, forthwith executed.

RESOLVED, that a Subscription be opened for raising, not exceeding £300 for the sole purpose of repairing the College Edefice.

The President and Jabez Bowen were appointed a committee "to procure a Tutor, as soon as possible on the best terms they can"; they engaged Ashur Robbins, a graduate of Yale in 1782, who later entered the law, becoming United States district attorney in 1812, and representing the state in the national Senate from 1825 to 1839.

The college now began anew to struggle upward, but the path was rough and progress slow. For a while the state of things was almost desperate, for both students and funds were lacking. A public Commencement, at which six graduated, was held in 1783; but the students in college at the outbreak of the war and those who had recently been under Manning's private instruction having nearly all taken their degrees, the number in attendance was now very small, only twelve in November, 1783, and no more Commencements could be held until 1786. The productive funds at that time yielded barely £60, and there was also a great lack of books and apparatus.

Various methods of increasing the income were open to the Corporation, and they tried them all. We have seen how persistently, and how long in vain, they sought to recover damages from the national government. At the meeting in September, 1782, a committee was appointed to sell the college lands in various parts of the state, the gifts of Esek Hopkins and others; but this plan offered little prospect of relief, for agriculture was still prostrate. Because of the general impoverishment there was also small hope of raising much money by subscription in this country, and it was not a favorable time to ask Englishmen to aid an American college. Yet Manning laid before the Corporation on January 27, 1783, a plan for soliciting funds abroad, offering to attempt the task in person. The Corporation agreed to the proposal, provided some suitable person could be found to preside over the college in his absence; but this was not easily done, and the plan was never carried out. The President tried instead the persuasive powers of his pen. On November 8, 1783, he wrote to the Rev. John Ryland: "Can you find no Gentleman of Fortune among you who wishes to rear a lasting Monument to his Honour in Amarica? If you can direct his attention to the Hill of Providence in the State of Rhode Island, where are [= whereon] an elegant Edifice is already erected, which waits for a Name from Some distinguished Benefactor The Corporation are determined to do this Honour to its greatest." On the same day he wrote to Thomas Llewelyn, of London: "Cambridge College was so fortunate as to attract the Attention of an Hollis; New Haven of a Yale & New Hampshire of a Dartmouth: who have given their Names to these Seats of Science. We should think ourselves no less happy in the Patronage of a *Llewelin*. *Llewelin College* appears well when written & sounds no less agreeably when spoken." But this might-be benefactor had died three months before, and the ears of others seemed equally deaf.

At a meeting of the Corporation on January 8, 1784, a comprehensive scheme was adopted. Mr. Howell was appointed to go to Europe to solicit funds, being promised his expenses "exclusive of his Cloathing" and seven and a half per cent of all moneys he turned in. The President was "to try his Hand in New England," being "esteemed a *Poor Beggar*," as he humorously wrote to Howell the next day. William Rogers, the first student matriculated, was asked to solicit "to the Southard"; and the Rev. William Van Horn, an honorary Master of Arts in 1774, was given an opportunity to show his gratitude by collecting funds in the Middle States. Manning might truthfully write to Rogers, on January 9, "You see we are determined to sweep the Board now." On the same day he wrote a persuasive letter to Howell: "Mr. Mullet, an English Mercht: of great Character, & a Baptist, . . . tells me he thinks our Prospect is flattering, if there is no Time lost in the Application, which should be made before the People are gulled out by other Soliciters, who are flocking over in Crouds — Dr. Witherspoon is, I am told, already gone. I fear we shall again make it an Afternoon Business, if delayed beyond the Spring." But Howell and Rogers both declined, and little came of the attempt as a whole.

The Corporation tried yet another plan: they appealed to the king of France. Fantastic as the scheme seems now, there were facts which made it appear feasible then, even to the hard-headed business men of the Corporation: the French king had been our recent ally; his invalid soldiers and seamen had found a hospital in the college building; French officers, including some members of the nobility, being quartered in Providence for a year or more, had become the warm friends of leading members of the Corporation; and it was reported that the king had made an offer of aid to Yale College, which had been declined. A resolution was therefore passed, at the annual meeting in 1783, "that an Application be made to his most Christian Majesty to patronize this College; and that the President, Revd: Mr Stillman & Doctr: Waterhouse be a committee to draught a Petition to him for that Purpose." At a meeting on January 7–8, 1784, the address to the king and an accompanying letter to Franklin, then our minister at the French court, were read and approved; and it was voted that a duplicate of each be sent to Howell, in Congress, "to be communicated to the French Minister at Philadelphia, soliciting his influence in our favour." Manning wrote to Howell the day after, "The Idea is to feel the Minister to know whether our Proposal will take, & not to let him know of the real Application, unless he encourages it." Howell replied, on February 20, that the minister received him courteously and agreed to forward the letter and the address to Franklin with his next dispatches. Nothing more was heard of either; it is probable that both were swallowed up in Franklin's massive common sense. Undiscouraged, the Corporation renewed the attempt to catch the ear of his Most Christian Majesty two years later, when President Manning was in Congress; he and his colleague were asked to forward the address to our new minister in France, Thomas Jefferson, with a request for his aid. Jefferson's reply, on July 22, 1787, courteously pricked the bubble: "I thought it necessary to sound, previously, those who were able to inform me what would be the success of the application. I was assured, so as to leave no doubt, that it would not be complied with. . . . Upon such information I was satisfied, that it was most prudent not to deliver the letter, and to spare to both parties the disagreeableness of giving and receiving a denial." Thus ended the first and last attempt of Brown University to get aid from the crowned heads of Europe.

While these various methods to increase the funds and

improve the equipment of the college were being tried, the income remained practically the same. But help was slowly coming from a humbler but surer source, an increase in the number of students, with a small advance in the price for tuition. The growth was fundamentally due to the reviving prosperity of the country, but a secondary cause was better facilities for instruction. In the autumn of 1783 Mr. John Brown offered to pay half the sum necessary to buy "a compleat Philosophical Apparatus & Library" if the Corporation would raise the other half, and in a few days about £700 was secured for this purpose. As a result of this timely gift, some valuable instruments and about fourteen hundred books were soon added to the equipment.

The next year the Faculty was much strengthened by the appointment of two professors, "both of whom," writes Manning, "engaged to give Lectures in their respective Branches, without any Expence to the College while destitute of an Endowment." They were Joseph Brown, one of the Brown brothers, described by Manning as "a philosophical Genius," who was appointed professor of experimental philosophy; and Benjamin Waterhouse, a doctor of medicine of the University of Leyden and professor of the theory and practice of physic in Harvard College. The Corporation voted on September 2, 1784, "That this Corporation will proceed to establish Professorships in the various branches of Learning, in this College, as fast as suitable persons can be found to undertake them; and that the President & Professors be requested to enquire after suitable Persons for such places." Professor Waterhouse served through Manning's administration. Professor Brown died in 1785, and was succeeded the next year by Peres Fobes, a Congregationalist clergyman, who had been acting president earlier in the year during Manning's absence in Congress.

Benjamin West was appointed professor of mathematics and astronomy in 1786. These professorships, although they heightened the reputation and efficiency of the college, were lectureships merely; the daily recitations had to be conducted by the president and tutors. For four months in 1785–86 the college had the services of a second tutor, Robert Scott, a graduate of the University of Edinburgh, who taught the languages, arts, and sciences. He was followed in 1786 by Abel Flint, a graduate of Yale, who withdrew in 1790 to enter the Congregationalist ministry, and was succeeded by Josias L. Arnold, a graduate of Dartmouth. Meanwhile, in 1787, a third tutor had been added to the Faculty, Jonathan Maxcy, of the class of 1787, soon to become president.

Tutors could not be had for nothing, although professors might be; and it was the increase in the number of students that made possible as well as necessary this enlargement of the teaching corps. Manning's letters during these years show that the college was steadily growing. On July 3, 1784, he says there were twenty-three college students, besides nearly twenty in the grammar school; a year later, thirty-seven; in April, 1786, about fifty; in September, 1787, sixty; in June of the next year, "more Students than ever it had"; and on Christmas Day, 1789, the number lacked "but two of Seventy." The root out of dry ground was proving that it had life in it, and would yet grow into a great tree.

But the relief from increase in receipts for tuition and room rent was slow at first, and often uncertain, particularly when students could not, or would not, pay their bills promptly. From these and other causes (chiefly the refusal of the legislature to pay him in good money for his recent services in Congress), the winter of 1786–87 was the most distressful in Manning's life. On January 18, 1787, he writes thus to Hezekiah Smith:

Of all the Arreerages of Tuition for the last year, & the quarter advanced in this I have not recd, Ten Pounds. I was taken sick the day after the second great Snow. With no provisions in the Cellar, except 100 Wt. Cheese, 2 Barrels of Cyder & some Potatoes, with not a Load of Wood at my door: Nor could I command a single Dollar to supply these Wants. The kindness of my Neighbours, however, kept us from suffering. But when a man has hardly earned money to be reduced to this abject state of Dependance, requires the exercise of more grace than I can boast of. . . . I have serious thought of removing to the farm at the Jerseys, & undertake *digging* for my support. Should things wear the same unfavourable aspect next year, I believe I shall make the experiment if my Life is spared.

Unpublished letters to the Rev. Samuel Jones, who was establishing a school in Kentucky and perhaps planning for a college there, and who wanted Manning's aid, show that he was deeply dissatisfied with conditions in Providence during the years 1785 to 1787, and that the college narrowly escaped losing its president:

Providence Nov. 12th: 1785 . . . I really wish, should my Life be spared, that my connections here would any how admit of my going out with you in the Spring. I feel my Spirit moved to it, but as yet see no way open, but by disengaging myself at once from Providence at all events; & I see not how I can consistently do this, at least, before the next commencmt: My feelings have long since prognosticated that I shall not spend all the remnant of my days in Providence, unless they are few indeed. . . . The labours of my present Situation, are, I feel most sensibly, too great for me to support.

Providence Feby 27th: 1786. . . . My determination to accompany you to Kentucky was so fixed, that I was making my arrangements for it before your Letter arrived; but I find it totally impracticable to procure money sufficient for my Journey & to supply my Family during my Absence. And, of course I must give up the design for this year. I had not communicated my intentions to the Corporation, nor to the Church & Society; nor did I intend doing it till near the time of my departure, as I did not intend to have been stopped by any remonstrances from that quarter; but the want of the *Unum necessarium* is a knock me down Argument, the force of which I cannot resist. . . . You cannot imagine how much I have been pleased with the thoughts of being your companion in travel. But I must groan it out at Providence, for ought I can see, for the present. My prospects here are not more chearing than heretofore. I expect, with all the Oeconomy of which I am Master to sink money again this year, unless the Corporation grants me relief, which I have not much reason to expect.

Providence July 23d: 1787 . . . The College Horizen, to me, is cloudy at Providence, but what will be the final result God only knows. I expect some trying scenes between this & Commencement. I have lately expelled two Students, for a flagrant violation of the College Laws, one of them a senior, is of this Town has many connections, and amongst them some of the most powerful families, of these some by Mr. Howels means, who has seized this opportunity to raise a clamour against me, & has advised them to appeal to the Corporation for a reversal of our Judgment, are warm, this they are now pursuing, under Howels advice & assistance. John Brown has become interested for the young men, & though he wishes to do me no Injury, I expect the spirited manner in which he has taken it up will carry him great lengths. He has conferred with me several times on the subject, & I have told him plainly that if I must be subject to the pointed censure of David Howel, whether I execute, or dispense with the Laws (which has been of late the case); & if he must lay hold of every opportunity to injure the Authority of College, & be supported in it by the influential men in the Corporation, they may take the Presidential Chair that choses, for I will not hold it; — That I will [not] be browbeaten by that mischief making man; & that I do not care two pence for the consequences. What will be the issue of this affair I am yet to learn, but, I am determined to resent any affront offered me on this subject, by that assiduous Antagonist. It is the opinion of many that he wishes to displace me from the College. This I believe is the truth; but it is not so agreeable to be pushed out.

The situation soon after improved in every respect, and the President regained his usual equanimity.

Commencements were resumed in 1786, when a class of fifteen took their degrees. This year the seniors first wore academic costume, in accordance with the following vote of the Corporation on March 13 : "RESOLVED that in future the Candidates for Bachelor's Degrees, being Alumni of the College, shall be clad at Commenct : in black, flowing robes. & caps, similar to those used at other Universities." The largest graduating class under President Manning was that of 1790, numbering twenty-two, a record not equaled for several years. The total number of graduates from 1786 to 1791 was ninety-two, as against seventy-three for all the years up to that time. The Commencement of 1786 is noteworthy for the presence among the candidates of Nicholas Brown, Jr., the future benefactor of the college, who appropriately took for the subject of his oration, "The Advantages of Commerce." The contact of these early Commencements with contemporary events was illustrated in this year by the forensic dispute on the question, "Whether it would not have been better for America to have remained dependent on Great-Britain" and by a "Tribute to the Memory of our late departed Friend General Greene." The procession was made splendid by the presence of "the United Company of the Train of Artillery, under Arms, in complete Uniform" ; and the catholicity of the college was symbolized by "a Choir of Singers, from all the Societies in Town," who "performed" an anthem. The attendance of a military company and of singers continued to be features of Commencement for several years. In 1787 two innovations appeared on the program, an oration in Greek and a poem. The latter, "The Prospects of America," with the valedictory addresses (also in verse), was by Jonathan Maxcy; he "was induced with reluctance to consent to its publication," says his editor, who adds that at Commencement it

"gained the universal Applause of a large, crouded and polite Assembly." The urgent political problem of the day was
discussed by one of the orators, who spoke "An Oration on
the present Appearance of public Affairs in the United States
of America," advocating "the great foederal Measures"
then being so hotly debated in the Constitutional Convention, urging "the Disuse of foreign Goods," and "soliciting
the fair Daughters of America to set the patriotic Example
. . . by banishing from their Dress the costly Gewgaws and
Articles of foreign Production." The following year all the
members of the Corporation were provided with seats on
the stage. This change threatened to crowd the graduating class off, and they petitioned to be allowed to sit on the
stage, like former classes; adding that they hoped for a favorable answer, "knowing that you, as well as themselves,
are interested in the eclat of that day." There is no evidence
whether the request was granted or not; but in 1790 a committee was appointed to erect a stage "for the accommodation of the Corporation & Candidates at the next Commencement."

The interest of the students in "the eclat of that day"
sprang in part from the fact that Commencement was to
them Class Day as well. This aspect of the occasion was
recognized by the Corporation, who voted on September 6,
1787, "that in future the Salutatory Oration at public Commencements, be assigned by the President; that the Valedictory and intermediate Orations, be assigned by the Classes;
—And that the Syllogistic and Forensic Disputes, and such
other Exercises as they may judge necessary, be assigned
by the President and Tutors." The program of 1788 may
fairly be called polyglot, containing orations in Hebrew,
Greek, Latin, French, and English. It had variety in other
ways, for it comprised a "Poem on Liberty," a "Burlesque

Poem, on Political Projectors," a "Tribute to the Memory of our departed Heroes," "A Dialogue in blank Verse, on the Situation and Prospects of America," a "Comic Dialogue,—to ridicule false Learning," and "A Sketch on Creation." After this display of versatility it is not surprising that the Corporation voted, the next day, "that the Graduates of this College write, or procure to be written fair copies of their Commencement Exercises, and have them bound in an handsome volume, annually, at their expence, to be deposited in the College Library."

The Providence Gazette in speaking of this Commencement noted that "as the Day was fine, so the Concourse of People was prodigious." The disorder may in consequence have been greater than usual; at any rate the Corporation saw fit on the day before the next Commencement to take extra precautions for the maintenance of order, voting "that James Arnold Esquire be requested to take charge of the Baptist Meeting House to morrow, & that Major Allen, & Mr: Martin, the Deputy Sheriffs together with the Town Seargeant be requested to assist him, with such others as they may employ." Even these formidable safeguards proved not enough, and in 1790 a committee was appointed to "apply to the General Assembly, to authorize and direct the Sheriff of the County of Providence to attend on this Corporation, on Commencement days, in future, and, by himself or deputies, to preserve the peace, good order, and decorum, on Commencement days, in, and about the Meeting house, in which the Public Commencement may be celebrated." At the same meeting the Corporation tried to strike at the underlying cause of much of the disorder by a resolution "That it be recommended to the Baptist Society, in future, to take effectual measures to prevent the erection of Booths, or receptacles for liquors, or other things for sale, and other disorderly practices on the Baptist Meeting-House lot, on Commencement days."

The Commencement of 1790 was notable for several things. The size of the class has already been mentioned; the program was naturally longer than any before it, consisting of thirteen numbers, and the subjects were curiously varied. Moses Brown, Jr., true to the traditions of his family, spoke an oration "On the History of Commerce and Navigation"; Asa Messer, later to be president, grappled with Job Nelson in a dispute on the question, "Would Mankind have been more happy than they now are, had the Earth spontaneously yielded her Fruits necessary for the Support of Man"; one oration consisted of "Reflections on Happiness"; Franklin, who had recently died, was made the subject of a "Panegyric"; a candidate for the master's degree spoke on "The Expediency of establishing a Federal University in America"; the salutatorian followed up his Latin address by an English oration "congratulating the State of Rhode Island upon their Accession to the federal Government"; and the Greek oration was on "The Slave Trade."

The event referred to by the salutatorian had brought a distinguished visitor to Rhode Island a few weeks before, in the person of George Washington, who came to Providence on August 18, accompanied by Jefferson, his Secretary of State, and other public men. It was a holiday throughout the town; and in the evening, according to the *Gazette*, " the President and many others took a Walk on the College Green, to view the Illumination of that Edifice, which was done by the Students, and made a most splendid Appearance." The next day the students escorted him to the college, where President Manning made him an address of welcome, to which he replied, expressing his "ardent wishes that Heaven may prosper the literary Institution under your care.'' At Commencement, a fortnight later, Washington was given the degree of LL.D.

The Commencement of 1790 was the last presided over by President Manning. For some time before his death he seems to have had intimations that his work was almost done, and at their meeting in September, 1790, according to Howell, he requested the Corporation to make arrangements to fill his place; but the end came suddenly at last. On July 24, 1791, while at family prayers, he was stricken with apoplexy, and died five days later. The Corporation met at once and arranged for the funeral service, which occurred the following day at the college. A great number of the Corporation members, graduates, students, and citizens attended the body to the North Burying Ground, where it was laid beside that of Nicholas Brown, Sr., who had died a few months before. Howell wrote of the funeral, ''It was the largest & most solemn that I have ever seen in this place.''

A sketch of President Manning, published in *The Providence Gazette* of August 6, and attributed to Judge Howell, said:

His Countenance was stately and majestic, full of Dignity, Goodness and Gravity; and the Temper of his Mind was a Counterpart to it. —He was formed for Enterprize—his Address was pleasing, his Manners enchanting, his Voice harmonious, and his Eloquence almost irresistible. . . . The good Order, Learning and Respectability, of the Baptist Churches in the Eastern States, are much owing to his assiduous Attention to their Welfare.—The Credit of his Name, and his personal Influence among them, perhaps have never been exceeded by any other Character. . . . In State Affairs he discovered an uncommon Degree of Sagacity, and might have made a Figure as a Politician. In classical Learning he was fully competent to the Business of Teaching, although he devoted less Time than some others in his Station to the Study of the more abstruse Sciences: In short, Nature seemed to have furnished him so completely, that little remained for Art to accomplish. The Resources of his Genius were great. In Conversation he was at all Times pleasant and entertaining. He had as many Friends as Acquaintance, and took no less Pains to serve his Friends than acquire them. . . . Few Persons ever enjoyed a more excellent Constitution, or better Health. Increasing Corpulence, occasioned chiefly by his Confinement to the Labours of his Station (for he was temperate in his Diet) gave him some Complaints of ill Health, of late Years.

This sketch may be confirmed and amplified from other sources.

President Manning's countenance is well known from the portrait in Sayles Hall, which was bequeathed to the college by Mrs. Manning at her death in 1815.[1] "Doctor Manning was 32 years old when his picture was done," wrote Solomon Drowne, his pupil and close friend. "You will see it was not the production of an eminent artist, though deemed a pretty good likeness at that time. He wore his own graceful hair, and there was a dignity in his port and countenance which that picture by no means reaches." The suggestion of robust vigor in the portrait is confirmed by tradition. Professor Goddard says, "He sometimes made his own stone wall; and in the use of the scythe, he acknowledged no superior among the best trained laborers in the meadow." His prowess as a maker of stone walls is attested by this entry on the Corporation records of September 3, 1777: "President Manning laid before the Corporation an Accompt for making thirty two Rods of Stone wall on the College Land." Even in his later years, according to one of his pupils, "his motions and gestures were so

[1] Manning's portrait, and that of Mrs. Manning which hangs beside it, were painted, according to Dr. Guild, by Cosmo Alexander, Gilbert Stuart's first teacher.

easy and graceful, that ordinary observers thought not of his immense volume of flesh, and those who criticised, admired the manner in which it was spontaneously wielded." His mingled grace and dignity when presiding at Commencement are said to have called forth an admiring "*Natalis praesidere*" from a French gentleman who was once present.

"He was of the most happy disposition and temperament—always cheerful—much inclined to society and conversation," wrote Ashur Robbins, Manning's first colleague after the Revolution; "in conversation more disposed to pleasantry than seriousness; fond of anecdote, especially if illustrative of character, of which he had a store." The cheerfulness and animation of his mind in lighter moods are well illustrated by a letter of May 5, 1773, to his old college friend, Hezekiah Smith: "Now therefor, as I am tied to College, pray take Mrs. Smith, the Heir Apparent & the new Chaise and come and take your Station for a Week or two, on the Hill of Providence, where I will ensure you excellent good Water; the best my House affords & our good Company—Pray what more would you have? If any thing, in my Power, to render the visit still more agreeable, depend on it, you shan't be wanting it—I have made a Tour into ye hither Parts of Connecticut this Vacation, & preached 15 times, in 14 Days. 7 of them in Presbyterian Meeting Houses. What do you think of that? See what it is to be catholic like me; while you with brandishing Weapons take the field of Mars, like an old Veteran that scorns to let his Sword rust—Good Success to you if you must draw."

The tolerant breadth of mind and temper which Dr. Manning here playfully claims showed itself in many ways. In his charge to the graduating class of 1773 he said, "Challenge the glorious prerogative of thinking for yourselves in religious matters, and generously grant to others without a grudge what you yourselves deem the dearest of all blessings." What he preached he himself practiced, within the limitations of his day and place. At the end of a controversial letter on baptism he writes thus: "You may probably esteem me rigid from this Specimen, & greatly attached to Externals: but I think otherwise of myself; I think I love the followers of the Lamb, under whatever Denomination they pass amongst Men. I esteem them my Brethren; and feel disposed to make all proper Allowances for the Prejudices of Institution, and ye Weaknesses of human Nature, knowing that I myself also am in the Body; and peculiarly need the Candour of my Xtn. [= Christian] friends." It was consistent with this spirit that, in a time marked by ardor in sectarian theology, Manning's sermons were practical rather than doctrinal. Mr. Robbins said, "He occasionally touched and dwelt upon some doctrinal point; but it was incidentally, as it were, and subordinate to some practical view, the scope of his discourse."

It must not be inferred, however, that Manning was out of sympathy with his sect. On the contrary he agreed with it in all essentials, and stoutly stood up for its rights. "Dr. Manning," wrote Robbins, "was the acknowledged head of the Baptist clergy of his time. He was so considered in England as well as in this country." It was doubtless in recognition of his leadership that the University of Pennsylvania gave him the degree of D.D. in 1785. This preëminence was of course due in part to his position as president of the only college connected with the denomination; but it was fundamentally the result of his personal gifts—his genuine goodness, his breadth of mind, his administrative ability, his knowledge of human nature, and his power as a writer and speaker. Even President Ezra Stiles, in the midst of a prejudiced estimate of Manning in his diary, admits that he was "somthg in Oratory & belles Lettres," and "a popular Preacher." Of his fluency and power as a speaker there is no question. President Maxcy said : "His eloquence was forcible and spontaneous. To every one who heard him, . . . it was evident that the resources of his mind were exceedingly great." Robbins said : "His pulpit discourses were all *ex tempore*. . . . His manner was earnest, but never vehement. He made no effort at oratory, or at display of learning." On the last day of the Massachusetts constitutional convention, when President Manning was invited by Governor Hancock to offer a closing prayer, he poured out "a strain of exalted patriotism and fervid devotion, which awakened in the assembly a mingled sentiment of admiration and awe." Professor Waterhouse, who tells the incident, adds that "the praise of Rev. Dr. Manning was in every mouth," and that " nothing but the popularity of Dr. Stillman prevented the rich men of Boston from building a church for Dr. Manning's acceptance."

David Howell, himself a member of Congress and a judge, speaks of President Manning's capacity for public affairs. His fellow citizens recognized this ability by thrice intrusting him with political duties. The first occasion, during the war, has already been described. His election to the federal Congress in March, 1786, is said by Robbins to have come about because he chanced to "look in upon the Assembly " one afternoon when there was a vacancy in the delegation, and Commodore Hopkins, suddenly struck with his fitness for the place, nominated him then and there. He attended to his political duties with able and conscientious thoroughness, but was so deeply incensed at the conduct of the state in neglecting to support him, either with money, colleague, or instructions, that a congressional career of seven months was more than enough for him. He resigned his seat on October 25, but was still boiling in January, when he wrote to Hezekiah Smith: "The Paper Money of this State has run down to 6 for one, notwithstanding which the Legislature continue it as a tender. . . . At the last Session I petitioned them to pay my Advances, & the remainder of my Salary as Delegate, amounting to upwards of 400 Dollars, this they offered to do in their paper, but no other way. . . . A more infamous set of men, under the Character of a Legislature, never, I beleve, disgraced the Annals of the World." Yet when Rhode Island, having delayed ratification of the Constitution, found its exports to other states subject to a tariff, and the seaport towns had to petition Congress for exemption, President Manning was chairman of the committee that drafted the petition from Providence, and was one of the delegates appointed to present the document. In this mission, again, most of the work fell upon him, and his zeal and shrewdness carried it through.

Manning's interest in public affairs was so deep, and his desire for a stronger national government so great, that he worked with voice and pen for the ratification of the new Constitution. He wrote to Isaac Backus on October 31, 1787, requesting him to use his influence to have the minutes of the Baptist Association of Philadelphia "read publickly in all the Congregations" in order that "by the notice taken of the new form of the federal Governmt: recommended by the Convention, our friends in New England may see the remarkable Unanimity of our western Brethren in the adoption of it." On February 11, 1788, he wrote to Hezekiah Smith: "I felt so deeply interested in the adoption of the new federal constitution by your State, that I attended the Debates in Convention more than a fortnight, & expected to have seen you at Boston on that Occasion. I considered Massachusetts the hinge on which the whole must turn." He was not merely a spectator: most of the Baptist clerical delegates were opposed to the Constitution, and he labored to bring them over to the federalist side.

President Manning also did public service in connection with the schools of Providence. When the college was founded there was still no system of free public schools in any part of Rhode Island. In 1768 a plan for the establishment of four free schools in Providence was defeated by popular vote, and for many years longer the town had none. Some of the private schools, however, received aid from the public funds and some oversight from a school committee; and Manning served on this committee for many years, much of the time as chairman. In June, 1791, a petition was presented in town meeting for the establishment of free schools; it was referred to the school committee, who made a favorable report on August 1, two days after Manning was buried. The report, which was signed by him and was doubtless largely or wholly his work as chairman, may be considered his final word in behalf of the cause of education to which he had devoted his life; and although free schools were not established in Providence until nine years later, this report of Manning's must have helped to prepare the way.

As administrator of the college, President Manning's success was freely recognized by his contemporaries. Howell, in a letter of August 3, 1791, speaks of his being "celebrated for many shining abilities which peculiarly qualified him to preside," and says, "We are apprehensive that the Institution may suffer a temporary relapse unless some known & established Character can be induced to supply the Vacancy soon." Isaac Backus wrote to an English friend on August 19, 1791, "We have no idea of obtaining any man who will equal President Manning in all respects, at least soon," and specifies his "gift of governing so as to be both feared and beloved by all" as one of the things which "rendered him the most accomplished man for that station of any one that I ever saw." President Maxcy said, "In the College over which he presided, his government was mild and peaceful; conducted by that persuasive authority, which secures obedience while it conciliates esteem."

In scholarship Manning was not great: he was too busy for that.[1] His own description of his manner of life, as reported by Dr. Waterhouse, helps one to realize how crowded his days were:

I shall never forget what Dr. Manning, in great good humor, told me were among his trying "experiences." He told me that . . . he performed all the duties of President of the College; heard two classes recite, every day; listened to complaints, foreign and domestic, from undergraduates and their parents of both sexes, and answered them, now and then, by letter; waited, generally, on all transient visiters into college, &c. &c. Nor was this all. " I made," said Dr. Manning, "my own garden and took care of it; repaired my dilapidated walls; went nearly every day to market; preached twice a week, and sometimes oftener; attended, by solicitation, the funeral of every baby that died in Providence; visited the sick of my own Society, and, not unfrequently, the sick of other Societies; made numerous parochial visits, the poorest people exacting the longest, and, in case of any seeming neglect, finding fault the most."

But although not a profound student of any one subject, he was a good all-round scholar, as his standing in New Jersey College showed, with special gifts in the languages and, as we have seen, in oratory. Dr. Stiles admitted that "He was a pretty good Linguist," praise which meant much,

[1] The inventory of his effects after his death estimates his books and maps at £15 11^s 6^d, or less than $52.

coming from so learned a man. Robbins gave this interesting reminiscence of him as a teacher: "I well recollect to have heard the students of the classes whom he chose to take through Longinus particularly, often speak with admiration of his comments upon that author, and of the happy and copious illustrations he gave of the principles from which Longinus deduces the sublime. I could readily believe the admiration was merited; for I know he had paid great attention to the general principles of oratory, and particularly to those of elocution, of which he was an admirable preceptor." An example of his thought and style in his lectures on philosophy, taken from Solomon Drowne's note-book (copied from Theodore Foster's) of the year 1772, may aid us in estimating Manning's power as a teacher:

If we take a short Survey of the World we live on; What a glorious Proof of the divine Existence is the Air? That soft, thin and yeilding Body, so fit for vital Motion, that it seems the very Nourishment of Life, and so transparent that the Rays of the Sun pass thro' it without any Difficulty; tho' placed at an immense Distance? What Wisdom tempered it so nicely, as at once to be a proper Vehicle for Light, and Nutriment for Life? What Power has made it so thin and fluid an Element, the safe Repository of Thunder and Lightning, Winds and Tempests? By what skilful Hand is the Water, which is drawn from the Sea, curiously distilled, and bottled up in the Clouds, to be sent on the Wings of the Wind, and scattered over the Face of the Earth in gentle Showers? . . . Who painted and perfumed the Flowers? How comes it that the same Water or Air, dies them with different Colours, the scarlet, the purple, the carnation, and whence have they those sweet Odours which they breath with insensible subtlety, and diffuse into the Air for our Delight?

It is probable that, whatever the subject, his deepest interest, even in the class-room, was not intellectual but ethical and religious. Simeon Doggett, in his "Oration, on the Death of the Rev. President Manning" at the Commencement of

1791, said: "How naturally at our College exercises would a very slight connection lead his discourse to moral and religious subjects! Upon these subjects, with what additional ardor would he discourse! These occasions seemed to add new life to his faculties. They would add warmth to his heart, brightness to his understanding, and eloquence to his tongue."

It remains to sketch the inner life of the college during the administration of President Manning. The Laws of 1783, printed in the Appendix, give a comprehensive view, and may serve as a background to the sketch.

The spirit in which the institution was administered by the Corporation deserves mention at the outset. The work that the first fellows and trustees did, with small means and in the face of great difficulties, must forever claim admiration and gratitude; and in particular they deserve praise for standing so consistently by the principle of religious freedom laid down in the charter. At the first annual meeting in the city of Roger Williams, on September 6, 1770, they voted "That the Children of JEWS may be admitted into this Institution and intirely enjoy the freedom of their own Religion, without any Constraint or Imposition whatever." In candor it should be added that the vote was called forth by an inquiry from a Jewish merchant in South Carolina, who sent a small gift, and said that if the rumored catholicity of the new college was a fact, his liberality should "exceed beyond ye: bounds of yr: Imagination." The Corporation must have known, however, that catholicity might repel as well as attract gifts. At all events they stood loyally by the charter; and although nothing more was heard from the prospective benefactor, they took care to guard jealously the religious scruples of Jews, Quakers, and members of other sects, as the following extracts from the Laws of 1774 prove:

That every Student attend publick Worship every first Day of the Week steadily at such Places as he, his Parents or Guardians shall think proper; provided that any who do not attend with any Officers of Instruction, produce Vouchers when Demanded of his steady & orderly Attendance.

N . . B . . Such as regularly & statedly keep the Seventh Day, as a Sabbath, are excepted from this Law; & are only required to abstain from Secular Concerns which would interupt their fellow Students.

That, no Student wear his hat within the College Walls; excepting those who steadily attend the F[r]iends Meeting.

That if any Student of this College shall deny the being of a God, the Existence of Virtue and Vice; or that the Books of the old and new Testament are of divine Authority, or Suggest any Scruples of that Nature or circulate Books of such pernicious Tendency, or frequent the Company of those who are known to favour such fatal Errors, He shall for the second Offence be absolutely and forever expelld from this College. Young gentlemen of the Hebrew nation are to be excepted from this Law.

From the last law it is manifest that the Corporation's liberality did not extend to deists and atheists, who must suppress their opinions or leave the college. Herein they fell short of the spirit of Roger Williams, with his magnificent declaration that "It is the will and command of *God*, that . . . a *permission* of the most *Paganish, Jewish, Turkish* or *Antichristian consciences* and *worships*, bee granted to *all* men in all *Nations* and *Countries*." They were, however, within the letter of the charter, since atheists and deists do not belong to any "Religious Denominations"; and the preamble to the law shows that they based their action on the broad ground that infidelity was a moral pest, which it was their duty to keep out of the college.

In another important respect the Corporation and the President acted in absolute harmony with the unsectarian provisions of the charter. No sectarian instruction in the class-room was allowed or attempted. The college was assailed from time to time as narrow, as wholly under the control of the Baptists, as building with public funds a parsonage for a Baptist minister, etc. ; but no enemy, so far as is known, ever accused it of making sectarian principles a part of the course of study. Solomon Drowne's note-book affords direct proof that President Manning, in his lectures on natural theology and the credibility of miracles, avoided the least reference to the distinctive tenets of the Baptists.

As interpreters and administrators of the charter in its relation to the officers of government and instruction, the Corporation evinced a broad spirit. When electing members and officers of their own body, they interpreted generously the terms describing the different religious denominations, making no distinction between the various stripes of Baptists, not inquiring into the orthodoxy of Congregationalists, and putting into the chancellorship a man whose standing in his own sect, the Quakers, was at least doubtful. In the clause of the charter declaring that places on the Faculty, that of the president excepted, shall be "open for all Denominations of Protestants," they interpreted "Protestants" to include Jews; for in a letter drafted by Manning at the direction of the Corporation, in 1770, replying to the inquiry of the Jewish merchant, the committee express willingness to appoint a Jew as professor of Hebrew. Twelve years later, in a rough draft of a letter to a French nobleman, Manning asks him to assure the French king that the charter's discrimination against Roman Catholics on the Faculty was adopted in "the Times of our Ignorance," and that if the state constitution were amended so as to remove all disabilities from Roman Catholics, as then seemed probable, he had small doubt that the college charter would be amended also. This passage in the letter was finally canceled, but at least it showed the spirit of the head of the Corporation. In the appointments which were actually made to the Faculty no sectarian narrowness appears. Of the seven tutors in Manning's time, four were not Baptists; and when it was necessary to choose a vice-president during Manning's absence in Congress, the Corporation selected a Congregationalist clergyman, whom they soon after made professor of natural philosophy. In bestowing honorary degrees, also, they showed the same liberality; although a decided majority went to leading Baptist clergymen at home and abroad, as was natural enough when they were trying to arouse interest in the college throughout the denomination, yet thirteen were given to clergymen of other folds, including three of the English Church — Henry Foster of Oxford University, John Newton, Cowper's friend, and Augustus Toplady, the hymn-writer — and one Unitarian, the pastor of King's Chapel, Boston.

The personnel of the Corporation changed greatly during Manning's administration, twelve fellows and thirty-six trustees resigning or dying. At the death of Stephen Hopkins in 1785, Jabez Bowen, a graduate of Yale and a former chief justice of the Rhode Island supreme court, was chosen chancellor. Dr. Eyres resigned the secretaryship in 1776, and was succeeded by Thomas Arnold, who served until 1780, when David Howell was elected. The first treasurer held office only three years; Job Bennet served until 1775, and was succeeded by John Brown.

No record exists of the requirements for admission to Rhode Island College before the Revolution, but it is safe to assume that they were similar to those in New Jersey College at the time Manning was a student there. The requirements at the latter in 1764, at least, were almost identical with the following at Providence in 1783: "No person may expect to be admitted into this College, unless, upon examination by the President and Tutors, he shall be found able to read accurately construe and parse *Tully* and the Greek Testament, and Virgil; and shall be able to write true Latin in prose, and hath learned the rules of Prosody and Vulgar Arithmatic; and shall bring suitable Testimony of a blameless life & conversation.'' The requirements at King's College in 1755 and at Yale in 1759 were similar. It will be noted that the work for admission, although of very limited range, was definite, and the examination tested power rather than memory; if the conditions were enforced, the freshmen of those days must have had a real command of the Latin language. How much of each Latin author was read cannot be determined; at King's College three orations of Cicero and the first three books of the *Aeneid* were specified, and that may have been the usual amount.

The curriculum also was restricted in range. Our knowledge of it in the early years of Manning's administration is derived almost entirely from the following memoranda collected by a descendant from the papers of Solomon Drowne, of the class of 1773; it should be observed that he was in college only a little more than three years, and that the record of his last year is incomplete:

1770. After examination in June, by the Rev. James Manning and Prof. David Howell, entered Rhode Island College July 2d. Began Horace, Longinus & Lucian in October, and French in December.

1771. . . . Commenced Geography in January; Xenephon in February; Watts Logic in May; Ward's Oratory in June; Homer's Iliad in July; Duncan's Logic in August; Longinus in October; Hill's Arithmetic same month; Hammond's Algebra and British Grammar in December.

1772. Began Ethics, January; Euclid's Elements, February, also Metaphysicks, Trigonometry, Cicero de Oratore; Martin's Philosophy in May; Martin's Use of the Globes, August; Hebrew Grammar, December.

The Laws of 1783 give the whole course of study at that time as follows:

THE President and Tutors, according to their judments, shall teach and instruct the several Classes in the learned Languages and in the liberal Arts and Sciences, together with the vernacular Tongus— The following are the clasics appointed for the first year, in Latin, Virgil, Cicero's Orations and Horace, all in usum Delphini. In Greek, the new Testament, Lucians Dialogues & Zenophon's Cyropaedia;— For the second year, in Latin, Cicero de Oratore & Caesars Commentaries;— In Greek Homer's Iliad & Longinus on the sublime, together with Lowth's vernacular Grammar, Rhetoric, Wards Oratory, Sheridan's Lectures on Elocution, Guthrie's Geography, Kaims Elements of Criticism, Watts's and Duncan's Logic.— For the third year, Hutchinsons moral Philosophy, Dodridges Lectures, Fennings Arithmatic, Hammonds Algebra, Stones Euclid, Martins Trigonometry, Loves Surveying, Wilsons Navigation, Martins Philosophia Britannica, & Ferguson's Astronomy, with Martin on the Globes.— In the last year, Locke on the Understanding, Kennedy's Chronology and Bollingbroke on History; and the Languages, Arts & Sciences, studied in the foregoing years, to be accurately reveiwed.

Oral examinations were held quarterly.

An extract from a letter of the President on March 18, 1784, gives a more intimate idea of the teaching of these subjects:

If Mr Wood means to enter the Sophimore Class next Fall I advise him to read with great Attention Cicero & the Greek Testat: and make himself Master of the Grammar of each Language; also to study with great Attention Lowth's English Grammar, & Sterling's, or Turner's Rhetoric, as preparatory to Wards Oratory.— To read Horace, & Zenophon's Cyropedia, & accustom himself to compose in English. We use Guthrie's Geography & Watts & Duncan's Logic: But we don't commonly study those before the 2d Year, as we wish to have their Knowledge in the Languages well advanced in the first Year.

Should the Class advance faster, I will let you know. I think a further Attention, at present, to mathematical Studies, may not be advantageous.

What strikes the modern reader most forcibly on a first view of this course of study is its meagerness. English literature, other modern languages and literatures, most of the natural sciences, and all the social sciences are absent, and slight attention is given to history and metaphysics. But on further inspection it seems even more singular that relatively so little time, after all, is allotted to Greek and Latin. They do not appear in the last two years, except by way of review in the senior year; and in the first two years, although they receive the greater share of the time, only four Latin and four Greek authors are studied, the dramatists, historians, and philosophers being totally untouched. Another surprise is that mathematics is taken up so late in the course, and carried such a little way, arithmetic, algebra, geometry, and their applications all being crowded into the junior year. In the curriculum, as in the entrance requirements, the example of New Jersey College was followed; but the studies in the other Amercian colleges were substantially similar, although at Harvard and King's College there was a somewhat wider range in the classics.

One important feature of the curriculum, the training in English composition and public speaking, is not adequately shown by the preceding statements. John Brown, in resigning from the Corporation in 1803, wrote, "The most beautiful and handsome mode of speaking was a principal Object, to my certain knowledge, of the first Friends to this College." His statement is borne out by these provisions in the Laws of 1774: "That, every evening two shall pronounce on the Stage, begining with the Senior Class and proceeding Alphabitecaly down through all the Classes. . . . That, on

the first Wednesday of every Month each Student shall publickly pronounce an Oration, which he shall have previously
Committed to Memory. . . . The Senior & Junior Classes
shall each of them write a Dispute every Week, & read the
same, upon such Subjects as shall be appointed them.'' In
the Laws of 1783 it is specified that at the monthly speaking
''the two upper classes shall make use of their own compositions''; and it is added that '' all the members of the College
shall meet every Wednesday afternoon in the Hall, at the
ringing of the Bell at 2 OClock, to pronounce before the
President & Tutors, pieces well committed to memory, that
they may receive such corrections in their manner, as shall
be judged necessary.'' This emphasis upon public speaking
was then common in American colleges, which were educating men chiefly for the ministry and the law, in times that put
a high value upon skill in the use of voice or pen. The training was not wholly in English, for in addition to translation
from the classic languages there were frequent '' disputes ''
in Latin. One of the Laws of 1774 says that '' Latin Syllogistic disputes are to be kept up & duly cultivated.'' How
often they occurred is not certain, but there must have
been a good deal of practice if the students were to acquit
themselves well in the Latin dispute which before the Revolution formed a part of every Commencement program.[1]

[1] It was '' omitted for want of time '' in 1786, and then dropped altogether. But
the custom of printing on a '' broadside '' a formidable list of Latin theses, which
the candidates for degrees were supposed to be ready to defend against all
comers—a curious survival from the Middle Ages—lasted well into the next
century. In pre-Revolutionary days one of these theses was the subject of the
Latin disputation at Commencement; and another, turned into English for
the benefit of the unlearned, was debated in the vernacular. On the broadside
the two theses which were to be discussed were printed in italics or large type;
in 1769 the subject for the debate about American independence was thus
phrased: '' Americanos in rerum statu praesenti res novas moliri, Reipublicae
administrandae solertiae male convenit.'' The theses were grouped under
many heads—'' Grammatica,'' '' Rhetorica,'' '' Logica,'' '' Mathesis,''

The method of instruction in all subjects was chiefly by recitations from textbooks, but in philosophy and logic, at any rate, the President supplemented the textbook by lectures of his own; and the professors appointed after the Revolution gave lectures only. The President's lectures in philosophy, so far as Drowne's note-book reproduces them, contained a compact and clear, though rather superficial, résumé of the more important doctrines of psychology, intellectual and moral philosophy, ontology, and natural theology. The shortness of the course is shown by Drowne's memorandum on the front cover: "Began to write it February ye: 1st: Began to Study it Feby. ye: 26th:: Anno Domini 1772—Finish studying it. March ye: 6th. 1772." On the back cover is the entry, "Our Class say the last Recitation in this Book. March ye: 6th. Domini 1772."

The sciences, so far as they were taken up at all, must have been studied mainly from textbooks, for laboratory work was impossible; but Corporation, Faculty, and students early realized the need of apparatus for the performance of illustrative experiments. The Corporation in 1768 requested the President to write to Morgan Edwards, then collecting funds in Great Britain, and ask him to "purchase an Air-Pump a Telescope and a Microscope out of the Monies at any Time in his Hands by the Consent of the Donors," the money to be replaced by funds raised in America. The next year the students showed scientific ardor and business enterprise by circulating a subscription paper with the following preamble:

"Physica," "Theologia," "Politia," etc.,—and included all sorts of topics, from favorite problems of the schoolmen to burning contemporary questions, such as the lawfulness of the slave trade ("Africanorum invectio coloniis hisce nostris incommoda est et illicita"), or the tyranny of taxation without representation ("Senatui populis vectigalia imponendi, qui in illo senatu non repraesentantur, jus non est").

Whereas there are a Number of Students in Rhode Island College, engaged in the Study of natural Philosophy, & desirous of pursuing the same to the greatest Advantage; and Sd: College, by Reason of it's present infant State, is destitute of some Conveniences, which others on the Continent enjoy—

These are therefore to Solicit all Gentlemen, who are well-Wishers to the Design, to Contribute towards purchasing an Electrical Apparatus, which would be of immediate Utility to the Students, & Curiosity to such transient Gentlemen, as have turn'd their Attention to the popular Subject of Electricity.

N.B. An Account of the Subscribers, will be enter'd upon the General List of Donors, to Sd: College.

Warren, 19th. of August, 1769.

Nine students subscribed £2 11^s, and two "Gentlemen of Newport" and seven of Warren £5 14^s, making a total of £8 5^s, or $27.50. Some if not all of these instruments were secured, for in a letter of February 21, 1772, President Manning wrote: "Our Apparatus consists of a pair of Globes, two Microscopes and an Electrical Machine: to this we are desirous of making the Addition of an Air Pump, if one reputable can be purchased for £22.10 Sterl:; a Sum which two young Gentleme[n] informed me they intended to give towards an Apparatus, or Library." The college owned a telescope in 1782, as appears in a letter of July 13 from Joseph Brown to David Howell: "I dont know whether I ever told you of the Ingury our Tellescope has receved in attempting to have the tarnish or rust taken off the mettal Speculums . . . When I come to putt them to tryal I could see through the Tellescope scarcely at all but only jest bearly to descearn a large object very indistinctly and so this Exelent instrument has been rendered totally usless for about a year."

It may have been the condition of the telescope which incited John Brown and other members of the Corporation to raise a sum for the purchase of the "compleat Philosophical Apparatus" in 1783. By Manning's letters in the following year we learn some particulars about these new instruments. On March 18 he writes: "The Air-Pump with its Apparatus complete is arrived. It cost £50 Sterlg: in London, & is, perhaps, the completest in America, made on the New Construction. Mr Joseph Brown has not yet compleated his List of the Apparatus, for want of some Information, on that Subject, which he has not yet been able to obtain." On September 13 he writes: "The amount of upwards of £200 Sterl: was also ordered in a necessary philosophical Apparatus, in Addition to what we already have—Consisting chiefly of a Telescope, an Air Pump & its Apparatus, Globes, & a Thermometer."

For many years the college was almost as destitute of books as of scientific apparatus. In 1768 Morgan Edwards was authorized to buy in Great Britain "such Books as he shall think necessary at this Time not exceeding Twenty Pounds value." No other appropriation for books was made until 1784, and the collection grew very slowly. In 1772 Manning wrote that the library consisted of about two hundred and fifty volumes, "and those not well chosen, being such as our friends could best spare." Small and poor as the library was, it was carefully guarded during the Revolution, as we have seen, and at the end of the war was brought back to town. The new tutor, Mr. Robbins, wrote years afterwards: "At the reorganization of the College, in the autumn of 1782, I was appointed to the office of tutor, and took charge of the Library as librarian. It was then kept in the east chamber on the second floor of the central building; the volumes it contained were quite limited in number — these mostly the primary editions of the works in folio and quarto. The precise number I am not able to recollect; my impression is that it did not exceed two or three hundred." His memory was at fault as to the number, for Manning says, in a letter of November 8, 1783, "Our Library consists of about 500 Volumes most of which are both very antient & very useless, as well as very ragged & unsightly." In the archives is a catalogue of books, in Manning's hand, which appears to have been made at this time. It shows that there were then 607 volumes, most of them theological, these being the works which the friends of learning even in those days "could best spare"; but the Greek and Latin classics were well represented, especially Ovid; Molière and Pascal were included; while Hooker, Hobbes, Jeremy Taylor, Bunyan, Milton, and *The Spectator* were the only English classics.

With the raising of £700 for the purchase of philosophical apparatus and books, in 1783, came a great change for the better. About fourteen hundred volumes, selected chiefly by the President and the Chancellor, were ordered from London in 1784; they covered a wide range, and must have come like showers on a thirsty land to the Faculty and students of Rhode Island College. A few titles, taken almost at random, will illustrate the variety and richness of the additions: Ossian, Addison, Anson's Voyages, Burke on the Sublime and Beautiful, Life of Clarendon, Montesquieu, Robertson's Charles V, Rousseau's Inequality of Mankind, Winckelmann on Painting, Gay's Fables and Poems, Blackstone's Commentaries, Young, Thomson, The Turkish Spy, Robinson Crusoe, Pope's Complete Works, Colley Cibber's Works, Congreve's Works, The Chinese Spy, The Jewish Spy, The Idler and Rambler, Lady Mary Wortley Montagu's Letters, Otway's Works, Hume, Swift, Goldsmith, Junius, Dryden, Hudibras. In the same year Moses Brown gave some forty-six volumes, including the works of Fox, Barclay, Penn, Woolman, and other Quakers; and John Tanner, of Newport, gave a hundred and thirty-five volumes of miscellaneous works, some of them especially valuable for the study of New England church history. In 1785 a hundred and forty-nine volumes, including several of the church fathers, Sale's translation of the Koran, Bayle's Dictionary, Chambers's Cyclopaedia, and the Biographia Britannica, were received from the Education Society of Bristol, England.

The college now having a valuable library of two thousand volumes or more—and Harvard at this time had only twelve thousand—the Corporation passed special votes regarding the arrangement and care of it. In November, 1784, they voted and resolved, "That the old books which stand on the right hand, as we enter the Library room, be, & they are hereby ordered to be taken down by the Librarian, & the new Books set up in their place, that the Students may have immediate access to them." The following year they adopted new by-laws for the library, including these:

VOTED & RESOLVED, that (that in Addition to the former regulations for the College Library) the Librarian keep the Library room neat & clean; and, in delivering out Books, he shall suffer none of the Students to derange or handle them on the Shelves; nor shall the Students pass into the Library room beyond the Table at which the Librarian sits.

HE shall demand & receive a fine of six pence for every time it shall come to his knowledge, that any Student hath suffered a Library book, by him taken out, to be uncovered in his possession.

No student or Graduate, shall presume to lend to any person a book belonging to the Library, on penalty of forfeiting the value thereof, and the priviledge of the Library till such forfeiture be paid.

HE shall open the Library room on such day of the week, as the President shall from time to time direct; and shall keep it open from one to three OClock in the Afternoon.

The charge to students for the use of the library was raised in 1788 from six shillings a year to twelve. Whether any part of the money thus obtained was used for the purchase of new books cannot be determined; but there was no great increase in the library during the rest of Manning's administration.

Undergraduate life in these early years was regulated by the English idea of a college as a large family, sleeping, eating, studying, and worshiping together under one roof; the undergraduates were the children, the President was the father, and the tutors were the stern and learned elder brothers. At the beginning a handful of students recited to the President in his own house, the parsonage in Warren. When the academic family moved to Providence the President's house was on the "home lot" and close to the students' hall. The professor was encouraged to reside in the hall, and the tutors and the steward were required to do so. The college set a table, the so-called "Commons," where most of the students took their meals; the steward was expected to eat with them and to "exercise the same Authority as is customary & needful for the Head of a Family at his Table." Every student was required to come to family prayers, or "chapel," morning and evening. During the day they all, whether sleeping in the college edifice or at home, had to pass study hours at college, and were charged with room rent. They were expected to keep steadily at work, as the following Laws of 1774 show:

That the Hours of Study, between the Fall & Spring Vacation, shall be from morning Prayers, one hour before Breakfast: from Nine oClock A.M. until 12 oClock; from 2 oClock P.M. until Sunset, & from 7 until 9 oClock in Evening; & between the Spring & Fall Vacation, one Hour after morning Prayers; from 8 oClock A.M. until 12 oClock; from 2 P.M. until 6: & none Shall be out of his Chamber after 9 oClock in the Evening.

That no Student read any Book in Study Hours excepting the Classics [*i.e.*, textbooks used in the classes], or those which tend to illustrate the subject Matter of his Recitations, for the time being.

That, each one Continue in his Room in the hours of Study, unless to do an Errand, in which he Shall be speedy; or to attend Recitations.

That, each one attend Recitation twice in a Day at such Time & Place as shall be appointed.

That, no one be absent from any Collegiate exercise without first rendering his excuse to his Instructor, or go out of the College Yard, without Liberty, in the time of Study.

In means for carrying out this conception of a college as an academic family, the American colleges fell far behind their English models in two respects : the officers of instruction did not usually dine in hall with the students; and the college buildings did not form a quadrangle, with only one exit guarded by an argus-eyed porter. An attempt was made to remedy the latter defect by requiring the tutors to visit the students' rooms at frequent and irregular intervals. Hence the following rule of Rhode Island College in 1774, based upon one at New Jersey College:

That, no Student refuse to open his Door when he shall hear the stamp of the Foot or Staff at his Door in the Entry, which shall be a Token that Some Officer of Instruction desires admission, which Token every Student is forbid to Counterfit, or imitate under any Pretence whatever.

While the means for enforcing obedience were inferior, the rules were in some respects more strict and Puritanic. In the English universities wine parties were allowed or at least winked at if not too noisy. At New Jersey College in 1764 a student was not allowed " to make any treat or entertainment in his chamber, on any account." The Yale *Statuta* of 1759 even forbade the student to drink tea in any company out of his own chamber, on penalty of one shilling : " Et si quis, in aliquo Coetu extra Cubiculum suum, Theam potaverit, mulctetur uno Solido.'' Harvard was more lax, the Corporation voting in 1759 that ''it shall be no offence if any scholar shall, *at Commencement*, make and entertain guests at his chamber with punch''; and even the restriction as to the season was removed two years later, on the ground that punch, ''as it is now usually made, is no intoxicating liquor.'' Rhode Island College again followed the lead of New Jersey College, enacting in 1774, ''That no one practice attending Company in his Room in Study hours: or keep Spirituous Liquors in his Room without Liberty obtained of the President.''

In spite of paternal discipline and strict rules, youth would have its fling even in the earlier years of Manning's administration, when most of the students were supposed to be sober-minded youth preparing for the ministry.[1] In a letter of December 12, 1770, the President wrote:

One Scott, a youth under my tuition, some time ago riding through Smithfield, . . . rode up to, and, in a most audaciously wicked manner, broke the windows of the Friends' meeting house in said town, of which meeting I understand you are clerk. . . . You will be so good as to let me know when the first meeting of business is held, that I may send him up to appear before them, and make not only reparation, but such a confession before the Meeting as shall be fully satisfactory. . . . When this is settled, we shall discipline him with the highest punishment we inflict, next to banishment from the society; and with that, if he does not comply with the above. . . . I am sorry for his friends, and that it happened to fall to my lot to have such a thoughtless, vicious pupil.

In the archives is a paper which the President read in public to five culprits in 1774:

When every method for the Reformation of Delinquents, in a private way, has been used to no Purpose the Good of Society and the

---

[1] The average age of the students at graduation was somewhat less then than now, being 20.43 years before the Revolution, and 21 years after it.

Honor of Government, as well as the Interest of the Delinquents, require those more public and mortifying Exertions of Authority which must either reclaim, or prove, that obstinate Offenders must be cut off as Pests to the Body—John Hart, Daniel Gano, William Edwards, Walter Wigneron and Pardon Bowen, walk forward into the Ally—Whereas you have persisted for a long time notoriously to violate the Laws of this College in sundry Instances as follow—

John Hart, for habitually neglecting your Studies, being out of College in the Evening in Town beyond the Time specified in the Laws and absent from his Room in Study Hours and making Disturbance by Noise or otherwise, and suffering others to spend their Time idly in his Room at Entertainments or otherwise

Daniel Gano for habitually neglecting his Studies, being absent from his Room in Study Hours, making a Noise after 9 OClock at Night in the College; by assisting others to hoist a Carpenters Bench in the Entry, & breaking a Window from without

Walter Wigneron for habitually neglecting his Studies, being absent from his Room in study Hours; making a Noise in College; by assisting others in hoisting a Carpenters Bench in the Entry after 9 OC at Night and suffering others to spend their time idly in his Room at Entertainments and otherwise

William Edwards, for habitually neglecting his Studies and being absent from his Room in Study Hours,

These crimes being made to appear against you severally upon Examination, & all private Admonitions proving ineffectual; at a Meeting of the President & Professor on the second Day of March AD. 1774; Resolved, That the aforesaid, John Hart, Daniel Gano Walter Wigneron & William Edwards for the Crimes aforesaid be publicly admonished in the Hall; and that this Admonition and an Innumeration of the said Crimes be registered in the Black Book.

We may smile at the Puritanic solemnity of the college authorities in this piece of discipline, but we must admire their impartiality. One of the students thus publicly disgraced was the son of Morgan Edwards, so prominent in the founding of the institution. John Hart was the son of an eminent Baptist clergyman, Manning's close friend, who in a letter four months before had thanked the President for the pains he had taken with his son, including "Trial of the Discipline of the Rod"—doubtless one of the "private ways" of reform that had proved inadequate. Daniel Gano was the son of Manning's own brother-in-law. These three were still further punished by the withholding of their degrees for one year. Of the students as a whole, however, Manning wrote in 1773 that they were, "take them together, a Sett of well behaved Boys."

For a few years after the Revolution there was no marked change in the order of the college. In March, 1785, Manning wrote, "I believe our students are as orderly, industrious, and as good scholars as at any one period of the Institution." But in September of that year the Corporation saw cause to pass the following vote: "VOTED & RESOLVED, that the Steward to be appointed shall have the supervisal & direction of the College Edefice, to prevent any damage being done thereto; & for this purpose shall cause hinges & a Lock to be put on the Scuttle on the Roof; & that he take care of the Key." And in 1788 the President wrote, "As the number increases my difficulties increase, especially in the Government of ye College, and collecting Tuition, &c." The year before he had had a serious case of discipline, referred to in the letter quoted on page 84; in the archives is a memorandum that these offenders were expelled for "having offered an Insult and Abuse to one of the Tutors." The members of the Corporation who intervened did not, at least openly, question the justice of the punishment, but asked for mercy because of the students' previous good record; both finally received their degrees. In the last year of Manning's administration there seems to have been a growing tendency to violate the laws of the college, a tendency due, no doubt, to the growth in numbers and perhaps to some change in the character of the students. At a meeting of the Faculty on April 4, 1791, it was ordered that five students be fined one shilling each for "attending a Treat in Leonard 2dus: & tertius' room last Saturday Night, in direct violation of the laws of College." The record continues:

Fairbanks is fined also 6/ for permitting, some time since, liquor to be brought into, and to be drunk in his room. . . . That Howell be fined 6/ for . . . being guilty . . . at late Hours in the night of running through the College, beating against the doors, hallooing and using prophane language. . . . Admonish all the College for irregularities, in being out of College in the Hours of Study; making unnecessary noise in the College Edifice; neglecting prayers & Recitations;—And especially associating together in each others rooms in study Hours; and for a growing neglect of public Worship—Also for making no distinctions, in their intercourse, between the higher & lower Classes.

On April 2, probably in the same year, three students were fined fourpence each for "misbehaviour at prayers." Another memorandum of about the same time reads:

Hunter King & Hazard primus, for riding out on Sunday fined three shillings each.—Baileys & Ellis, for allowing a combination in their room fined two shillings each.—Reprimand the three under Classes for insulting the Seniors, & the Junior Class in particular for entering into a Combination to transgress the regulations of College. Reprimand the whole for profane language.

The last item of the program seems perilously like the process which Burke condemned, of bringing an indictment against a whole nation, and was a strange necessity in a college founded chiefly to educate young men for the ministry. A stray "Recitation Bill" of this period shows that in one class during one week there were fifty-six absences out of a possible one hundred and sixty-five, a very high rate.

The system of "Commons" was a wretchedly inadequate substitute for the English system. Instead of a large and venerable dining-hall, beautiful in architecture and rich with the associations of centuries, the place of meeting was a small, bare room, still fresh from the hands of mason and carpenter.[1] Instead of dining with the officers and guests of the college, the students usually ate alone except for the presence of the steward, for whom they had no reverence, and whom they often disliked. In a round-robin, dated December 31, 1773, a committee representing all the classes protested to the Corporation that the steward was not furnishing the food prescribed. Another petition, apparently some years later, complains that "the Steward is a person difficult to deal with, . . . frequently insulting us by his reflections—frequently injuring us by his complaints." The steward, on the other hand, often reported that the students did not pay their board bills. In such conditions the amenities of the table were not likely to be observed. For many years things seem to have been doubly cheerless in cold weather, the Corporation voting in 1789 that "in future, during the cold season," the commons room should be " suitably warmed." The food was plain and lacked variety, and, if the student petitions say true, it was not always well cooked or well served. In short, college commons were merely a cheap boarding club for students, with the bad manners and boisterousness usually characteristic of such places. The Corporation recognized the evil and tried to lessen it by rules, the very need for which betrays the conditions. The following regulations were included in the Laws of 1774:

That the Steward call on whome he thinks proper to ask a Blessing, and return thanks at Table, during which no Studant shall meddle with any of the Provisions or Table Furniture, but behave with Decency and Sobriety.

[1] Commons room was what is now 6 University Hall, but only one story high and without galleries.

That the Senior Class be divided and some sit at one part of the Table and others at another Part; and that they, or such others as shall be appointed, only, shall call for what may be wanting at Table; and all others are forbid either calling or using any other signs of calling, except Decantly mentioning it to the above named, what is wanting: and provided any Person or Persons shall use indecent Gestures at Table; or in any wise transgress the orders of the Table, the Senior siting at the Head of the Table shall immediately order him to sit next to him, that he may observe his, or their future conduct and behavior.

That the whole Body be so divided as that a determinate Number only, in succession through the whole, shall carve; this being done in Alphabitical order, the next to him shall distribute the Meat, & Sauce; no one else being allowed to take them him-self; and the same Person, for the Day, shall pour out Coffee, Tea, &c and put in a proper Quantity of Sugar.

In spite of the minuteness and legal precision of these regulations, they evidently failed of their end; and in 1789 the Corporation voted that the tutors must sit at table in commons "and preserve order and Decorum," and also that students might be allowed by the president and tutors to board in town if they wished.

The expenses of students, especially if they boarded in commons, were low, even when allowance is made for the high purchasing power of the dollar in those days. In 1773 tuition was $12 a year; room rent in the college edifice, $5 a year; board in commons, $1 a week: a total, exclusive of books, firewood, and incidentals, of about $56 for a year of nearly thirty-nine weeks. After the Revolution tuition went up to $16; room rent went down to $4, but there was a charge for the care of rooms. The total expense for the college year is thus stated by President Manning in a letter of February 11, 1788: "The Expence of boarding in Commons, Tuition, Room Rent & Library & Apparatus

Privileges, deducting 1/4 of a Year for the Vacations,[1] amounts to just £20–5–9 Lawful Money at present, but I expect the Commons will be lowered as soon as stability in Government takes place — A Period, I now hope, not very distant — Wood is about 12/ pr Cord; and, other incidental Expences as moderate here, or more so than at Dartmouth.'' The cost of firewood is mentioned because the students had to supply their own, as is shown by the following vote of the Corporation on December 12, 1786, which also gives a glimpse into the conditions of student life then: ''From a representation made to this Corporation, by the officers of instruction, that the Students are absolutely unable to pursue their respective s[t]udies on account of the scarcity of firewood at this very inclement season, the Corporation . . . Resolved that four cords be immediately brought from Mr Waterman's lot, to be distributed by the Steward as may be necessary; and be, by him, charged to those who may receive it in their next Quarter bills.'' In a letter of December 8, 1790, Manning writes, ''Our Vacation commences a fortnight sooner than usual on Acct: of the Extremity of the season, & scarcity of wood, wch: is now at 10/ & 12/ pr. load.''

It is evident that in the youth of the college its charges for tuition were relatively low, being about one-third of the price of board. Rhode Island College, as was natural in a young institution connected with a poor religious denomination, sought to provide an education at the lowest possible price, its charges being about the same after the war as those of

[1] The vacations specified in the Laws of 1783 amount to fourteen weeks and four days: ''THE times of Vacation shall be from Septr: 6th: to October 20th; — From December 24th: to January 10th; — and from April 21st: to June 1st.'' In 1786 the winter vacation was lengthened to six weeks, but it was changed back to a month the next year, the spring vacation being two weeks in 1787 and three weeks in 1788.

New Jersey College were ten years before it. In a letter of February 15, 1791, to the Rev. Dr. Richard Furman, of South Carolina, Manning says, "I have taken pains to procure certain information of the expences in all the colleges from Philadelphia eastward and am convinced, that the whole expence usual [for] a public education is much less with us than in [them]."

Of the life of the students in their relations with one another very little is known. The only undergraduate society of which there is evidence was the "Pronouncing Society," for mutual improvement in the art of speaking; it is referred to in the papers of Solomon Drowne, who was chosen president of it in 1771. Athletic, musical, and dramatic clubs were undreamed of, and indeed there would have been little leisure for them with the prescribed routine. One feature of undergraduate life—the relations of the classes to one another—which is now left wholly to student control except when restraint becomes necessary, was in these early years made the subject of academic regulation: the college laws taught the freshman his place. One of the Laws of 1774 reads, "That, the freshmen Class in alphabetical order kindle a fire seasonably before morning Prayers, in the Room where they are attended During the Winter Season"; and in 1783 the ringing of the college bell was added to the duties of the freshmen. By the Supplement to the Laws of 1793 freshmen were required to carry the disciplinary billets sent by seniors and juniors to lower classmen; "to wait on the Corporation when they meet"; and "to attend the Librarian on the days on which the library shall be opened." The gradations between the other classes likewise were recognized and enforced by the following Laws of 1774:

That, due respect be paid to those of a Superior standing, by Inferiors, by giveing them the Precidence & Choice of Seats.

Ordered that the Senior Class have authority to detain in the Hall after Evening Prayers such of the under Classes as they shall observe in breaking any of the Laws of College, and there admonish them of such Offences, as well as correct and instruct them in their general Deportment, correcting their Manners in such minute particulars of a genteel Carriage & good breeding, as does not come within any express written Law of the College. which Admonitions Corrections & Instructions the Delinquents are to receive with Modesty & Submission, & punctualy observe.

That the under Classes always wait for those of the Superior Classes to go in first [*i.e.*, into the dining-room], provided any of them be in sight when at the Door: and that they observe the same Decorum in returning.

The proof of a college is in its graduates. What kind of scholars came out of Brown University during its first quarter century? what training for their work in life did they get in the college? what work did they do in the world? To these questions some answers can be given, though partial and imperfect.

The training in Latin and Greek seems to have been thorough as far as it went. The entrance work laid a good foundation, and on this the college built a solid though not lofty superstructure. Great emphasis was laid upon the actual use of Latin as a language to be written or spoken; and there is no reason to suppose that the law was a dead letter which said, in 1774 and again in 1783, "That, in the Hours of Study no one speak to another except in Latin in the College or College-Yard." An interesting bit of evidence on this point is found in the note-book of Solomon Drowne, copied from that of a former student, which has a Latin as well as an English title: "Compendium Metaphysicorum et Ontologiae, Manuscriptum Solomonis Drown, Junioris, primo Die Februarii, Anno Domini 1772do." His admonitions to himself, at the bottoms of the pages, when he fears he is not

[121]

copying fast enough, afford amusing proof that he is accustomed to express himself and perhaps to think in Latin. Thus on February 5 he writes, "Perge, perge, Solomon, et scribe occjus, vel non finias hac hebdomade." On finishing the Second Part he scribbles in the margin, "Fessus Sum. Sic finit Ontologia, et maxime Gaudeo octava nocte Februarii." At the conclusion of the whole he writes, "Hoc Compendium Metaphysicorum et Ontologiae, cum Perfectionibus et Attributis DEI, Proprium est, Solomonis Drown Junioris; qui Membrum est Collegii, Providentiae, intra Col. Ins. Rhod. et Prov. Plant. Nov. Anglorum. Manuscripta sua, ab Exemplare Theodori Foster, Artium Baccalaureus." And in the margin he heaves a Latin sigh of relief: "Tandem finivi, et Occasio est Mihi maximi Gaudii." All this is no proof, of course, that the early graduates of the college were finished classical scholars having the culture of European universities; but it is evidence that one of the world's great tongues was something more real and vital to them than a mere set of printed characters in books, and that in the study of it they must have received considerable discipline in thought and expression. The same in less degree may be said of their training in Greek and Hebrew.

In English composition and public speaking, also, the pupils of President Manning had much practice, under the guidance of an expert; and there has survived ample material for judging of their proficiency in the use of their mother tongue. When we examine their spelling, grammar, and other beggarly elements, it is something of a shock to find that these students, of native American stock and of classical nurture, are far from impeccable. After due allowance is made for difference in usage then and now, the number of errors is surprisingly great. A member of the first graduating class, in a letter to his professor shortly after Commencement, runs from one sentence into another without a capital and with only a comma between, and uses "who" for "whom" in so simple a phrase as "who I expect Daily." In a letter to Manning, fifteen years later, a letter carefully written, with corrections, he commits a double negative—"to neither of which I have not Recd. any Reply." The valedictorian of the same class, in his Commencement address, constantly misspells common words, as in the following extract from the original manuscript:

Oh! could you but for a moment, transport yourselves to Athens, & immagin you there behold that Oracal of Greece; that prince of Orators ascend the Rostrum, Surrounded by the gaping multitude; could you here the terrific thunder of his Voice; and See the light flash from either Eye; while all the members of his Agitated body, proclame the huge immotions of his Mind—Could you here him discharge those thundering Vollies of Execrations on the devouted head of an usurping philip, that Invader of Greecien Liberty: . . . you would cease to wonder at the prodigious Influence of that renowned Patriot, over his fellow Citizens.

It is surprising that this classical scholar and admirer of the Greek orator never once spells his hero's name correctly, always writing it "Demosthines." The habit of misspelling words derived from the classic languages also appears in a letter by Theodore Foster, in 1770, where occur "Collonies", "Lattin", "Derector", "Desturbed", "Despute", "insensable", and "juvinile". In Drowne's note-book there may be found, in addition to an individual stroke of genius—"grocer" for "grosser",—many of the misspellings so familiar to every teacher nowadays: "concious", "Peice", "seperated", "opperation", "immitation" and "imatation", "cheifly", "beleive", "existance", "dispise", "emminent", "enimies", "sensative", "Cataline". Here, too, quite in the modern style, "effect" is misused for "affect" and "lays" for "lies", and singular verbs are unequally yoked together with plural subjects. After the Revolution things were no better. In 1786, when Manning had been elected to Congress, some of the students respectfully urged him not to accept, on the ground that the college needed him, and their very spelling added strength to their plea, with such errors as "underwriten", "percieved", "preperation", and "oppertunity". The valedictorian of the class of 1787, Jonathan Maxcy, in resigning his tutorship in 1791, could write, "Under which your kindness has already lain me." His successor in the presidency, Asa Messer, of the class of 1790, had not mastered the art of spelling in college, and to the end of his days, in private and official letters, committed such mistakes as "shepard", and "birth" for "berth". But Rhode Island College was not alone in failing to secure accuracy in all the fundamentals of English scholarship; there is abundant evidence in the Corporation records, and elsewhere in its archives, that the graduates of other colleges were in the same case. Modern teachers of English, when weary with cropping the hydra heads of bad spelling and bad grammar, may at least comfort themselves with the thought that their dragon foe is of ancient lineage.

In the style of these early graduates there is much that is sophomoric, the natural tendency of youth toward the florid and bombastic being then reinforced by popular taste in a new country, at a time of strong political excitement. A few specimens may be interesting.

The valedictorian at the first Commencement talked in the learned Latinized style:

For tho'ugh Logic, Mathamatics, Metaphysics and philosophy, furnish knowledge for, & add Strength to the Mind, yet, these are rather calculated for entertainment in Solitude; and Seperate from a proper

Method of Communicating our Ideas, would be as Superfluous to Society, as elaborate volumes on those different Subjects in a language perfectly unintelligible.

Barnabas Binney, who became a surgeon in the Continental army, when he delivered his valedictory in 1774 had not yet learned to use the knife on his style, which is infested with swelling tumors like the following (on the preservation of religious liberty): "Hear it! O Americans! Hear it! O ye unborn millions; and hearing, feel; and feeling, swear by heaven's great fire, that what *he* gave you'll still preserve." In his wrath against oppression he passed the bounds of nature, and represented a patient animal, that has long borne the tyranny of man, as doing something quite beyond its powers: "To sit sucking our fingers, 'till our burdens press so hard that we can neither support them, nor throw them off, is characteristic rather of asses than of men." The windy style reached almost cyclonic proportions in an oration by a member of the junior class, in 1788, full of empty commonplaces on death and high-flown expressions of grief over the loss of a classmate drowned at Fox Point.

But there is much that is admirable, even to a modern reader, in these youthful productions. The thought, while neither original nor profound, is usually sensible and vigorous; and there is on the whole a rather surprising gift of expression—a fluency, an amplitude, a force, a general maturity—hardly to be expected in writers so young. One can easily credit President Manning when he says, writing in 1782 about the college just before the Revolution, "The Reputation it had acquired, for producing good Speakers, promised in the Course of a few Years, to render it equal in Numbers, and the Rival of American Colleges founded long before it"; or when he says to the Rev. Dr. Furman, in a letter of February 15, 1791, "If I am not deceived

in point of public speaking, the palm is almost universally
yielded to us, even by the alumni of other Colleges.''

In versifying, too, the students had some knack. Barnabas Binney's valedictory address to his classmates draws a
rather pretty picture of student life "on the hill":

> No more!—at ease reclin'd on yonder hill,
> Where verdent grass perfum'd with sweetest flowers,
> By faithful nature's provident command
> Prepares a couch unknown to rankling care;
> While o'er contented heads, those shady trees,
> Seem pleas'd to spread their num'rous waving bows,
> Or sweetly blushing in their vernal bloom,
> Or gently bending, with their ripen'd fruit!
> Alas! no more, in those fair, fertile fields,
> Where zephyrs gently fan the sultry heat,
> Shall we in harmless jolity and mirth,
> And converse free, of all the mighty minds
> Of ancient times, talk down the summer's sun!
> In wint'ry storms, by gen'rous fires, no more
> Together turn the grave historian's page!
> Nor search the greek and roman classics more!
> Nor swell with rapture at the poet's song!

Jonathan Maxcy, in his valedictory poem of 1787, "On
the Prospects of America," attempts a loftier note. In coup-
lets having much of the smooth eloquence characteristic
of the school of Pope, he sketches the great future which
awaits the New World, including this picture of the college
at Providence:

> There shall bright learning fix her last retreat,
> Her joyous sons, a num'rous concourse meet;
> Each art shall there to full perfection grow,
> And all be known that man shall ever know;
> There shall religion pure from heav'n descend,
> Her influence mild thro' all degrees extend;

Each different sect shall then consenting join,
Walk in her domes, and bend before her shrine;
Virtue shall reign, each heart expand with praise,
And hail the prospect of celestial days.

The most convincing test of the quality of a college's
product is the work which its graduates do in the world.
Judged by this standard, Brown University has no reason
to be ashamed of its beginnings. So far as the records show,
very few of its early sons were idle or inept; nearly all found
honorable places in the professions or in trade, while a relatively large number attained more or less distinction. The
first student, William Rogers, after being pastor of the First
Baptist Church in Philadelphia and chaplain in the Continental army, held for twenty-two years the professorship
of oratory and belles-lettres in the University of Pennsylvania; he also served in the Pennsylvania house of representatives, and was vice-president of societies for the abolition of slavery and for prison-reform. Theodore Foster,
1770, represented Rhode Island in the United States Senate for thirteen years. Solomon Drowne, 1773, a surgeon
in the Continental army, a student of medicine in Europe
for several years, a vice-president of the Rhode Island Medical Society, and a member of the American Academy of
Arts and Sciences, served his Alma Mater as professor of
materia medica and botany for twenty-three years and as
fellow for half a century. Dwight Foster, of the next class,
represented Massachusetts in the national House and Senate. Pardon Bowen, 1775, was an eminent physician in
Providence for some forty years, and president of the Rhode
Island Medical Society. Samuel Snow, 1782, was United
States consul in Canton, China. Levi Wheaton, of the same
class, was professor of medicine in Brown University for
thirteen years and a trustee for fifty-three years. Nicholas

Brown, 1786, presidential elector, a founder of the Providence Athenaeum and the Butler Hospital, was the munificent patron of the college, which takes its name from him. Samuel Eddy, of the next class, long a trustee and fellow of the college, represented Rhode Island in Congress for three terms, was its secretary of state for twenty-two years, and chief justice for eight years. Jonathan Maxcy, his classmate, was president of Rhode Island College, Union College, and South Carolina College. Jabez Bowen, 1788, was chief justice of the supreme court of Georgia. James Burrill, of the same class, was chief justice of the Rhode Island supreme court and a United States senator. James Fenner, 1789, was United States senator, governor of Rhode Island for thirteen years, presidential elector twice, and president of the Rhode Island constitutional convention in 1842. His classmate, Jeremiah B. Howell, was brigadier-general of the Rhode Island militia, and United States senator. Asa Messer, of the following class, was president of Brown University for twenty-four years. The last class under Manning included William Hunter, United States senator and minister to Brazil, James B. Mason, member of Congress, and Jonathan Russell, commissioner to negotiate the treaty of Ghent in 1814, member of Congress, and minister to Norway and Sweden.

These are the more prominent names, surely a distinguished list when we consider that there were but one hundred and sixty-five graduates in all during this period, and that most of them had neither wealth nor family station to give them a start in life. But this roll by no means tells the whole story, which is better given by the following statistics showing the occupations of all these alumni so far as known. It should be premised that, since the main purpose of the figures is to indicate the work which these men did in the world, some are counted more than once, being entered under

all the occupations in which they engaged. Clergymen, 43:
Congregationalist, 26; Baptist, 12; Episcopal, 1; Unitarian,
1; of unknown denomination, 3. Lawyers, 29. Physicians,
19. Teachers, 19. State legislators, 18. Members of the college Corporation, 17. Judges, 12: United States judges, 2;
state supreme court judges, 4; judges of lower courts, 6.
Business men, 12. College professors, 6. United States senators, 6. Congressmen, 6: in Continental Congress, 1; in
United States House of Representatives, 5. United States
ministers, 2. College presidents, 2. General state officers,
2. Governor, 1. United States consul, 1. Librarian, 1. Certainly the college under its first president fulfilled its purpose
of "preserving in the Community a Succession of Men duly
qualify'd for discharging the Offices of Life with usefulness
and reputation."

CHAPTER IV

PRESIDENT MAXCY'S ADMINISTRATION

UPON the death of President Manning the thoughts of the Corporation turned at once to the Rev. Dr. Samuel Jones, of Pennsylvania, as a fitting successor. Dr. Jones had already served the college by remodeling its charter, and would have made a very able college president. He was a man of imposing presence; he had guided young men for years in their theological studies; he was a powerful preacher and a wise administrator. It is interesting to surmise what the development of the college might have been under the guidance of so vigorous and mature a man. But it was not to be. Dr. Jones declined, chiefly on the ground that his age made it imprudent for him "to enter on a new Scene of Life." The Corporation then deferred the election of a president, making temporary arrangements meanwhile. On August 2, 1791, they voted that the Rev. Peres Fobes, professor of natural philosophy, who had acted as vice-president in 1786, "be requested to attend the College from this time 'till Commencement to supervise the Instruction of the Students & perform prayers &c."

David Howell, secretary to the Corporation, and professor of law since 1790, was appointed to officiate at Commencement. He made an address to the graduating class, full of kindly, pointed wisdom, bespeaking the scholar and man of affairs. A few sentences from it will supplement what has already been said about the character and ability of the college's first professor:

Be cautious of bandying into parties; *they* regard neither the abilities nor virtues of men, but only their subservency to present purposes;

they are a snare to virtue and a mischief to society. With this caution on your mind, you will never revile or speak evil of whole sects, classes, or societies of men. . . . Never aim to rise in life by depressing others; it is more manly to rely on the strength of ones own abilities and merit. Avoid publishing, or even listening to scandal. To mention, with pleasure, the virtues even of a rival, denotes a great mind. . . . It is a mark of vanity to speak lightly of revelation. Not to admire those ancient and sublime books shews a want of taste in fine writing, as well of real judgment in discerning the truth. And here let me caution you never to ridicule whatever may be held sacred by any devout and judicious man. If you cannot join with him, at least do not disturb him by your irreverence.

During most of the next year the college had no formal head. Jonathan Maxcy, who had served as tutor since his graduation four years before and had just been appointed professor of divinity, was requested, by a vote of the Corporation on September 8, "as often as he conveniently can without interfering with his duties as Pastor of the Church he serves to attend & accasionly Lecture on Sundays Morning & Eveng. prayers in the College Hall in Compensation for which services he be allowed the occupation of half the Presidents house & half of the College Lands." On June 6, 1792, Mr. Howell was "appointed to superintend the Government & Instruction of the Institution from this period untill Commencement day" and also "to officiate as President from [= for?] the ensuing Commencement." At the annual meeting in September, 1792, Jonathan Maxcy was elected president *pro tempore;* he served as such until September 7, 1797, when he was chosen president. On September 2, 1802, he resigned, to become the head of Union College in Schenectady, New York. After two years in this position, he was chosen the first president of South Carolina College, which he served with great success until his death on June 4, 1820.

At the time of his election Maxcy was probably the youngest college president in the country. "At the Commencement succeeding his inauguration," says his biographer and editor, Professor Elton, "the College was illuminated, and a transparency was placed in the attic story displaying his name, with — 'President 24 years old.' " He was born in Attleboro, Massachusetts, September 2, 1768. His grandfather was greatly respected in the community, for many years representing the town in the colonial legislature; his parents were of strong character and intellect, and his father had some literary talent. Jonathan showed precocity as a scholar and orator, and was therefore put into the academy at Wrentham. Although only fifteen years old when he entered college, he stood high in scholarship, being noted for his versatility and his excellence in English composition; at graduation he delivered the valedictory addresses. He was at once appointed tutor, and in this office was the intimate and favorite of President Manning. His position as Manning's successor in the pastorate of the Baptist church, and his union of scholarship with eloquence, naturally pointed him out for the presidency; but his youth gave pause, and was doubtless the reason for his being president *pro tempore* until after five years of trial.

President Maxcy's chief service to Rhode Island College was his teaching of oratory and belles-lettres and widening the fame of the institution by his personal reputation as an orator and divine. One of his colleagues in South Carolina College said in a memorial sketch: "As a teacher, Dr. Maxcy enjoyed a reputation higher, perhaps, than that of any other president of a college in the United States. His pupils all dwelt with admiration, on the clearness and comprehension of his ideas; on the precision and aptness of his expressions." The testimonies to his eloquence are numerous and all of the same tenor. Tristam Burges, himself famous as an orator, spoke thus of his former teacher in an oration before the Federal Adelphi in 1831:

There is an eloquence altogether corporeal: It belongs to the voice and to the stature. The tongue seems to *form* the thunderbolt and the hand *to wield it*. The eloquence of Maxcy was not of this character. . . . He was little of stature. His voice seemed not to have reached the deep tone of full age. . . . The eloquence of Maxcy was mental: You seemed to hear the soul of the man; and each one of the largest assembly, in the most extended place of worship, received the slightest impulse of his silver voice as if he stood at his very ear. So intensely would he enchain attention, that in the most thronged audience, you heard nothing but him, and the pulsations of your own heart. His utterance was not more perfect, than his whole discourse was instructive and enchanting.

The following letter, written on July 9, 1819, by a Southern gentleman, and published in the Charleston *City Gazette* of July 15, shows that in the last years of his life President Maxcy had still his early power:

Last Sunday we went to hear Dr. Maxcy. It being the 4th of July, it was a discourse appropriate to that eventful period. I had always been led to believe the Doctor an eloquent and impressive preacher; but had no idea, till now, that he possessed such transcendant powers. I never heard such a stream of eloquence — It flowed from his lips, even like the oil from Aaron's beard. Every ear was delighted, every heart elated, every bosom throbbed with gratitude. . . . I was sometimes in pain, lest this good old man should outdo himself and become exhausted; but as he advanced in his discourse, he rose in animation, till at length he reached flights the most sublime, and again descended with the same facility with which he soared. . . . In short, I never heard anything to compare to Dr. Maxcy's sermon in the course of all my life; and old as I am, I would now walk even twenty miles through the hottest sands to listen to such another discourse. I am persuaded, I shall never hear such another in this life.

The Southern colleague already quoted said:

Dr. Maxcy was a remarkably powerful and fascinating Preacher. Few men have ever equalled him in the impressive solemnity, and awful fervour of his manner. There was nothing turgid, or affected, or fanatical. . . . But though the general manner of Dr. Maxcy was rather mild than vehement, and rather solemn than impetuous, yet there have been occasions upon which he exhibited an eloquence animated and impassioned in the last degree, and which carried with it, as with the force and rapidity of a torrent, the hearts and feelings of his audience.

The following extract from a sermon on the existence of God, delivered in 1795, is a fair example of President Maxcy's more poetical style:

All parts of creation are equally under his inspection. Though he warms the breast of the highest angel in heaven, yet he breathes life into the meanest insect on earth. He lives through all his works, supporting all by the word of his power. He shines in the verdure that cloathes the plains, in the lily that delights the vale, and in the forest that waves on the mountain. He supports the slender reed that trembles in the breeze, and the sturdy oak that defies the tempest. His presence cheers the inanimate creation. Far in the wilderness, where human eye never saw, where the savage foot never trod, there he bids the blooming forest smile, and the blushing rose open its leaves to the morning sun. There he causes the feathered inhabitants to whistle their wild notes to the listening trees and echoing mountains. There nature lives in all her wanton wildness. There the ravished eye, hurrying from scene to scene, is lost in one vast blush of beauty. From the dark stream that rolls through the forest, the silver scaled fish leap up, and dumbly mean the praise of God. Though man remains silent, yet God will have praise. He regards, observes, upholds, connects and equals all.

His more intellectual style, together with his theory of government (in which he seems to have been a disciple of Burke), is well illustrated in this passage from an oration on July 4, 1799:

In governments where there is but one branch of power, there is no security for liberty. Simple democracies, whether managed by the whole people assembled, or by their representatives, have always proved as tyrannical as the most despotic monarchies, and vastly more mischievous. It is in vain to substitute theoretical speculations in the place of facts. The modern zealots of revolutionary reform may tell us that the science of government is of all others the most simple; that a nation, in order to be free, needs only an exertion of will; but the experience of ancient and modern times will tell us that the science of government is of all others the most intricate; because it is to be deduced from principles which nothing but experiment can develope: and that a nation, in order to be free, needs some wisdom as well as will.

The superior of Manning in fancy, elegance, and intensity, though hardly his equal in virile force, Maxcy was broader of outlook and more liberal in thought. In his address to the seniors at Commencement in 1794 he said:

Should any of you assume the character of a minister of the gospel, let me advise you to form your faith immediately from the sacred scriptures. Emancipate your souls from the force of prejudice, annihilate all attachment to particular systems, exalt yourselves to a noble independency of thought. . . . Let not the peculiarities of your religious faith confine your benevolent affections and exertions within the narrow limits of a party. Neither let a cynical moroseness, nor a fanatical zeal, impoverish your hearts, and rob you of the elegant commerce and rational enjoyments of human life. The sour scowl of a hypocrite is as offensive to heaven as the open profanity of an infidel.

In defending certain of his views that had incurred displeasure, he must have horrified most of his brethren still more by recognizing Priestley and other Unitarians as fellow Christians. He said:

All men have full liberty of opinion, and ought to enjoy it without subjecting themselves to the imputation of heresy. For my own part, I can safely say, that I have never been disposed to confine myself to the peculiar tenets of any sect of religionists whatever. . . . An entire coincidence in sentiment, even in important doctrines, is by no means essential to christian society, or the attainment of eternal felicity. How many are there who appear to have been subjects of regeneration, who have scarcely an entire, comprehensive view of one doctrine in the Bible? Will the gates of Paradise be barred against these, because they did not possess the penetrating sagacity of an Edwards, or Hopkins? Or shall these great theological champions engross heaven, and shout hallelujahs from its walls, while a Priestly, a Price, and a Winchester, merely for difference in opinion, though pre-eminent in virtue, must sink into the regions of darkness and pain?

It speaks well for the liberality of the Corporation that the next year they elected Maxcy to the full presidency.

"As a scholar," says Professor Elton, "Dr. Maxcy was one of the most learned men which our country has produced. Criticism, metaphysics, politics, morals, and theology all occupied his attention. His stores of knowledge were immense, and he had at all times the command over them." This statement must have been more true of him in his later years than during his presidency of Rhode Island College; it is noteworthy, however, that Harvard College conferred on him the degree of S.T.D. in 1801, when he was only thirty-three years of age.

"In his person," Elton says, "Dr. Maxcy was rather small of stature, of a fine form and well proportioned. All his movements were graceful and dignified. His features were regular and manly, indicating intelligence and benevolence; and, especially, when exercised in conversation or public speaking, they were strongly expressive, and exhibited the energy of the soul that animated them." No likeness of him exists except a silhouette, which shows a rounded head, rather full lips, and a somewhat prominent nose, slightly aquiline.

Under such a president the study of rhetoric and oratory would naturally be given great prominence and be taught with much success. The fact that more than half the graduates of Maxcy's time entered the law or the ministry affords striking proof that this was the case. His most distinguished pupil in the oratorical art, Tristam Burges, the man who as Congressman from Rhode Island successfully stemmed the tide of John Randolph's sarcastic eloquence, spoke thus of the instruction in public speaking under Manning and Maxcy:

It was not the Philosophy of Rhetoric, (falsely so called,) which in their time, gave lustre to instructions; it was Rhetoric itself; the divine art of persuasion, which, on their tongues, inspired their disciples with the desire to imitate, and the hope to resemble them. . . . You all remember the elevated advanced stage where the speaker took his stand, when, under supervision of the whole authority, surrounded by the entire collegiate assembly, awed by the continued and pervading spirit of the hour and the occasion, he gave utterance to his own, as soon as the last echo of the voice of devotion had ceased to whisper in the ear of the listening audience. It was not to all the assembled Greeks, it was not at the Olympic Games that he spoke; but the pupil, who passed through this ordeal, under the eye of Manning or Maxcy, has never since that time, with more anxiety prepared himself for any other; or gone through it with more fear and trembling. . . . In belles lettres and eloquence, where was the institution in our country, the character of which stood more permanently distinguished.

The same comfortable opinion of the excellence of the oratory in Rhode Island College is found in a letter of James Tallmadge, Jr., who wrote to a classmate in 1798: "I attended the Commencement at Newhaven and find it though much celebrated, not equal to ours. The students speak formally and likewise theatrically. Their compositions were very poor, scarcely equal to our Sophomore productions." This is at least proof that the ideals of speaking, under Maxcy, included simplicity and naturalness.

It must be admitted, however, that the subjects of the Commencement speeches at this time grew more and more general: "Mental Improvement" was treated in 1792, 1795, 1797, and 1800, and such topics as "War," "Education," "Enthusiasm of Opinion," occurred frequently. But the programs still had subjects of a more definite and local nature, as "An Oration recommending Rhode Island College to the Patronage of the State," and "An Oration, on the Indignities offered America by France." The exercises also retained their old-time variety, English, Latin, and Greek jostling one another, while orations and dissertations were intermingled with disputes, conferences, dialogues, and poems. The Latin dispute had been given up; but in English the young disputants attempted such questions as "Is it for the Interest of the United States to assist the French Revolution against its Enemies in the present War?" "Whether the Use of Spirituous Liquors is advantageous to Mankind?" and "Is Marriage conducive to Happiness?" The dialogues often introduced a humorous element, as in a "Dialogue, designed to ridicule Quackery in Professions," "The Bachelors," and "The Fall of Fashion." Even the conferences were sometimes facetious, as in "Astronomy burlesqued." Humor must have been a welcome relief in a program of twenty or more numbers; and it was allowed even in the poems, some of which would now be considered too undignified for the occasion.

Several of the speeches of this period have survived, being "published by request," and enable us to form an estimate of college rhetoric under Maxcy. Modern judgment on them cannot be wholly favorable. They seem inflated, occupied more with words than with thoughts, and the words are commonly too long and too learned. The imagery is often profuse and occasionally ridiculous. The sequence of thoughts is sometimes confused; the thoughts themselves are usually commonplace; there is no close grapple with facts, and the reasoning is generally loose. Yet fluency and a kind of power there certainly are in these productions, while the defects are chiefly those of youthful exuberance. Some specimens are moderate and sensible throughout; and occasionally the floridity itself held a promise realized in later years, as in these sentences from the Commencement oration of Tristam Burges in 1796:

By imagination, man seems to verge towards creative power. Aided by this, he can perform all the wonders of sculpture and painting. He can almost make the marble speak. He can almost make the brook murmur down the painted landscape. Often, on the pinions of imagination, he soars aloft where the eye has never travelled; where other stars glitter on the mantle of night, and a more effulgent sun lights up the blushes of morning. Flying from world to world, he gazes on all the glories of creation: or, lighting on the distant margin of the universe, darts the eye of fancy over the mighty void, where power creative never yet has energized, where existence still sleeps in the wide abyss of possibility.

Whatever the present judgment on Commencement oratory of that time, the Commencements were increasingly popular, forming a conspicuous feature in the life of the college and the town. The following extracts from reminiscences of them near the end of Maxcy's administration, written by "Old Citizen" and first published in *The Providence Journal*, July 2, 1851, give vivid pictures of these vanished scenes:

Commencement formerly was *the* Festival of Providence. . . . The town was filled with strangers. . . . The principal mode of conveyance was the square top chaise, long since discarded for the bellows top chaise and other carriages. They would begin to arrive on Monday, but on Tuesday toward sunset every avenue to the town was filled with them. In the stable yards of the "Golden Ball Inn," "The Montgomery Tavern," and other public houses on Wednesday morning, you could see hundreds of them, each numbered by the hostlers on the dashers with chalk, to prevent mistakes. . . .

How long the twilight of Tuesday used to appear. . . . Before it is fairly dark the College yard is filled with ladies and gentlemen of all ages and sizes. Not a light is to be seen at the College windows. Anon the College bell rings, and eight tallow candles at each window shed their rich luxuriant yellow light on the crowd below. The curtain rises from the box at the pediment, and there emblazoned in light is our national emblem, the spread eagle, talking Latin to this same crowd. In later times, the eagle gave place to "the temple of science." Loud was the cheering and long did it continue, even until several taps on a bass drum intimated the presence of the band of music which the graduating class had hired to discourse music on Commencement day. The band arrange themselves on the front steps of the old chapel, and make the welkin ring again, with Washington's March, Hail Columbia, and other appropriate tunes. At a given signal from the College bell, the music ceases, the lights are simultaneously extinguished, and the spectators and auditors left in darkness that could almost be felt to find their homes. . . .

Day breaks at last and the rising sun is saluted by two of the brass field pieces which Burgoyne surrendered at Saratoga. An old revolutionary drummer and fifer are playing the reveille through the principal streets of the town. . . . The boys can scarcely be stayed for their breakfasts. Their imaginations are too much excited to leave any appetite for ordinary food. Before nine o'clock Commencement morning the current is again setting towards the College. The great gate has been thrown wide open, the turn-stile would not afford space enough for those who are now going to pay their morning devoirs to Alma Mater. . . . The military escort has halted without the gate. The procession is formed now as it was in former times, excepting only the escort. They proceed down College street, up Main street and President street, and enter the Old Baptist at the South door. The Trustees and Fellows, that "learned faculty," occupy a stage on the North side of the pulpit, the graduating class one on the South side, while in front is that on which the speakers are to appear. The band of music are in the West gallery where the Organ now is.

After describing the morning speeches and the return of the procession to the college, "Old Citizen" goes on:

They changed front at the dining-hall door. — From this the undergraduates were excluded. The hall was generally well filled in a very short space of time, each old graduate well prepared to keep down the interest on the four dollars he invested in the commencement dinner fund when he was in college. There used to be wine, too, on the tables, and doctors in divinity, after the unusual labors of the morning, deemed it not improper to indulge in one glass, and in at least one more, to enable them to undergo the fatigues and pleasures of the afternoon. We generally had "short commons" on this occasion, not in food, quantity or quality, but in time, as the undergraduates were waiting to take our places. Not a word is uttered at the table, except "the grace," and "the thanks;" each seems ambitious to show forth his faith by his works. The graduates, trustees, &c., wait in the chapel while the undergraduates swallow what they have left on the dinner tables, then the procession is again formed as before, and again to the meeting house. The rest of the class now speak "their pieces," occupying two or three hours. . . . Again the procession is formed and proceeds to the College, and thus ends commencement proper. . . .

Many an aching head longs for its pillow commencement night. . . . We arose on Thursday morning resolved to be cured by a repetition of a similar round of literary excess. At ten o'clock, "The Federal Adelphi" met at College to elect their officers, and then to go in procession to some meeting house, and hear an oration from some old graduate. This society was supposed to consist of the most talented, as well as the most wealthy children of Alma Mater. Associated under their half English name, decorated with blue ribbons, and no silver medals, professing mysterious rites of initiation and advantages unutterable to the initiated, and always meeting the day after commencement and having a good dinner, if not a good oration, and good wine in plenty, the society was a very popular one. . . . Thus closed the literary exercises of commencement.

Such was Commencement week under President Maxcy. That the growth of the college, and the growing interest in it on at least one day in the year, brought new difficulties both within and without the meeting-house is shown by votes of the Corporation in 1791 and 1795:

Voted. That in future, all the exercises of the Commencement, be previously exhibited to the faculty of the College for correction &

approved of by them & that they do not in the whole exceed two hours in the forenoon & the same time in the afternoon.

Voted, That the Town Council of the Town, be requested to prevent any Booths, or other recepticles for persons or vendible articles from being erected in the public Streets, North and South of the Baptist Meeting-house, or in the main street or back street East and West of said Meeting-house, and between the extremities of the aforesaid cross streets, or in the gang-way leading to the river between the house's of Messrs. Nathan Angell and Jonathan Tillinghast.

The increase in number of students was fairly steady, so far as can be told by means of stray references which have escaped the burying hand of Time. In 1793–94 the number was 83, as shown by Maxcy's college account-book; in 1798 it was about 100, according to Peres Fobes, in a letter to the Corporation of later date; in October, 1800, when the first catalogue of undergraduates was published, in "broadside" form, it was 107; and in a financial estimate for the next year it is set at 112. This growth was not due wholly to the reputation of President Maxcy and the Faculty: for several years Professor Fobes was employed to turn students toward the college, a work which his position as head of a school in Massachusetts enabled him to do with advantage. The catalogue of 1800 affords proof that the college was not yet drawing students from a very wide area: 93 per cent came from New England; of these all but four came from Rhode Island and Massachusetts, and the four were from nearby Connecticut. It is rather surprising to find that Massachusetts supplied 74 students, and Rhode Island only 22. One student came from New York State, 2 students from Virginia, and 4 from South Carolina.

The increase in income from growing numbers is clearly shown by two contemporary statements. One, in the Corporation records for October 8, 1793, gives the income for the preceding year thus: tuition, $1088; library fees, $204; interest of fund, $366.67; a total of $1658.67. The other, preserved among some miscellaneous papers, is indorsed, "Estimate of The Funds of the College Septr 1801": "Tuition Room Rent & Library of 112 Schollers" are entered as $2688 (tuition at $16, room rent at $4, and library fees at $4); "Product of Permanent funds," $500; total, $3188. This gain in resources, modest as they still were, enabled the Corporation to raise salaries. President Maxcy's salary in 1792 was £100, or $333.33; in 1795 it was $600; in 1801, $1000; in each case the fees from the graduating class, and the use of the president's house and the adjoining land, were added. The resident professor received £90, or $300, in 1792, $357 in 1795, and $600 in 1801. The salary of a tutor rose from £65, or $217, in 1792, to $287 in 1795, and $350 in 1801.

These salaries were still low compared with those in other professions and even in some of the other colleges. The Faculty could not be much enlarged, and there was little left for other needs: in 1800 the appropriation for the library was $200; the next year it was $100, "for New Books & Repairing & Binding Books." In these circumstances it is not strange that the old device of a lottery was thought of. On December 23, 1795, a committee was appointed to pray the General Assembly for "the grant of a Lottery to raise the sum not exceeding 25,000 Dollars, to be applied to the use of this institution." The plan matured slowly, for it was September 5, 1798, when the Corporation voted, "That the College Lottery shall Commence drawing the second Wednesday of October next, and continue till the same be completed." President Maxcy took 303 tickets to sell, at six dollars apiece, and sold 168 of them. The final account of the managers, rendered on November 8, 1800, showed a total business of $33,548.50, with a "Neat drawback" of $8000.

The hope for a generous benefactor also lingered still in the minds of the Corporation. On September 3, 1795, they voted "That any person giving to this Corporation the sum of Six thousand dollars, or good security therefor, before the next annual Commencement, shall have the honour of naming this university." How much effort was made to find a patron is unknown; but on October 26, 1795, President Maxcy wrote thus to the Rev. Dr. Richard Furman, a prominent man among the South Carolina Baptists:

Our College flourishes as to numbers, but is very barren as to funds. A lottery has been suggested as a sure method of increasing them. Do you think it would meet with encouragement in your part of the Country? We extremely need funds for the establishment of 2 or 3 professorships. This I conceive the only way in which education can be carried on as it ought to be. Nothing injures an institution more than a perpetual change of instructors. This will always be the case, unless friends can be procured to afford sufficient encouragement to men of capacity. This College is still without a *name*. No benefactor has appeared. The corporation at their last meeting past a resolution that if any person would previous to the next Commencement, give to the College $6,000, he should have the right to name it. Have you no eminent rich man among you, who might be disposed?

The great benefactor was to arise nearer home, but not for some years. Meanwhile there were various small gifts for special purposes. In 1792 Nicholas Brown gave the college a law library, comprising some three hundred and fifty volumes, which he imported from England at a cost of £138 sterling, or nearly $700. The college, however, did not get the benefit of the books at once, for they were placed by the donor "for a term of time" in Mr. Howell's office; but in 1804 they were delivered up, whereupon the Corporation advised that "a conspicuous alcove" be prepared for them in the "Library-Room," and voted that no part of the collection should be taken out "by any person whomsoever." In 1793 a catalogue of the whole college library was published, which showed a total number of 2173 volumes. Little money could be spared for its increase and upkeep during Maxcy's presidency, and there seems to have been some laxity in the care of it. A report of the library committee on September 4, 1797, complains that books have been kept out for "several years past," although the persons keeping them had been notified; the chief offenders were a professor and a fellow. Another report at about the same time urges the enforcement of the legal penalty for failure to return books; and says that "some of the books particularly a Number of old folio Volumes are injui'd by the Worms which they Conceive may be prevented in future by having the books together with the shelves Carefully brush'd at Certain Periods." The freshmen, meanwhile, were granted new privileges by a vote of the Corporation on September 6, 1796, "That the Freshman Class be in future admitted to the use of the College Library on the same terms as the other Students."

The scientific apparatus and collections fared somewhat better, although an entry in the Corporation records of 1795 reveals a pitiful gratitude for small favors : "Voted, That the thanks of this Corporation be presented to Mr. Jones Welch of Boston, Merchant, for his present to this Corporation of a preserved bird called the Curlieu of Cayenne, and a Calabash curiously wrought by the Natives of Cayenne, to be deposited in the Museum." On such casual windfalls did the illustration of the truths of natural history then depend. Natural philosophy received more ample support. When Professor Fobes resigned his chair in 1798, and was succeeded by Professor Messer, he left his apparatus at the college, receiving $50 a year for the use of it. In 1799 Mr. Samuel Elam, of Newport, gave $500 for the purchase of apparatus, and $300 more the next year. The Corporation authorized the President to get the aid of the Rev. John Prince, of Salem, in buying the instruments, and to "have conspicuously engraven thereon the name of the Donor." They also requested Dr. Prince to have "the Air pump and telescope, now belonging to this College, repaired and fitted for use," and appointed a committee "to procure a room in the College to be suitably repaired and fitted for the Philosophical apparatus, and for the exhibition of Lectures, &c." The original list of articles bought with Mr. Elam's donation, still on file in the archives, includes these items and prices, some of the latter scrupulously carried out to mills: An electrical machine, with ten-inch cylinders, $37.33.3; "inflammable air pistol," $2.16.7; "mounted flask for Aurora Borealis," $1.87.5; "An artificial Eye," $9.10; "An improved wind mill for airpump," $10.40; "An hydrostatic machine for shewing the spouting of fluids in parabola & semiparabola," $30.00; "an orrery on brass stand," $202.33.

The curriculum and methods of instruction under Maxcy seem to have been substantially the same as under Manning. But some new light is thrown on the intellectual life of the undergraduates by the records of the library, which begin at about this time, and show that a great deal of solid reading was done. David R. Williams, governor of South Carolina in 1814–16, who was a student in Providence for two years, took out books nearly every week, and came back for the successive volumes of works in sets; before vacations he laid in a stock for the weeks when the library would be closed. The quality of his reading may be seen by the following list, which is complete:

1793. Nov. 16: Robertson's Charles V., vol. 4. Nov. 23: Female Ruin, vol. 1. Nov. 25: Gibbon, vol. 2. Dec. 5, 12, 21: Shakespeare, vols. 2, 3, 5.—1794. Jan. 4: Shakespeare, vols. 7, 10; Pope's Odyssey, vols. 1, 2; Robertson's America, vol. 3; Vertot's Revolution in Sweden; Marshall's Travels, vol. 1. Feb. 8: Marshall's Travels, vol. 2; De Witt's Political Maxims. Feb. 18: Anderson's History of France, vol. 2. Mar. 2, 8: Robertson's Scotland, vols. 1, 2. Mar. 15, 22: Moore's Travels in France, vols. 1, 2. Mar. 29: Rousseau's Inequality. April 1, 5: Moore's Travels in Italy, vols. 1, 2. April 12, 19, 26, May 2: Addison, vols. 1-4. May 8: Vaillant's Travels, vol. 2; Rollin's Roman History, vols. 1, 2. June 7: Vertot's Revolution in Portugal; Vertot's Revolution in Rome, vol. 2. June 21: Montagu's Letters; Life of Queen Anne, vol. 1. July 3: Thomson's Poems, vols. 2, 3. July 9, 16: Young's Poems, vols. 3-6. July 25: Congreve's Plays, Otway's Plays. Oct. 31, Nov. 8: Rollin's Roman History, vols. 5, 6. Nov. 15, 22: Rollin's Belles Lettres, vols. 1-4. Nov. 29, Dec. 6: European Settlements, vols. 1, 2. Dec. 13, 20, 27: Kaimes's Sketches of the History of Man, vols. 1, 3, 4. Dec. 27: The Spectator, vols. 1, 2.

Two undergraduate societies were formed during Maxcy's administration. The Misokosmian Society, founded in 1794, was remodeled in 1798, and changed its name to the Philermenian Society. It held fortnightly meetings, for debates, speeches, and declamations, and the reading of essays and poems, and began in 1798 to collect a library. On the day before Commencement occurred its anniversary meeting, at this time held in the chapel, when an oration and a poem were delivered by undergraduate members. Membership was limited to forty-five, and the society was practically secret, with certificates of membership drawn up in sonorous Latin. In 1799 a branch of the Philandrian Society was established in the college. This made more of the social life, but also gave much attention to speaking: it held four quarterly meetings, at which there were always a lecture on politeness and a debate; at the anniversary meeting, which was not usually held in Providence, there were as a rule an oration and poem, and might be debates, dialogues, and such exercises.

The first organization of graduates also had its beginning in this decade. Certain of the younger alumni, including Samuel Eddy, William Hunter, Paul Allen, and Tristam Burges, with Professors Howell and West and the former tutor, Ashur Robbins, formed the society of the Federal Adelphi in November, 1797. The purpose of the society, according to its charter, was "Improvement in the Arts and Sciences"; Tristam Burges, in his oration before it in 1831, said the society was founded to give a higher degree of perfection to studies begun in college, and the context shows that he referred chiefly to the study of oratory. Membership was limited to holders of college degrees, members of the learned professions, and seniors and juniors in Rhode Island College. Professor Howell was the first president, serving from 1797 to 1802. The society took itself seriously, and for many years its meeting formed an attractive addendum to Commencement. In the archives is a letter from the society to the Corporation, inviting them to attend the meeting in 1799, when Tristam Burges gave the oration; so far as is known, this is the first communication to the Corporation from an organized body of alumni.

The growing sense of solidarity which led to these student organizations might easily lead also to growing resistance, more or less organized, against college authority and laws. President Maxcy's government, according to Elton, "was reasonable, firm and uniform, and marked in its administration by kindness, frankness and dignity. He did not attempt to support his authority, as is sometimes done, by distance, austerity and menace, but his pupils were addressed and treated as young gentlemen." The pupils, however, did not always choose to be "young gentlemen," and there was undoubtedly some relaxation of the bonds of discipline and some lowering of moral tone among the undergraduates as a whole. In the laws themselves there was no relaxation. The Supplement to the Laws of 1793, extracts from which may be found in the Appendix, fastens the fetters more firmly upon the freshmen, and seeks to strengthen the distinctions between all the classes. It is likely that the need for such legislation sprang from a tendency on the part of the students to disregard what was then considered due deference to superior station.

The rules forbidding students to leave the college yard in study hours seem to have been well obeyed by the better men, if we may judge by the case of Tristam Burges, 1796, who, in a letter to John Howland in 1849, said that he knew little of Providence until after his graduation: "For," he wrote, "though I had resided in the town more than three years at that time, yet my residence was at the college; nor was I in the street more than once a week, and then on the Sabbath." On the other hand, a student writing in 1799 says of two of his fellows: "Old Die Shins around among the girls with the utmost freedom. Young Daniel throws Glass bottles, & is raking about every night." It was possible, too, to defy authority and follow nature while staying within the college walls. Tristam Burges's biographer thus describes a "merry meeting" and its interruption: "The first night after the class met, in the first term, there was a grand festival (as it was then represented) of the whole class. . . . In the midst of their jollity, as the table was covered with decanters, pitchers, glasses, wine and all kinds of fragments, the tutor's cane was heard, at the door, and in a moment Mr. Messer stood before them." In connection with this anecdote the following vote of the Corporation a year before has greater significance : " Voted That the Steward shall not be permitted on any pretence to sell any Spirituous Liquors to the Students except Cyder." But all precautions failed to keep some students from intemperance, although there is no evidence that the vice was common. "I am sorry to inform you," writes a student in 1798, "that Corporal Trim has drowned his grief with liquor so often this quarter that Maxcy has had him at the tribunal bar, and last night admonished him and fined him 6 shillings."

Another extract from the same letter illustrates the undergraduate attitude toward dishonesty in academic work, and the spirit of the students in general :

Anxious for advancement our class appear like a drove of deacons. All are attentive to their books, all are anxious to gain favour. If one of the authority walk in the odoriferous Grubstreet, the seniours all prepare to meet them that they may shew respect by bowing with profound adoration. No art remains untryed to obtain favour — enough — Webb's exhibition piece is proved to be stollen from *St. Pierres Studies of Nature* and Cary's Poem on *chance* consisting of 150 lines is found in *Blackmore on Creation* 90 lines verbatim, Thomson is so proud that he did not steal his that by the request of the Freshmen and Sophomores it is put to the press and will be out tomorrow, Mr. Carter offers them at 2 cents each. I hope therefore there will not be so much grass pulled up this summer for — fodder. . . . It was diverting the other day to hear Cary and Webb dispute. They twited each other of appearing in borrowed feathers at exhibition &c . . . and came nigh to fighting.

The government seems to have viewed the offense lightly, too, for there is no record of the offenders' being punished, and both got their degrees with their class, one receiving the valedictory honor.

The following extracts from letters written in the spring

of 1798 show how seriously the undergraduates took the assignment of Commencement parts, and how disrespectful they could be to college officials. Incidentally the letters prove that the class no longer was allowed to choose the valedictorian.

After prayers they all looked with anxious expectation. If you have ever seen the sable cat from under the barn floor glare with her flaming eyeballs, imagine if you can endure the thought, 27 of them in one row with eyes if possible more terrible than usual looking you full in the face, and you will have a good representation of our class and the deplorable situation of little *Jock*. He at length summoned a sufficiency of mind to proclaim the following arrangements. . . . Maxwell is high, talked with Maxcy and at length told him it was a damned partial distribution.

The irreverent spirit of youth! To the undergraduate the President of the college, the eloquent Jonathan Maxcy, was no more but "little Jock"! Another senior writes to the same correspondent:

As Mr. Tallmadge has given you a catalogue of the parts I shall not trouble you with another but will recite some of the transactions since. The next night after; the locks that are on the doors that lead to the bell were filled with lead so that we had a long morning before the ringing of the bell, the entries nightly resound with crashing of bottles and the hoarse rumbling of wood and stones. We have found out that Father Messer was the principal man in giving out the parts and for that reason he is treated with contempt by the students. Mr. Maxcy has been unwell the last week so that he did not attend prayers and Messer officiated and he has both been hissed and clapt.

If a professor in chapel was treated thus, what might a young tutor expect? A partial answer is found in a letter of 1799, in which both the college building and the tutor receive expressive nicknames:

The Old Brick resounds very frequently with the breaking of glass bottles against Tutor T's door, If he can be called a Tutor. We have given him the epithet of Weazle. He is frequently peaking through the knot holes & cracks to watch his prey. The cat that crafty animal gives him a douse in the chops not infrequently. She has not yet been able to be in full possession of him. But if Mr. Weazle is not more careful his destruction is certain.

Student rowdyism did not confine itself to the college walls. The minutes of the Corporation for April 16, 1798, record that a committee from several churches reported, "That a number of the Students are not only remiss in a punctual attendance on Public Worship, . . . but that they frequently behave during Divine Service, with great indecency." On April 6, 1801, the Corporation appointed a committee to request at least one of the tutors to "take the seat that is assigned them in the Gallery of the Benevolent Congregational meeting house every sunday," and aid in "keeping order in the time of public Worship." On September 6, 1804, the Corporation voted, "That the Treasurer be directed to pay a bill brought against the Benevolent Congregational Society by Grinnell and Taylor for repairing damages done by the Students of the College in said Society's meeting-House, for eight Dollars, nineteen cents ; and that the President collect as much of the money as he can from the Students who attend that Meeting."

The college commons continued to be a source of complaint and disorder. The unfriendly attitude of the students toward the steward is reflected in a vote of the Corporation, in 1797, that students living in college "be liable and chargeable for all damages done to the Stewards furniture or property within the College Walls." The rise in the price of board frequently caused discontent. It was at $1.75 per week in the autumn of 1795, and rose to $1.92 the next spring. It fell and rose several times after that, the students demanding a reduction, and the steward maintaining that he could not furnish board for less without loss. In 1798 the chronic irritation became acute. The students rebelled and forsook commons in a body, despite threats of expulsion. The President finally concluded a "Treaty of Amity & Intercourse," whereby the students agreed to return to the board of Alma Mater, and the President promised to do his best to improve conditions. A worse situation arose two years later, as we learn from a letter written March 21, 1800:

We have had shocking times such as the Old Brick never experienced before. . . . No study! No prayers! Nothing but riot and confusion! No regard paid to Superiors. Indeed, Sir, the spirit of '75 was displayed in its brightest colors. . . . The Steward's inattention to his duty and the long enmity that has existed between him and the students became intolerable. . . . At length 13 of March, the memorable 13 of March—we inconsiderately carried headlong by passion framed an instrument which contained all the names of those who boarded in Commons With This Declaration. We Solemnly Swear that we will not attend to any duties of the said College till the Steward is removed from his Office ! ! ! ! . . . They were in the Chapel when he [the President] came to beseech the Lord! They began to retire. He found it in vain to command. He requested them to stop. He addressed us in as mild language as he could possibly considering the causes of provocation. He told us we were trampling upon all law. He pledged his fidelity, that our grievances should be removed, as far as it was in his power to remove them, if we would return to duty.

The students stood out stoutly; one was expelled, and five were rusticated. The senior class thereupon decided to leave college unless these were restored, but one of the trustees induced the seceding rebels to remain until the next meeting of the Corporation. Some *modus vivendi* was evidently reached, for all the students disciplined got their degrees, except one who died, and the writer of the letter became a tutor immediately after graduation, the next autumn.

Perhaps all these ebullitions were due to the powerful

individualities of the students. At any rate, the record of their later achievements shows that they must have been all the while preparing themselves with some earnestness for the work of life. Of the 227 graduates from 1792 to 1802 the great majority entered professional or public life, as follows: Lawyers, 66. Clergymen, 56: Congregationalist, 34; Baptist, 11; Episcopal, 1; Unitarian, 1; of unknown denomination, 9. Teachers, 32. State legislators, 31. Physicians, 23. Judges, 17: United States judge, 1; state supreme court judges, 4; judges of lower courts, 12. United States representatives, 11. College professors, 4. Editors, 3. College presidents, 2. Authors, 2. United States senators, 2. Army officers, 2. Naval officers, 2. General state officers, 2. Lieutenant-Governors, 2. Governor, 1. United States minister, 1. United States consul, 1. Mayor, 1. Librarian, 1. Sixteen served on college governing boards, 11 for Brown University and 5 for other institutions. Twenty-two were merchants or business men. A few of these alumni deserve separate mention. Paul Allen, of the class of 1793, became an author of some note, publishing *Original Poems*, a *History of the Expedition under Lewis and Clark*, a *History of the American Revolution*, etc. The fame of Tristam Burges as Congressman and orator has already been mentioned. Jeremiah Chaplin, 1799, became the first president of Waterville (now Colby) College. In the last class that graduated under Maxcy was a youth who received at Commencement only the honor of an intermediate oration, but who later developed into one of the profoundest thinkers of his generation —Henry Wheaton, minister to Prussia, and an authority of world-wide fame in international law. If Rhode Island College during the decade of President Maxcy's administration had done nothing else but give this intellect a collegiate training, its existence would be amply justified.

CHAPTER V

PRESIDENT MESSER'S ADMINISTRATION

ON the same day that President Maxcy's resignation was received, the Corporation elected Asa Messer president *pro tempore*, and two years later made him president. President Messer was born in Methuen, Massachusetts, in 1769, the son of a farmer. His preparation for college was acquired under the Rev. Hezekiah Smith, of Haverhill, and in an academy at Windham, New Hampshire; he entered Rhode Island College as a sophomore, and graduated in 1790. He was licensed to preach by the First Baptist Church in Providence, in 1792, and was ordained in 1801, but never had the care of a church. At the time of his election to the presidency he had already served the college eleven years — as tutor from 1791 to 1796, as professor of the learned languages from 1796 to 1799, and as professor of mathematics and natural philosophy since 1799, also acting as librarian from 1792 to 1799.

The conspicuous facts of the new administration are that near its beginning Rhode Island College became Brown University, and near its end the second college building was erected: the institution had at last found its patron, and was by his help led on to larger things. On September 8, 1803, the Corporation passed the following vote: "That the donation of $5000 Dollars, if made to this College within one Year from the late Commencement, shall entitle the donor to name the College." One year later, on September 6, the day after Commencement, the following letter was read in the Corporation meeting:

[155]

Providence Sept. 6: 1804

Gentlemen—

It is not unknown to you that I have long had an attachment to this Institution as the place where my deceased Brother Moses and myself received our Education—This attachment derives additional strength from the recollection that my late Hond. Father was among. the earliest & most zealous patrons of the College: & is confirmed by my regard to the Cause of Literature in general—Under these impressions I hereby make a Donation of Five Thousand Dollars to Rhode Island College to remain to perpetuity as a fund for the establishment of a Professorship of *Oratory* & *Belles Letters*—The Money will be paid next Commencement, and is to be vested in such funds as the Corporation shall direct for its Augmentation to a sufficiency in your judgment to produce a competent annual Salary for the within mentioned Professorship—

I am very respectfully Gentlemen with my best wishes for the prosperity of the College

Your obedt: friend

Honbl. Corporation
   of Rhode Island College

Nicho Brown

In selecting oratory as the chair to be endowed, Mr. Brown was doubtless influenced by the wish of his uncle, John Brown, expressed the previous year in a letter to the Corporation written only a few days before his death, in which he said, "And as the most beautiful and handsome mode of speaking was a principal Object, to my certain knowledge, of the first Friends to this College, I do wish that the Honorable the Corporation may find means during their deliberations of this week, to establish a Professorship of English Oratory." The fund was put at interest for several years until the income from it was judged sufficient for the purpose specified by the donor.

In fulfillment of their previous vote, and in gratitude to Mr. Brown, the Corporation at the same meeting voted, "That this College be called and known in all future time by the Name of Brown University in Providence in the State of Rhode Island, and Providence Plantations.'' If it seem to any modern reader that the sum given was too small for so great an honor, it should be remembered that $5000 was worth far more then than now, that the day of very large gifts to colleges was not yet, and that Mr. Brown continued his benefactions through many years, until their total was in the neighborhood of $160,000. The new name had, furthermore, a peculiar propriety. Mr. Brown was a devout man, although he never joined any church : he believed in the distinctive doctrines of the Baptists, and constantly attended their places of worship ; but ''no sectarian attachments,'' says his friend, Professor Goddard, ''were suffered to fetter the exercise of his truly liberal and catholic spirit.'' The name ''Brown University,'' therefore, carries in it a reminder of the religious and denominational origin of the college, and of its catholic spirit as well. Mr. Brown was also a Rhode Islander through and through. He came of an old Rhode Island family, bone and sinew of the colony and state ; and he himself, for fifty years a great merchant, whose ships were seen in all the waters of the globe, a man of strictest probity, an educated gentleman and a philanthropist of wide interests, stands out with modest dignity as a foremost representative of the qualities of head and heart which have made the smallest state in the Union one of the richest, most powerful, and most honorable. In becoming ''Brown University,'' therefore, the institution did not cease to be ''Rhode Island College.''

The Corporation in President Messer's administration was for the most part less active than in the stirring earlier days. The annual meetings were occupied chiefly with matters of routine, and the meetings of ''minor quorums'' almost wholly ceased. The personnel of both branches had largely changed: of those who took office under President Manning, only eight fellows and ten trustees held over into President Messer's administration, and many of these soon fell out because of old age or death. The second chancellor, the Hon. Jabez Bowen, died in 1815, and was succeeded by Bishop Alexander V. Griswold, of the Episcopal Church. There was also a change in the secretaryship, Judge Howell giving way in 1806 to the Hon. Samuel Eddy. Nicholas Brown continued to serve as treasurer until 1825, when he was succeeded by Moses B. Ives. The new members and officers proved themselves worthy successors of the old by continuing the administration along essentially the same liberal lines. At the annual meeting in 1826 the Corporation, for some unknown reason, departed from the uniform practice of previous years in the mode of conducting business. The two branches met in separate rooms of University Hall. The trustees sent one of their number to inform the fellows that they were duly organized and had elected a clerk. Several votes were then passed by both branches, each branch voting separately: the votes when passed by the trustees were signed by their clerk; when passed by the fellows they were signed by the secretary of the Corporation. This dual meeting occurred on September 7, and seems to have been an experiment, for on the day before both branches had met in joint session as usual. The experiment evidently proved unsatisfactory, and was never repeated.

For several years after Messer's accession to the presidency there was no great change in the affairs of the college. The number of students slowly increased; the average number of graduates during the first nine years was twenty-five, while under Maxcy it had been twenty-one. The Faculty was no larger: it consisted of the President; the professor of jurisprudence, David Howell, who gave no lectures, although several times requested by the Corporation to do so; the professor of the learned languages, Calvin Park, who served as such from 1804 to 1811; two tutors; and the steward, who after 1803 was also called register.

In 1811 came an innovation. A Medical School was established, by the appointment of three professors: Solomon Drowne, professor of materia medica and botany; William Ingalls, professor of anatomy and surgery; and William C. Bowen, professor of chemistry. There had been no considerable increase in the available funds or in the amount received from tuition, and the yearly income barely sufficed to pay the salaries of the former members of the Faculty. How, then, it will be asked, was this enlargement possible? Could a medical school in those days be founded on nothing? Apparently this one was founded on nothing but goodwill and student fees. There is no record that the Corporation even considered salaries for the medical professors before 1815, and in 1816 Professor Drowne received but $200; in 1823 he was allowed $100 and fees; in 1825, $250. The truth is that these medical professors were lecturers only, and their duties at the college did not interfere seriously with their practice, while the distinction of holding professorships was doubtless of some pecuniary value to them as physicians.

The standard of medical education in this country was then low, or a medical school so scantily equipped would not have been tolerated in a reputable institution of learning. At the time of its founding, in 1811, there were only two medical schools in New England — one at Harvard, founded in 1782, and one at Dartmouth, founded in 1798. Many practitioners had no medical degree, but were merely licensed, after an apprenticeship of three or four years to some physician of established reputation. Yet even by contemporary standards the Brown University Medical School was open to criticism; and its inadequacy was the first point of attack in a friendly but severe "Letter to the Corporation" from an "Alumnus Brunensis" in 1815, two years after Professor Bowen had resigned the chair of chemistry. At this time only two medical students had as yet completed the course and taken their degrees; and the critic finds good reason why other schools are preferred: "Ours is incomplete. The departments of Chemistry, and of the Theory and Practice of Medicine, remain to be filled. . . . Two able Professors fill the other departments. But will medical students extensively resort to a school 'but half made up'? . . . Not a moment ought to be lost in completing the establishment; especially since not a single serious obstacle appears to oppose its completion." He proposes that the professors receive salaries, instead of being humiliated by precarious dependence upon fees, and that their lectures be free to juniors and seniors in the college. He realizes that lectures by non-resident professors ought to be supplemented by a study of textbooks and a drilling by tutors; but laboratory work and clinics are not so much as hinted at.

Whether or not the Corporation had needed this prodding, they did, a few weeks after the "Letter" came out, appoint Dr. Levi Wheaton as professor of the theory and practice of "physick," and Dr. John M. Eddy as "adjunct" professor of anatomy and surgery. The chair of chemistry, for which a committee of the Corporation had been seeking a professor since 1813, was filled in 1817 by the selection of John D'Wolf, of Bristol. The Medical School, thus strengthened, continued through President Messer's administration and into the second year of President Wayland's. Its professors were able men of excellent training. Professor Drowne was a graduate of the University of Pennsylvania Medical School, served as a surgeon in the Continental army, and studied under eminent physicians in Europe for four years; he was also a famous botanist, having a remarkable botanical garden at his home on Mount Hygeia, in Foster. Professor Ingalls, who took the degrees of A.B., M.B., and M.D. at Harvard, was a prominent Boston physician, especially skillful in surgery, and one of the earliest opponents of the practice of bleeding. Professor Bowen, who came of a family of eminent Providence physicians, was educated in Rhode Island College and Union College, studied and practiced in Providence, and then went to Europe, where he took a medical degree in the University of Edinburgh, studied in Paris, and was a private pupil of the great London surgeon, Astley Cooper; Dr. Usher Parsons wrote of him, "In the death of Dr. William C. Bowen, Rhode Island lost its brightest ornament of the medical profession." His successor, Professor D'Wolf, studied in Brown University, but did not take a degree; his knowledge of chemistry was acquired chiefly under Dr. Robert Hare, of Philadelphia, a celebrated chemist, later professor of chemistry in the University of Pennsylvania. Dr. D'Wolf was a brilliant lecturer. "He always had a full attendance," wrote a member of the class of 1826. "He opened to the eyes of the student, in his peculiarly attractive manner, the wonders of a new and brilliant science. . . . Sometimes in drawing practical deductions from the science he was teaching, he would suddenly electrify the class by illustrating its truths in glowing and eloquent words, so impressive and graphic as not to be easily forgotten." He also gave popular courses of lectures, which drew large audiences, in Providence, New Bedford, and Savannah. After leaving Brown he held the chair of chemistry in medical schools in Vermont and St. Louis. Professor Wheaton, of the class of 1782, studied medicine with a Rhode Island physician during the Revolution, and acquired valuable experience in a military hospital and as surgeon on a privateer and a prison-ship; he contributed many articles to the Boston *Medical and Surgical Journal* and other professional periodicals. Professor Eddy, who died in the second year after his appointment, was a man of high promise, and one of the original fellows of the Rhode Island Medical Society. Professor Parsons, Eddy's successor, after studying medicine in Boston under Dr. John Warren, a professor in the Harvard Medical School, served with distinction as surgeon in the War of 1812; he received the degree of M.D. at Harvard in 1818, walked the hospitals in Paris and London, and in 1821 became professor of anatomy and surgery at Dartmouth, whence he removed to Brown University the next year as adjunct professor of those subjects, becoming full professor in 1823. "If we may accept the testimony of two surviving pupils of the school," modestly writes his son, Professor C. W. Parsons, "the opening of courses by Dr. Parsons gave new life to the institution. He made arrangements, through channels over which a veil of secrecy had to be thrown, for a supply of anatomical material." Dr. Parsons became eminent as a surgeon and consulting physician, and his prize medical essays made his name widely known; in 1853 he was chosen first vice-president of the American Medical Association.

This was surely a brilliant Faculty for a medical school without endowment; and it is not surprising that the school had a considerable measure of success. The following extracts from a circular recently given to the university library show the methods and ideals of the professors; the circular is undated, but belongs to the years 1822–25:

THE Medical Lectures in Brown University will commence in the Anatomical Building, in Providence, on the first Thursday in February, and be continued daily for nearly three months.

Theory and Practice of Physic and Obstetrics, by Dr. WHEATON,	$10 00
Chemistry and Pharmacy, by Professor D'WOLF,	10 00
Anatomy, Physiology and Surgery, by Dr. PARSONS,	15 00
	$35 00

. . . The Anatomical Museum has recently received very important additions from various parts of Europe, and now contains every preparation, plate and instrument necessary to a teacher of anatomy. Students will be accommodated with separate sets of bones, and allowed ample opportunities in Practical Anatomy. . . .

The lectures on Surgery will comprise about one fourth part of the course, and nearly every instrument now in use will be exhibited and described. When practicable, students will be allowed to attend surgical operations, and cases of sickness. . . .

The conditions on which Medical Degrees are conferred are the following:

1st. That the candidate sustain a good moral character.

2. That he furnish the Professors with satisfactory evidence of his possessing a competent knowledge of the Latin language and Natural Philosophy.

3. That he shall have attended two full courses of lectures on Anatomy and Surgery, Chemistry and the Theory and Practice of Physic.

4. That he shall have studied three years (including the time of lectures) with physicians of approved reputation.

5. That he shall have submitted to a private examination held by the Professors during the last week of the lectures, or on the Monday and Tuesday preceding Commencement—and received their recommendation.

6. That he shall have written a dissertation on some medical subject and read and defended it in the College Chapel before the President, or such College officer as he may appoint, and the Medical Professors and such other professional or literary gentlemen as choose to attend.

A Brown University Medical Association, consisting of pro-

fessors, students attending the medical lectures, and resident physicians, was formed in 1811 and lived until 1825.
It held weekly meetings during the lecture season, and had
a library from which books were lent.

The graduates of the Brown University Medical School
numbered eighty-seven, not counting the recipients of honorary medical degrees, of whom there were thirty-one during the years 1804–28. Most of the graduates became useful members of their profession, and several attained to
eminence. Jerome V. C. Smith was professor in the Berkshire Medical Institution, port physician of Boston for
twenty-three years, editor of the Boston *Medical and Surgical Journal* for twenty-eight years, and the author of many
medical works. Alden March was a founder of the Albany
Medical College and professor of surgery in it for thirty
years, president of the American Medical Association, and
originator of various surgical appliances. Lewis L. Miller
was an eminent physician in Providence for forty years,
and president of the Rhode Island Medical Society. George
Capron practiced in Rhode Island for half a century; he
was physician in the United States Marine Hospital at
Providence, president of the Rhode Island Medical Society, and author of numerous medical publications. Johnson
Gardner was a Rhode Island physician for forty years,
and examining surgeon for the state recruits during the
Civil War. Francis L. Wheaton was appointed surgeon-
general of Rhode Island during the Mexican War, and was
a surgeon in the United States military service throughout
the Civil War. The most famous of all was Elisha Bartlett,
of the last class under President Messer; he held professorships in several medical schools, including Dartmouth, the
University of New York, and the College of Physicians and
Surgeons in New York City; he was also prominent as an

author, producing, says Dr. Parsons, "two works of great importance and permanent value," one on the "Fevers of the United States," which established the distinction between typhus and typhoid, and the other an "Essay on the Philosophy of Medical Science."

The Medical School was not the only department of the University for which the vigorous "Alumnus Brunensis" of 1815 had pointed suggestions to make. Turning to the college as a whole, he urges that a non-resident professor of rhetoric and oratory be appointed at once; advises that "a concise course of Lectures on Law" be given, and hopes that "it would be the commencement of a *Law School*, which is much needed"; thinks that "probably no immediate alteration is expedient" in the department of mathematics and natural philosophy, of which President Messer had charge, but "in almost every college, it has a professor specially devoted to its interests." He would also have "summary and concise" courses of lectures on mineralogy and zoölogy given by the professors of chemistry and botany. The professor of moral philosophy and metaphysics, Calvin Park, seems to have confined the course to recitations from a textbook; for "Alumnus" says he has "only to remark, that a course of lectures on this subject, should the worthy professor of it be inclined to engage, would be a valuable addition to the circle of discipline." He has just views of the function and needs of a college library: "A Library, not to be retrograde, must keep pace with the progress of science and of other similar institutions. The college Library ought therefore to have an annual appropriation for its regular increase." He has other ambitions for the college, but does not expect to see them realized at present—a cabinet of minerals, a botanic garden, and an additional college building. The most modern suggestion is that about "Miscellaneous Lectures,'' which incidentally shows that the relations between officers and students were then less intimate and friendly than now:

Persons generally enter a college young and comparatively inexperienced. In the choice of books, in the direction of their studies, in their attention to diet and exercise, in the selection of companions, in their judgment of mankind, and in the formation of their social and moral habits, how much assistance might be given by one whose experience has instructed him on these points, and whose affectionate solicitude for the welfare of his pupils would call forth all his abilities and all his experience in their behalf. . . . Such a course of lectures would especially have one good effect. It would tend to narrow the distance between the instructor and instructed. It is an unfortunate fact, that these two stations are viewed by many as two hostile camps. An entrance into college is thought almost a declaration of war: letters of marque and reprisal certainly scarcely come up to their ideas of the state of their relations. Perpetual hostilities must be kept up.

All these thoughtful and progressive recommendations doubtless had a stimulating effect. Plans had already been made to meet some of the needs, however, and others were met as they became more apparent. When the two new medical professors were appointed, Tristam Burges was also selected for the chair of oratory and belles-lettres. In 1819 Jasper Adams was made professor of mathematics and natural philosophy. The botanic garden had been under consideration by a committee since 1813, and a plot near the southeast corner of the campus was later devoted to it. Even the cabinet of minerals was assigned a room in the new college building in 1823.

The entrance requirements under President Messer remained the same as under Presidents Manning and Maxcy. The curriculum prescribed by the Laws of 1803 differed from that of 1783 chiefly in the omission of Lucian, Caesar, and Homer; the Greek prescribed was the New Testament,

Xenophon's *Cyropaedia*, and Longinus. By 1823, however, the course of study was considerably enriched, the laws then enacted specifying the following works, some of which had already had a place in the curriculum for several years:

The Freshman Class, after revising a part of Virgil, Cicero and the Greek Testament, shall study Graeca Minora, Xenophon's Cyropoedia, Sallust, Cicero de Amicitia and de Senectute, Horace, Roman Antiquities, Sheridan's Lectures, Arithmetic and English Grammar.

The Sophomore Class shall study Morse's Universal Geography, Blair's Lectures, Cicero de Oratore, Homer, Algebra, Euclid, Kaim's Criticism and Hedge's Logic.

The Junior Class shall study Paley's Moral Philosophy and Natural Theology, Enfield's Natural Philosophy, Campbell's Philosophy of Rhetoric, Steward's Philosophy of Mind, Chemistry, Trigonometry, Surveying and Navigation.

The Senior Class shall study Butler's Analogy, Burlamaqui on the Law of Nature, The Federalist, Paley's Evidences, and Vattel. They shall also revise their preceding studies.

Noteworthy points about this curriculum are the addition or restoration of several classical works, the inclusion of a study of government and international law, and the strong emphasis still laid on elocution and rhetoric, the laws prescribing weekly declamations by all the classes, weekly exercises in English composition by the three older classes, and weekly practice in ''making Latin'' by the freshmen.

As to methods of instruction, we have this vivid statement by Barnas Sears, of the class of 1825: ''Our professors were more portly men, going on to sixty. Sitting cross-legged in an arm-chair, against which a silver-headed cane leaned, they would insist on your giving them the exact words of Blair (false English and all), or of Kames, and of Stewart and Hedge. Our president, who heard us in Enfield's philosophy, was more communicative and even facetious. . . . In languages, beyond making Latin, after

Clarke's Introduction, there was nothing, if we except scanning, but translating and parsing; no true philology, nothing of the necessary meaning of words from derivation and usage, or of the force of grammatical forms and construction. Everything depended on translation, generally guessed out, often stolen.'' The courses referred to were those conducted by the resident teachers, in which the students were treated like school-boys, with set tasks and set times for doing them each day. But the instruction by the non-resident professors in the Medical School was given by lectures, to which the academic students were admitted. In 1821 the professor of oratory and belles-lettres, Tristam Burges, also a non-resident, began a course of lectures; and a letter from him to the Corporation on November 19, 1826, referring to his work of that year and protesting against a proposal to deprive him of the professorship, gives interesting facts about his methods and ideals:

I commenced the instruction, by a course of Lectures on Rhetorick. I still continued to hear their declamations; & to declaim before them, as I had done; & to hear their weekly compositions read in the Chapel, & to correct them. . . . I am . . . solicitous, that the instruction, from the Rhetorical Professor, in the University, should be confined to a certain part only of the year; & not be extended over the whole of every collegiate term. It might embrace a course of Lectures; & the hearing of declamations, of such original compositions, as might, under the instruction of the Professer, be, during that time, prepared by the pupils, for that purpose. The weekly compositions, & declamations, may be continued. These may, as was the case before 1821, be heard, & examined, by the other officers of instruction. This labour will then be divided. At present, it is all thrown on my shoulders; & I have, not unfrequently, gone from the Chapel, with thirty sheets of paper in my pockets, to read correct, & criticise, in the course of the next week. The young men are, some times, considerate; & do not *all* write; & the two present Classes relieve me, in a more creditable manner; that is by writing very correctly. . . . I must be permitted to say, that no practical man, either in the desk, or at the bar, could have done what I have done, unless he, as I have, give up his practice. You may obtain a mere theorist, who will undertake to do it; but a theoretical orator will succeed no better, if as well, in teaching eloquence, as a theoretical anatomist will, in teaching surgery.

How heavy was the labor of correcting compositions, which before 1821 fell wholly on instructors teaching other subjects, including the president himself, is shown by this extract from a letter of 1815 by President Messer, who seems to have been imposed upon by some waggish student: "I should also be glad to know the Reporter of the story of blank Composition. The year before last I received on each week of term-time, 49 pieces of composition; and hence, during the year, more than 1400 pieces. Since an Officer of the Institution, I have received nearly twenty thousand Pieces. Now, though it is possible that I may have neglected 50, or 100, or 500 of these Pieces, I should still be glad to know the reporter of this *one* of them, though, as the story says, a *blank!*"

By the Laws of 1803 there was a vacation of four weeks beginning with Commencement day, which came always on the first Wednesday in September; a second vacation, beginning on the last Wednesday in December and continuing six weeks; and a third of three weeks, beginning on the first Wednesday in May. By a vote of the Corporation in 1807, the winter vacation was lengthened to eight weeks, while the spring one was shortened to two weeks and began on the third Wednesday of May. The examinations came at times determined by the vacations. The seniors were examined in the languages on the Wednesday preceding the spring vacation, and in the liberal arts and sciences on the second Wednesday in July; the rest of the time before Commencement they were supposed to be busy preparing their Commencement parts. The three under classes were examined on the Monday preceding the spring vacation, and on the Monday (after 1823 the Friday) preceding Commencement.

The library grew considerably during President Messer's administration. In 1805 Nicholas Brown gave $500 for the purchase of books, and the Corporation voted as much more. In 1812 $400 was appropriated for new books, and three years later $500; in 1820 $100 annually was voted "particularly to subscribe for . . . the best scientific periodical works now publishing." In 1824 a decided improvement was made in the care of the library. The librarians heretofore had been college tutors or preceptors in the grammar school, usually serving only a year or two; but now Horatio G. Bowen, just appointed professor of natural history, became librarian, and he held the office for sixteen years. He at once set to raising a fund, and in a few months had secured subscriptions of $840. The library was also enriched by various bequests of books. The Rev. Isaac Backus left a part of his library to the college, including a copy of Roger Williams's *Bloody Tenent yet More Bloody* with this inscription in Williams's hand: "For his honoured & beloved Mr John Clarke an eminent Witnes of Christ Jesus agst ye bloodie Doctrine of Persecution &c." In 1818 the valuable library of the Rev. William Richards of England was received. Dr. Richards was a broad-minded Baptist and an ardent advocate of religious freedom, whose correspondence with President Manning had predisposed him in favor of the young college, and as his end drew near he made inquiry whether the institution still maintained its liberal principles. President Messer replied vigorously in the affirmative, and the library was accordingly bequeathed to the university. It consisted of thirteen hundred volumes, and contained, said Librarian Jewett, "a considerable number of Welsh books, a large collection of valuable works, illustrating the history and antiquities of England and Wales; besides two or three hundred bound volumes of pamphlets, some of them very ancient, rare and curious." In the last years of President Messer's administration some two hundred costly volumes on anatomy, biology, mathematics, and theology were given to the library by John Carter Brown, Robert H. Ives, the Rev. Thomas Carlile, and Messrs. Brown and Ives. The second printed catalogue appeared in 1826, and showed that the library then consisted of about five thousand volumes. In 1825, after the appointment of the new librarian, the Corporation made a few changes in the rules for the use of the library: it was to be opened on three days a week (instead of two) in term-time, and on Saturday in vacation; and members of the Corporation and Faculty might take out ten volumes at a time, and renew them.

The number of students in the college continued to grow. The catalogue of 1821–22 shows an attendance of 152, not counting medical students; of the 152, furthermore, 49 were freshmen. An additional college building was now much needed, and on September 6, 1821, the Corporation appointed a committee, including the President, Nicholas Brown, and Thomas P. Ives, "to consider on the propriety of erecting another College edifice." At an adjourned meeting a few weeks later, the committee were authorized "to select and if necessary to purchase a suitable site for another College edifice," "to erect the edifice on such plan and of such dimensions as they may think proper," and "to solicit donations and draw on the Treasury for the above purpose." The result showed the wisdom of leaving so much latitude to a committee of which Mr. Brown was a member. On January 13, 1823, the committee reported that a lot had been purchased of Nathan Waterman, and that on it had been erected, "by Nicholas Brown Esq. the distinguished patron of the University," "an elegant brick building, . . . length 120 feet Width 40 feet four stories high and containing 48 rooms." At the same meeting the following letter from Mr. Brown was read:

To the Corporation of Brown University.

It affords me great pleasure, at this adjourned meeting of the Corporation to state, that the College Edifice, erected last season, and located on the land purchased by the Corporation of Mr. Nathan Waterman, is completed. being warmly attached to the Institution where I received my education, among whose founders and benefactors was my honoured Father deceased, and believing that the dissemination of letters and knowledge is the great means of social happiness— I have caused this Edifice to be erected wholly at my expense, and now present it to the Corporation of Brown University to be held with the other Corporate property according to their Charter. As it may be proper to give a name to this new Edifice, I take leave to suggest to the Corporation that of "Hope College."

I avail myself of this occasion to express a hope, that Heaven will bless and make it useful in the promotion of Virtue, Science, and Literature, to those of the present and future generations, who may resort to this University for education. — With respectful and affectionate regards to the individual members of the Corporation,

I am their friend,

Brown University   Nicholas Brown.
January 13. 1823.

The Corporation at once passed a resolution, "That the members of this Corporation, entertain a very high sense of the liberality of this Patron of Science, in the gift of this new building, in addition to his former large donations to this University." A committee appointed to devise a means of manifesting the Corporation's gratitude to Mr. Brown reported in favor of having his portrait painted and "placed in an apartment of one of the Colleges," and also recommended "That a monumental marble be placed in the front of Hope College with a suitable inscription." Mr. Brown's modesty defeated the second plan, and delayed the execution of the first for some years.

The new building took its name from Mrs. Hope Ives, wife of Thomas P. Ives, the only surviving sister of Mr. Brown. It is reputed to be one of the purest specimens of colonial architecture in New England, less massive than University Hall, but light and graceful in its lines. It was designed as a dormitory; for many years, however, its rooms were not all needed for lodgings, and some served other purposes, the Philermenian and United Brothers Societies having quarters on the top floor of the north division. The building cost about $20,000; the lot, $5189.

At the same meeting at which Hope College was received and named, the Corporation voted "That the old College Edifice be named 'University Hall'." Since the completion of its inside finishing in 1788, a bell had been placed in the old building, and necessary repairs had been made from time to time. The early laws imply that the college had a bell; but either it had been broken or was deemed too small, for in 1790 a committee was appointed "to procure a Bell for the College, as soon as may be." The next year they were instructed to get a bell of "the weight heretofore ordered (about 300 lbs.) as soon as may be." Just when this essential to college life arrived and was hung in its place, does not appear; but on September 8, 1791, the committee was authorized to "complete the Copola," no doubt to fit it for its guest; and on December 6, 1792, the Corporation voted "that the President employ one of the Students to ring the College Bell, & that such Student be allowed his Tuition & Room rent for that Service." In September, 1795, a committee was appointed to report what repairs to the roof were needed, and to "cause necessary repairs to be immediately made on the roof over the Library." A year later the treasurer was authorized to hire a sum not exceeding $1500 for the repair of the building, which was leaking badly, and he was instructed to "sell on the best terms he can, the slate now on the roof of the College"; he and another were made a committee to repair the edifice and the president's house "without delay."

A painting formerly in the family of President Messer gives a view of the college grounds as they were about the year 1800.[1] The campus is little more than a field, roughly graded, with very few shade trees; it is inclosed by a fence on the west, and by walls elsewhere — doubtless the same that President Manning made; and College Street is still only a lane. A well that is represented at the southeast corner of University Hall was as old as the building, the accounts of Nicholas Brown and Company showing that it was dug in 1770. In 1803 it was planned to put the well to a new use, the treasurer being instructed to apply to the town "to take measures for establishing a pump in the College Well for the use of the College and the neighbouring buildings in case of fire."

The first addition to the grounds was made in 1815, when the Corporation bought for $600 a lot about 50 feet wide and extending north from George Street about 130 feet to the college lands; it is the land lying just behind Rhode Island Hall. In the same year, on October 24, occurs the first reference in the Corporation records to trees on the campus: "Voted, That the Committee appointed to keep the College Edifice in repair cause such of the trees in the College Yard to be cut down as they may think expedient."

[1] A reproduction of the painting is given in Guild's *Brown University and Manning*, page 157, and in *Memories of Brown*, page 15.

The lot for Hope College was a large addition to the grounds, being 123 feet wide and extending east from Prospect Street 400 feet; and on September 5, 1822, while the new building was nearing completion, a committee was appointed "to cause the College yard, to be enclosed with a suitable fence and planted with trees at their discretion." Another important change made in this year was the continuation of Prospect Street from Meeting Street (where it had stopped in 1785) to College Street; and on September 5 it was voted, "That this Corporation confirm the doings of the Town Council of the Town of Providence in continuing prospect Street through the College lands, westward of the Presidents House, and that they release all claim to damages for the lands belonging to them through which said Street passes." The appearance of the college neighborhood a few years earlier is clearly described by Samuel B. Shaw, of the class of 1819: "No other street but Angell then led directly to the river. What is now Waterman street was chiefly a pasture for horses.[1]. . . The only houses on Prospect street were those of Colonel Thomas Halsey and his son-in-law, Captain Creighton. From George street to Power, through Brown, the brick house then occupied by Mr. Moses Eddy was the only one then erected on the latter, and on College street as far as Benefit the only house was that occupied by a Mr. Jenckes."

The finances of the college during President Messer's administration were still straitened. Mr. Brown's fund for a professorship of oratory lay dormant for many years, and the new building yielded income only in the form of room rents, which were very low. Tuition, also, remained at the old figure of $16 a year until 1822, when it was raised to

[1] Waterman Street was opened from Benefit Street to Prospect Street in 1833, from Prospect Street to Hope Street in 1841.

$20. Furthermore, the payments for tuition and room rent often came in slowly. In 1821 there was due the college from undergraduates and graduates $2783.84, of which about $600 was considered bad debts; and $3126 was due the steward for board, of which nearly $400, it was thought, could not be collected. Hence there was often a lack of ready money. The following letter to Nicholas Brown as treasurer pictures the state of things:

Sir, June 11th. —

Our quarter day has returned, & I have not money enough to meet the demands of the officers. Notwithstanding I have actually advanced of my own Money from four to five Hundred dollars, there is still a balance due of nearly three Hundred dollars. I suppose, however, that with $200, I might give a general satisfaction. If you will direct the course to be taken in the case, you will oblige your friend & Servant.

Nicholas Brown Esqr. Asa Messer.

Another undated letter of like import ends with the pointed query, "Will you send it up, or shall I call and take it myself?"

The productive funds were still small, and they increased slowly. In 1809 they were $14,086, exclusive of the fund to endow the chair of oratory. In 1824 they were only $15,578, yielding but $936 a year. There seems to have been no serious attempt to secure a larger endowment; in 1811 a lottery was again proposed, but nothing came of it. The reliance upon tuition and room rents for increase of income was to some extent justified: the attendance kept on growing for several years, reaching 162 in 1823–24, besides 38 medical students;[1] the next year the graduating class numbered 60, of whom 48 took the degree of Bachelor of Arts — the largest class until 1870. These numbers, with tui-

[1] At Harvard College the number of students in 1825-26 was only 234.

tion at $20, brought in a respectable income when the bills were all paid. Hence the salaries of the officers rose gradually under President Messer. In 1823–24 the president's salary remained at $1000, with the usual perquisites, but the two resident professors, Park and Adams, now received $840 each; four of the non-resident professors received little or nothing, but Tristam Burges, professor of oratory and belles-lettres, was paid $600, and Professor D'Wolf, of the chair of chemistry, the same; the tutors received about $500 each, which was the salary of the masters of the Providence public schools.

The public days of the institution continued to be as popular as ever. The processions at Commencement were still enlivened by the escorting bodies of militia, although after 1803, by a vote of the Corporation, the senior class had to get the consent of the Corporation before inviting these glittering warriors to attend. The following newspaper notices and vote of the Corporation give glimpses of Commencement at various times:

Voted, That at the next Commencement the doors of the Meeting House be open from 9, oclock in the morning for the admission of Ladies but that the Pews to the eastward of the middle aisle be reserved for the Gentlemen composing the Procession. (Corporation Records, September 5, 1816.)

We have on no similar occasion welcomed so great a concourse of strangers. The procession was escorted to the first Baptist Meeting-House by the new company of Light Infantry. . . . In the evening, the receipts at the Theatre exceeded five hundred dollars. (*Providence Patriot and Columbian Phenix*, September 5, 1818.)

At no time within our recollection has there been a greater number of strangers in town attracted by the exercises of commencement. Yesterday the spacious house in which the performances took place was crowded even with more than its usual excess. Among the auditors there were several strangers of distinction from abroad. — In point of elocution we have never seen a class graduating on the stage, who gave better specimens of correct taste, and energy in delivery. . . . The interesting little youth who pronounced the Greek oration, but 15 years of age, attracted much interest; there was a musick in his delivery which gave a charm to that beautiful language even to the ear totally incapable of receiving a particle of its meaning. (*Manufacturers and Farmers Journal*, September 8, 1825.)

In spite of contemporary praise, there was a change for the worse, according to modern ideas, in the subjects of the Commencement speeches. Few were taken from current life, and nearly all were too broad for brief treatment. The War of 1812 inspired none of the orators, debaters, or essayists; only a poem in 1816, "The American dead," may have dealt with those who fell in the war. Most of the disputes were upon questions which admit of no definite solution, such as "Which is the most injurious, Hypocrisy or Pride?" or "Is Sensibility the source of excellence?" Some of the debaters, however, took more concrete questions: "Are Factories beneficial to the United States?" "Has the reign of Napoleon been advantageous to Europe?" "Are Capital Punishments useful?" In the orations there was for several years a curious fondness for dealing with "abuses" —of religion, of merit, of genius, of liberty, of reason. Some topics were almost incredibly general, as "Man," "Jurisprudence," "The Fine Arts," "Thinking." A new tendency, especially noticeable after the establishment of the Medical School, was the choice of topics relating to modern science: "Influence of Science on Liberty," was a subject in 1815, "Science of geology" in 1817, "Are the Inducements for cultivating Science in the United States equal to those in Great Britain?" in 1819, "Do Meteorites originate from sources connected with the earth?" in 1821. Much of the variety in forms of discourse and in languages was preserved. The orations in Hebrew and French had been discontinued under President Maxcy, and the semi-dramatic and often humorous dialogues disappeared after 1805; but orations, dissertations, essays, disputes, conferences, and poems still diversified the exercises, and orations or essays in Latin and Greek were pronounced or read nearly every year.[1]

If the Commencement programs show some decline, those of another occasion improved. The "Exhibitions" by seniors, and by juniors and sophomores together, which began in President Maxcy's time, grew more and more popular, and called out a livelier display of talent than the more staid Commencement exercises. The sophomore-junior exhibitions occurred in April and August: the sophomores recited selected pieces; the juniors delivered original orations and poems, engaged in disputes and dialogues, and even acted scenes from plays. After the spring of 1820 the sophomores no longer took part. The senior exhibition came in December. The place was at first the college chapel, but after 1806 often the town-house. The titles of some of the pieces presented show how much freedom was allowed the students on these occasions. At the sophomore-junior exhibition in the spring of 1803 four poems were read, and a dispute was held on the question, "Ought those, who are old Bachelors from Choice, to support those, who are old Maids from Necessity?" At the August performance four juniors had a "conference" on "The Comparative Disadvantages of

[1] Although the Latin theses had disappeared from the programs after the Revolution, the seniors were required even in the Laws of 1803 to "collect, prepare, and publish" them, delivering two each week (on penalty of a fine of eight cents for every omission) to students appointed to receive them. How long the hunt for these academic flora and fauna was compulsory is not certain, but they were printed until 1817; in the Laws of 1823 the collection of them was made conditional — "if the President shall direct."

personal Beauty, Wit, Coquetry and early Marriage''; and there was ''A Colloquial Discussion, in Latin, on the Policy of carrying on a War with Tripoli.'' In the senior exhibition of 1804 ''An Oration on religious Persecution'' came between a conference on ''The comparative Demerit of Quack Legislation, Quack Divines, Quack Physicians and Quack Lawyers'' and a dialogue, ''The young Man of Sixty.'' It is evident that the lighter parts of the programs supplied to college life some of the elements which now appear in the events of Class Day and Junior Week. This impression is confirmed by the following reminiscences of ''Old Citizen,'' published in *The Providence Journal* on July 1, 1851:

Many a time have I attended "exhibitions" of the undergraduates, in the old town house. On these occasions, a temporary stage was erected in front of the pulpit, and some neighbor was called upon for the loan of a carpet, to cover the naked boards. In the South East corner under the gallery, was the dressing room, screened from vulgar eyes, by a fair chintz curtain. From behind this came forth the youthful orators, who have since edified churches and charmed senates and courts, trembling like aspen leaves and blushing like young maidens. . . . At the close, a select number from each [class] " acted a play" or "spoke a dialogue," dressed in character. There in the pulpit sat the President and the Professors and the Tutors. . . . Over the dressing room, in the gallery, usually sat the musicians, as many in number as the exhibitors could afford to hire, who would occasionally discourse such music as is now seldom heard. I have seen that old town house crowded as full of ladies, bright eyed ladies too, and gentlemen as the "Old Baptist" used to be on the afternoon of Commencement day; not a vacant seat in those old square pews, nor a place to stand in those broad aisles.

In the undergraduate life of the period the most conspicuous new feature was the growth of societies. The Philermenian Society, founded under President Maxcy, continued to thrive. Its library gradually increased, until in 1821 it contained 1594 volumes, including such works as *Tom Jones*, *Tristram Shandy*, and Byron's poems; the books were kept in the college library-room until 1823, when they were removed to the society's quarters in Hope College. The fortnightly debates and other literary exercises aroused great interest, and were believed to afford valuable discipline. Membership in this society was limited to forty-five; and as there were more undergraduates whose thirst for public speech was not slaked by the required exercises at chapel, exhibitions, and Commencement, another society, the United Brothers, was formed in 1806. These two great rivals divided the student body between them for many years, surviving into the days of President Sears. A tincture of political controversy sharpened their rivalry, the older society inclining to the aristocratic Federals, the younger to the Republicans, the democrats of that day. Both organizations had anniversary meetings on the day before Commencement; after 1810 these were held in the Congregational church on Benevolent Street, and the orators and poets were more or less distinguished alumni or other persons. The societies took themselves very seriously, as indeed they had a right to do in that oratorical age, and invited eminent persons to come and speak before them and be made honorary members. Among the Philermenian documents preserved in the college library is a bundle of faded letters containing polite declinations from Henry Clay and other busy dignitaries, but acceptances, also, from many lesser lights. The students continuing to increase in number, they outran the constitutional limits of both societies, and a third, the Franklin Society, was established in 1824; it never had the vitality of the other two, however, and died after ten years. A Philophusion Society, for research in science, existed from 1818 to 1827. One of the minor suggestions of

"Alumnus," in his "Letter to the Corporation" in 1815, was that an association be formed to aid poor students, particularly by lending them textbooks. The seed fell into fertile soil, for a few weeks later was held the first meeting of such an organization, called the Philendean Society. Well-known names appear among the autographs of the early members — Robert H. Ives, John Carter Brown, Samuel G. Howe, Edwards A. Park, and others. The dues were only a dollar a year; but a goodly number of textbooks were gradually collected, and many poor students were glad to use them — Barnas Sears for one. The records of the society show that it lent books until 1848. In the early years it, too, had its anniversary meeting for oratorical delight, when a senior delivered a "lecture." The religious life of the students also took organic form at this time: a Praying Society was formed in 1802, which had prayer-meetings twice a week, and exchanged letters with similar societies in other colleges; in 1821 it was succeeded by a Religious Society.

The college rules for the conduct of students remained much as before. "To encourage and assist the students in their literary pursuits, to promote in them a regular conduct and diligent use of time," ran one of the Laws of 1803, "the officers shall, as often as they judge necessary, visit their chambers, as well in study hours as at other times." Absence from rooms, recitations, and chapel, tardiness, neglect to "exhibit composition" or attend disputations, were punished by fines ranging from three cents to $1.50, followed in obstinate cases by admonition, rustication, or "degradation." If a student should "presume" to exhibit anything on the stage which had not been approved, he was "liable to a fine not less than fifty cents, and to be publicly admonished before the audience"; and he incurred the same punishment if he used "any profane or indecent language on the stage." For declamations in chapel no piece likely to excite laughter was to be chosen, on penalty of sixteen cents. The chapter of the laws entitled "Of Criminal Offences" invented several new crimes; and in addition to the fundamentals of right living the undergraduates were instructed in some of the refinements of the academic life:

No student shall keep any kind of fire-arms or gunpowder in his room, nor fire gunpowder in or near the College, in any manner whatever.

If any scholar shall wilfully insult any of the officers of government or instruction, if he shall strike them, or break their windows, he shall be immediately expelled.

No student shall play on any musical instrument in the hours allotted for study, on the penalty of eight cents for every offence.

All students are strictly forbidden to make indecent, unnecessary noises in the College at any time, either by running violently, hallooing, or rolling things in the entries or down the stairs.

Every student is strictly forbidden to throw any thing against the College edifice, to attempt throwing any thing over it, or to throw water or any thing else from the College windows, or in the College entries.

All students are forbidden to enter the chapel, except at the times of devotional and collegiate exercises, or without permission to enter the Library, Musaeum or Philosophical Chamber.

Rules unfortunately do not enforce themselves; and in spite of this formidable array of prohibitions and penalties, there were many infractions of discipline under President Messer, especially in his later years. His letter-books are full of notices of rustication, which was then carried out with literal accuracy, quite in the fine old English style, the purpose being to send the offender away from distracting and too stimulating influences, and to allow him to regain his equipoise of soul in rural seclusion and pursue his studies aided

by some scholarly clergyman. Some of the disorder was innocent enough. A guileless farmer, unacquainted with the
ways of the learned world, found his ox-sled and load of
wood transported to the roof of University Hall. The President's horse was led to the top story of the building and
left there over night: its guide on this perilous journey was
Samuel G. Howe, who was soon after doing heroic service
in the Greek war of independence and was later the teacher
of Laura Bridgman; but even in mature life, says his daughter, "there was no keeping the twinkle out of his eye, as he
told how funny the old horse looked, stretching his meek
head out of the fourth-story window, and whinnying mourn-
fully to his amazed master passing below."

But sometimes there was vandalism, rowdyism, or riot.
Soon after the completion of Hope College, a committee
of the Corporation reported that "the outside doors in the
New College have been injured in a shameful manner & the
Committee are sorry to remark, there appears a disposition
to cut waste & distroy the Buildings." "Your son, since
his return," writes Messer in 1819, "has thrown a stone
through the window of one of the Tutors, and has put into
his bed a shovel of ashes; though the Tutor had given him
no Provocation; nor did even know him." In the same year
he writes to a clergyman: "Some time since a large number of our Students combined together for the Purpose of
subverting a regular recitation; and from them we selected
twelve supposed to be prominent, and fined them each four
dollars. Your Son is one of the twelve." The lot of the college tutor had not improved when Williams Latham, of
the class of 1827, was an undergraduate, for in his diary
he remarks of one of the tutors, "His talents and good
deportment gained for him a respect which in a measure
compensated his want of bodily strength — having a white

[184]

swelling on his ankle which unfit him for resisting the violence of our College bullies.''

In December, 1817, there occurred a disturbance which aroused the citizens as well as the college officers. The details are best given in a letter by President Messer to the father of one of the students implicated: ''The building which was burnt, and which you call a *nuisance* stood adjacent to the stewards barn, and between it and his hog-pen. From thence it was carried into the middle of the college-yard; and then, having been filled with hay & corn-stocks, it was consumed by fire. The blaze, it is said, rose as high as the college edefice; and, if the wind had favored it, it might have endangered ei[ther] that, or the adjacent barns; and it is here thought to be not a small thing to alarm in the night, and by the cry of fire 10 or 12 thousand People.'' In a postscript to a statement read in chapel he says, ''Being at Midnight the burning excited in the Town such indignation, that two of the Persons suspected, were arraigned before the civil tribunal.'' The college expelled one student, rusticated four others, and fined three.

In the spring of 1819 there was another and worse outbreak. The President's letter to the parent of one of the culprits describes the affair thus: ''I hasten to state, That, some weeks since, our chapel and dining-hall doors were, during the darkness of night, burst in, and carried off; that the furniture was carried from the latter, and some of the seats, and even the Pulpit, from the former; that the gates and bars of the college yard, and the blinds of the college-house were carried off. The day after this had occurred, a notification, probably stuck up the day before, was found in the college-entry; and the features of it may be collected from the consideration that it was a notification of a meeting of 'Hell fire rummaging club at half past twelve this night.'

It was for this notification that your son was sent away; and it was the unanimous opinion of the government that he wrote it."

These disturbances, however objectionable, had in them nothing of bitterness or deliberate hostility. But in 1824 there broke out an ugly quarrel in the academic family, which lasted for months and finally led to the President's resignation. The quarrel seems to have been aggravated by antagonism to Messer's theological opinions, which for several years had been deemed heretical. In 1818 the Hon. Samuel Eddy, secretary of the Corporation, reputed author of an heretical pamphlet on the divinity of Christ, was given "liberty to withdraw" from the First Baptist Church, and did withdraw. Suspicion then attached to the views of his close friend, President Messer, who for some time had been in the habit of making prayers in the First Congregational Church, which since 1815, at least, had been openly Unitarian. In 1819 the First Baptist Church passed a vote disavowing fellowship with those who "openly and avowedly deny the Deity of our Lord Jesus Christ," and he supposed that the vote referred to himself; but he was not named in it, and actually remained a member of the church until his death.

President Messer's position is best stated in a postscript to a letter of December 10, 1818: "The difference between me and others respecting the character of Christ would be settled by a settlement of the question, not whether he possesses the divinity, for I hold that in him dwelt all the fulness of the godhead, or *divinity* bodily, but whether he possesses it by his Father, or by himself? whether he proceeded forth and came from God, or, whether, not like God, but God himself, he exists per se? Following the former, I have the satisfaction to know that I follow John, Paul, Peter, and *Jesus;* and, what some perhaps, may though wickedly think is more, that great leader of the Baptists, Dr. John Gill." In brief, he held that Christ was not God, but in a preëminent sense the Son of God, a position very like that of Channing and other Unitarians of his day, if not identical with it. "He then is a *Son*," he writes in a letter of March 20, 1819; "and, as God has given him ; so I would give him a name, which is above every name." On December 23, 1820, he writes, "Unless you should suppose me idiotic, you surely will not now inquire, whether I believe that that *Son* of the living God, is the living God himself, the great Father of all, the self-existent, almighty, independent, underived, most holy, only wise God?"

Such opinions naturally alarmed many, who became unwilling that the holder of them should remain at the head of Brown University, particularly at a time when Unitarianism was rapidly spreading in New England. The President, on the other hand, stood up stoutly for liberty of thought. The following extract from a letter of December 16, 1818, to William Hunter, United States senator and a trustee, presents the case as he saw it: "Will you, on that occasion [the next Commencement], again favor us with your company? . . . A storm of bigotry, you must be sensible, is now raging around us; and, unless prevented by the energies of men of liberal minds, it may tear up by the root the best tree ever planted by our Fathers. *God* forbid that a Spanish Inquisition should ever stand on a soil sanctified by the bones of Roger Williams." On November 17, 1819, he writes thus to the Rev. John Evans, of England: "A violent contention respecting the Trinity has been raging among us; and it has not yet wholly subsided. . . . Notwithstand[ing] the charter of our University forbids all religious *Tests*, some, zealous for what they call the word of God, had determined that, unless willing to change my creed, which yet is that very, unadulterated word, I should be compelled to leave that Institution. I, however, though daring to maintain that 'Jesus is the Christ, the *Son* of the living GOD,' still remain in statu quo.'' It was indeed not easy to dislodge him. The college charter merely provides that the president shall be a Baptist; and Messer still adhered firmly to the distinctive tenets of the denomination, holding that a personal profession of belief should precede baptism and that the scriptural mode of baptism was immersion. He was therefore strongly intrenched, and open opposition after a while died down; but the fire still smouldered, and the President's receipt in 1820 of the degree of S.T.D. from Harvard College, now controlled by the Unitarians, must have tended to keep the embers warm.

What connection, it will be asked, had this theological quarrel with the undergraduate disturbances of 1824? It may be that it really had none; but President Messer thought otherwise. The disorders themselves differed from those that had preceded in being deliberate, organized, and protracted. Messer gives a brief account of them in a letter of October 29, 1824, to the presidents of Williams College and Union College: ''During our last spring and summer Terms unusual disorder prevailed among our students. They broke open the Library: they beat down the Pulpit: they prevented or disturbed for several weeks a regular recitation: they even assailed our house, in the night, and broke the windows. Severe punishments were, therefore, inflicted; and order was restored. —Many, however, formed combinations for the redress of what they called grievances; and, failing in this, some, it is reported, are now making application for admittance into other institutions.'' The students' side is given in an anonymous pamphlet, ''A True and

Candid Statement of Facts,'' published in January, 1826, in New Haven. It asserts that the instruction given to the junior class in the spring of 1824 was inadequate because of the resignation or absence of certain professors, and that a petition to the Corporation on the subject, lodged with Judge Howell, resulted in the rustication or suspension of several of the petitioners by the ''tyrannical'' President. The concluding sentence, with a punning allusion to the recent retirement of Professor Calvin Park, glances at Messer's theological views : ''Though we would rather see the Rev. President *calvinistic* in his religion, than in the abdication of his office; yet we hope, that, for the honor of human nature, literature and religion, it may please Heaven, so to overrule events, that soon the tyrant may be shaken from his throne.''

The pamphlet contains no explanation why it was brought out a year or more after the events it describes; but it was doubtless called forth by certain communications which had appeared in Providence newspapers during the year 1825. One, by ''Vindex,'' in *The Independent Inquirer* of May 5, asserts that a small party in the Corporation, chiefly from ''a particular class of a particular denomination of Christians,'' have ''for long time'' constituted a ''determined and untiring opposition'' to the President. ''In proof of this, let the history of last year be referred to. During that time, were not *certain* students, or persons who were then students, again and again closeted with *certain* members of the Corporation? Were they not frequently taking sweet counsel at the fountains of legal science, or theological mystery? Were they not told, that the Corporation were ready and anxious to remove the faculty, and were only waiting for a suitable occasion, and that a certain famous wonder-working petition, would be just the thing?'' ''Alumnus,'' in the same paper, on August 18, says: "It is well known to the friends of Brown University, that, for several years past, there has been a division of sentiment in the corporation with respect to its executive Governor. . . . But what is the cause of this opposition? . . . It is simply, because these gentlemen imagine that he differs from them in matters of Religion. This is the foundation upon which their opposition is built, and from this has arisen a course of conduct that any party might well blush to avow."

How much truth, if any, there was in these charges, it is now impossible to determine. It is certain that President Messer himself believed that his theological opponents had deliberately hindered the growth of the college, for in a letter of October 10, 1825, addressed to a Baptist clergyman in England, he said: "Brown University continues in statu quo. Its progress has been retarded by orthodox exertions for exterminating heresy. O when will popery entirely leave the earth. . . . What the future effect of those exertions will be on the University I cannot say; but I can say that, for myself, I fear none of them; determined, as you quote from Milton, to 'proceed right onward,' maugre all the dangers which may be threatened." This does not specify what form these "exertions" took — it might or might not refer to such acts as "Vindex" alleges. But in another anonymous pamphlet, "An Exposition of Certain Newspaper Publications," appearing in August, 1826, the assertion is boldly made that "Vindex" and "Alumnus" were tutors in Brown University, and that President Messer had approved of and even revised their articles. While this is hardly credible, and the pamphlet itself says the President denied it to a member of the Corporation, the fact that his defenders connected the student disorders with the theological opposition to the President is significant. And finally, Messer's first letter of resignation, quoted below, seems to imply belief in such a connection. In any case, the charges and counter-charges made a very disagreeable situation for the man at the center of the storm. The second anonymous pamphlet attacked him openly and with venom, and called for deci-sive action at the approaching Commencement. "It is need-less to recapitulate all the grievances which exist. — They are generally but too well known, and their effects too deeply felt. They can be all comprised in these few words: THE INCUMBENCY OF THE PRESENT PRESIDENT. 'The head is sick and the whole heart' fainteth."

Here was a coil to weary and disgust the most patient man. The last straw was laid on the President's broad back at the Corporation meeting in September, 1826, when a Baptist trustee asserted that the charges against him in the pamphlet could be proved. On September 20 Messer wrote to this trustee: "Having just read the annonymous Pamphlet concerning which you volunteered your testi-mony at the late meeting of the Trustees of Brown Univer-sity, I hasten to state to you, the reputed author of it, that that Pamphlet contains respecting me infamous falsehoods; and that I am preparing to institute such Process in the case as may seem due to truth, as well as to self." But he was evidently weary of the whole affair; and on September 23 he wrote two letters to the secretary of the Corporation, resigning the presidency. The first, which he did not send, contains these sentences: "The pungency of the reflection that I am leaving an office which I have held 24 years, and a College of which I have been either an officer or a pupil 39 years is, I can assure you, greatly increased by the belief that the perplexities which induce me to leave them grow out of the consideration that I can not allow that there [are] more Gods than one; or deny that Jesus Christ is the son of God. . . . I would not do either for all the offices in the world. . . . I wish to live where I may, without molestation, serve the living and true GOD, and wait for his son from heaven." The letter sent is as follows:

Providence Sept. 23d. 1826

To the Hon. Saml. Eddy,
    Secretary of Brown University
dear Sir.

I take the liberty to request you to inform the Hon. Corporation of Brown University that I resign my office in that Institution. On leaving an office which I have held 24 years, and an institution of which I have been either an officer, or a pupil 39 years, I, though inclined to make many reflections, shall now make but this one; that probably I feel somewhat like one who is breaking up long, dear friendships, and bidding the world farewell. I pray that, when the time for my doing this shall actually arrive, and it may arrive in a day, or an hour, I may be enabled to think that I have served my GOD as faithfully as I have served Brown University; and I also pray that He, who was the GOD of Abraham, and, if I may be allowed to utter a little heresy, the God of Jesus, may have that seat of literature and all its Patrons, as well as you and me, in his holy keeping.

Asa Messer

The resignation was not formally acted upon until December 13, when, at a meeting of the Corporation in the President's house, he being absent, it was accepted without comment. Alva Woods, professor of mathematics and natural philosophy since 1824, had already been made president *ad interim*, and served until the accession of a new president early in the next year.

Of Dr. Messer as a man and a college president it is possible to form a picture from his letters and from descriptions of him by his pupils. The portrait of him in the possession of the university, painted by James L. Lincoln from miniatures, gives the impression of homely strength rather than of finish or grace; and this is confirmed by all that is known of him. Professor Edwards A. Park, his pupil, says of his appearance: "No one who has ever seen him can ever forget him. His individuality was made unmistakable by his physical frame. This, while it was above the average height, was also in breadth an emblem of the expansiveness of his mental capacity. A '*long* head' was vulgarly ascribed to him, but it was breadth that marked his forehead; there was an expressive breadth in his maxillary bones; his broad shoulders were a sign of the weight which he was able to bear; his manner of walking was a noticeable symbol of the reach of his mind; he swung his cane far and wide as he walked, and no observer would doubt that he was an independent man." "He had some marked peculiarities of manner," says President Sears, "such as . . . a swelling of the cheeks when displeased, accompanied with a quick, gruff utterance."

Intellectually he was characterized by native vigor and masculine sense, not by suppleness, imagination, or culture. He was a man of practical wisdom—a judicious farmer, a shrewd man of business; and by these qualities, combined with thrift and economy, he got together a snug fortune. He owned a farm or two and shares in a cotton factory, and his letters show that he looked after his material interests very keenly. To his nephew, the lessee of one of his farms, who had made a proposal about stocking it, he wrote in 1816: "You must not think that your uncle Asa, though he is growing old, has yet become either so old or so silly, that he will buy cows, and put them on a farm of his own, in the expectation of receiving for each only two dollars, and an half pr. year." On the management of the factory he wrote thus, in 1815, to a fellow-owner: "On acct. of our debts our agent is generally obliged to make his purchases and his sales very much like a man on the verge of

Bankrupcy; and can any man prosper, who is obliged to pursue a course like this? . . . This consideration alone compels me to fear, that, in the present state of the cotton business, every turn of our wheel turns us farther into the mud. . . . I wish to inquire, whether we ought not to ascertain *with certainty* whether the mill is swimming, or sinking? and if she should be sinking, whether we had not better put under her some buoys, or bladders, or *bank-bills*, or something, or other, and prevent her going to the botom."

In his public addresses Messer never attempted flights of imagination or poetical fancies; but his thought was judicious, his reasoning solid, and his style plain and strong. These qualities may be illustrated by a passage from his oration, in 1803, before the Providence Association of Mechanics and Manufacturers:

Are we willing to live in a state of dependence on other nations? No. We abhor, we despise the suggestion. We glory in our independence, as well national as individual; and we are determined to defend it even at the hazard of our lives. But can we be independent of other nations, while we depend on them for almost all the clothing of our bodies, and for almost all the furniture of our houses? Can we be independent of other nations, while we cannot print a book without their types, nor make a pen without their penknife, nor a shirt without their needle, nor even a shoe without their awl? No. While we depend on them for any article of necessity, our independence is defective.

His delivery fitted his thought and style. "He gesticulated broadly as he preached," writes Professor Park; "his enunciation was forcible, now and then overwhelming, sometimes shrill, but was characterized by a breadth of tone and a prolonged emphasis which added to its momentum, and made an indelible impression on the memory." "In earnest public discourse," says President Sears, he had "a muscular force and over-strained emphasis, with a peculiar gesture, as if he would grasp his subject in the extended downward curvature of his right hand and arm.''

He was not a profound scholar, but had a firm grasp upon a wide range of subjects. He received the degree of D.D. from Brown University in 1806, of LL.D. from the University of Vermont in 1812, and of S.T.D. from Harvard University in 1820. ''For what is termed polite literature,'' writes Professor William G. Goddard, his pupil and colleague, ''he had no particular fondness, but he was a good classical scholar, and was well versed in the Mathematics, and the several branches of Natural Philosophy. In moral science, also, we have known few better reasoners or more successful teachers.'' ''He was a powerful and sound moral reasoner,'' says President Sears, ''and no thoughtful young man, who listened to his Sunday evening discourses, could fail to carry away impressions not easily removed.'' He seems to have been lacking in subtlety of mind and the higher philosophical faculties, but within his limits he was an acute reasoner, as is shown by his articles in *The Providence Patriot and Columbian Phenix*, in 1818, on mysteries in religion, which he deemed absurdities. In science, also, his gift was practical rather than theoretical. In 1817 he was consulted about the proper height for the lighthouse at Jamestown, and in several letters expounded the physical laws governing the case. He made some inventions, including a ''Messer's Pneumatic Engine, or Philosophical bellows,'' and ''a new & useful improvement in the mode of using water wheels & furnishing them with water,'' and was granted a patent for the latter.

Of President Messer as a teacher not much is known. Governor William L. Marcy, one of his earlier pupils, says: ''He always met his class . . . with a kindly spirit and manner, and never assumed any offensive official airs, or did any thing that seemed designed to impress us with a sense of his superiority. He was often very familiar in our recitations, and sometimes introduced anecdotes, by way of illustration, that we thought more remarkable for good-humour and appropriateness than for the highest literary refinement." The Rev. Dr. James W. Thompson, of the class of 1827, said of him at Commencement in 1877: "I assure you he was . . . 'every inch a man,' of learning ample for his day and place, of logical power all compact, a model, in fact, of clear, close reasoning in his lectures to the students." President Sears, who also came under him in his later years, calls him "a genial, pleasant teacher," and adds what is really high praise: "As he was independent himself, so he wished his pupils to be. He had no imitators, he wished to have none. The many eminent men educated under him had no other resemblance to each other, than freedom from authority. There is among them no uniform style of thought, resulting from its being run in the same mould. Even among the undergraduates, there was a personal independence of character and thought, and a manliness of deportment and self-respect that gave a certain air of dignity to the two upper classes."

The same shrewd common sense which President Messer showed in business characterized him as a college disciplinarian and administrator. President Sears writes:

In discipline, in his best days, he was adroit, having a keen insight into human nature, and touching at will, skillfully, all the chords of the student's heart. Rarely was he mistaken in the character of a young man, or in the motive to which he appealed, in order to influence him. Foibles and weaknesses, he treated with some degree of indulgence; but vice and willful wrong, he treated with unsparing severity. In government he followed no abstract principles,—which so often mislead the theorist,—but depended on his good sense in each case, giving considerable scope to views of expediency. The student who attempted to circumvent him, was sure to be outwitted in the end. On account of his great shrewdness, he was sometimes called 'the cunning President.' One of the many anecdotes related of him is, that he kept in his room a bottle of picra for sick students; and that every one who came to him to be excused from duty on account of headaches, found it necessary to swallow a dose before leaving the room.

In spite of his severity he was popular with the great majority of the undergraduates. Governor Marcy says: "Dr. Messer sustained his position as President of the College in a highly creditable manner, and was generally esteemed and beloved by the students. He was regarded as a man of even temper, honest in his purposes, free from prejudice, and well adapted to exercise that kind of authority which pertained to his office." Professor Edwards A. Park, one of his latest pupils, speaks much to the same effect: "I have seldom known a veteran in the government of a College, who was so strict a disciplinarian, so clear-headed a diplomatist, and at the same time so apt in uttering kindly words to the boys whom he met in the street, so ready with a cheering proverb or a sprightly turn with the care-worn and down-hearted." It may be that he grew somewhat capricious and arbitrary toward the end, although the charges of tyranny and double-dealing are probably the exaggerations of enemies in the heat of a quarrel.

His letter-books afford pleasing evidence that in the first half of his presidency, at least, he felt a fatherly interest in the students and watched over their physical and moral welfare with tender care. A few selections will show this gentler side of his nature. To an anxious mother he writes thus, in 1812:

To your favor of the 9th. inst. I hasten to reply, That, though I have examined the case, I cannot find that Henry is addicted to Gambling. I hope, therefore, that this charge is without foundation. . . . Though the Progress of Henry is not such as we wish it to be, I still do not know that any reasons of dissatisfaction exist at present greater than actually existed when I sent you my last letter. I, at any rate, feel as willing *now*, as I felt *then*, to give him a further trial. Whether this will be best for him, I cannot determine. If I must err at all, I had rather err in the way of tenderness, than in the way of severity.

The following was written to the father of a Virginian lad, in 1813:

On the morning after I wrote my letter of 25th. ult. which I suppose you have received before now, I visited your son, and found him in a very unpleasant condition. I, indeed, was alarmed. And fearing that he might not, at his room, obtain the best accommodations, I invited him to come to my house, and to remain in my family until his indisposition should be removed. After expressing much thankfulness for the invi[t]ation, he observed that Mr. Lippitt had just before given him an invitation to go to his house, and that he had accepted it, though unable to go that day. Being the next day a little more comfortable, he was bro't from his room, put into my carriage, and carried to Mr. Lippitts.

Several weeks later, when the young man was able to go home, although still weak, the President and his wife "rode twelve, or fourteen miles to the Tavern where he expected to breakfast, with the view both of showing him respect, & and of seeing the manner in which traveling might affect him."

The following extracts from letters of 1811–13 illustrate at once Messer's patient attention to troublesome details and the extravagance of a young Southern blood in a Northern college:

I have requested your son to give me an estimate of the money he will need the ensuing year. This he has actually given, and it amounts to $550. In this estimate he has placed $150 for pocket-money, and $50, for boots and shoes. One dollar a week, however, for pocket-money is better than a larger sum; and twenty dollars a year I should think would answer for boots and shoes. Be this as it may, I am still confident that no Principles either of Interest or honor, would require him to expend more than $450. I do not, indeed, know a single scholar among us, who expends a sum so large as this; and were *your* son, *mine*, I would rather you would give him, in this view, $300, than $450.

I have requested your son not to contract any other debts without my knowledge; for I find that the value of Money has not yet engaged his attention.

Since my last, several applications have been made similar to that of Mr. Braman. The amount of them all would much surpass the amount of money remaining in my hands. Your son, indeed, says that he owes in Boston about $600. In my opinion, this sum is at least as small as the reality.

Your son, in general, enjoys good health, and a good flow of spirits. . . . Though on the score of expense, I cannot bring him within the limits I could wish, I cannot persuade him to think that he is inclined to extravagance. He seems actually to think himself economical.

A boot and shoe Maker's bill, amounting to $116, (to what use so many boots and shoes could have been applied I do not know) on which, however, $40, had been paid, has actually been lodged with an Attorney in this Town for collection. . . . From information lately handed me, I am induced to believe that your sons debts in Providence are greater than I had anticipated. Since the Commencement of our vacation he has, I am told, gone on a visit to New-York; and I am also told that, for this visit, and for expenses incurred at other times, he has borrowed of one man nearly $200 in cash. . . . He does not seem sufficiently to feel the value either of money, or of time. . . . I am often exhorting him on the subject; and he is always ready to confess, and to promise; but.————.

President Messer showed his common sense in the large lines of his academic policy, which was that of an intelligent conservatism, attempting no impracticable innovations, but seeking to build on the old foundations as solidly and as high as the available means allowed. His wisdom and success in this are ably set forth in the following extract from an anonymous pamphlet, "Brown University under the

Presidency of Asa Messer, S.T.D., LL.D.," published in 1867, and attributed to the Rev. Silas A. Crane, of the class of 1823, who was a tutor from 1824 to 1828:

His policy was that of demand and supply. He offered the country such a college education as it could pay for; and such, too, as the necessities of its condition then compelled it gladly to accept. Here we have the rule by which he fixed the requirements for matriculation, and the whole subsequent course of undergraduate studies. Here, too, we see the reason for that system of rigid economy, which under his management pervaded every department of the institution.[1] . . . Hence, too, the disposition of the *vacations*, assigning the *long* one to the winter, that the students might help out their scanty means by teaching the common schools of the country, then taught almost only in that season of the year. . . . It is not easy for us now to feel the full force of the reasons which led to this policy, nor to picture to our minds the full extent and magnitude of the happy results that then followed it. Under its benign influence, hundreds of young men who had otherwise been doomed to a life of comparative ignorance and inefficiency were able to lay the foundation of intellectual culture and future usefulness; and the whole country, not less than themselves, shared in the wide-spread and lasting benefits.

Upon his resignation of the presidency Dr. Messer removed to the western part of the town, where he bought a small farm with a fine colonial mansion on it, near the street which now bears his name. Here he lived quietly, occupied with his business affairs, and for many years serving as alderman. While he was still president, in 1818, he had been appointed chief justice of the supreme court of the state, but had declined the office, partly because it was incompatible with his "collegial functions." In 1830 he ran for governor on the "National Republican & Landholders Prox," and was defeated. In the last year of his life he was again offered the nomination, but declined. He died on October 11,

[1] In the catalogue of 1825–26 is the statement, "Tuition, Library, Room Rent, and Board, less than $100 per annum."

1836, after a short illness, and was buried in the North Burial Ground. At a special meeting on October 14, 1836, the Faculty passed the following resolution: "That the Faculty of Brown University learn, with deep regret, that the Rev. Dr. Messer, an eminent son of this University, and for a long course of years its presiding officer, is no more; that we are impressed with a strong conviction of his acknowledged merits as an Instructor, of his vigorous intellect, and of his solid learning; and that we gratefully recognize his title to the best distinctions of the Citizen, the Man, and the Christian."

In the twenty-four years of President Messer's administration 693 men graduated in the regular course, 301 more than during the twenty-eight years in which degrees were granted under Presidents Manning and Maxcy. Those who reached distinction were fewer in proportion to the whole number than in the early years of the college, but the list is nevertheless honorable. It includes six college presidents: Barnas Sears and Alexis Caswell presided over their Alma Mater; Jasper Adams, after resigning his professorship in Brown University, was president of the College of Charleston, South Carolina, and of Geneva (now Hobart) College; Wilbur Fisk became president of Wesleyan University, Rufus Babcock of Waterville (now Colby) College, and Horace Mann of Antioch College. The last named, however, did his greatest work as secretary of the Massachusetts Board of Education from 1837 to 1848, remodeling the school system of that state and thereby profoundly affecting public-school education throughout the nation. Seven men attained to more or less eminence as professors in colleges and seminaries: William G. Goddard and Romeo Elton served Brown University for many years under President Wayland, the latter as professor of Greek and Latin, the former as professor of moral philosophy, metaphysics, and belles-lettres; Solomon Peck became professor of Latin and Hebrew in Amherst College; William Ruggles taught in Columbian College, Washington, for fifty-two years as tutor and professor of various subjects, besides performing the duties of acting president at three different periods; George W. Keely held the chair of mathematics and natural philosophy in Waterville College for twenty-three years; Enoch Pond was professor in Bangor Theological Seminary for thirty-eight years and president for fourteen; Edwards A. Park, a giant in body and mind, was professor in Andover Theological Seminary for forty-five years. Authors and editors of some note were not lacking: David Benedict published *A General History of the Baptist Denomination* (1813), besides several other historical works; William R. Staples brought out his *Annals of the Town of Providence* in 1843, and performed other valuable historical labor; Albert G. Greene published various poems, including "Old Grimes," and began the Harris Collection of American Poetry; David Reed was for forty-five years editor of *The Christian Register*, the leading Unitarian newspaper; George D. Prentice, by his brilliant conduct of the Louisville (Kentucky) *Journal* for forty years, exerted a far-reaching influence through the Southwest, besides writing a life of Henry Clay, and delivering orations which every school-boy was declaiming a generation or two ago. In educating Benjamin B. Smith and George Burgess the college was helping to prepare two Episcopal bishops for their life-work, the latter as bishop of Maine for nearly twenty years, the former as bishop of Kentucky for over half a century. In Messer's administration, too, graduated the brilliant and heroic missionary to Burmah, Adoniram Judson. Samuel G. Howe had hardly left his mischievous boyhood behind when he plunged into the Greek war for independence, later serving as surgeon-in-chief to the Greek fleet; he came home to do a great humanitarian work in his native city, as superintendent for forty-four years of the Perkins Institution for the Blind. Into the business world, too, the college sent its representatives of distinction in the persons of such men as Moses Brown Ives, John Carter Brown, and Robert H. Ives, all liberal-minded merchants and public-spirited citizens of Providence, and Isaac Davis of Worcester, mayor, legislator, railroad director, bank president, college trustee, and much else besides. Public life was enriched by many graduates of these days : among the more notable were Theron Metcalf, on the bench of the Massachusetts supreme court, and Job Durfee and Samuel Ames, both chief justices of the Rhode Island supreme court; in Marcus Morton the college furnished Massachusetts with a Congressman, a justice of its supreme court, and a governor; Jared W. Williams served the state of New Hampshire as governor, Congressman, and United States senator; Rhode Island had a governor and a United States senator in John B. Francis; William L. Marcy held the same offices in New York, and was also Secretary of War to President Polk and Secretary of State to President Pierce.

CHAPTER VI

PRESIDENT WAYLAND'S ADMINISTRATION

IN the diary of Williams Latham, a senior in Brown University, occurs this entry under date of March 1, 1827: "Francis Wayland has taken the presidential chair — and seems to be well qualified for his station, He has made great alterations in the course of studies, in the regulations of College and in the manner of reciteing — He carries no book into the recitation room nor suffers any of the students to do it — We are obliged to keep in our rooms all study hours, they being visited as often as twice a day by some officer." Six days later he records this experience: "Since 9 Oclock I have been into Peter Minard's room and have had a little singing with him — But we were interrupted by the President who thought we could not be permitted to sing between nine and ten Oclock in the evening — Thus he has deprived us of a privilege which we esteemed very valuable." May 9 he sums up thus: "This term has been the most profitable one, since I have been in College — not only on account of the great improvement that has been made in the various studies here attended to But good habits of study have been formed, We have laid a good foundation for prosecuting our future studies with advantage."

These entries give evidence that a powerful driving force had come to Brown University in the personality of Francis Wayland, one of the greatest college presidents of his century. The new president was still young, only thirty-one years of age; but he had had a varied training which, added to his natural gifts, peculiarly fitted him for the work that lay before him. He was born on March 11, 1796, in New York City, of English parents who had come to the United States three years before. They were of the middle class, and belonged to the Baptist denomination; the father, for many years a currier, became a Baptist minister in 1807. President Wayland got his early training chiefly from his mother, an intellectual and devout woman. A few years in school fitted him to enter Union College as a sophomore in the spring of 1811, and he graduated in 1813 in his eighteenth year. He next studied medicine under two physicians in Troy, and in the winter of 1814–15 attended medical lectures in New York City; but he had hardly begun the practice of his profession when an awakening of his religious nature led him to abandon medicine and prepare himself for the Christian ministry. He entered Andover Seminary in the autumn of 1816, and spent one year in rigorous and enthusiastic labor under that profound scholar and master teacher, Moses Stuart, devoting himself to the study of the Old and New Testaments in the original. Poverty compelled him, at the end of this year, to leave the seminary and become a tutor in his Alma Mater, where he served for four years, teaching a wide range of subjects and learning much from intimacy with the rugged and sagacious President Nott. In 1821 he accepted a call to the First Baptist Church, Boston. Here he struggled for two years against many obstacles, without much apparent success; but the hard work made him grow, and the solid intellect and masculine strength of the man slowly gained him recognition among the discerning few. One stormy evening in the autumn of 1823 he preached the annual sermon before the Baptist Foreign Missionary Society of Boston. No great effect was produced at the time; but when "The Moral Dignity of the Missionary Enterprize" was published, its strength of style, breadth of view, and heroic note soon made it famous. Followed as it was, a year and a half later, by two powerful discourses on "The Duties of an American Citizen," it gave its author a commanding position in the Baptist denomination and considerable reputation in a wider field. In September, 1825, he was made a fellow of Brown University; and when President Messer resigned, the minds of many naturally turned to Francis Wayland as his successor. He had just left his pastorate and returned to Union College as professor of mathematics and natural philosophy; but being elected head of Brown University on December 13, 1826, he accepted, and assumed his new duties at the beginning of the next term, in February, 1827.

President Wayland's first work was to tighten the reins of moral and mental discipline, which in the last few years had been somewhat relaxed. The old rule requiring the officers of instruction to visit the students' rooms, which had been omitted in the Laws of 1823, was revived and made more strict in the Laws of 1827, and the officers were required to "occupy rooms in College, during the hours appropriated to study." The President himself set the example, and could regularly be found hard at work in his room in Hope College. The officers were required to make daily reports to the President of all absences and other violations of the laws which came to their knowledge. If a student's general conduct was unsatisfactory, the laws authorized the President to inform his parents and "dismiss him without public censure or disgrace."

But the soul of the new moral regimen was not a code but a man—intense, fearless, strong in intellect and will. The influence of Wayland upon the individual student and upon groups of students was tremendous. He had a vast amount of primitive power in him, made more effective by passion, wit, and a gift of trenchant speech. All who knew him agree that his books give no adequate idea of his immense personal force; but Professor George I. Chace, his pupil in the first three years of his administration, conveys some sense of it in the following description:

Another means employed by President Wayland for awakening impulse, and correcting, guiding, and elevating public sentiment in college, was addresses from the platform in the chapel. These were most frequent and most characteristic, in the earlier days of his presidency. . . . President Wayland was at that time at the very culmination of his powers, both physical and intellectual. His massive and stalwart frame, not yet filled and rounded by the accretions of later years, his strongly marked features, having still the sharp outlines and severe grace of their first chiselling, his peerless eye, sending from beneath that olympian brow its lordly or its penetrating glances, he seemed, as he stood on the stage in that old chapel, the incarnation of majesty and power. He was raised a few feet above his audience, and so near to them that those most remote could see the play of every feature. He commenced speaking. It was not instruction; it was not argument; it was not exhortation. It was a mixture of wit and humor, of ridicule, sarcasm, pathos and fun, of passionate remonstrance, earnest appeal and solemn warning, poured forth not at random, but with a knowledge of the laws of emotion to which Lord Kames himself could have added nothing. The effect was indescribable. No Athenian audience ever hung more tumultuously on the lips of the divine Demosthenes. That little chapel heaved and swelled with the intensity of its pent-up forces. The billows of passion rose and fell like the waves of a tempestuous sea. . . . At length the storm spent itself. The sky cleared, and the sun shone out with increased brightness. The ground had been softened and fertilized, and the whole air purified.

The intellectual tonic which the new president administered was equally powerful. The laws of 1803 and 1823 held the juniors to only two recitations a day after the spring vacation; the seniors to only two a day until April, and but one a day thereafter. The new laws declared, "There shall be three recitations in every Class in the University throughout the year." Instructors and pupils both had come to depend unduly upon the textbook. "No text book shall ever be brought into the recitation room," said a new law, "except at the recitation of the Learned Languages." This Spartan rule put teacher and taught upon their mettle to master the substance of the lesson, and encouraged original phrasing and free discussion. President Wayland's own statement of his method deserves quoting:

Our practice was, in all recitations from text-books, to accustom the student to make out the analysis, skeleton, or plan of the lesson to be recited. He was expected to commence, and, without question or assistance, to proceed in his recitation as long as might be required. The next who was called upon took up the passage where his predecessor left it; and thus it continued (except as there was interruption by inquiry or explanation) until the close. . . . It was also customary to commence the recitation by calling on some one to give the entire analysis of the lesson. . . . Accompanying the habit of analyzing every lesson, and making this analysis a distinct feature of the recitation, was that of frequent review. It was my custom in the class-room to require, first of all, the lesson of the previous day, whether that consisted of a lecture or a portion of a text-book. This fixed every lesson in the mind of the pupil. As we advanced, I would begin the book, and call for the analysis of several portions of what we had gone over. When we had overtaken our advance, we commenced anew from the beginning. In this manner we were enabled to review the whole book frequently during the course of a single term, thus strengthening materially the habit of generalization.

To-day we should think that most of the time thus spent in reviewing and re-reviewing one textbook might more profitably have been given to wide reading or to special research. The famous "analysis," furthermore, was but making an outline of matter already arranged, and demanded far less mental effort than organizing crude material for argument or debate; but at that time, in comparison with com-

mon methods, it doubtless had great merit. Still more valuable, however, was the President's habit of encouraging free
discussion: "I also caused it to be understood that our subject was one in which they and I were equally interested.
Therefore I not only allowed, but encouraged, my pupils
to ask questions with reference to any portion of the lesson
recited, or of the lecture delivered." Wayland was too
experienced a teacher not to know that the method might
be abused. "This, however," he writes, "may be easily prevented by an instructor. It is only necessary to answer a
fool according to his folly, in order to make the experiment
too dangerous to be repeated." A sample of this kind of answer is given by his biographers: "At another time he was
lecturing on the weight of evidence furnished by human
testimony. He was illustrating its authority and sufficiency
even for the establishment of miracles. A member of the
class, not entirely satisfied of the correctness of the teaching, suggested a practical application of the doctrine: 'What
would you say, Dr. Wayland, if I stated, that, as I was
coming up College Street, I saw the lamp-post at the corner
dance?' 'I should ask you where you had been, my son,'
was the quiet reply in the instructor's gravest manner." But
sensible and honest discussion he always welcomed. "I
rarely passed through such a discussion," he says, "without great advantage. Sometimes I was convinced that I had
been in error. . . . It not unfrequently happened that when
the subject under consideration was especially interesting or
important, two or three days were consumed upon a single
lesson."

But Wayland's stimulating effect upon his pupils came
primarily, not from any particular method in the class-room,
but from his personal resources. From the first he supplemented the textbooks by extempore talks; and he soon be-

gan to elaborate some points by formal lectures, which finally grew into the books that made him famous. The Hon. John H. Clifford, a member of the first class that Wayland instructed, says: "It was quickly perceived by us that he was, in truth, the 'master,' and far in advance of the books from which he taught. This was one great source of the new spirit with which he inspired his pupils, namely, that he was thoroughly the master of his subject, and not a mere conduit of another man's thoughts." His method as a lecturer and his effect on the students, a few years later, are vividly described by Professor Silas Bailey, of the class of 1834:

At the time to which I refer, his recitation-room was on the first floor of the middle hall of Hope College, and in the rear of his own study. It had been a dormitory, but was afterwards furnished with benches, and what served for writing-desks — narrow pine boards upheld by pine uprights. . . . The entire furniture of the room did not exceed ten dollars in value. Entering by a door connecting the recitation-room with his study, he was in his chair at the moment, and he required the same promptness of each pupil. . . . All being present, and subsiding instantly into silence, the work began. He had no table, but sat with his manuscript for the lecture of the hour resting upon his knee. At this period none of his text-books had been published. The members of the class, in succession, recited the lecture of the preceding day, or perhaps one still farther back in the series. . . . This exercise concluded, there was a rustling all around the room; papers were adjusted, and preparation made for writing. The president's manuscript was opened, and the well-known *a-hem* was the signal for all to be ready, and for the work of the hour to begin. . . . These lectures seemed to us more wonderful than anything we had ever heard. They carried all the conviction of a demonstration. To have believed otherwise would have seemed absurd. Some of us at a later day found reason to modify the views then received and accepted. But at the time the conviction was complete. His definitions were clear, simple, and easily remembered. His analysis of any obscure but important part was exhaustive, omitting no essential element. His progress through either of his favorite sciences was that of a prince through his own dominions. At intervals, not regular in

their occurrence, yet sure to occur somewhere, he suspended his reading for a few minutes, and, waiting for a short time, until each member
of the class could complete his notes and give his attention, he would
relate some incident or anecdote strikingly illustrating the point last
made. In this department he was always most happy. The confirmation imparted to the argument was often unexpected, and even irresistible. These anecdotes were drawn from any source that offered the richest supply; from history, from romance, from poetry, from common,
unrecorded, every-day life. Often they were mirthful, sometimes ludi-
crous. Frequently statistics would be given, conclusively verifying the
position which had been assumed. . . . Whether in these exercises
Dr. Wayland stirred up the intellect of his pupils, it was not difficult
even for a stranger to determine. As they issued from the lecture-room,
and went by twos and threes to their own apartments, the subjects
which had just been discussed became the theme of most earnest conversation. . . . His manner was simple and childlike. There was no
indication of special concern that others should assent to his views.
Yet the mind that was not quickened by contact with his, that did not
gird itself for more strenuous and elevated endeavors under the inspiration of his presence and teachings, must have been hopelessly dull.
The recitation-room was his empire, and he reigned with imperial
dignity.

The ideal which the President so rigorously followed himself he expected his colleagues to follow with equal rigor.
His conception of college life was that of the academic family. He wished to establish close personal relations beween
officers and students and thereby secure strict though kindly
supervision over the latter's mental and moral life. What,
then, should be done with the non-resident professors in the
Medical School and in the departments of oratory and natural history? One plan might have been to let them remain,
and rely on the rest of the Faculty to do the work of supervision. The advantages of such a plan, combining academic
drill with invigorating breezes from the outside world of
public and professional life, were possibly not appreciated

by President Wayland; it probably seemed to him that the non-resident professors were a part, if not a cause, of the lax discipline which he sought to cure. Another reason for dismissing them is given in his "Reminiscences": "The regular officers were competent to perform all the required duties, and by thus dispensing with outside services, they found their means of subsistence materially increased." Accordingly, on March 15, 1827, the Corporation passed the following vote:

Whereas it is deemed essential to an efficient course of instruction, and to the administration of discipline, in this University, that all its officers be actual residents within the walls of the Colleges, therefore Resolved, That no salary or other compensation be paid to any Professor, Tutor, or other Officer, who shall not, during the whole of each and every term, occupy a room in one of the Colleges (to be designated by the President) and assiduously devote himself to the preservation of order, and the instruction of the students, or the performance of such other duty as may belong to his station.

Copies of this vote were sent to the non-resident professors. Their names stood in the catalogue of the next year without change, but in 1828–29 were starred, and a foot-note said, "The gentlemen to whose names the asterisk is prefixed, are not of the immediate government; and do not, at present, give any instruction in the University." This premature promotion to the ranks of the *stelligeri* was doubtless annoying, and doubtless was meant to be. Dr. Wheaton withdrew before the next catalogue appeared, Dr. Parsons the year after; and in 1832–33, by vote of the Faculty, all the names were dropped except that of Professor Bowen, who was librarian. Thus was the Medical School in Brown University killed by a president who had been trained for the profession of medicine.

Radical changes like these could not be made abruptly

without arousing opposition. Professor Chace, of the class of 1830, gives some amusing details of undergraduate disapproval:

Indignant protests were made against the innovations. . . . One of the mildest of these modes of expressing public sentiment, was delineation on the walls of the halls, and the lecture rooms when these could be entered. I recall a spirited sketch executed by a class-mate, which represented very well the prevailing current of opinion and criticism. It comprised two figures. Dr. Messer, seated in his old chaise, with reins fallen, and whip lost, was jogging leisurely on. Directly before him and in clear view, lay the gulf of perdition. Near by was Dr. Wayland, in a buggy of the newest fashion, harnessed to an animal on whose build and muscle two-forty was plainly written. He was headed in the same direction, and with taut rein and knitted brow and kindling eye, was pressing with all his might forward. But the students soon learned with whom they had to deal. . . . The greater number presently became reconciled to the new order of things, and forgot their angry feelings in the general enthusiasm for study, which already began to be awakened.

The opposition outside the college walls, which focused upon the policy of cutting off the non-resident professors, lasted longer. At first it expressed itself chiefly in fears that the students were not getting proper instruction in oratory, being no longer taught by the favorite Rhode Island orator, Tristam Burges. But in the Commencement week of 1830, when it seemed likely that the newly established chapter of Phi Beta Kappa would kill the local society of Federal Adelphi, of which Burges was a conspicuous member, the pack broke out in full cry. The new president's personal peculiarities were attacked in a communication in the *Rhode Island American, Statesman & Providence Gazette* of September 7: "Some carped at his Oxonion Cap, others insisted that his side pockets were not the proper place for his hands when engaged in the public services, and that his morsel of narcotic, that mark which distinguishes man from all other animals, should not have been ruminated at such a time." Most of the attacks, however, were directed against the new policy of the college. *The Providence Journal* of September 10, 1830, said: "We have understood that Mr. Burges tendered his services to President Wayland, after his salary and compensation had been stopped by the Corporation, and that he was told, the institution did not require them. Of that fact certainly the President ought to have been best qualified to judge; the public, however, entertained a different opinion. . . . The vote of the Corporation, together with Dr. Wayland's answer to Mr. Burges, have deprived the University of the services of one of its best and ablest professors." The *Daily Advertiser* of the same date, regretting the lost lecturers, said: "In these classes were not unfrequently mingled citizens of the town; an arrangement certainly not calculated to injure the popularity of the College beyond its walls, or to limit the extension of knowledge. When President Wayland took the chair, Messrs. Burges and D'Wolf were probably the most popular persons, connected with the institution." In the same issue is a long anonymous communication urging that another university be set up in the state, to furnish a broader and more practical education; the plan curiously anticipates most of the ideas which Dr. Wayland advocated and partly put into effect twenty years later. A beginning should be made by the establishment of classical, medical, and chemical lectures, a workshop and farm, and by the application of chemical and mathematical science to mechanics and agriculture. "We have at hand the very persons, required for such an undertaking, in the learned and worthy professors who have been *reformed* out of their academic employment by the new rules of the College." In the *Daily Advertiser* of

September 20, "E Pluribus Unum" complains that "young men, instead of being taught eloquence, (that source of power and influence in this Republic) and induced to become ambitious of emulating the excellence of ancient and modern orators, have been kept down to the cool calculations of Euclid, the demonstrations of conic sections, and the differential and integral Calculus!" Finally, "A True Friend to the College," in an issue of the same paper five days later, lets a political cat out of the bag; after describing various evils in the present régime, he continues: "Some of the friends of the College . . . see all this, and yet it all does not affect them so painfully as one other fact which can no longer be kept in the dark — viz: that the College is becoming *a nursery of anti-American doctrines*, a mill for the manufacture of young theorists, ready to meet the world in arms, and fight for the principles of free trade!"

But the President held to his course in silence, effecting various changes besides those already mentioned. The entrance requirements were somewhat increased: in 1827 Jacob's *Greek Reader* and Caesar were added, and in both Latin and Greek emphasis was laid upon a knowledge of the grammar; ancient and modern geography and English grammar were also mentioned as supplementary subjects; in 1828 algebra to quadratics was added. After this there was no material change, except that in 1843 the New Testament (or the option in Xenophon which had been allowed for some years) was struck out and nothing put in its place. Several changes were made in the curriculum in 1827. The review of the Latin and Greek required for admission was omitted. Algebra was put into the first year, and studied three terms instead of one; trigonometry, conic sections, and calculus were added. A term in astronomy was introduced. The range in the classics was widened by the introduction of Xenophon's *Anabasis*, Herodotus, Thucydides, Plato, Aristotle, Euripides, Tacitus, Juvenal, and Perseus. Two terms of French were offered, with an option of calculus in one term and Hebrew in the other; but French was dropped from 1831 to 1842, and Hebrew after 1834. A two-term course in political economy, taught by the President, was added in 1828. In the catalogue of 1827–28 is the significant statement, "Lectures are delivered upon the various branches of study, in connexion with the regular Recitations." Three years later this is expanded into an announcement that "Lectures are delivered, during the Course of Instruction, on the following branches, viz. Intellectual and Moral Philosophy; Political Economy; Rhetoric; Roman Antiquities—Greek and Roman Literature; Natural Philosophy; Chemistry; Physiology."

The curriculum as announced in the catalogue of 1842–43 is fairly representative of the whole period from 1827 to 1850:

FRESHMAN YEAR

First Term. Plane geometry; Livy; Latin grammar reviewed; abstract of Roman history; Xenophon's *Cyropaedia;* Greek grammar reviewed.

Second Term. Solid geometry; algebra; Livy; abstract of Roman history; exercises in writing Latin; Xenophon's *Memorabilia;* exercises in writing Greek.

Third Term. Algebra; Tacitus; exercises in writing Latin; the *Odyssey;* exercises in writing Greek.

SOPHOMORE YEAR

First Term. Algebra; plane and spherical trigonometry; Horace; exercises in writing Latin; the *Iliad;* exercises in writing Greek.

Second Term. Mensuration, surveying, navigation, nautical astronomy; the *Iliad;* exercises in writing Greek; Horace; rhetoric.

Third Term. Analytical geometry; *de Amicitia* and *de Senectute:* exercises in writing Latin; rhetoric; Euripides.

Junior Year

First Term. Mechanics; animal physiology; logic; modern languages.

Second Term. Pneumatics and hydrostatics; chemistry; Sophocles or Æschylus; modern languages.

Third Term. Optics; chemistry; vegetable physiology; Juvenal; modern languages.

Senior Year

First Term. Intellectual philosophy; astronomy; Æschines or Demosthenes; modern languages.

Second Term. Moral philosophy; Butler's *Analogy* and Paley's *Evidences;* rhetoric; modern languages.

Third Term. Political economy; evidences of Christianity; geology; American constitution; modern languages.

The quality of work done by those who went through this course of study cannot be determined with much precision, but there are fragmentary data which throw some light upon it. In the first place, proficiency in college studies could hardly have been expected of young men so ill prepared for them as were some of those admitted to the university. President Wayland, in a special report to the fellows in 1841, said of the study of rhetoric: "This branch of learning would be materially improved if the requirements for entrance . . . were more rigidly enforced. Students frequently enter college almost wholly unacquainted with English grammar and unable to write a tolerably legible hand." A committee appointed by the fellows, in 1842, to consider changes in the conduct of the institution, reported that "students are frequently admitted very ignorant of the grammars and are able in general to read but a very small portion of Latin & Greek at a lesson." "The writing of Latin," they add, "is not required at all of the candidate for entrance. . . . Instruction in the University is too much confined to the mere rendering of the ancient languages into English and . . .

not sufficient attention is paid to elegance of rendering, and to the cultivation of the taste of the pupil.'' That laxity in entrance examinations was rather general among the New England colleges appears from a communication sent to them by a committee representing a meeting of classical teachers held in Boston on May 28, 1844; this calls for more uniform and rigid requirements, saying: ''All the colleges, at times, receive Students with much less than the required amount of preparation; in some cases even less than half the usual preparatory course is admitted as sufficient, while in others nearly the whole is required.''

Dr. Wayland was strongly impressed, on a visit to England in 1840–41, with the enormous stimulus applied to school and university students by means of prizes, scholarships, fellowships, and other rewards for high attainments; and on his return he devised a system of prizes for undergraduates in Brown University. In the catalogue of 1842–43 premiums to the total value of $250 were announced; and the next year the system was extended. President Wayland had founded the President's Premiums for excellence in preparatory studies, by the gift of $1000, which provided prizes of $15 and $10, to be awarded after a special examination, in both Latin and Greek. University Premiums, derived from one of Nicholas Brown's bequests, were offered as follows: freshman premiums of $15 and $10, in Greek, Latin, and mathematics; sophomore premiums of like amounts in the same subjects, and a premium of $15 for English composition; junior premiums of $17 and $15 in mechanics, physical science, and English composition, and a premium of $17 in either Greek or Latin; senior premiums of $20 each in astronomy, history, physical science, and in either Greek or Latin. The awards in astronomy, mathematics, and mechanics were to be determined by examination; in the other subjects, by essays. Two premiums of $25 each, established the year before by the Rev. Henry Jackson, were also offered to seniors for essays in philosophy and political economy. The total value of these prizes was $458.

The results did not speak very well for the intellectual ambition of the students, however thoroughly they may have done their routine work for the class-room. Very few entered the contests, especially after the freshman year; two or three was the usual number, and sometimes there were fewer competitors than prizes. The competition for the Jackson premiums was so slight that the donor became dissatisfied and discontinued them after 1850. The quality of the work done by the prize men was not remarkably good according to modern standards. The essays on literary, historical, economic, and philosophical subjects show industry and considerable maturity of style, but little originality or independent research. The essays in Latin, according to the present professor of that subject, are full of English idioms set over into Latin words, and are on the whole inferior to what would now be expected in a prize contest. "The essays in Greek," writes a professor in the Greek department, "are not startlingly original, and there are a good many cases of the transfer of English locutions to a foreign style; but there are few things wrong, and the physical perfection of the Greek handwriting itself reflects a careful, scholarly attitude that is not unimportant." Of the examination papers in mathematical subjects a member of that department says: "The dexterity required in the handling of algebraic and trigonometric expressions is very slight. In all the papers, solution of problems rather than development of theory is called for. The questions seem to indicate a good grounding in fundamental principles of that day, but a decidedly moderate standard as to the amount of work covered in a given year. The standards in pure mathematics are far higher now; many of the premium questions of the 40's could now be answered by matriculants.''

Brown University owes a great debt to President Wayland for his wise and energetic efforts to build up the library. It had grown to considerable size by occasional gifts of books and money; but it had no permanent fund or regular income, and there was no settled policy regarding it. In the President's report to the Corporation ''in behalf of the Faculty,'' on September 2, 1829, the inadequacy of such a ''miscellaneous collection'' was pointed out, and two sources of income for the purchase of books were suggested — the students' library fees, and the interest of a permanent library fund, to be raised by subscription. The Corporation at once voted that $200 of the money received from library fees be appropriated annually for buying books; and at a meeting of the Standing Committee of the Corporation on January 10, 1831, it was resolved, ''That immediate measures be taken to raise by subscription, the sum of *twenty-five thousand dollars*, to be appropriated to the purchase of books for the Library and apparatus for the philosophical and chemical departments of Brown University.'' President Wayland and Thomas P. Ives were made a committee to carry the resolution into effect. The proposal was magnificent, almost to audacity, for no such sum had ever been raised by subscription in the interests of education in Rhode Island. But a new day was dawning. Nicholas Brown promptly subscribed $10,000; Thomas P. Ives and John Bowen gave $1000 each; and many other subscriptions, varying from $300 to $10, were secured, chiefly by the exertions of President Wayland and Professor Caswell. The sum of $19,437.50 was raised; it was put at interest until it had grown to

$25,000, when it was invested as a permanent fund, the income from which, beginning in 1839, was devoted to the purchase of books and apparatus. Provision had already been made to secure a consistent policy in directing the growth of the library. At the September meeting of the Corporation in 1834, the committee on the library, anticipating the time when "large additions will be made every year to the number of Books," urged that it was "of great importance that these books should be selected in conformity with some approved plan, so that the Library may present a view of the progress & attainments of the human mind." The report continues: "The number of visitors which may hereafter be attracted to the Library, as well as the convenience of the officers of instruction suggests the importance of having the Library at all times accessible to the faculty & to strangers. They therefore recommend that the Librarian be required to occupy a room in the College buildings." The Corporation appointed a committee, including the President, to carry out these recommendations; and voted that, after the library had been removed to the new building, the librarian must attend in the library room from 10 to 12 o'clock every week day in term time. In 1837 it was voted that $500 from the income of the library fund be spent annually for books, under the direction of a joint committee of the Corporation and Faculty. Mr. Charles C. Jewett, of the class of 1835, was appointed librarian in 1842, also holding the professorship of modern languages after the first year. A catalogue prepared by him was published in 1843; it showed that the library contained 10,235 volumes. Mr. Jewett became the librarian of the Smithsonian Institution in 1848, and from 1858 till his death in 1868 was librarian of the Boston Public Library. He was succeeded at Brown University by Reuben A. Guild, of the class of 1847.

The new building referred to above was Manning Hall. The time had come when it was imperative that the library should have better quarters, for its room in University Hall was, in President Wayland's words, "crowded to excess, unsightly and inconvenient, and wholly unsuited for the purpose to which, from necessity, it was devoted." A chapel was also much needed. Nicholas Brown met both needs by erecting Manning Hall, at a cost of $18,500. The building, somewhat in the style of a Greek temple, was named at Mr. Brown's request after the first president, and was dedicated on February 4, 1835. It was built of stone and covered with cement. The lower room, sixty-eight feet in length and thirty-eight in width, was designed for the library; the upper room was the chapel.

It was doubtless because the new building had a cement covering that University Hall, standing next to it, received a similar covering at this time. The report of a committee, on June 14, 1834, says: "The Building seems to have arrived at that State of decay that very considerable repair is necessary to prevent it from going to entire destruction— the window frames must be taken out, in order to prevent the water from getting in, over them. the bricks should be painted or covered with cement—the mortar has come out from between the bricks, & many of the bricks are much decayed." A bill of March 3, 1835, shows that the repairs cost $4684.

President Wayland, because of his training, was deeply interested in the teaching of natural science. His influence doubtless appears in the vote of the Corporation on September 6, 1827, when a committee was appointed to expend $500 in instruments and apparatus such as the committee might "judge necessary for the immediate wants of the University." Soon afterwards a set of apparatus costing about

$3000 was presented to the college by Nicholas Brown and Thomas P. Ives; and in consequence the catalogue of 1828–29 contained the following statement: "The Philosophical Apparatus is extensive and complete. A large number of Instruments, constructed on the most approved plans, by distinguished artists in London and Paris, has been recently imported at individual expense, and presented to the University. The advantages of instruction in Natural Philosophy, thus presented, it is believed, are equal to those possessed by any similar institution in this country." Another need of the scientific departments became acute in 1836, when Professor Chace brought back from a tour through the West a valuable collection of fossils and found no suitable room for them. "The University was almost destitute of a Chemical laboratory," wrote Wayland in 1841, "and the lecture rooms for the Professors of Chemistry and Experimental Science were small and inconvenient." In September, 1836, a committee of the Corporation was appointed "to devise means for erecting a building for Lecture rooms, and rooms for the reception of Geological and Physiological specimens." By 1838 about $2500 had been raised, but there the movement stayed. Once more the patron of the university came forward with a generous and stimulating offer, contained in the following letter:

Providence, March 18. 1839

Moses Brown Ives, Esq
   Treasurer of Brown University
               Dear sir,
                         In Common with a number of the friends of Brown University, I desire the Erection of a suitable Mansion House for the President, and likewise of another College Edifice for the accomodation of the Department of Natural Philosophy, Chemistry, Mineralogy, Geology and Natural History.
   As it is highly important that these Buildings, so necessary to the

welfare of the Institution, should be Erected without delay, I hereby tender to the acceptance of the Corporation Two Lots of Land on Waterman Street, as a Site for the Presidents House, and the Lot of Land, called the Hopkins Estate on George Street, as a Site for the College Edifice,—and I moreover pledge myself for the sum of Ten Thousand Dollars, viz Seven Thousand Dollars for the Presidents House, & Three Thousand Dollars towards the Erection of the College Edifice, the suitable improvement of the adjacent grounds, and the increase of the permanent Means of Instruction in the Departments of Chemistry, Mineralogy &c, *provided* an equal amount be subscribed by other friends of the University before the 1st: day of May next.

I am with affectionate Regards
and great personal Respect to all the
friends & patrons of the University,
Respectfully

Nicho Brown

The response was prompt. Before the date set more than the needed amount had been subscribed; and "the whole sum," according to Dr. Wayland, "with the exception of about six hundred dollars, was contributed by the citizens of Providence and its vicinity." The appropriate name of "Rhode Island Hall" was given to the new building, which was dedicated on September 4, 1840; it was made of stone, covered with cement, and cost $11,250. The president's house, standing on the northwest corner of Prospect and College Streets, cost $7000; it was finished in season for the President to hold his reception in it on the evening of Commencement in 1840. The old president's house, according to tradition, was moved down College Street, where some still identify it as the third house below the corner of Benefit Street, on the north side.

At this time also "the grounds were graded and adorned," to quote the President speaking in 1841, "and the surrounding premises placed in the condition in which we now behold them." The "adornment" consisted partly in the building of a new fence around the grounds and in the planting of the elms that are now one of the chief glories of the campus.

The gifts in connection with Rhode Island Hall and the president's house, and the gift of another valuable lot on George Street, in 1840, were Mr. Brown's last donations to the college during his lifetime; he died on September 27, in the following year. Nicholas Brown was born in Providence, April 4, 1769, the son of Nicholas Brown, Senior. At his graduation from Rhode Island College in 1786, he was less than eighteen years old; and when he was chosen a trustee of the college, in 1791, he was only twenty-two. He served as trustee until 1825, and as fellow from then till his death; from 1796 to 1825 he was also treasurer. After the death of his father, in 1791, he and his brother-in-law, Thomas P. Ives, formed a partnership in what grew to be one of the largest mercantile houses in New England. "Up to the year 1836," wrote Professor Goddard, "when he withdrew almost entirely from all concern in foreign commerce, no man, it is believed, possessed so extensive and accurate a knowledge of the commercial marine of the whole country." The firm was one of the pioneers in developing an American trade with China and India, and after the beginning of the century became more and more deeply engaged in cotton manufactures in Rhode Island. Of Mr. Brown as a merchant Dr. Wayland said: "His disposition was ardent, and his plans frequently adventurous. Yet the success of his diversified operations sufficiently testified that boldness of enterprise may be harmoniously united with vigorous and deliberate judgment. He was endowed in an unusual degree with that quality, which I know not how better to express than by the term, largeness of mind. A plan or an enterprise was attractive to him, other things being equal, in proportion to its extensiveness." Professor Goddard gives this discriminating account of his mental habits, which were clearly those of a man of action: "He had no relish for general reading, or for prolonged conversation, or for mixed society. On paper, he expressed himself, always with freedom and clearness, and sometimes with force. His power of observation was singularly quick and searching; and he seemed to reach his conclusions, generally sagacious, without the aid of intermediate processes, or without being able to communicate such intermediate processes to others."

Mr. Brown took a broad interest in life outside the world of business. In politics he was first a staunch Federalist and then a Whig, and for many years he served as a member of the state legislature; his last political act was to cast his vote, as presidential elector, for President Harrison. He was a deeply religious man, although he never joined any church "in consequence," says Professor Gammell, "of certain peculiar views which lingered in his mind." "I do not think," says President Wayland, "that there was any branch of human knowledge with which he was so well acquainted as theology." "His heart," Wayland writes, "was the abode of active sympathy for every form of human suffering. He not unfrequently visited the sick in their own dwellings, while his door was frequently thronged, and his steps waylaid, by the poor and unfortunate of every age. I think I do not at all overstate the fact, when I assert, that for the last twenty-five years, whenever any person among us, in almost any rank of society, was in pecuniary distress, the first person to whom he would spontaneously apply for relief was Nicholas Brown. . . . His benevolence was frequently requited by ingratitude; yet, under the most irritating provocations, he was never known to indulge in the language either of harshness or reproach. He seemed always disposed to look upon human nature in its most favorable aspects, and when no favorable aspect could be discovered, to contemplate the spectacle in silence.''

Mr. Brown's public benefactions were by no means limited to the institution which bears his name. He contributed to the endowment of Columbian College, Waterville College, and Newton Theological Institution. When the Providence Athenaeum received its charter, in 1836, he united with Moses B. Ives and Robert H. Ives, the sons of his deceased partner, in offering to the library its present site and $10,000 toward the erection of a building and the purchase of books. In his will, besides many bequests for religious and educational purposes, he left $30,000 toward the endowment of an insane asylum, and was thus the originator of a movement which resulted three years later in the foundation of Butler Hospital. Brown University was also remembered in his will, receiving $10,000 in money, payable in ten years, the income for ten years from certain estates worth about the same sum, and land lying between Thayer and Hope Streets and valued at $42,500. These bequests brought up his total gifts to the university to nearly $159,000, and Professor Gammell estimated that his entire benefactions to public institutions and objects amounted to not less than $211,500. Even more significant is the wisdom shown in bestowing his gifts. ''He seemed habitually to look at results,'' writes President Wayland, ''and frequently at results long distant. . . . He sought not so much to build up, as to lay the foundations.''

The university is fortunate in having a good likeness of its benefactor. After the erection of Manning Hall the Corporation renewed their request to Mr. Brown to sit for his picture. He consented ; and the familiar portrait now hanging in Sayles Hall was painted in 1836, by Chester Harding, one of the best American artists of the day, and placed in the library. What President Wayland said of the living face may be applied to the pictured one: "The leading traits of Mr. Brown's character were, I think, distinctly revealed in his countenance. In his ample brow and well-developed forehead, you could not but observe the marks of a vigorous and expansive intellect; while his mouth indicated a spirit tenderly alive to human suffering, and habitually occupied in the contemplation of deeds of compassion."

When Mr. Brown resigned the treasurership, in 1825, he was succeeded by Moses B. Ives, who retained the office throughout President Wayland's term. Chancellor Griswold, however, retired in 1828, and three other chancellors served during this administration — the Hon. Samuel W. Bridgham, of the class of 1794, who died in office in 1840; the Hon. John B. Francis, of the class of 1808, who acted from 1841 to 1854; and Dr. Samuel B. Tobey, who took the chancellorship in President Wayland's last year, and held it through the administration of his successor. The secretaries of the Corporation under Dr. Wayland were yet more numerous, including Judge Samuel Eddy, who resigned in 1829, the Rev. Dr. Nathan B. Crocker, who served from 1829 to 1837 and from 1846 to 1853, Judge Theron Metcalf, who served from 1837 to 1843, Professor William G. Goddard, whose term was still shorter (1843–46), and John Kingsbury, who, beginning in 1853, held the secretaryship under four presidents until his death in 1874. Until 1844 professors of the college were eligible for membership in the Corporation, and several actually served as fellows; in that year the Corporation voted that no professor of the university should thereafter hold a seat in the Corporation, the two offices being deemed "from their very nature" to be "incompatible."

What of the Faculty and students in these years during

which the material equipment of the institution, under the hand of its patron, was growing so fast?

We have seen what happened to the non-resident professors. Of the three resident professors when President Wayland came, one, Alva Woods, of the chair of mathematics and natural philosophy since 1824, resigned in 1828, to take the presidency of Transylvania University; he was succeeded by Alexis Caswell, who became one of Dr. Wayland's staunchest supporters and intimate friends. Professor Goddard, of the department of moral philosophy and metaphysics from 1825 to 1834, when he became professor of belles-lettres, resigned in 1842 because of his health; his relations with the President were peculiarly close. The third professor, Romeo Elton, a scholarly man but not a powerful teacher, served as professor of Greek and Latin from 1825 to 1843. For a few years the Faculty consisted of the President, three professors, two tutors, the librarian Mr. Bowen, and the register and steward Lemuel H. Elliott, who served from 1826 to 1864. A fourth professor, Solomon Peck, who taught Latin, and a third tutor were added in 1832. The next year Professor Peck retired; and George I. Chace, who had been tutor since 1831, became adjunct professor of mathematics and natural philosophy. In 1834 the President was formally made professor of moral and intellectual philosophy; Professor Goddard assumed his new title; and Professor Chace took the chair of chemistry. The next year the classical department was much strengthened by the appointment of the brilliant Horatio B. Hackett as adjunct professor of Latin and Greek, who became professor of Hebrew and classical literature for the years 1837–39; and William Gammell, tutor since 1832, was made assistant professor of belles-lettres. The Faculty now consisted of ten officers of instruction — the President, six professors, and three tutors,—five of whom were recent graduates of Brown University, trained by the methods of the new régime. This was about its numerical strength until 1842, when it began to decline, chiefly by a reduction in the number of tutors.

Three of the young men whom President Wayland gathered around him in the first half of his administration— Chace, Gammell, and John L. Lincoln, who became a tutor in 1839 — were to fill large places in the history of the university; from the first they brought in fresh life, and did much to win support for the new order of things. Dr. Wayland, like all natural leaders, knew how to pick his aides and how to value them. Masterful as he was, he did not commit the folly of supposing that one man could make a college, and he gave his colleagues due honor and influence.[1] Professor Gammell, writing in 1867, speaks thus of the official relations of the President and the Faculty:

It was the habit of Dr. Wayland to consult very freely with members of the Faculty respecting every measure of importance relating either to the internal or the external affairs of the institution. . . . Until that time [1850] I do not recall a single instance in which the nomination of an officer, whether professor or tutor, was made to the corporation without the advice of the Faculty, or in which any measure of importance that concerned the interests of the college was decided upon without their sanction and coöperation. . . . He encouraged no appeals from professors or tutors to the president. No fear was felt, on the part of either, that he would ever seek to promote his own popularity or comfort at the expense of that of his associates. . . . Whenever it became necessary, he bore unflinchingly and magnanimously the odium of every measure, no matter what was its origin, which the good of the college seemed to require.

[1] It is under Wayland that the records of the Faculty meetings begin, with a meeting on May 7, 1829, for the assignment of Commencement parts; but for years the meetings occurred at very irregular intervals.

Professor Gammell also gives an interesting account of the social relations between the President and the members of the Faculty :

To them all, I may say, his house was a place of frequent and familiar resort, although his relations to them differed with different persons in their degrees of intimacy. To the younger members of the Faculty, I remember, he was particularly attentive, and ever mindful of the solitary life they led, residing, as they did at that time, within the walls of the college. In those earlier days we dined with him almost always on Saturdays. Very often, after evening meetings of the Faculty, . . . he would invite us to remain at his house, and share in some extemporized entertainment, as an offset to the weary routine of college affairs. . . . His familiar friends, and especially members of the Faculty, were in the habit of visiting his garden very frequently ; and he was never happier or more genial than when narrating passages of his horticultural experience. . . . At other seasons of the year he was exceedingly fond of walking in the country, always seeking companionship on such occasions. The evening prayers of the college, until they were abolished in 1850, were invariably at five o'clock. On the dismissal of the students, he would very commonly summon some of us to join him in the walk to the Seekonk River, going by one road and returning by the other. . . . This ancient road, five and twenty or thirty years ago, was rural and secluded, full of attractive scenery of meadow and grotto, of wooded hill and flowing river, and pervaded throughout its whole extent with the tranquillity always so grateful to reflective and studious minds. In these walks, which were continued through many years, he would often do all the talking himself, especially when accompanied only by his juniors. . . . Grave as were his daily studies, and serious as was his habitual tone of thought, those who mingled thus freely in his society amidst the scenes to which I have alluded, knew him to be exceedingly fond of both humor and of wit, and to be capable of a mirthfulness that was in singular contrast with other moods of his mind.

Salaries were somewhat higher from the first under the new administration. The President received $1500, besides the graduation fees and the use of the presidential house and garden. In 1827–28 the stopping of the salaries of non-

resident professors, and an increase in the price of tuition to
$36 a year, enabled the Corporation to raise the salaries of
the resident professors to $1000 each. But the next year,
because of a deficit of $900 partly due to decrease in receipts
from tuition, these salaries were lowered to $1400 and $900,
and the new professor received but $800; other economies
were also effected. That year the number of students sank
to 98; then it began slowly to rise until 1836–37, when it
reached 196; afterwards it declined for some years, with
consequences to be recounted later. By 1833–34 the President again received $1500, and the three senior professors
$1000; the "adjunct professor" in that year was paid $600,
the two tutors $400 each, and the librarian $175. About
this scale was maintained for many years. It was impossible to pay out much more in salaries without a large increase in productive endowment, and of that there had been
almost none. President Wayland stated, in a special report
of 1841, that the entire property of the university was then
worth more than $150,000, a great gain since ten years
before; but the productive funds, amounting to $32,300,
had increased only $1000 in the same time. Here was a
situation sure to become increasingly distressful as the cost
of living rose.

Intellectually and morally the college community seems to
have had a healthy hardihood, but perhaps it had too little
play. The tallow-candle illumination on the night before
Commencement, which had apparently been for some time
a source of anxiety to the authorities, was stopped at once
by Wayland. The other features of the gala week remained
almost unchanged, except that the President made an effort
to give the exercises of Commencement day more dignity
and decorum. The *Rhode Island American & Providence
Gazette*, in the issue before his first Commencement, said:

"It is earnestly hoped that those who attend the Commencement will go there for the purpose of HEARING, and not merely to display fine clothes, fine faces, and fine chat." After Commencement it said: "Though it was difficult, and in most cases impossible for the speakers to be heard beyond their immediate circle, an attentiveness and decorum were preserved by the whole assembly. . . . The barbarous mode of expressing applause, by stamping and clapping, was, at the special request of the President, wholly dispensed with."

The diary of Williams Latham gives a complete picture of this Commencement week as seen by a member of the graduating class:

Sept. 1, 1827, Started from home this morning at 4 Oclock and reached Providence at half past 9, Just time to rehearse my piece in the Chapel with most of my classmates. . . .

On Sunday sept. 2 went to meeting Mr. Edes with friend Minard and sung a little—in the afternoon went to Mr. Pickerings and heard a fine sermon about the love and benevolence of God—This day has passed off rather heavily On Monday rehearsed our pieces in the Baptist meeting house Philips being absent after his intended wife. . . .

Tuesday—This morning the students were dismissed and many of them have gone home, violating a particular law of the *old system* so much deprecated—There are three Literary Societies in College, Viz. Philermenian, United Brothers, and Franklin, The two first celebrate this day, the other being disappointed in the Orator—The Philermenians this forenoon Professor Burgess being the Orator, He diliverd a fine oration on the history and power of eloquence—The Brothers had a Mr. Burton of Oxford on the progress of intellectual improvement—

S[t]rangers and Alumni have been numerous, this evening They flocked into the College yard thinking there would be an illumination as usual but were disappointed, yet they kept up an old custom by burning a *tar barrel* which induced the President to come out into the yard and try to drive them out but without success—

Wednesday Sept. 5, 1827. The long wished day has arrived and almost past—The day is pleasant—at ten a procession was formed and some with gowns and some without them, marched to the Baptist meeting house es[c]orted by music—and there heard the President make a solemn prayer—9 spoke in the forenoon of which number I was one—at noon My class were all seated at one table on the lower floor south end of the Old College—Grace was said by Thresher and the table was dismissed by Bishop—A sumptuous table without strong drink, excepting good cider—but this was not sufficent and of course wine was called for and producd—a few songs were sung and much noise made—Mr —— [a member of the class, a theologue] made a communication to the Class in which he expressed his thanks and best wishes for the favour they had confered upon him Viz a suit of black clothes—he being indigent This afternoon the house was uncommonly crouded, every inch of ground was occupied—This evening My Class were invited to the Presidents *levee* or party and accordingly went and were treated in the best style—

Thursday every thing was still and all were preparing to take a meloncholly departure—This day Thresher started for N. Y. where he is to marry a lady of respectability—This evening Weeded [=Weeden], Putnam, Minard, and myself went to Mr Burrows and bid farewell by taking a glass of wine—

The absence of Class Day festivities in this account is noticeable. But the class had appointed an orator and a poet in the autumn of 1826, for a celebration at Bristol some time in the spring; and had recently had a meeting and a supper before separating for the summer, as appears from the following entries in the diary:

Thursday May 10th. 1827—

This morning was held a meeting of the Senior Class at the Pump, at which it was resolved, that this class choose a corresponding committee consisting of two persons, Viz. John H. C[l]ifford Esq. chairman John H Weeden deputy to perform the duty of the committee in the absence of the chairman

Resolved, that each individual of the class, *anually*, address a line to the chairman on the first day of January stating his prospects in life—

Resolved, that the committee answer all the letters he receives, on the first day of February — ...

After the [Commencement] parts were given out, the class were invited down to Mr. C[l]ifford's where they went and partook of cold ham and stimulus of the first rate — The following toast was given by Gilman who was very much dissatisfied with his part, "Those who wished to abolish the old system and prayed for the new one have jumped out of the frying-pan into the fire" —

As the years went on, certain changes were made in the Commencement program. In 1829, since the class was small, all the speeches were delivered at one session ; and this became the custom, the number of speeches delivered being limited to fifteen or sixteen. In 1835 there were but five orations, including two for the master's degree, for the seniors, with three exceptions, declined their degrees because the competitive system of Commencement parts impressed them as appealing to "the unworthy passions of the heart"; all were finally awarded degrees — some, at the request of friends, after they had graduated from this world. The Classical Oration was introduced in 1838, the Philosophical the next year. The variety in form was much less than in the earlier administrations: conferences appeared for the last time in 1839, disputes were now wholly a thing of the past except for a solitary revival in that year, and poems became rare; essays and dissertations were common for a while, but after 1850 all the speakers delivered "orations." In subjects, however, the range grew wider and wider, and the topics were also more specific and modern. Philosophy, ethics, politics, history, and the fine arts all received attention, and much more often than before the themes were drawn from literature.

Although the popular interest in Commencement week gradually declined, its social attractiveness increased for those in the academic circle. *The Providence Journal* said of the Commencement of 1841: "The meeting house was as crowded as ever. The speakers did their best to make themselves heard above the noise from the movements of the crowd and the talking of the ladies, who would chat with the gallants circulating about the house in spite of Marshals, Sheriffs, and Constables. The meeting house is a fine place to receive yearly calls from their old admirers among the graduates, and this to them is full as important a matter as the speaking." The programs from 1847 to 1850 had this request, or its equivalent, printed on the first page: "Persons occupying pews in the church are requested not to stand upon the seats, or to converse aloud, during the exercises." The Commencement dinner gained yearly in numbers and in social features. The records of the class of 1841 say: "The eating was despatched in ½ an hour or so & then all joined in singing the 100th. psalm as printed & distributed to each person. After this was sung & an abortive attempt at Auld Lang Syne the dinner broke up." In 1847 about one hundred and sixty persons attended the dinner, and there were speeches, one by Charles Sumner. Two years later the dinner was in Rhode Island Hall, which was completely filled, and there were six speeches and a poem, followed by an alumni meeting in Manning Hall; in the evening came the President's reception in his "hospitable mansion." This Commencement was attended by two alumni of President Manning's day, William Wilkinson, of the class of 1783, and Simeon Doggett, of the class of 1788. In this year the election of the Phi Beta Kappa Society came in the morning of the day before Commencement, and was followed by an oration in the First Congregational Church. In the same place, in the afternoon, an oration was spoken before the Philermenian Society and the United Brothers, and a missionary sermon was preached in the First Baptist Church in the evening.

Thus the exercises of Commencement week were gradually approaching the form which they were long to hold. The chief difference still was the absence of Class Day; but the records of the class of 1841 show that one of the main features, the class supper — or dinner — had already become a well-established custom, for the dinner is there called "a venerable relic of the past." It was held in the City Hotel, on the day after Commencement, and lasted from 3 to 6 p.m. Toasts were drunk, and songs sung — "Fill, fill the sparkling brimmer," "Oft in the stilly night," "Auld Lang Syne," and the class ode. "As the last two verses were being sung all walked around the table & each gave his hand to all the others." Class officers were chosen — a president, five vice-presidents, and a secretary — and the meeting adjourned for three years.

At this period, also, the first alumni association was formed. Several years before, it is true, the alumni had taken concerted action to establish prizes for declamation and composition. The Corporation records of September 2, 1824, say that "At a numerous meeting of Alumni of Brown University, holden in the Philosophical Lecture room of the University on the third day of September A.D. 1823. The Reverend William Rogers a graduate of the first commencement of the University, Chairman," a committee was appointed to raise a fund of $1000, the income of which should be used for the purchase of medals to be awarded to the winners of contests in declamation and composition. The contests were to be held on the day after Commencement; the committee of award were to be the professor of oratory and belles-lettres and four graduates not connected with the government of the college; on the medals was to be engraved,

"Alumni fund of Brown University." The Corporation approved, and the movement went forward. On October 26, 1824, the Corporation voted, "That the Alumni Fund Society be permitted to occupy the College Chapel on the Tuesday Evening previous to the next commencement." And on September 8, 1825, the fellows appointed a committee to award the medals "at the anniversary exercises of the Alumni Society." There is no record of a contest that year; but one occurred in 1826, as appears from the following entry in Williams Latham's diary, under date of November, 1826: "A great discovery, one of the prize pieces of composition found to be a plagiarism. This piece of composition was taken from an english magazine and presented to the Committee of the Alumni as original by —— of the Sophomore Class—Strange to relate, this learned Committee for awarding medals did not discover the imposition—The other medal was awarded to Mr. Phillips of the Junior Class. Among those who competed for the prize in declamation G. Green and T. Hunter bore the palm—and all acquitted themselves with honour." A program in the archives shows that the contest occurred on September 5, in the chapel, and that four sophomores and four juniors competed.

But this organized action of the alumni aimed at only one specific object, and was short-lived, for after the advent of President Wayland nothing more is heard of the society or the contests. During Commencement week of 1842, however, an association of alumni for general purposes was formed; and on Tuesday, September 5, 1843, its first anniversary meeting was held. The members met in Manning Hall, in the morning, and marched to the First Baptist Church, where John Pitman, of the class of 1799, delivered an oration on the history of the college. A dinner was then served in commons hall, at which addresses were made by President Wayland, Ashur Robbins (tutor under President Manning), William Wilkinson, the mayor of Providence, and others. "Alma Mater" was not yet written, but "a spirited song," by a member of the class of 1832, "embodying various reminiscences of college life," was sung. A similar meeting and dinner occurred the following year; but from 1845 to 1852 only business meetings for election of officers were held, with reading of the report of the committee on necrology. The association was well officered, in 1847 electing a president, three vice-presidents, a secretary, and eight "councillors." Early in 1853 some of the alumni met in Manning Hall, "with the view of making arrangements for an Alumni Festival" at the next Commencement, and a committee of distinguished alumni was appointed to take charge of the matter. The committee met at the office of *The Providence Journal*, on January 15, 1853, and "decided that there should be an Oration and Poem on the occasion of the proposed festival." At the "festival," on September 6, there was no poem, but the Hon. Benjamin F. Thurston gave an oration; and the committee was reappointed to "devise plans &c for a continued celebration by the Alumni from year to year." Soon after, however, the association and the Phi Beta Kappa Society agreed to hold literary exercises in alternate years, beginning with the latter in 1854.

The senior and junior exhibitions were continued, though there was now but one a year of the latter, and interest in them declined. The literary societies, on the other hand, were at the height of their prosperity during the greater part of Wayland's administration. The Franklin Society, it is true, died in 1834, after a life of only ten years; but the two older ones, the Philermenian and the United Brothers, were centers of keen intellectual life, their debates and other exercises arousing much interest. President Ezekiel G. Robinson, of the class of 1838, in an article in *The Forum*, December, 1886, said:

The most intimate of my friends, though pure in their lives and morally wholesome as associates, were low in their aims as scholars, satisfied with very little and very superficial work. They had been sent to college to prepare for the ministry. . . . They . . . dropped into the wretched cant of "laying aside ambition as unworthy the servants of the Lord." But . . . it was my good-fortune to be a member of a debating society composed of a very different sort of men from those who were my most intimate friends. In direct education for the real work of life, no influences of my college-days were equal to those of this society. . . . Nothing yet devised has filled, or can fill, as a means of education, the place of the great debating societies, composed of representatives from every class in college, at once imposing and inspiring from their numbers, which were so marked a feature of the college of forty or fifty years ago.

These societies also did much to cultivate a taste for reading. The Philermenians' library, of which a printed catalogue was issued in 1849, had then 3224 volumes, and was a good general collection of history, biography, poetry, essays, and novels, a valuable supplement to the college library. The United Brothers' library was similar. The anniversary meetings, furthermore, stimulated oratorical and literary ambition by bringing to the college such men as President Mark Hopkins, in 1835, John Neal, in 1838, Edwin P. Whipple, in 1846, and Charles Sumner, in 1847; N. P. Willis came as poet in 1831.

Not content with the existing opportunities for debate, James B. Angell, Lloyd Morton, and other freshmen formed a class debating society on October 2, 1845, which survived until January 9, 1847. It met Saturday mornings and thrashed out such questions as "Should the American

Indian claim more of our Sympathy than the Slave of the South?'' or ''Do the plays of Shakspeare, on the Stage exert a good influence on a nation?''

A chapter of the Phi Beta Kappa Society was organized in Brown University on July 21, 1830. The new society not only stimulated scholarship among the undergraduates by the annual election of juniors and seniors to membership, but it added to the brilliancy of Commencement week by securing as orators and poets men of wider fame than had usually spoken before the Federal Adelphi, which it soon supplanted. Oliver Wendell Holmes, George S. Hillard, Caleb Cushing, Henry Wheaton, Professor Edwards A. Park, and George William Curtis were among the Phi Beta Kappa orators and poets.

Undergraduate Greek-letter fraternities took root in the college in Wayland's presidency. Alpha Delta Phi established a chapter in 1836, Delta Phi in 1838, Psi Upsilon in 1840, Beta Theta Pi in 1847, Delta Kappa Epsilon in 1850, Zeta Psi in 1852, Theta Delta Chi in 1853. This new feature of student life evidently excited some alarm. Dr. Wayland wrote letters to the presidents of various universities, in 1836, asking if they allowed secret societies, and what they thought of them. The replies were of varied tenor, and no adverse action was taken at that time. In 1844, however, the Corporation voted, ''That this Corporation disapproves of the establishment of Secret Societies by the Undergraduates of this University or of their participation therein and that the Faculty of the University be requested to adopt such measures as they may deem advisable for the suppression of said secret societies.'' The Faculty seem to have found suppression impracticable or inadvisable; for two years later the Corporation adopted the policy of regulation, instead, passing rules for the government of the societies, and empowering the President to visit their meetings at any time.

The intellectual life of the undergraduates found expression in still another way under President Wayland. In July, 1829, was published the first number of a college magazine, *The Brunonian*, " edited by Students of Brown University." It ran through twelve numbers, which came out monthly at first and then at longer intervals, the last number appearing in March, 1831. The purpose of the publication was " to secure to the Students, the facility of appearing before their friends, through the medium of the press, and to place within their reach, what, in subsequent life, may prove an interesting memento of early attachments." The price was $3 a year. The neat brown covers inclosed twenty-eight or more pages, some of them closely printed, and affording a wide variety of material. A few of the articles are recent Commencement orations, one, on "Southern Slavery," being a defense of the institution by a student from South Carolina. There are long and rather heavy essays on "The Druids," "Effects of Intellectual Culture," "The American System" (an argument for free trade), and the like. Poems on "Mount Hope," "Narragansett Bay," "Twilight," "The Dying Maiden's Lament," etc., relieve the youthful bosom of perilous stuff. Critiques on Burns, Lytton, American literature, etc., show reading and some sense for style. Light sketches and tales of a melodramatic cast—"The Pirate," "The Suicide," "The Anchorite"—supply more readable matter. College news and comments on college life are almost wholly absent; but during the newspaper attacks on the new administration the editors say that the criticisms show spleen, and that "never before has such universal satisfaction been felt by the students respecting the affairs of the College." The most entertaining page is the last of all, on which the editors, "Viator" and "Philander," take farewell of the public: "If our efforts have relaxed for a moment the stern visage of Gravity, or prompted a readier smile on the countenance of Gaiety, if fair bosoms have throbbed over our pages and soft sighs been breathed over our Tales, we have not labored in vain. . . . Our patrons will accept our warmest gratitude; our subscribers are entitled to the same—when they shall have paid their bills; our fellow-students who have assisted our efforts, receive our thanks; to our friends, we proffer our regards, to our foes our indifference; to all, we, as *editors*, with unmingled joy bid an eternal Farewell."

A reading-room association was formed in 1840 by a meeting of students in the chapel, when a committee was appointed to procure and fit up a room; what room was secured does not appear, but it was supplied with eleven periodicals and twelve newspapers. In 1841, it was voted to discontinue the periodicals because of the "abstraction" of them by unprincipled members; a year later the admission fee was changed "by graduating the price to the several classes"; in 1843 resident graduates were given the privileges of undergraduates. At that time it was also voted to establish a "Record of College news &c and place the same under the *sole* care of an Editor"; and from this have been gleaned the foregoing facts about the association. The "Record" also shows, by its "Definitions, not found in Webster," how ancient are some still extant college terms and habits: "*Flunck*—a forced confession of an empty head. *Pony*—a small steed for cripples,—unsafe, obsolete. *Study-hours*—intervals of time between the ringings of the college bell." The record seems to have been discontinued after a few months; how long the association lived is not known.

The Society of Missionary Inquiry was organized in 1834

and lived until 1891. Musical organizations were formed from time to time. Williams Latham notes in his diary, on November 24, 1826, "Harmonic Society got excused from singing in the Chapel any more this term"; on March 25, 1827, "At 11 O,clock the Harmonic Society to Mr Edes's Meeting house, where with the use of the Organ we sung many tunes out of Bridgewater Collection to the gratification of Rev. Mr. Edes and some others"; and on Sunday, April 15, "To day non [= noon] the Harmonic Society met in the projection room old College." At the Commencement of 1828 the music was furnished by a student band. At the junior and senior exhibitions in Manning Hall, in 1837, there was music by "The Brunonian Band." Dramatic clubs would probably not have been tolerated; but Latham's diary contains this record of a moot court in 1826: "College Court instituted and holden at No 56 U. H. on the 5 day of Nov. Commonwealth versus Charles Gilman for an assault and battery upon the person of Wms: H. Spear and thereby endangering his life. This case was conducted by Weeden Attor. Gen. and Lovering Solic. on the part of Commonwealth and Colby and myself for the defendant. After having a fair and impartial trial he was found guilty of two of the three charges set forth in the indictment — The sentence of Court was, to treat the whole College and the high sheriff was ordered to see that it was performed in all its parts. Joseph Phillips chief-Justice C. Carpenter H. Sheriff."

"Junior Burials" had not yet been devised, but what seems to be their historic forerunner was already in existence. "This forenoon," writes Latham on May 5, 1827, "we burnt our compositions which afforded much light and heat to warm and enliven this garden of science Parker was the high priest, Putnam the marshal and Thurber the Poet."

The granddaughter of a former steward of the college, Joseph Cady, witnessed a similar ceremony, and described it thus:

The first thing I remember about college affairs was the burning of the essays by the students when I was about seven years old. It was probably at the end of the spring term of 1831. . . . One morning I noticed two tall poles standing on the east side of Hope College with bundles of white paper tied on them. Soon I heard music, and running up the garden promptly climbed the fence to investigate. A procession of students, dressed in fantastic costumes, came around University Hall, not a lengthy procession like those of the present day, but quite as enthusiastic, and the music (probably Washington's March, as that was always played on great occasions) was very inspiriting. They went by the old well up the back campus and halted; probably there were speeches. Then the papers were lighted, and made a very pretty bonfire. I was told afterwards that the bundles contained the essays that the students had written during the year. I do not remember ever seeing such a procession afterwards.

Sports were still unorganized. Latham records on March 22, 1827, ''We had a great play at ball to day noon.'' On Monday, April 9, he says: ''We this morning . . . have been playing ball, But I never have received so much pleasure from it here as I have in Bridgewater They do not have more than 6 or 7 on a side, so that a great deal of time is spent in runing after the ball, Neither do they throw so fair ball, They are affraid the fellow in the middle will hit it with his bat-stick.'' On April 25 he writes: ''Yesterday five or six of us went down to the Observatory to roll nine pins — This is a very good exercise and not very expensive.''

President Wayland, because of his medical training, might be expected to realize the value of systematic physical exercise, and he clearly had ideas ahead of his time in this regard; for he had hardly been inducted into office when the Corporation voted, on March 15, 1827, ''That the

President, Treasurer and Mr. Dorr, be a Committee, with authority to establish a Gymnasium in this Institution." In a circular of information for 1827–28 is the statement, "A very complete Gymnasium, with every variety of apparatus for exercise, has lately been erected on the College grounds." This was evidently an announcement before the fact, for in the next catalogue there is no reference to the matter, and in 1830 a communication in the *Daily Advertiser* of September 25 speaks of "an idle waste of money on gymnastic projects that were no sooner conceived than abandoned." There was no college gymnasium, nor any arrangement with gymnasiums in the town, for many years to come; and athletic sports in the modern sense were almost as long delayed. The Rev. James C. Seagrave, of the class of 1845, in memoranda made shortly before his death in 1913, wrote, "We had games of foot ball organized in two minutes, engaged in by most of the students residing in the College Halls, and when the game was over, every man was ready to take up any work on hand." The Rev. Henry I. Coe, valedictorian of the class of 1846, in a recent letter says, "I never heard of athletics while in the University; my exercise was walking." Alexander J. Robert, of the class of 1849, makes the following statement: "Football was the only sport engaged in: sophomores vs. freshmen. No ground was appropriated for the game. The rear of Hope College & the college fence on the east were utilized as the bounds. No one was ever invited, & no one ever came to witness the game. There was no gymnasium. In the spring of '48 a club of young men in Bristol wanted to sell their boat as they had all married & wished to retire to business life. Twelve of us formed a club & purchased the boat. This was the first boat ever owned by the students of Brown. It was a daily custom of the students & many of the citizens to promenade on the north side of Westminster St. after 5 p.m. This was our principal exercise.''

In spite of limited outlet for youthful spirits in the way of sports, there was little disorder during the greater part of Wayland's presidency. In general the students were busy and well-behaved, for fear of the majestic Head intimidated would-be evil-doers. ''He was disobeyed with fear and trembling,'' writes Charles T. Congdon, of the class of 1841, in his *Reminiscences*, ''and the boldest did not care to encounter his frown. . . . He had a heavy foot for a student's door when it was not promptly opened after his official knock. Once, when we were bent upon illuminating the college in honor of some festive occasion, and contrary to his express injunctions, he exhibited his abilities in this way most effectually. '*Aequo pulsat pede*,' we quoted from Horace as we fled from his wrath, and saw one row of lights extinguished after another.'' Mr. Seagrave says of Wayland as a disciplinarian : ''To us watching him it seemed perfectly easy to administer the affairs of a college. To know him well was to recognize a man most forbearing toward the weak and erring. Look at him — you would not wish to encounter his rebuke or his frown. But go to his study, state your perplexity, — not another man of all your acquaintance would listen more attentively or help you more truly and kindly. How he dealt with unruly or dissolute students was another thing, but the other fellows were not expected or likely to know much about it, for discipline was an unseen element in our college life.''

In his last years, nevertheless, Wayland seems to have grown somewhat autocratic and arbitrary. President James B. Angell, who was his pupil in the late forties and his colleague soon after, in a recent interview said that he was imperious and often rough, sometimes unreasonable and unjust; especially was he jealous of his authority — question that, and he swelled with anger. Weariness with routine made him more and more brusque toward the end. The journal of William G. Dearth, of the class of 1855, pictures him thus in the year 1854: "Went up to Dr. W. after recitation to explain the cause of my absence. 'The reverend and respected Sir' was surrounded by several of the rest of the class, wishing to propound various question[s] for his consideration; but after answering a few, he began to walk off into his office, with the greatest coolness and disregard for us undergraduates. I tried to stop him; but had to follow him into the room to say my couple of words; — for he wouldn't be stopped. Characteristic."

The social station of the undergraduates as a whole must have risen somewhat under Wayland; but few of them had intercourse except with their fellows. President Angell says: "Students rarely went into society in the city before their senior year, and not many even then. We found our social delights in our college intimacies." The close personal relations between professors and students, of which so much is often made in speaking of college life half a century ago, seem to have been confined chiefly to the class-room. Mr. Seagrave, in his memoranda, says: "Our social life was largely confined to ourselves. We did not often visit the professors in their homes." Mr. Coe, in the letter already quoted, writes, "I never while in the University entered the home of the President or any Professor." The experience of Mr. Robert, a Southerner, was somewhat different: "It was my good fortune to visit in some families of the best society. Wherever I met some of the professors at their parties, they would ask me to join them in a glass of wine. There was never a dance & but one social event in the college during my college course. The Registrar, Mr. Elliott, who with his family occupied the lower east rooms of University Hall, held a reception on Christmas eve in honor of his niece, to which we, who occupied our rooms during the short vacation, were invited.''

In Messer's day the expenses were kept down to the lowest possible limit. The long vacation, of eight weeks, was put in the winter, expressly that poor students might teach school; how generally they availed themselves of the opportunity appears from Latham's diary, in which occurs the entry in December, 1826: ''It is rather lonesome here in College, Most of the students have gone out to keep school.'' One of President Wayland's first acts was to shorten this vacation to six weeks; and in his report to the Corporation, in 1829, he argues in favor of shortening it still more: ''If it be said that the indigent students will lose *more* time by such an arrangement, we grant it; but we answer that those who are not indigent, will lose *less* time. And it deserves to be considered, whether the rights of one party are not as worthy your attention as those of the other.'' By 1834 the vacation had been shortened to three weeks. At the same time the expenses of the student had been increased to $120 or more, besides a matriculation fee of $5. In 1832–33, perhaps because of public clamor that the college was now too costly for the poor man's son, two tables were set in commons, one at $1 a week, and one at from $1.50 to $1.61. The cheaper rate brought the total annual cost of the intellectual life down to $103.50, while the young plutocrats at the better table paid $122.50 to $128. This system was retained for several years, in spite of the criticism that it violated academic democracy. ''Most of us took our meals in Commons Hall,'' writes President Angell, ''the room now used as a classroom on the first floor in the middle of the east side of University Hall. Each class had its own table.

If the fare was not very sumptuous, it was not costly, and the conversation was lively. Occasionally it became so boisterous as to stir the amiable steward, Mr. Elliott, known familiarly to us as 'Pluto,' to bring down his big bread-knife with a loud resounding whack on his table, and to shout with his husky voice, 'Order, order.' I cannot say that the usages in Commons Hall were conducive to elegant manners. But the plain meals were spiced with the flavor of excellent companionship." Commons were abolished in 1850.

President Wayland has already been described as an administrator and teacher; something should be added about his personal life at this time and his books and addresses. His life was one of almost incessant toil. He wrote to his sister in 1832: "I am, my dear A., a perfect dray-horse. I am in harness from morning to night, and from one year to another. I am never turned out for recreation." He did, however, take daily exercise. "For many years," write his biographers, "this was his sole relief from study. Indeed, his only idea of relaxation was exercise in the open air. . . . If the weather was unfavorable for gardening, he resorted to sawing and splitting wood." He not only worked his brain many hours daily, but he held doggedly to the task set for each hour and concentrated all his energy upon it. By this rigorous method he did a large amount of work. In addition to performing the regular duties of a college president and professor, he brought out *The Elements of Moral Science* in 1835, *The Elements of Political Economy* in 1837, *The Limitations of Human Responsibility* in 1838, *Thoughts on the Present Collegiate System in the United States* in 1842, and *Domestic Slavery*, a series of letters between himself and a Southern clergyman, in 1845. He was also called upon for many sermons and addresses, most of which he prepared for publication. Among these may be mentioned an address before the American Institute of Instruction in 1830; a discourse on "The Philosophy of Analogy," before the Brown chapter of Phi Beta Kappa in 1831; an address, "The Dependence of Science upon Religion," at the dedication of Manning Hall in 1835; two sermons on "The Moral Law of Accumulation," preached during the panic of 1837; a discourse at the opening of the Providence Athenaeum in 1838; an address before the Rhode Island Society for the Encouragement of Domestic Industry in 1841; "The Affairs of Rhode Island" and "A Discourse on the Day of Public Thanksgiving" in 1842, both dealing with the Dorr War; a memorial address on Nicholas Brown in 1841, and one on Professor Goddard in 1846; and "The Duty of Obedience to the Civil Magistrate," three sermons preached in 1847, referring to the war with Mexico. Among his unpublished addresses were the Dudleian lecture at Harvard University in 1831 and an address before the Harvard chapter of Phi Beta Kappa in 1836. He also contributed articles to various newspapers and magazines. He had a prominent part in improving the public schools of the state in 1828, was a founder and for years the president of the American Institute of Instruction, served as examiner at West Point in 1837, and the next year, at the request of the Secretary of State, gave advice about the organization of the Smithsonian Institution. He took an active interest in local charities, and performed many labors in the church and affiliated societies.

In the autumn of 1840 President Wayland sailed for Europe, returning in April of the next year; Professor Caswell served as president *pro tempore* during his absence. As a vacation the tour was not wholly successful. Dr. Wayland had never learned how to play; the art and the rich material civilization of Europe meant little to one so Puri-

tanic and practical; and he could not study continental life
deeply, being ignorant of the languages. In fact, he visited
no continental country but France, resisting a friend's invitation to go to Italy because "life is too short to devote
much of it to sight-seeing." In England he fared better.
He met his uncle, an Anglican clergyman, and many of the
dissenting clergy. He became acquainted with various distinguished men — Senior, the political economist; Sir James
Lubbock, then president of the Royal Society, a meeting
of which he attended; Professor Whewell, Dr. Chalmers,
and other university dignitaries in Cambridge, Oxford, and
Edinburgh, some of whom he heard lecture. Of his visit
to Oxford, the Hon. Isaac Davis, who was with him, said:
"Here he was most cordially welcomed by the magnates of
the university. I need not tell you with how eager an interest
he visited the chapels, libraries, and printing establishments
of this ancient university, or with what patient attention he
examined the discipline, courses of study, and educational
advantages thus fully open for his inspection." He also went
to Rugby and had an interview with Dr. Arnold; and he
met a few authors, including Miss Edgeworth and Blanco
White. He preached several times, with great effect, and
everywhere seems to have made a strong impression. "I
well remember," wrote Mr. Davis, "that Dr. Wayland had
more invitations to dine with distinguished men in Liver-
pool than it was possible for him to accept." There is reason
to think, as will appear later, that his European experiences
widened the President's outlook and materially affected his
educational views.

When Dr. Wayland returned, Rhode Island was in the
early stages of a political struggle that was to end in the
Dorr Rebellion. Weary of the obstructions by which the
legislature had long blocked the way to constitutional re-

form, the popular leaders — chief of whom was Thomas W. Dorr, a man of good Rhode Island family and a Harvard graduate — ignored the venerable constitution and appealed direct to the people as the ultimate source of political power. In November, 1841, a People's Convention assembled in Providence and framed a brand-new constitution, abolishing the property qualification for suffrage and equalizing representation in the legislature. The following April Dorr was elected governor under this constitution; and, having failed to secure recognition and support from the federal authorities, he made two formidable attempts, in May and June, to obtain the people's rights by force of arms. In this contest it was natural that the sympathies of the university officials should be chiefly on the side of the conservatives. Most of them, however, took no active part in the struggle; but Professor Goddard, a man of strong convictions and a facile writer, battled vigorously for what he considered good government. "His essays for the daily press, during this period alone," said Dr. Wayland, "would fill a moderately sized volume. Day after day, he explained to his fellow citizens the principles of rational liberty; he laid bare, with a masterly hand, the distinction between liberty and licentiousness; and when at last the crisis arrived — with an eloquence that fired the soul of every true hearted man, he urged us all to unite in defence of that heritage of civil and religious liberty which God had bestowed upon our fathers." President Wayland expressed his own view in a sermon preached in the First Baptist Meeting-House the Sunday after the first crisis of the rebellion. His attitude was judicial and broad-minded. "My own opinion," he said, "as many of you know, has always been in favor of the extension of suffrage"; he affirmed, too, that the representation of the towns "had become palpably unequal," and that there

was "good reason for a revision of this whole subject."
But although he sympathized with the aims of the popular party, he dissented utterly from their methods. "It was
no more in the main a practical question how far the right
of suffrage should be extended," he declared, "but the abstract question whether the asserted majority of the people,
a majority determined by no forms of law, has a right at any
moment to overturn the whole fabric of existing institutions
and form a government at will."

The second crisis of the rebellion touched the life of the
college closely, as is set forth in a circular letter of July 7,
sent to the parents of the students. After rehearsing the main
facts about the gathering of the insurgents and the calling out of the state troops, the letter says: "On Saturday,
June 25th, about two thousand troops had arrived in this
city, and the number was hourly increasing. All the means
for their accommodation, at the disposal of the Government,
had been exhausted. In this emergency, an official request
was made by the Executive Council, that a part of the College buildings might be appropriated to their use. Study,
from the nature of the case, had become impossible. The
lives of the students might have been exposed to peril by
a longer continuance in the city; and, anticipating what we
supposed would, in such a case, be the wishes of parents, it
was determined to suspend for a season the exercises of the
Institution." The Faculty records state that "the troops were
quartered in the college for several days." Thus did Art
and Science once more lend aid to Mars; and the veteran
University Hall, dreaming of the past through all its old
bricks and timbers, might well have fancied that the Revolutionary days of its youth had come again.

Professor Goddard retired from the Faculty shortly after
the storm had overblown. Four years later, in 1846, he died.

On his mother's side he was descended, through James Angell, from one of the founders of Rhode Island. His father, William Goddard, was a newspaper proprietor and editor in Providence, Philadelphia, and Baltimore, and also held the office of first comptroller of the United States Post Office. Professor Goddard was born in Johnston, Rhode Island, in 1794. After graduating from Brown University in 1812, he began the study of law in Worcester; but finding his strength insufficient for the legal profession, he returned to Providence in 1814, and became proprietor and editor of *The Rhode Island American*. In 1825 he was appointed a professor in the university; upon his resignation in 1842, he was chosen a trustee, and fellow and secretary the next year. He was also a director and vice-president of the Providence Athenaeum, a director of the Rhode Island Historical Society, a member of the Providence school committee, a representative in the state legislature, and long a warden of St. John's Church, although never a church member. Bowdoin College gave him the degree of LL.D. in 1843.

Although first appointed to the chair of philosophy, Professor Goddard felt that he had no peculiar aptitude for that subject, and by mutual arrangement with his colleagues, says Dr. Wayland, he was soon relieved of instruction in it, giving himself instead to teaching rhetoric, the evidences of religion, and the constitution of the United States. His mind was rather intuitive than logical; but so keen was his insight, so just were his instincts, that President Wayland, although of a very different type of intellect, greatly admired his writings, saying of his address on the new state constitution in 1843, "I do not remember any commentary upon the nature of our free institutions, which, in so few pages, contains so much that is of permanent value." Dr. Wayland praised even more highly his literary gifts: "If I have correctly estimated the character of Mr. Goddard, its most remarkable feature was delicate and discriminating sensibility. . . . His critical perceptions were more exquisitely delicate than those of any man whom I have ever known." Most of Professor Goddard's writings now seem too formal, with words too long and sentences too elaborate; but correctness and finish are everywhere apparent, and in his public letters on political subjects the style becomes simpler and more racy, as in the following extract from a letter in *The Providence Journal* of October 29, 1841:

The secret of all this agitation about Free Suffrage in Rhode Island, is coming to be pretty well understood. An air of suspicion has been thrown around the whole movement, by the extremely active participation therein of certain gentlemen, who have never been remarkable for taking very good care of the people, except when they expected the people to take very good care of them. These gentlemen, in the late Convention, trampled upon some of their favorite theories, with an audacity so calm and collected that, under circumstances less grave, there would arise in the public mind, a struggle between admiration and merriment. As things are, however, the predominant sentiment is indignation — indignation, that those who have preached up, till they were hoarse, the doctrines of undiluted democratic equality, should not hesitate, for the sake of expediency, to turn their backs upon their own principles.

His academic addresses bear the impress of a broad and cultivated mind. His oration at the dedication of Rhode Island Hall is a wide and just survey of the social benefits of scientific study; his Phi Beta Kappa address, in 1836, is noble in spirit, pleading for the higher and finer life in the midst of commercial materialism.

"The manners of Professor Goddard," wrote President Wayland, "were courteous and refined. His personal habits, without being painfully exact, were scrupulously neat, and in perfect harmony with the character of a literary citizen.

His conversation, sometimes playful, never frivolous, was always instructive, and at times singularly forcible, captivating and eloquent. His tastes were simple and easily gratified; and I think that he preferred a book in his study, or a conversation at the fireside with a friend, to any form of more exciting and outdoor enjoyment. . . . He carried into daily practice the sentiment which he uttered only a few days before his death. 'The longer I live,' said he, 'the more dearly do I prize being a Christian; and the more signally unimportant seem to me the differences by which true Christians are separated from each other.' "

CHAPTER VII

PRESIDENT WAYLAND'S ADMINISTRATION

[CONTINUED]

IN the year 1849 President Wayland was at the height of his powers and reputation. He was universally respected and admired in the community ; his addresses and books had spread his name far ; and he was widely known as one of the most successful college presidents in the country. The condition of the university was supposed to be excellent. It was therefore a shock to the community and the alumni, and a surprise to a wider circle, when, the day after Commencement, President Wayland resigned. One reason for his action is given in his own words to the Corporation: "The undersigned deems this a suitable occasion to carry into effect a purpose which for some years he has had in contemplation and devote the remainder of his life to pursuits which require the uninterrupted command of his time." But there was more behind. For several years Dr. Wayland had been deeply dissatisfied with the policy of the institution. In 1841, the year of his return from Europe, he had made a formal report on the subject to the fellows, and the matter had been discussed at length but without radical results. Since that time the steady decrease in the number of students, which fell from 196 in 1837 to 140 in 1845, and was only 152 in the year of his resignation, had convinced him that there was something fundamentally wrong. With the decrease in students the income fell off, and there was growing difficulty in meeting expenses. In 1846, as a partial relief to the treasury, the

[258]

tutors were dismissed; and two years later, when the professor of modern languages resigned, an instructor supported wholly by fees was appointed in his place. The salaries, furthermore, were inadequate. In September, 1848, the three senior professors addressed a memorial to the Corporation, saying that they could not support their families on their salaries, the cost of living having increased twelve or fifteen per cent in recent years; that other professional salaried men in the city got from fifty to a hundred per cent more than they did; and that while their salaries had remained the same, their work had been increased by the reduction of the teaching staff, so that they now had three or even four recitations daily instead of two. In response the Corporation attempted to raise a fund of $50,000, but failed completely. In these circumstances President Wayland's resignation was doubtless meant to be a call to action.

The effect was electrical. The Corporation at once expressed a unanimous wish that he would withdraw his resignation. He consented on the understanding that the whole matter would be referred to a committee empowered to confer with him; and a Committee of Advice was thereupon created for that purpose. One of the first acts of the committee — after Wayland had investigated the salaries at other New England colleges [1] — was to vote that the President's salary be raised to $1600, Professor Caswell's to $1250, and the other four professors' to $1200 each. The whole situation was then discussed; and on December 18 "The present condition and embarrassments of the University were laid before the Corporation in a written communication, by the President." The subject was thereupon referred to a committee of eleven, headed by Dr. Wayland. At an-

[1] The correspondence shows that professors received $900 at Amherst, $1140 at Yale, $1200 to $2000 at Harvard.

other special meeting, on March 28, 1850, President Way-land, as chairman of this committee, read his famous "Report to the Corporation of Brown University, on Changes in the System of Collegiate Education." The report was ordered published, and formal action on it was deferred until May 7.

The report begins with a survey of university education in Great Britain and its relation to the American colonial college. The English university was originally designed to educate the clergy; the studies were chiefly Greek, Latin, and mathematics; each college was an academic family. The American college naturally followed the English model; but the college building was not an open quadrangle with only one entrance, and the officers were not required to live with the students. "The result of our departures from the original idea has been in every respect unfortunate. In the first place, we assume the responsibility of a superintend-ence which we have rendered ourselves incapable of fulfill-ing; and we have lost the humanizing effect produced by the daily association of students with older and well bred gentlemen, so obvious in an English college." Yet the colo-nial colleges did effective work. "They nurtured the men who, as jurists and statesmen and diplomatists, in the in-tellectual struggle that preceded the Revolution, shrunk not from doing battle with the ablest men of the mother coun-try, and won for themselves, in the contest, the splendid eulogy of Lord Chatham, the noblest of them all. . . . It ought not here to escape remark, that these colleges were almost wholly without endowment. They were nearly self-supporting institutions. The course of study was limited, and time was allowed for deliberate investigation of each science. The mind of the student was suffered to invigorate itself by reflection and reading, and hence, with far less perfect means than we now possess, it seems to have attained a more manly development.''

''But, with the present century, a new era dawned upon the world. A host of new sciences arose, all holding important relations to the progress of civilization.'' These new subjects had to be given a place in the college curriculum. How should it be done? By extending the length of the course? or by allowing the student to select certain subjects and omit others? or by keeping to the traditional four years, enlarging the number of subjects, and reducing the time allowed to any one? The last method was the one adopted, and the results had been evil. ''It seems to us evident, that the effect of this mode of instruction must be unfortunate on the mind of both student and instructor. The student never carrying forward his knowledge to its results, but being ever fagging at elements, loses all enthusiasm in the pursuit of science. . . . We have now in the United States . . . one hundred and twenty colleges pursuing in general this course. All of them teach Greek and Latin, but where are our classical scholars? All teach mathematics, but where are our mathematicians? We might ask the same questions concerning the other sciences taught among us. There has existed for the last twenty years a great demand for civil engineers. Has this demand been supplied from our colleges? We presume the single academy at West Point, graduating annually a smaller number than many of our colleges, has done more towards the construction of railroads than all our one hundred and twenty colleges united.''

Meanwhile a new and startling phase of the matter developed; the colleges ceased to be self-supporting. ''Two courses were again open before the colleges. The first was to adapt the article produced, to the wants of the community.

. . . The other course was to appeal to the charity of the public, and thus provide funds by which the present system might be sustained. The second course was adopted. . . . Hence, if it be desired to render a college prosperous, we do not so much ask in what way can we afford the best education, or confer the greatest benefit on the community, but how can we raise funds, by which our tuition may be most effectually either reduced in price, or given away altogether?'' New England responded generously to this appeal, and several of her colleges are now liberally endowed. Yet the results have been disappointing. The proportion of college graduates to the whole population is decreasing, and the average of ability in the learned professions is no higher than it was thirty years ago. "We are, therefore, forced to adopt the . . . supposition, that our colleges are not filled because we do not furnish the education desired by the people. . . . Is it not time to inquire whether we cannot furnish an article for which the demand will be, at least, somewhat more remunerative?''

The report then turns to the case of Brown University in particular. The history of the college since 1827 is sketched, with due emphasis on the improvement in equipment. But there has been no considerable increase in productive funds, and the attendance has decreased; hence the institution is financially embarrassed. "Proceeding at this rate, the fund must soon be exhausted, and the institution become bankrupt.'' What means shall be adopted for its relief? The means recommended, constituting the radical portion of the report, may best be stated by giving considerable extracts from the report itself:

Were an institution established with the intention of adapting its instruction to the wants of the whole community, its arrangements would be made in harmony with the following principles.

1. The present system of adjusting collegiate study to a fixed term of four years, or to any other term, must be abandoned, and every student be allowed, within limits to be determined by statute, to carry on, at the same time, a greater or less number of courses as he may choose. . . .

3. The various courses should be so arranged, that, in so far as it is practicable, every student might study what he chose, all that he chose, and nothing but what he chose. . . .

4. Every course of instruction, after it has been commenced, should be continued without interruption until it is completed.

5. In addition to the present courses of instruction, such should be established as the wants of the various classes of the community require. . . .

The courses of instruction to be pursued in this institution might be as follows:

1. A course of instruction in Latin, occupying two years.

2. A course of instruction in Greek, occupying two years.

3. A course of instruction in three Modern languages.

4. A course of instruction in Pure Mathematics, two years.

5. A course of instruction in Mechanics, Optics, and Astronomy, either with or without Mathematical Demonstrations, 1½ years.

6. A course of instruction in Chemistry, Physiology and Geology, 1½ years.

7. A course of instruction in the English Language and Rhetoric, one year.

8. A course of instruction in Moral and Intellectual Philosophy, one year.

9. A course of instruction in Political Economy, one term.

10. A course of instruction in History, one term.

11. A course of instruction in the Science of Teaching.

12. A course of instruction on the Principles of Agriculture.

13. A course of instruction on the Application of Chemistry to the Arts.

14. A course of instruction on the Application of Science to the Arts.

15. A course of instruction in the Science of Law. . . .

That such a change as is here proposed, would add to the number of its pupils, seems to your committee probable, for several reasons.

1. The course of instruction will, it is hoped, present a better preparation for the learned professions, than that pursued at present. There is no reason, therefore, why this class of pupils should be diminished.

2. Opportunity would be afforded to those who wished to pursue a more generous course of professional education, to remain in college profitably for five or six years, instead of four, as at present.

3. Many young men who intend to enter the professions, are unwilling or unable to spend four years in the preparatory studies of college. They would, however, cheerfully spend one or two years in such study, if they were allowed to select such branches of science as they chose. This class would probably form an important addition to our numbers, and we should thus, in some degree, improve the education of a large portion of all the professions.

4. If we except the ancient languages, there are but few of the studies now pursued in college, which, if well taught, would not be attractive to young men preparing for any of the active departments of life. If these several courses were so arranged as to be easily accessible to intelligent young men of all classes, it may reasonably be expected that many will desire to spend a term, a year, or two years, under our instruction.

5. It is not probable that the courses of instruction in agriculture, or chemistry, or science applied to the arts, will, of necessity, occupy all the time of the student. Many of these persons will probably desire to avail themselves of the advantages so easily placed in their power. Another source of demand for the courses in general science would thus be created.

Should these expectations be realized, it will be perceived that the addition to our numbers will come from classes who now receive no benefit whatever from the college system, as it at present exists. . . .

If reasons need be offered for attempting the changes in our collegiate system that have been here indicated, the following will readily suggest themselves.

1. IT IS JUST. — Every man who is willing to pay for them, has a right to all the means which other men enjoy, for cultivating his mind by discipline, and enriching it with science. . . . And yet we have in this country, one hundred and twenty colleges, forty-two theological seminaries, and forty-seven law schools, and we have not a single institution designed to furnish the agriculturist, the manufacturer, the

mechanic, or the merchant with the education that will prepare him for the profession to which his life is to be devoted. . . .

2. IT IS EXPEDIENT. — . . . Civilization is advancing, and it can only advance in the line of the useful arts. . . . A knowledge universally diffused of the laws of vegetation, might have doubled our annual agricultural products. Probably no country on earth can boast of as intelligent a class of mechanics and manufacturers, as our own. Had a knowledge of principles been generally diffused among them, we should already have outstripped Europe in all those arts which increase the comforts, or multiply the refinements of human life. . . .

3. IT IS NECESSARY. — To us, it seems that but little option is left to the colleges in this matter. . . . Men who do not design to educate their sons for the professions, are capable of determining upon the kind of instruction which they need. If the colleges will not furnish it, they are able to provide it themselves; and they will provide it. In New York and Massachusetts, incipient measures have been taken for establishing agricultural colleges. . . . What is proposed to be done for the farmers, must soon be done either for or by the manufacturers and merchants. . . .

It will at once appear, that if an extended and various system of education, such as has been indicated above, be adopted, the relation of the parties [*i.e.*, Corporation and Faculty] to each other must be made more simple and definite. The corporation cannot pretend any longer to hold themselves responsible for the support of every professor; nor can they pretend to oversee him in the discharge of his duty. . . . The officer who accepts of a professorship will then be entitled to whatever income is attached to it, and he will look to his fees for instruction for the remainder of his compensation. Like every other man, the instructor will be brought directly in contact with the public, and his remuneration will be made to depend distinctly upon his industry and skill in his profession. . . .

We proceed, in the last place, to consider the subject of academical degrees. . . .

We, in New England, insist upon requirements never thought of in any other country. There has not, probably, been a first class man in either Oxford or Cambridge for a century, who could sustain an examination in one half of the studies required of the candidate for a degree in one of our New England colleges. And, on the other hand, none, even of our highest scholars, could sustain the examinations required of a senior wrangler or first class man in these universities. . . .

By adopting . . . a system of equivalents, we may confer degrees upon a given amount of knowledge, though the kind of knowledge which makes up this amount may differ in different instances. Thus, for instance, suppose a course should be prescribed, containing a given amount of Latin, Greek, Mathematics, and Natural and Moral and Intellectual Philosophy, and Rhetoric, as the basis of requirement for degrees. In determining upon equivalent courses, a certain amount of some other study might compensate for Latin, or Greek, as a certain amount of some other study might be a compensation for the higher mathematics, or intellectual philosophy, and so of the rest. An arrangement of this kind would seem just, and to us it seems not to be impracticable.

The objection that would arise to this plan, would probably be its effect upon the classics. It will be said, that we should thus diminish the amount of study bestowed on Latin and Greek. To this the reply is easy. If by placing Latin and Greek upon their own merits, they are unable to retain their present place in the education of civilized and Christianized man, then let them give place to something better. They have, by right, no preëminence over other studies, and it is absurd to claim it for them. But we go further. In our present system we devote some six or seven years to the compulsory study of the classics. . . . And what is the fruit? How many of these students read either classical Greek or Latin after they leave college? . . . Is there not reason to hope, that by rendering this study less compulsory, and allowing those who have a taste for it to devote themselves more thoroughly to classical reading, we shall raise it from its present depression, and derive from it all the benefit which it is able to confer?

As the conclusion of the whole matter the report affirmed that "This college cannot, under any circumstances, be long sustained without large addition to its funds"; and that "There is reason to hope that the same amount of funds which would be necessary to sustain the college under the present system, might, if the system were modified in the manner above suggested, add greatly to the number of students, and, at the same time, confer inestimable advantages on every class of society.'' The committee therefore recommended to the Corporation the adoption of this resolution: ''Resolved, that the system of instruction in Brown University be modified and extended in the manner indicated in the above Report, as soon as the sum of $125,000 can be added to its present funds.''

The report made a stir throughout the country. And yet it contained little or nothing that was new in theory. Dr. Wayland had himself presented the kernel of the matter in his report to the fellows in 1841, containing the following sentence: ''It is the opinion of your committee that an effort must soon be made by the more advanced American colleges to adapt their courses to the different capacities and wants of students, giving to each officer the opportunity to carry his course of instruction to as great a degree of perfection as he is able, fixing certain acquisitions as necessary to graduation but making such arrangements as will enable those not candidates for a degree to obtain in the various departments of knowledge such instruction as may qualify them for the occupations for which they were designed.'' In 1842 he had covered the whole ground in his little book, *Thoughts on the Present Collegiate System in the United States.*

In practice, too, nearly everything that the report advocated had been anticipated even in American colleges, to say nothing of European. In Rhode Island something had been done from early times to bring the benefits of the college to the whole community. In 1785 and 1786 Professor Waterhouse had given courses of popular lectures on natural history, and in 1790 Professor Fobes had given a similar course on natural philosophy. These first attempts at ''university extension,'' although falling far short of what President

Wayland had in mind, yet affirmed the principle. The lectures in the Medical School, under President Messer, went farther and offered to the community extended courses of instruction in subjects of practical value. Professor D'Wolf, of the chair of chemistry, was authorized by a vote of the Corporation in 1822 "to admit to his Lectures, others beside members of the University, with the Presidents approbation," and other courses were also opened. President Wayland's reforms swept away these privileges for a time; but when the professors, under his stimulus, began to give lectures to their classes, the community was again remembered. In the Faculty's report to the Corporation, in September, 1833, they inquire "whether it might not be desirable to issue tickets of admission to the courses to be delivered during the current year so that the advantages of the university might be more extensively enjoyed by those who do not wish to attend the regular recitations"; and the Corporation at once acquiesced. In 1840–41 Professor Chace gave in Rhode Island Hall a course in chemistry, "with suitable illustrations" (says Dr. Wayland), which was "well received by the public." Three years later Professors Caswell and Chace gave lectures on natural philosophy and chemistry before the Providence Mechanics' Association, using by permission the college apparatus.

Students were admitted to the college for a partial course by a vote of the Corporation in September, 1830, and by 1846 seventy-two special students in all had been in attendance. In that year an attempt was made to attract more students to the partial course. A committee of the Faculty reported in favor of changing the name to "English and Scientific Course," presented an outline of study for one year and another for two years, and recommended that for the purpose of bringing the course "more distinc[t]ly before the Public" a descriptive circular be published with the catalogue and in other ways be "spread through the community." The catalogue of 1847–48, accordingly, contained the following announcement:

There has been established in the University, in connection with the regular Collegiate Course, an English and Scientific Course, designed for the benefit of those who do not propose to enter either of the learned professions, but who desire to prepare themselves, by a thorough education, for some one of the more active employments of life. This Course embraces every department of English study pursued in the University, together with the several branches of Mathematical and Physical Science; and moreover, opens to the student all the advantages of the Library, the Cabinet of Natural History, and the Courses of Lectures on Chemistry, Natural Philosophy, Physics, Intellectual Philosophy, and the Evidences of Christianity. It is believed that such a Course will furnish to those who are preparing for Mercantile pursuits, or for the higher employments of Agriculture and Manufactures, the means of securing, at a moderate expense, an education specially adapted to their wants. The Course is arranged for a residence of either one or two years, according to the wish of the student.

Between 1846 and 1849 twenty-two students had entered the course.

There is evidence that at first President Wayland was not in favor of a broad elective system. In 1831 he wrote to the father of a student who had failed in mathematics: "The literary world requires a knowledge of some portion of mathematics [as essential?] to a liberal education, and college discipline requires that the ultimate decision upon what shall be studied, rest somewhere else than in the student himself; at least, till the millenium approach somewhat near." The elective principle was, however, given limited recognition in the curriculum for many years, the students being allowed a choice between calculus and Greek, or Hebrew and Greek, or Hebrew and French, and sometimes between German and logic or rhetoric; but in all this there was, of course, no vital application of the principle.

At Harvard University the principle of elective studies had received much more ample recognition. In 1824 Judge Story, as chairman of a committee of the Board of Overseers, made a report recommending, "That the College studies shall be divided into two classes; the first embracing all such studies as shall be indispenable to obtain a degree; the second, such in respect to which the students may, to a limited extent, exercise a choice which they will pursue." New statutes based on this report went into effect in 1826; they allowed students, after the first third of the freshman year, to substitute modern languages for certain specified courses in Greek, Latin, topography, Hebrew, and natural science, and in the fourth year to take natural philosophy in place of a part of the course in mental philosophy. It was only in the department of modern languages that much range of choice was possible, but there the results were very satisfactory. In 1838 mathematics was made elective after the freshman year, and natural history, civil history, chemistry, geography and the use of the globes, Greek, or Latin might be taken instead. A similar provision was made the next year in regard to Greek and Latin. In 1841 the Faculty adopted a new scheme: in the freshman year all the subjects—mathematics, Greek, Latin, history—were required; in the sophomore year English grammar and composition, rhetoric and declamation, a modern language, and history were required, while electives were allowed from ten subjects; a similar choice was granted in the last two years. Even in this limited form the elective system aroused opposition in the Faculty, and in 1846 a compromise was reached. " It allowed every Senior," says President Eliot, "to select three from the following studies, namely, Greek, Latin, mathematics, German, Spanish, and Italian, and every Junior to select three from the same studies, Italian excepted. All other studies were prescribed.'' In April, 1850, the month after President Wayland read his report, further restrictions were adopted at Harvard; the juniors and seniors were allowed only one elective a year, and the time thus saved was given to required subjects.

The introduction of elective studies at Harvard University seems to have been due partly to the influence of a far more radical scheme in the University of Virginia, which was organized on principles conceived by the liberal mind of its first rector, Thomas Jefferson. Professor Ticknor, a leader in the movement at Harvard, had been for years the friend and correspondent of Jefferson, who offered him a professorship in the new institution. Writing to him on July 16, 1823, Jefferson said: '' I am not fully informed of the practices at Harvard, but there is one from which we shall certainly vary, although it has been copied, I believe, by nearly every college and academy in the United States. That is, the holding the students all to one prescribed course of reading, and disallowing exclusive application to those branches only which are to qualify them for the particular vocations to which they are destined. We shall, on the contrary, allow them uncontrolled choice in the lectures they shall choose to attend.'' When the University of Virginia was opened in the spring of 1825, it offered instruction in seven separate '' schools ''—ancient languages, modern languages, mathematics, natural philosophy, natural history, anatomy and medicine, and moral philosophy; others were added later. There was no fixed curriculum; students were given entire freedom of choice, although to get a degree they must pass the examinations in certain schools.

How far President Wayland was indebted to the experiments at Harvard University and the University of Virginia it is not possible to say. He must have had personal knowledge of what had been attempted at the former; and, furthermore, his report of 1850 quotes from a pamphlet published in 1825 by Professor Ticknor, *Remarks on Changes Lately Proposed or Adopted, in Harvard University*, which sets forth most of Wayland's leading ideas—the need of an elective system, the call of modern life for more varied and practical education, and the benefits of paying professors partly by student fees. But the Harvard system was fundamentally defective in keeping so many prescribed courses that the student's energies were dissipated among a host of unrelated subjects. Dr. Wayland pointed this out in his report; and President Eliot confirms the criticism, saying of the Harvard plan of 1846, "In trying to include the elements of the various new subjects which were pressing for admittance into the old curriculum of classics, mathematics, and metaphysics, the Faculty had overloaded the student and restricted him to superficial attainments."

There is little direct evidence that before 1850 President Wayland was acquainted with the system at the University of Virginia. Professor Ticknor's pamphlet contains this reference to it: "It were to be wished, indeed, that the choice [of studies] could be left without limitation, and that the period passed at College could be thus more intimately connected with the remainder of life, and rendered more directly useful to it; but this, perhaps, is not yet possible with us, though it is actually doing in the University of Virginia, and will soon, it is to be hoped, be considered indispensable in all our more advanced colleges." Dr. Wayland probably had read this statement; but there is no way of determining whether it had come to his notice before the main outlines of his own plan had taken shape, in 1842, and in any case it would give him no knowledge of the details of the Virginian system. The relation in 1850 is clearer. In the archives of the university is a letter of February 27, 1850, from Alexander Duncan, a trustee, to President Wayland, telling when he can go with him to the University of Virginia and implying that their intention had been to go earlier; and in the minutes of the Committee of Advice is a record that the President asked permission, on March 1, to be absent whenever he might find it necessary for the purpose of "obtaining information in respect to the proposed change in the college curriculum." But the visit was delayed until after the reading of the report on March 28; at some time between that date and May 7, Dr. Wayland went to the University of Virginia, accompanied by Zachariah Allen, a trustee of Brown University. "The result of his observation," say his biographers, "so far as it related to the practicability and efficacy of the system, was highly favorable." But although this visit doubtless gave him added confidence in the principles of his report, it shows that when he wrote the report his acquaintance with the Southern institution was imperfect. It is also noteworthy that both in 1842 and in 1850 he makes not the slightest reference to the University of Virginia. Yet the two plans are so like that there must have been some connection between them. The resemblance is not confined to fundamental matters already mentioned, but extends to details peculiar to the Virginian and the Brown systems: in each the principal degree was that of Master of Arts, the degree of Bachelor of Arts being of secondary importance; and each ignored the time element in conferring degrees, which were granted solely on the basis of attainments in certain groups of subjects. The degree of Bachelor of Philosophy, however, was at this time peculiar to

[273]

the Brown plan, which was also unique in some other respects.[1]

Whatever may have been President Wayland's final debt to the University of Virginia and to Harvard University, his first impulse toward a radical change in educational policy seems to have come from the universities of Great Britain. Before his visit to Europe his letters, reports, and addresses contain no suggestion of fundamental reform; upon his return he began at once to agitate the question. His report to the fellows in 1841 made many comparisons with the English universities. His radical review of the American collegiate system, in 1842, contrasts the superficiality of its course of study with the depth of the English, and urges the elective principle as a cure. In the report of 1850 are similar comparisons. In short, although he did not wish to copy their methods as a whole, the English universities seem to have set him to thinking how to secure their thoroughness. This view, based on Wayland's written or printed words, is confirmed by the opinion of President James B. Angell, a member of the Faculty when the New System went into effect, who in a recent interview attributed Dr. Wayland's discontent with the old system to his study of the universities of Great Britain.

There were several reasons for the effect of striking novelty in the doctrines of President Wayland's report, and for the wide sensation it made. The yet more liberal system in the University of Virginia was almost unknown in the North, doubtless because of the widening chasm between

---

[1] In the archives are two examination papers in mathematics, set at the University of Virginia in June, 1849, with explanations of the system of written examinations there. On the back of one paper is written in Wayland's hand, "Examinations in Minor Mathematics in Univy of Virginia." It seems likely that the documents were received after the New System had been adopted, when its details were being worked out.

[274]

the two sections; Dr. Wayland's monograph of 1842 had attracted little notice; and the system that he proposed in 1850 was far more radical than the one in force at Harvard. Furthermore, the report of 1850 was not a mere "academic" discussion, but an actual program for a well-known college. It was also a trenchant criticism of the collegiate system of the United States; it struck the democratic note strongly in its plea for an education that would fit the needs of all classes; and it sought to bring lecture-room and laboratory into vital relations with the material welfare of an immense new country awaiting development. The last two features won it popular favor at once. The newspapers greeted with applause the New Education that was to leave the cloister and walk among modern men at their daily toil. Merchants, manufacturers, farmers, artisans, legislators all saw something worth while in this "practical" form of instruction.

The archives of the university contain many communications expressing interest in the new plan and opinions about it. Some of them antedate the reading of the report, affording proof that the Corporation sounded the feeling of the community and of influential men elsewhere before making the plan public. Barnas Sears, then secretary of the Massachusetts Board of Education, wrote on December 17, 1849, giving his hearty approval and saying that Brown University must take such action to keep its hold on Massachusetts. George R. Russell, of the class of 1821, who had read the report in manuscript, wrote on January 31, 1850: "I believe that it will create a great sensation among those who have longed for this very thing. . . . We have gone along on a jog trot, in a path worn by our Fathers, . . . and if we have found any thing sticking to us at the end of the journey we have often been puzzled to know what to do with it in the active struggle of life." The Rhode Island General Assembly, at the January session, passed the following vote: "*Resolved*, That this General Assembly heartily approve the plan of education presented to this Assembly by the Rev. Dr. Francis Wayland, and proposed to be adopted in Brown University; and that the members of this Assembly will exert themselves to the end that said plan may be carried into successful operation." The Providence Association of Mechanics and Manufacturers reported on February 21 unanimously in favor of the new plan, because it would open higher education to a class now "almost entirely" precluded, and would advance the useful arts. The Franklin Society, in a committee's report of February 26, sounded a note of caution: "We fear that if these sciences were studied and taught only so as to answer the demands of the industrial pursuits of this country, and the knowledge were valued only as so much capital in business, many important branches would be neglected."

After the report had been published, letters about it came in from many quarters. George S. Boutwell, a leader in the Massachusetts legislature, writing to Wayland on April 22, said: "It cannot fail to have a marked effect on the colleges of New England and the whole country. I could not give the views you have so well expressed as prominent a place in the report of the Committee on Harvard College as I desired, on account of the lateness of the session, and the necessity of preparing the report without farther delay. In the debate, however, we shall derive great aid from them." University officials generally favored the plan. Professor C. Mason, of the University of New York, besides giving his own enthusiastic indorsement, quoted Professor Draper as saying to him, "Here is a clear expression of what you and I have been saying for many years, and vainly endeavoring to impress on the authorities of our struggling and sinking university." Professor Mason asked for a hundred copies of the report for distribution among university trustees in New York State. Certain gentlemen in Rochester, New York, wrote to Wayland, asking him to become the head of a new university on the new plan, for which $70,000 had already been raised. Dr. Leonard Bacon, of New Haven, wrote: "Allow me to say that you have spoken a word which needed to be spoken. . . . I have already, & for many months past, expressed to my friend Pres. Woolsey, & to other younger members of our college faculty, opinions so nearly related to those which you have now published, that it would not surprise me if I should be suspected of having been in communication with you on the subject." Professor A. C. Kendrick, of Madison (now Colgate) University, while agreeing with the general principles, regretted "the *utilitarian* tone of the Report," thinking the "useful arts" overemphasized in it. From Illinois came a letter from a farmer, once a "self-educated teacher," giving his approval of the new ideas. The Rev. Dr. Hague, a trustee, sent word from New Jersey that most men whom he had talked with were in favor of the plan, but that the Hon. William Frelinghuysen thought it "too revolutionary." President Nott, of Union College, wrote that he wished his old pupil success, partly, he added, because "we are already committed, in favour of a similar course."

The magazines were more conservative. *The New Englander*, in August, 1850, asserted that culture courses had been proved to be good preparation for active life, in the United States and in England; and it expressed a fear "that the partial courses will become so popular, that the full course will be in a great measure, if not wholly, deserted." *The North American Review* of January, 1851, said of the elective system as outlined by President Wayland: "This is certainly a bold innovation. We have great doubt whether it be practicable, or, if practicable, whether it will be a useful measure; and none at all, that it will, if thoroughly put in practice, be a most costly one.''

On the whole the response to the report was a strong encouragement to proceed. Meanwhile subscription papers had been passing around; and when the Corporation met on May 7, 1850, the Finance Committee reported that $77,000 had been subscribed, and that $10,000 more was practically pledged. Thereupon the Corporation passed the resolution recommended in March, ''That the System of Instruction in Brown University be modified and extended in the manner indicated in the above Reports as soon as the sum of $125,000 can be added to its present funds.'' They also appointed a committee of twelve, besides the President, to carry the proposed changes into effect.

Seven persons, John Carter Brown, Alexander Duncan, Mrs. Hope Ives, Mrs. C. R. Goddard, Moses Brown Ives, Robert H. Ives, and Horatio N. Slater, had subscribed $65,000 on condition that $60,000 more should be pledged by September 5. On August 6 the Committee of Thirteen published an appeal in *The Providence Journal*, saying that if the subscription were not completed, ''the whole design must fail and the University very soon be closed forever,'' but expressing confidence in ''the liberality of their fellow citizens.'' The confidence was justified. On September 4 the committee reported that the sum of $125,000 was so nearly subscribed that they were willing to assume responsibility for the deficiency; the total finally pledged was $127,995. The long list of those who came to the university's aid at this crisis contains many names well known in the history of the city and state; Dr. Wayland gave $1000,[1] and

[1] Dr. Wayland's large subscriptions on various occasions have given some the

Professors Caswell, Chace, and Gammell contributed liberally.

The President's resignation had thus brought about a sudden change in the prospects of the institution, and the future now seemed bright. But the task of translating an ideal into fact was a difficult one. The Committee of Thirteen invited members of the Faculty to deliberate with their sub-committees in working out the details of the New System, which was finally adopted, according to Professor Lincoln, only after "much agitated discussion in the Faculty." The result of the joint labors of the committee and the Faculty, with President Wayland as the master hand, may be seen in the Laws of 1850, enacted on August 1. These provided that courses should be given in Latin, Greek, modern languages, mathematics, natural philosophy, civil engineering, chemistry and physiology, English, moral and intellectual philosophy, history and political economy, didactics, application of chemistry to the arts, and theory and practice of agriculture. This list greatly enlarged the former curriculum, chiefly in science and its applications. A law school was to be established as soon as the funds allowed.

The most radical provisions had to do with degrees. These were to be Bachelor of Philosophy, Bachelor of Arts, and Master of Arts. The first was a new degree; the other two were now to be given on new conditions. "The Degree of Bachelor of Arts," say the laws, "is designed especially for those who desire to prepare themselves for the different professions, and yet, from unavoidable circumstances, are

impression that he had ample means. But in a letter of 1843 he said that he had only $7000, exclusive of copyrights, and that his wife's property was "not large by any means"; the year before he had given away all his income but $200, besides $1000 of his capital.

unable to pursue a complete course of liberal education. In order to render it accessible to such students, the number of studies is limited, and a large liberty of choice is granted, that they may be enabled to select such studies as will the better enable them to prepare themselves for a particular profession.'' Candidates for this degree must pass entrance examinations in arithmetic, ancient and modern geography, English grammar and the use of the English language, the Greek reader or an equivalent in some Greek author, the *Æneid*, Caesar's *Commentaries*, six orations of Cicero, and Greek and Latin composition. These requirements were those that had prevailed for years, with the notable omission of algebra; this was restored the next year, but at the same time students intending to pursue only one ancient language in college were excused from the entrance examination in the other. To get the degree of Bachelor of Arts the candidate ''must have attained the rank of proficiency [*i.e.*, above twenty-five per cent] in either of the following classes of studies'': 1. Two ancient languages for two years, mathematics for two years, English literature and two other courses of one year; 2. One ancient language for two years, two modern languages, mathematics for two years, English literature and two other courses of one year; 3. One ancient language for two years, mathematics for one year, one modern language, English literature and four other courses of one year. In other words, the candidate had his choice among three groups of courses, ranging from a maximum of ancient languages and mathematics, to a minimum of these and a maximum of modern languages and miscellaneous subjects. To get a degree the candidate had finally, at the end of his whole course, to be examined in three of the studies in which he had already proved himself ''proficient'' by the daily recitations and term examinations.

Candidates for the degree of Bachelor of Philosophy were to be admitted to college after passing examinations in arithmetic, ancient and modern geography, and English grammar and the use of the English language, with the addition, in 1851–52, of algebra as far as quadratics. To get the degree candidates must obtain testimonials of proficiency in the following studies: Two modern languages, mathematics of two years, English literature, and three other courses of one year each. Natural philosophy was allowed as a substitute for mathematics of the second year; and a course of two years in agriculture, or in science applied to the arts, or in chemistry applied to the arts, might be taken in place of the two-year course in mathematics and one modern language. The candidates must be examined, at the end, in three of the subjects in which they were proficients. The following statement is significant: " It is the design of the Corporation to require for the degree of Bachelor of Arts and of Philosophy, an amount of study which *may* be accomplished in three years, but which may, if he pleases, occupy the student profitably for four years."

The degree of Master of Arts had hitherto been given by Brown University, as by most other American colleges, "in course," to any Bachelor of Arts of three years' standing, who was of good moral character and who paid the fees. In most cases, however, the candidate had been pursuing professional studies since graduation. The new conditions deserve quoting in full:

The degree of Master of Arts is intended for those students who desire to pursue a full course of liberal education. In order to become a candidate for this degree, the student must have obtained certificates of proficiency in the following courses of instruction:—

In the Ancient Languages for two years, in one Modern Language for one year, in the Mathematics of two years, in Natural

Philosophy, English Language and Rhetoric, Chemistry and Physiology, History and Political Economy, Intellectual and Moral Philosophy.

He must also be examined in the Ancient Languages, in Natural Philosophy, and in three other studies of the course, to be selected by the Faculty; and he shall not be entitled to a degree unless his answers attain to 25 per cent. of the maximum established by the Faculty. The examination in the Ancient Languages shall include one author in Latin and one in Greek, which has not been read by the class in the regular course of instruction.

The candidate for this degree may be allowed to substitute a third year in an Ancient Language for a second in Mathematics, or a third year in Mathematics for a second in an Ancient Language; or to substitute one Modern Language for a year in an Ancient Language, or for a year in Mathematics.

It is the design of the Corporation . . . to require for the degree of Master of Arts an amount of study which *may* be accomplished in four years, but which, if generously pursued, may occupy the student with advantage a considerably longer time.

This course was almost identical in quantity with that previously required for the degree of Bachelor of Arts; the only difference was that the student was now expected to read a certain amount of Greek and Latin by himself, and on the other hand was excused from courses of one term each in astronomy, evidences of Christianity, Butler's *Analogy*, geology, and the American Constitution; he had also to stand a final examination in five of the subjects, in addition to the term examinations. Unless the outside reading in Latin and Greek was considerable (and we shall see that it was not), the total amount of work required for the Master's degree was not more than that formerly required for the Bachelor's degree.

It is disappointing, even humiliating, that a scheme of reform which set out to cure superficiality in collegiate education, and raise the standard of scholarship, should have resulted in degrading the degree of Master of Arts, which had at least stood for a certain mental maturity, in giving the degree of Bachelor of Arts for one fourth less work than before, and in creating a new collegiate degree which might be won by persons entering college with little more than a common-school education. The disappointment is the greater because the elective system, and the infusion of a larger amount of the scientific and practical into the curriculum, did not at all necessitate any lowering of standards, as President Wayland had himself affirmed in his treatise of 1842. Options among the old subjects might have been allowed freely, and new subjects might have been freely admitted, without making the requirements for entrance a whit less severe or lessening by an hour the amount of study required for a degree. Why were not modern languages or more mathematics demanded, in place of the omitted ancient languages, for admission to the Bachelor of Philosophy course? Why were not four years of study in college required for that degree and the degree of Bachelor of Arts? Why was not a fifth year made a requisite for the Master of Arts degree? The report of March 28 and the new laws show that there can be but one answer : the President wished to spread the benefits of collegiate education more widely among the people, and he wished to see more students paying tuition into the treasury of Brown University. To what extent the democratic motive dominated the pecuniary it is impossible to decide, but doubtless each was sincere and powerful. It will be seen later how far the New System brought higher education to the masses, and how far it brought lower education into the college. The increase in numbers during the rest of Wayland's presidency is shown by the following table :

	1850–51	1851–52	1852–53	1853–54	1854–55
Total number	174	225	240	283	252
Candidates for A.M.		118	119	126	119
Candidates for A.B.	174	33	43	48	42
Candidates for Ph.B.		19	27	25	16
Select course		55	51	84	75

How much of the increase was due to the New System and how much to the advertising that the college had received, is a question. The elective system attracted very few more candidates for the degrees of A.M. and A.B. than had formerly been in attendance as candidates for the degree of A.B. alone. Nearly all the additional students took advantage of the easier terms of admission to college.

The Laws of 1850 made other important changes. They created an Executive Board of nine members to be chosen from the Corporation, three being elected each year to serve for three years; the president was subsequently made chairman. This board was given large powers in administering the affairs of the university, subject to the approval of the Corporation; and the president and professors were required to submit reports to it at its monthly meetings. The Faculty were directed to meet weekly, and to keep a permanent record of their doings. It was proposed that each professor's salary should be supplemented by "the avails of the tickets for admission to his class," the purchase of tickets taking the place of payment for tuition; but this plan was never fully carried out. "Wherever the nature of the subject admits of it," say the laws, "the teaching will be by lecture and examination, with reference to text books and collateral authorities, accompanied by the writing of essays and exercises, and the solution of problems." The class-room period was to be an hour and twenty minutes, unless the Executive Board directed otherwise; at least twenty minutes were to be given to questions on the review and on assigned reading; "ten minutes of recreation" were to follow each period. Term examinations and final examinations for degrees were to be chiefly written, but an oral examination would be given in connection with each written one; the examination of each class was to be in the charge of a committee consisting of its teacher, another professor, and members appointed by the Executive Board. Three terms gave way to two — the first commencing on the first Friday of September and continuing twenty weeks, to be followed by a recess of four weeks; the second commencing on the fourth Friday of February and continuing twenty weeks, to be followed by a recess of eight weeks. Commencement was changed to the second Wednesday of July.

The laws also set forth certain high ideals for the conduct of courses, which may be illustrated by a few extracts:

Latin and Greek. "It will be the duty of the Professors in this department not to confine themselves to gramatical analysis, but to advance to the higher principles of interpretation, and cultivate in the student a taste for classical beauty and an acquaintance with the phases of civilization, the modes of thought and the leading political events to which these writings relate."

Modern Languages. "French, German, Spanish and Italian shall be taught. In the early part of the course, it shall be the object of the Professor to communicate a critical knowledge of the language, in order to enable the student to use it as a means of investigation. As the course advances, instruction will be given in the literature of the language."

Mathematics. "It is the design of the corporation that this study be so taught as to strengthen in the best manner the reasoning faculty of the student, cultivate the power of original demonstration, and render him familiar with the application of mathematical theorems to the practical business of life."

Natural Philosophy. "The solution of problems will . . . be required, and it is expected they will be of such a nature as to accustom him [*i.e.*, the student] to associate these studies with the practical business of life."

Civil Engineering. "It is intended that it [*i.e.*, the instruction] shall be accompanied by field labor, the examination of structures and machinery, and such attention to the solution of problems as shall enable the student in the best manner to reduce his theory to practice."

Chemistry and Physiology. "A private class will also be formed for instruction in practical chemistry, and also for original physiological research, under the immediate care of the professor, for such students as desire it."

Application of Chemistry to the Arts. "It shall be the duty of the professor to give instruction in the principles and practice of chemical analysis, so as to enable the student to prosecute investigations for himself. He will also explain the most important processes in the arts, exhibiting their defects, and suggesting the means by which they may be remedied."

Agriculture. "This course shall embrace instruction in the principles and practice of Agriculture; . . . it shall be its object to enable the student to conduct the operations of agriculture upon scientific and economical principles, with special reference, however, to the soil and climate of this portion of the United States."

Didactics. "The course in Didactics is designed at present especially for the benefit of teachers of common schools. There will be held two terms a year in this department of at least two months each. It shall be the duty of the professor of Didactics to review with the class the studies taught in common schools, and then to explain the manner of communicating knowledge to others. The other professors in the University will be expected to deliver to this class such lectures in their several departments as may be desired by the Executive Board."

The catalogue of 1850–51 shows that a beginning had been made in carrying out this ambitious program of the New System. William A. Norton, a graduate of West Point Academy and for sixteen years professor in Delaware College, had been appointed professor of civil engineering and natural philosophy. John A. Porter, who came highly recommended by Professors Liebig and Horsford, had been made professor of chemistry applied to the arts. Chairs of agriculture and didactics had also been created, but were not yet filled. The catalogue stated that the course in civil engineering would occupy a year and a half, and would include — besides theoretical instruction in mechanics, hydraulics, and "Engineering Proper" — considerable field work in surveying, locating a road, surveys for estimates of excavation, etc. The fee for the course was $30 a term, instead of $6 as in most of the courses. The class numbered ten the first term, and nine the second. Laboratory instruction in chemistry applied to the arts had to be deferred, as the laboratory was not ready. One was at length fitted up in Rhode Island Hall, at what seemed a vast expense; and the Executive Board said at the end of the year that "the arrangements for the prosecution of this branch of study are considered as perfect as those in any institution in this country." It was April, however, before the work could begin, and then a class of thirteen elected the course; of whom "the greater Part," said the President in his monthly report, were "persons preparing for the active duties of life." The fee for instruction was $30 a term, besides a charge of $55 for materials and incidentals. A course of lectures on the application of chemistry to the arts had also been planned, but Professor Porter found himself unready to give it the first winter.

This was not a very brilliant beginning. The next year showed some gain in the civil engineering course, which had nineteen students; but the class in chemistry applied to the arts numbered only eleven. The year ended unfortunately for these two departments; events which will be described later led to the resignation of both professors at the end of the first term, and temporary arrangements had to be made. In the following year the attendance in civil

[287]

engineering fell to five. For the other department, however, the Corporation had found a brilliant man in their professor of chemistry, the versatile George I. Chace. The laboratory class increased slightly under his direction; and he gave a series of popular lectures in the winter of 1852–53, which President Wayland described thus in his report to the Corporation: "One of the most interesting events in the history of the University during the year has been the brilliant success which has attended the labors of Professor Chace in the department of Chemistry applied to the Arts. . . . The class to which he first directed his attention was the workers in the precious metals. He visited their workshops and made himself familiar with the practice of their arts and the principles on which it depended. He then announced a course of Lectures on the Chemistry of the Metals. A class was immediately formed of more than 330 and the interest with which they listened to his instructions could hardly have been exceeded. At the close of the course they presented him with a splendid piece of plate." The department more than paid for itself that year; and Dr. Wayland expressed his conviction that it was only necessary to go forward, adhering firmly to the new plan as a whole.

Meanwhile more additions had been made to the Faculty. In the second term of 1850–51 Professor Gammell had been transferred to the newly created chair of history and political economy, the Rev. Robinson P. Dunn succeeding him as professor of rhetoric and English literature. Samuel S. Greene had been appointed to the chair of didactics in 1851, and in 1852 James B. Angell was made professor of modern languages. The Rev. Henry Day was now professor of natural philosophy and civil engineering. The chair of agriculture still remained vacant, however, and the law school was yet unborn. In 1853–54 the attendance was the greatest in the history of the college so far; but there were no additions to the teaching force except an assistant in chemistry. The following year, the last of Dr. Wayland's presidency, the number of students declined, and the professorships of didactics and agriculture were both vacant.

Although neither the elective system nor the scientific courses attracted the large numbers that had been so confidently hoped for, the college had gradually been finding a wider constituency, and the process was accelerated by the New System. The percentage of students from outside New England had always been small: 7 in 1800–01; 8 in 1810–11; 2 in 1821–22; 6 in 1831–32; 17 in 1836–37, the year of largest attendance up to that time; 12 in 1841–42; 22 in 1849–50, the last year under the old system. In 1851–52 it was still only 24, but rose to 28 in 1854–55; and it is significant that, in both these years, 14 per cent of the students came from the manufacturing and mercantile Middle States. The percentage from Rhode Island also gained. As far back as the catalogues go, Massachusetts had always furnished more students than Rhode Island: in 1800–01 the percentages were respectively 69 and 20; in 1810–11, 57 and 27; in 1821–22, 60 and 24; in 1831–32, 55 and 26; in 1836–37, 48 and 21; in 1841–42, 47 and 23; in 1849–50, 38 and 27. In 1851–52 and in 1854–55, however, the percentage from Rhode Island rose to 30, almost equaling that from Massachusetts, which was 31. The number of students from Rhode Island was 40 in 1849–50, 67 in 1851–52, 95 in 1853–54, and 75 in 1854–55. This increase, though encouraging, was far from satisfactory. Rhode Island had now a population of 147,545, of whom 41,513 were in Providence. The cotton and woolen industries had grown enormously in the last quarter-century; and the manufacture of tools, machines, and jewelry had also reached large proportions. The whole state was a workshop. It is not strange that so sagacious and practical a mind as President Wayland's felt that a university in the center of such a community should do far more than any other in America to guide the industrial life all about it by the application of science to the useful arts. But it is strange that he attached so much importance to popular instruction, which, however brilliant and delightful, could have no deep or lasting effect upon the practice of the arts. And it is stranger still that more of the young men of the state did not realize the value of thorough scientific education, by which they might learn, in class-room and laboratory, the applications of science to the industries they were to direct. But they did not realize it; and even if Brown University had had the funds necessary to equip it adequately for teaching science, its numbers at that time would doubtless have remained comparatively small.

In other respects, too, the New System was disappointing. Testimony that the students were of inferior quality because of lower requirements will be given in the next chapter. But even aside from that, the results were unsatisfactory. It had been expected that the elective system would stimulate a truer intellectual life, tending to transform the undergraduates from schoolboys conning tasks into university men studying great subjects. But no such effect was apparent. Where, indeed, were the forces adequate to produce such a result? The range of electives was narrow from the first, and after 1852–53 it was further restricted. In 1851–53 candidates for the degrees of A.B. and Ph.B. might elect four of the nine requisite year-courses, but after that only two; while for the degree of A.M. nine of the twelve courses were prescribed. But if all the studies had been elective, the result would have been much the same, for the courses offered in each department were so few that the student could not go far enough along any one line to become capable of independent research. The passing mark of twenty-five per cent, again, was surely a feeble incentive to intellectual effort. The substitution of written for oral examinations introduced tests that were fairer but not necessarily more stimulating.

Two features of the new regulations had in them large possibilities for good: the examination in a limited number of subjects at the end of the whole period of study, in addition to the term examinations in all subjects; and, for the master's degree, the reading of two authors outside the class-room and an examination upon them. Here was a crude approximation to the English system of honor examinations. If these examinations for degrees—three for the bachelor's and five for the master's—had been sweeping and thorough, requiring a mastery both broad and minute of a few subjects; if the student had been allowed to choose the fields in which he would thus specialize; and if a large amount of reading had been required in the two authors; then the abler students might have been inspired to manly labor in a spirit of high scholarship. But none of these conditions prevailed. The examinations were superficial; the subjects were either fixed at the beginning of the course or announced a term before the examination; and the amount of outside reading was very small—in 1854–55 consisting of a chapter in Campbell's *Philosophy of Rhetoric* and one book of Tacitus's *Historiae*. In 1855 a committee consisting of Professors Gammell and Dunn reported to the Faculty on the matter. They said that the candidates for the degree of A.M., who were to have been examined in five subjects at the end of the course, had never been examined in more than two; that good scholars estimated the study necessary to pass the examinations as equivalent to only four and a half days of uninterrupted labor; and that the examinations were made a pretext for neglecting the regular work. The committee recommended that the statute be repealed, which was done.

There are two additional pieces of evidence that the New System had done little or nothing to raise the intellectual tone of the college. It will be remembered that the results of the system of premiums had been disappointing under the old régime, few students having the ambition to compete. If the New System had done much to develop intellectual enterprise, there would have been more wrestlers for these awards; but there was no change, and in 1858 the Faculty converted the prizes into scholarships. The other evidence comes from a student's journal of the junior and senior years. The student was a bright young man, vivacious and witty, with intellectual interests in several fields; he was elected a member of Phi Beta Kappa in his junior year, and received the salutatory honor at graduation. Yet though he was above the average of his class in ability and scholarship, his journal shows a schoolboy worrying and shambling through his lessons, not a university man out on intellectual quests. To the last he is forever making hasty preparation for the next recitation, often in another class the hour before, writing the required essays in a rush, and doing almost no reading as a supplement to the textbooks. Both he and his classmates are constantly calculating their chances of being "called up" to recite, and are full of schoolboy hilarity when a class exercise is omitted. On December 31, 1854, he truly diagnoses his case as follows: "On the whole, I fear most of this year has been wasted. I have managed to work through my College duties; but have done nothing beyond the text-books & what I have done has been listlessly." This corresponds exactly to what

President Wayland had pictured as the result of the old system. Yet this student was under the New System throughout his course, and took the degree of Master of Arts at the end.

Some of the new laws directly affecting the Faculty also proved unsuccessful. One hour and twenty minutes as a class-room period evidently exceeded human powers of endurance; certain courses never had it, and in 1858 it was made optional in all. Written examinations met with general favor for a time. President Wayland reported in 1851 that the method was "universally allowed to be perfectly fair, and much more manly and scholarlike than the previous method." But some reaction soon appeared, and in 1853 the Executive Board permitted the Faculty to substitute oral for written examinations at will, "sufficient time being always allowed for entire thoroughness." How to get enough time for each student without unduly prolonging the examination period as a whole was the problem; the Faculty finally hit upon the device of giving an oral examination to one-third of the class, chosen by lot, and a written one to the rest. This system, although unpopular with the undergraduates, was retained for a while.

Student fees, as a partial substitute for salaries, excited strong opposition. The plan had long been a favorite one with Dr. Wayland, and the time had now come when it might be tried. For the year 1851–52 the professors were given their choice between a salary of $1200 and a salary of $500 augmented by fees from the students attending their courses. Professors Dunn and Porter chose the $1200; the rest tried the new plan. Just what the results were is not known; but for the next year the Executive Board recommended that the salaries be $900 plus *half* the fees. In 1853–54, when the number of students was greatest, the

President received $1839.50 in all; Professor Caswell, $1826; Professor Chace, $2014; Professor Gammell, $1400, to which $200 was added later; Professor Lincoln, $1440; Nelson Wheeler, the new professor of Greek, $800. Professor Gammell protested against the method in a letter to the Executive Board in May, 1853, saying that it gave him less salary than any other of the older professors, and less even than some of the younger, because the subjects he taught came late in the college course when the classes were always smaller. Professor Chace, although he had personally profited by the system, argued against it in a letter to the Executive Board on September 14, 1855: he said that it had been introduced by the Corporation and "pressed upon the Faculty by every argument at their command"; that it was unjust, and did not furnish "wholesome or beneficial stimulus"; and that he therefore looked to the board to secure him a certain salary the next year without fees. By 1856 the old plan, with salaries of $1200, was in force again.

In this time of reform the undergraduates wished to put into effect some ideas of their own, and the second year of the New System saw the outbreak of a serious revolt, the fundamental cause of which was a clash between the new spirit of freedom and certain old restrictions. In the spring of 1850 President Wayland reported that the inspection of rooms was less effective than before, while the students' temptations were greater: "Allurements to vice and dissipation have increased to a painful degree in our city. Two theatres are open every night, concerts, lectures, billiard rooms are exerting all their solicitations." A committee was appointed to consider the situation, and presented a rather hysterical report. "While the Professors adhered to celibacy, & slept in the Colleges, they were able to exercise a kindly supervision of the Undergraduates. But when they exchanged the always anxious & not seldom vexing duties inseperable from the government of a hundred young men, for the light cares of domestic life, the students were left in the exclusive possession of one of the Colleges, & in the other there was no one invested with authority except the Steward." This condition had existed for years, and "surely it is a fearful one"; it was true there had been no evidence of great wickedness, "but who can tell what scenes of iniquity are silently enacted?" The appointment of proctors was out of the question, for the salaries of three at $400 each would exceed by $200 the receipts from room rents; and the committee therefore recommended that all the students be lodged in private families. But the Corporation objected to emptying the dormitories and losing the rents, and so when the New System went into effect the Executive Board tried instead to enforce stricter supervision by the Faculty.

This was the situation in the autumn of 1851, when several causes of irritation combined to arouse the students. The literary societies issued a call for a petition against the rule forbidding undergraduate organizations to meet in the evening, and took a bold tone: "Let petitions couched in the strongest language and most forcible terms be presented to the president. Such petitions expressing the united sentiments of a whole community cannot be disregarded. . . . Shall the will of one man unsupported by reason overcome the settled convictions of hundreds?" The petition was rejected. The chapter of Psi Upsilon also petitioned to be allowed to meet at night, reminding the Corporation that "there is a potent charm in the stillness of the evening hours peculiarly favorable to literary exercises"; but this request, too, was refused.

While the students were smarting under these rebuffs,

their discontent was greatly increased by another occurrence, which had serious results. Professor A. L. Koeppen, formerly of the University of Athens, who had been granted the use of a college room for a course of lectures the year before, was for some reason denied a renewal of the privilege; and the Executive Board voted, on October 10, 1851, "That no Instruction or Lectures be given in Brown University except by the officers appointed by the Corporation." Action seemingly more opposed to the spirit of the New System can hardly be conceived. Professor Koeppen secured a hall, and invited the university students to attend his lectures free of charge, as they had done in the previous year. Some members of the Faculty excused the students from evening study hours that they might go, while others held to the rules. On November 7 the Executive Board appointed a committee to inform the Faculty that they were expected to do their visiting duty rigidly "and especially on Monday evening," when the lectures occurred. There followed the so-called rebellion of 1851, during which the students used "the most abusive epithets towards the President and Faculty," and made disturbances in chapel. In January the President conferred with the Executive Board on "the insubordination of the last term," and laid it chiefly to the lack of unanimity in the Faculty about the enforcement of discipline. A committee having confirmed his opinion, the board voted that it was "expedient" that Mr. Greene and Professors Porter and Norton "should terminate their connexion with the University." The three resigned forthwith. The acuteness of the crisis, as the Executive Board saw it, appears in their statement to Professor Norton that they "were unanimously of the opinion that it would not be safe to commence another term under the same circumstances as the last." The professors, on the other hand, denied that they had intentionally done anything to stir up rebellion; but they admitted that they regarded as "degrading" the rule which required them to report monthly to the Executive Board the number of "police visits" they had made. They added this very significant statement: "An impression may have existed, that men, coming from other Colleges, were likely to bring with them more or less of the spirit of the Institutions with which they had been previously connected. It is possible that such an inference was made from our manner and bearing, in our intercourse with Students." Here is doubtless the key to the whole situation. By adopting the New System, and bringing in such men as these, the Corporation had evoked a spirit of freedom which flew straight in the teeth of old restrictions. The Executive Board were probably right in thinking that the rules could not be enforced while men of this temper were on the Faculty; but the need to get rid of them is a severe commentary on the narrowness of the rules and the policy of the board.

It is apparently not a mere coincidence that the earliest extant "mock programs," satirizing the Faculty with humor almost as coarse as it is dull, date from this agitated time. Pranks of various kinds seem to have been more common then than they had been for a generation. "Junior Burials" of textbooks likewise began in this period, the earliest extant program being of the year 1853. The procession formed at half-past eight in the evening, at the corner of Hope and Waterman Streets, marched about the city, and finally took boat; the burial of textbooks by Whately and Campbell, with a Latin service and an oration, occurred off Fox Point. The burial two years later is thus described in the student's journal previously mentioned:

But it was growing dark, dressed up in my worst rig, & . . . started for the obsequies. . . . Procession formed in Hope St. Gave us Seniors the lead & I had the honor of bearing the new banner, fresh from Mark's hands, "The Supreme Canon of the New Analytic." — Represents Sir Wm: Hamilton, in the guise of the devil touching off with his fiery tail a cannon from the mouth of which fly in separate directions Messrs. Locke, Aristotle & Bacon. — The Hearse, a buggy with the top off, supporting a genuine coffin (Ch. Alden fecit), with a huge black pall (ornamented with a trio of skulls, each with its attendant couple of cross-bones) was drawn by four white horses, appropriately caparisoned, led by four impromptu darkies & driven by a genuine white man. . . . Have reason to think we made a good appearance. At all events our torches shed their glare upon a crowd of spectators, including many ladies. . . . Then a pleasant row down the bay, I not having to touch the oars, more trouble in drawing up around the channel post, when the services began. Back again to the landing. Rather chilly — Marched up to the colleges again, breaking the solemn stillness of the midnight. Broke up with appropriate shouts.

The senior and junior exhibitions still continued. The student's journal gives the following description of the senior exhibition of November 25, 1854:

Almost all in the library before me. Prof. Dunn impatiently tells me to put on my gown. I do so & feel like a criminal preparing for execution. . . . But while we are wandering round & round, nervous and terrified, the hall above is filling & one by one dignified Profs. & Members of the Corporation are entering the Library Door below. Cool, calm & collected they scarcely deign a look, much less a glance of pity, upon us; they care not how quickly the moments fly. . . . Soon the table is pushed one side, the doors swung wide open & I hear a voice calling.

President & Corporation of the Univ.

Regent & Members of the Faculty.

Speakers.

The Doctor is absent again & the Regent supplies his place. . . . We are at the top of the stairs & entering the room. As the speakers cross the threshold the ominous, measured Initiation Stamp begins about the door & continues while we slowly move up the broad aisle. . . . All subsides into momentary silence. The regent from his elevated seat behind our scaffold, nods towards the gallery and the band strikes up what seems a dirge. . . . The music stops, the Regent reads the first name on the programme & in 6 minutes perhaps, so far as Dearth is concerned, all is over & I am almost perfectly happy. I take my seat, on the *second* bench now, with a confused recollection of having made my way up to the platform & my bow to the regent & to the audience amidst a *very* moderate show of applause, then having yelled at the audience with gestures now and then for a few minutes, . . . making some terrible grammatical mistakes, seeing Marshall John Tobey standing composedly at the end of the aisle & girls giggling around, before me, and then making my final double bow & my exit. Sic transit.

Commencements under the New System had many interesting features, although the city no longer honored them by keeping general holiday. In 1851 and 1852 Commencement day, in accordance with the Laws of 1850, was the second Wednesday in July; in 1853 it was restored to the first week in September. A novel feature in the Commencement of 1851 was the awarding of the new degree of Bachelor of Philosophy to one student; it was done in English, and *The Providence Journal* observed, "If the enunciation lacked the sonorous reverberations of the Latin, it was pronounced with an unction that showed the gratification of the speaker." This year, for the first time, the Commencement dinner was served in a tent, capable of seating six hundred, which was pitched behind University Hall. At the dinner in 1853 four hundred and fifty persons were present; obituary notices of alumni who had died during the year were read by Professor Gammell, and there were besides nine speeches and a poem. In 1854 more than half the graduating class took as their first degree that of Master of Arts, now given for the first time under the new conditions. The literary exercises of the day before were of unusual interest. At the Phi Beta Kappa meeting, in the First Baptist Church, Professor Edwards A. Park was the orator, and George William Curtis the poet. The sermon that evening, in the same place, before the Society of Missionary Inquiry, was preached by Henry Ward Beecher; although the weather was stifling, his address, said the *Journal*, was "so eloquent as to hold in rapt attention, for nearly two hours, the most crowded and indeed the largest audience we have ever seen assembled in that church."

The Commencement of 1855 had a peculiar but painful interest, for it was known that Dr. Wayland had resigned and would never again preside in the old church. After the degrees had been conferred, Chancellor Tobey addressed the audience, reviewing the achievements of the retiring president; then turning to Dr. Wayland he said, in the quaintly impressive speech of his sect: "PRESIDENT WAYLAND, — on receiving thy resignation of the Presidency of Brown University and Professor of Moral and Intellectual Philosophy, a series of resolutions with some prefatory remarks were offered which the Corporation unanimously accepted, and directed that they be recorded and a copy of them furnished to thee. Believe me, when I assure thee, that they are not the record of mere formal words, but that they embody the heartfelt sentiments of those who have so long and so happily labored with thee to promote the interests of the College. They but feebly convey our sense of the good thou hast accomplished." He then read the resolutions, including the following: "*Resolved*, That in accepting this resignation the Corporation deem it proper to express their high sense of the fidelity, ability, singleness of purpose, and eminent success with which he has discharged the varied and important duties of his appointment — manifesting at all times his entire devotion to the welfare of the University — with unwearied assiduity watching over its interests — imparting to the students who have been educated here the rich treasures of his cultivated and original mind — imbuing them with that intellectual and moral culture which prepares for the fulfilment, with dignity and honor, of the duties which appertain to them as citizens, and giving them that religious instruction which qualifies for the discharge of their paramount duties to God.''

The scene at the Commencement dinner, where five hundred gathered under the tent, was also of exceptional interest. Resolutions adopted the day before by the alumni were presented to the President by Judge Benjamin F. Thomas, of the Massachusetts supreme court, a member of the class of 1830, who said: ''A quarter of a century has passed since I left these walls with your blessing. I have seen something of men and of the world since. I esteem it to-day the happiest event of my life that brought me here, the best gift of an ever kind Providence to me, that I was permitted for three years to sit at the feet of your instruction. Others may speak and think of the writer and scholar, my tribute is to the great teacher.'' Professor Felton, of Harvard, responded to the sentiment proposed by Dr. Wayland, ''Harvard University and Brown University—Near neighbors and excellent friends.'' Addresses were made by members of the classes of 1822, 1829, and 1838, the representative of the last being the Rev. Ezekiel G. Robinson, later president of Brown University. Barnas Sears was also present, and was greeted as President Wayland's successor with ''enthusiastic and reiterated applause.''

The resignation of President Wayland did not come as a surprise to his official associates or his friends, who knew that for some years the duties of his office had weighed upon him heavily. The formulation and launching of the New System had involved not only much labor but many worries and responsibilities. At the end of the first year he wrote, ''I would not, for any earthly consideration, go through the same work again.'' During 1852–53 every hour that he could snatch from college duties he gave to writing his life of Adoniram Judson, which appeared in the autumn of 1853. The next year he published his *Elements of Intellectual Philosophy*. Professor Caswell had been appointed regent in 1852, to relieve him of some cares, but this relief was not enough. In his letter of resignation on August 20, 1855, he wrote, "After more than twenty eight years of service the conviction is pressed upon me that relaxation and change of labor have become to me a matter of indispensable necessity." The Chancellor, in addressing the Corporation on the following day, said: "He has been admonished that continued persistence in one field of labor may interrupt the vigorous and healthy action of the best balanced physical and mental powers." His sons record that when the bell rang for the opening of the new college year, after his resignation, Dr. Wayland stopped and listened and then remarked, "No one can conceive the unspeakable relief and freedom which I feel at this moment to hear that bell ring, and to know, for the first time in nearly twenty-nine years, that it calls me to no duty."

For a year or two he lived in comparative leisure. In the spring of 1856 he moved into a house which he had been building, situated at the southeast corner of Angell and Governor Streets; and in the large garden he spent many happy and healthful hours. But it was impossible for him to rest long. His own nature and calls from without constantly summoned him to labors which, although less harmful than a continuance of his college duties would have been, undoubtedly hastened his end. He served as fellow of the college from 1855 to 1858. After Charles Sumner was assaulted in the Senate, Dr. Wayland addressed a meeting of the citizens of Providence, on June 7, 1856, and made a powerful impression. He attended the Commencement at Yale College that summer, where he spoke at a meeting of the alumni. Few Commencement speeches have ever had such consequences. One of his hearers was Andrew D. White, later the first president of Cornell University, who says: "He rose, and his appearance made an impression upon me, such that I doubt whether those who saw him constantly, now carry in their minds a more vivid portrait of him than I do at this moment. He spoke of the possible rise or decline of this nation, of the duties of educated men, and said that he believed this country was fast approaching a 'switching-off place' towards good or towards evil, and added that . . . the west was the place for earnest men to work in, to influence the nation. That was all; but it changed my whole life. I gave up law, literature, and politics, and thenceforward my strongest desire was to work anywhere and anyhow at the west in education."

This is proof enough that Dr. Wayland had not lost his remarkable power over young men. But his chief work, in the remaining years of his life, was to be religious and charitable. His publications were henceforth chiefly religious; and in February, 1857, on the death of the pastor of the First Baptist Church, Dr. Wayland consented to act as its pastor for a time. Into this work he threw himself, for sixteen months, with a zeal beyond his strength. The manifest effects of this strain warned him again that he must husband his powers, and he therefore declined, in 1858, an urgent call to the presidency of a new university. He resumed a leisurely revision of his *Elements of Moral Science;* but even this labor was too much, and in May, 1860, he had preliminary symptoms of paralysis. By rest and care, however, he slowly regained a large measure of strength, and occupied himself with writing his "Reminiscences." By Commencement week of this year he had so far recovered that he invited the alumni to visit him at his house, and a large number did so. This pleasant gathering henceforth occurred every year until the year of his death. At the Commencement of 1861 the bust of Wayland which is now in Sayles Hall was given to the college by alumni from nearly every class that had come under his instruction in Brown University; the Hon. William H. Seward, his pupil at Union College, was also a contributor. The bust was made by Thomas Ball, then at work upon the equestrian statue of Washington for the city of Boston, and was regarded as a very good likeness.

The charitable labors of these years of retirement reveal one of the most attractive sides of Dr. Wayland's nature. He continued to serve as a trustee of Butler Hospital until 1863, and he aided in the establishment of the Rhode Island Hospital in the same year. He took a deep interest in the Providence Reform School, visiting it every week, and often addressing the boys, whom he knew personally and who delighted to see and hear him. From 1851 to 1859 he was chairman of the board of inspectors of the state prison, and prepared the annual reports. Owing largely to his supervision, the sanitary, moral, and financial condition of the institution vastly improved during this period. Nor was his relation to the prisoners merely official: he often preached to them, and was for many years the superintendent of the prison Sunday-school and the teacher of a class; on the release of prisoners he aided them in various ways. During the hard times of 1857 he originated the idea of the Providence Aid Society, a kind of employment bureau, and acted as its president until his death.

The author of *The Elements of Moral Science* was bound to side with the party which set its face against the extension of slavery. Dr. Wayland voted for Fremont in 1856, and for Lincoln in 1860. He had for several years been president of the American Peace Society; but when the Civil War broke out, he stood staunchly by the government. To a friend he wrote in April, 1861 : " I have been this afternoon to two flag-raisings; on Wednesday I addressed the troops, and marched with them to the wharf; our flag goes up to-morrow or Monday. Mrs. Wayland cannot sew, but she and I have been making bandages." He followed the campaigns with interest so intense that he could not endure to read details of battles, but he was most deeply concerned for the moral issues at stake. As the time for a new presidential election drew near, he wrote to a friend : "To beat the Copperheads is nothing. They ought to be crushed. We have all the argument, the honesty, the character, the patriotism, and power of appeal to the American heart."

When the news of Lincoln's assassination reached Providence, on April 15, 1865, a committee called upon Dr. Wayland and asked him to address a public meeting in the city that evening; he declined, feeling that his strength was not sufficient. "Will you address them if they will come to your house?" He consented. Then was paid an impressive and unique tribute to the personal power of the man. At nightfall, in spite of pouring rain, some fifteen hundred citizens gathered and moved towards the plain house on Governor Street. What followed is best told in the words of Professor Chace:

The long dark column winds its way over the hill and into the valley. As it moves onward, the wailings of the dirge and the measured tread are the only sounds which fall upon the still air. Having reached the residence of President Wayland, it pours itself in a dense throng around a slightly raised platform in front of it. Presently he appears, to address for the last time, as it proves, his assembled fellow citizens. It is the same noble presence which many there had in years long gone by,

gazed upon with such pride and admiration from seats in the old chapel.
. . . The glorious intellectual power which sat upon those features is
veiled beneath the softer lines of moral grace and beauty. It is not now
the Athenian orator, but one of the old prophets, from whose touched
lips flow forth the teachings of inspired wisdom. The dead first claims
his thought. He recounts most appreciatively his great services, and
dwells with loving eulogy upon his unswerving patriotism and his high
civic virtues. Next the duties of the living and the lessons of the hour
occupy attention. Then come words of devout thanksgiving, of holy
trust, of sublime faith, uttered as he only ever uttered them. They
fall upon that waiting assembly, like a blessed benediction, assuaging
grief, dispelling gloom, and kindling worship in every bosom. God is
no longer at a distance, but all around and within them. They go away
strengthened and comforted.

On the last day of September Francis Wayland died of
paralysis; and many who had heard him that April night
attended his funeral services in the First Baptist Church
on October 4, and followed his body to its resting-place in
the old North Burying Ground. The Corporation, the Faculty, the undergraduates, and eminent men from various
walks of life and many regions united in paying him this
last honor.

The death of a man so long prominent in the educational
and religious world drew forth estimates of him and his
work from many sources. The Corporation, Faculty, and
alumni passed appropriate resolutions; commemorative sermons were preached by clergymen of various faiths; articles
appeared in countless newspapers and magazines. James B.
Angell, in *The Providence Journal* of October 2, wrote:

During the last forty years has any other life been such a force and
power in this city and this State as that, which is now quenched in
death? . . . His pupils will all testify that he was President in deed,
as well as in name. No one could look upon his face and his form
without feeling instinctively that he was born to command. . . . He
was not ordinarily an eloquent or even a fluent speaker. But we have

never listened to more eloquent or effective appeals than we have heard from his lips in the old chapel at morning or evening prayers and in the conference meetings. He lifted his hearers as by a resistless power up to his own level and animated them with his own spirit. . . . His class-room was not simply a place of recitations, but the scene of the highest intellectual enjoyment. The young men under his instruction learned not only the particular science he was teaching, but the best mode of approaching and studying any science. They learned how to use their minds. . . . But Dr. Wayland's preëminent power as an instructor lay in his almost unrivalled faculty of lending moral impulses to his pupils. . . . We believe it to be literally true that no student, however thoughtless, ever pursued the study of moral philosophy under Dr. Wayland without receiving moral impressions, which were never effaced. . . . Life, in his view, was made up of duties to be performed. Not that he took a gloomy view of life. He was fond of good companionship. We have known few talkers more entertaining, congenial and instructive than he was. He had a fund of good stories and amusing illustrations. He had an unusually sharp eye for the ridiculous. No man had a heartier laugh. His wit was as keen as a Damascus blade. He was as quick at repartee as he was prompt with an answer in discussion. But he believed that whatever duty was to be done was to be done with earnestness and with noble aims. He had little patience with those who fill their hours with trifling pursuits or give themselves up to mere dilettantism. Meanness of soul he utterly despised, and his rebukes of it were simply terrible.

Another pupil, Professor George P. Fisher, of Yale College, in a discriminating article in *The New Englander* of January, 1866, said:

He was unquestionably an able man intellectually. Yet he was not a subtle metaphysician. He had no great relish for the nice distinctions in which the metaphysician takes delight, and which are vital in his science. . . . Nor was Dr. Wayland an orator,—certainly not in the recognized and conventional use of the term. His intonations and gestures were conformed to no accepted standard, nor would they be considered pleasing. No more was he, properly speaking, a scholar. He did not aim to acquaint himself fully with the literature of any branch of knowledge. His reading was decidedly less extensive than is usual with persons of his ability and standing. Yet, for all this, Dr. Wayland was a great man. So every one felt who knew him. No one could be in the room with him and not be struck with his superiority. With no affectation of dignity, but with manners perfectly simple and even familiar, he commanded respect wherever he was. In the class-room, although he allowed full freedom and was quite willing to have his opinions controverted, he yet cast a spell over the minds of his pupils from which it was hard to break loose. . . . Nothing seemed to intervene between his mind and the truth, to warp his vision or bias his judgment. He certainly had little respect for authority. Perhaps he had too little; but he was saved from being cramped by an influence which has often enslaved the human intelligence. The usual forms in which Christian doctrine is stated, he thought open to criticism. He agreed substantially in his theology with the great body of Christians, but the *formulas* of theology had no sacredness in his eyes.

Professor Diman wrote thus in *The Atlantic Monthly* for January, 1868:

What power in his very presence, defying all description, as the most speaking faces defy the art of the photographer! What reserved force, sleeping in silent depths till stirred by great occasion! Such as know him only from his writings have gained no adequate impression of the man. . . . Never did Dr. Wayland seem so grand, one might almost say inspired, as in those unbidden gushes of emotion that would sometimes convulsively shake his great frame and choke his utterance. The finest paragraph in his missionary sermon would not compare for eloquence with some of those pungent appeals that at times electrified the students at their Wednesday-evening prayer-meeting. . . . There was never any cant of stereotyped exhortation, never any attempt to rouse a superficial emotion, but always direct appeal to conscience and to all the highest instincts of youthful hearts. In this most difficult task of dealing with young men at the crises of their spiritual history, Dr. Wayland was unsurpassed. How wise and tender his counsels at such a time! How many who have timidly stolen to his study door, their souls burdened with strange thoughts, and bewildered with unaccustomed questionings, remember with what instant appreciation of their errand the green shade was lifted from the eye, the volume thrown aside, and with what genuine, hearty interest that whole countenance would beam. . . . These were the moments when the springs of his nature were revealed.

A coldly critical opinion, apparently based on second-hand knowledge, was given in *The Nation* of November 28, 1867:

He had a good, serviceable intellect, hard worked at all times in its owner's life, deficient in imagination and humor, incapable, probably, of very high polish, strong rather than acute or delicate, and excellent in the executive faculties. . . . Intellectually, he was more than a common man, without being at all a great one; he wrote much, but he added to literature nothing of permanent value. . . . Morally considered, he was a man to be much admired; admirable rather than very lovable, perhaps, but certainly admirable, doing with all his might every duty which he thought to be laid upon him. The cause of good education, of good morals, had his intelligent, laborious, self-sacrificing service from his youth till his death.

The judgment of a critical but sympathetic outsider was expressed in *The North American Review* of April, 1868 :

Dr. Wayland's will always be a very considerable name, not only in the history of the respectable and influential denomination to which he belonged, but still more in the educational history of New England. . . . Yet Dr. Wayland does not appear to us to have been at all a man of genius, nor was his own education of a large or liberal type. The faults and the excellences of his character were strongly marked. He was hampered by a narrow creed; but his deep religious earnestness went far towards atoning for its imperfections. He was not a very learned man; but he had to the highest degree the power of using the learning he possessed. He was a born teacher and administrator; and he had those qualities which gain the confidence and conciliate the good-will of young men, — an honest simplicity of character, a hearty hatred of all pretence, an inflexible will, and an untiring perseverance. . . . It is, perhaps, as an educational innovator, as one of the first in this country to anticipate that change in the course and character of a liberal education which is now so rapidly taking place, that Dr. Wayland will be longest remembered. . . . He would have been a greater man, if he had not been a sectarian, and if the aesthetic side of his nature had early received its due share of cultivation.

For understanding of Francis Wayland posterity must rely chiefly upon what he did and what was said of him by men who knew him. But something may perhaps be added by one who studies him in his writings, unaffected by the magnetism of his personal presence and helped by the perspective of time. Such a critic is struck with his likeness to Samuel Johnson. The bottom quality in each was masculine common sense. The useful, the moral, and the religious appealed to both more than the imaginative, the aesthetic, or the speculative. Even in style the likeness holds: each had a gift of direct speech, sometimes delivered with the force of a knock-down blow. Johnson himself might have made the reply which Wayland gave to an English clergyman who apologized for not inviting him to preach, on the ground that the congregation disliked his views on abolition: "Sir," rejoined Wayland, "when I ask for your pulpit, it will be time enough for you to refuse it." The early written style of each was more formal and elaborate than the later. The later style of Dr. Wayland has been illustrated already; the following passage from his missionary sermon of 1823 may serve as an example of his earlier style:

The church has commenced her march. Samaria has with one accord believed the gospel. Antioch has become obedient to the faith. The name of Christ has been proclaimed throughout Asia Minor. The temples of the gods, as though smitten by an invisible hand, are deserted. The citizens of Ephesus cry out in despair, Great is Diana of the Ephesians! Licentious Corinth is purified by the preaching of Christ crucified. Persecution puts forth her arm to arrest the spreading "superstition." But the progress of the faith cannot be stayed. The church of God advances unhurt, amidst racks and dungeons, persecutions and death; yea, "smiles at the drawn dagger, and defies its point." She has entered Italy, and appears before the walls of the Eternal City. Idolatry falls prostrate at her approach. Her ensign floats in triumph over the capitol. She has placed upon her brow the diadem of the Caesars!

President Wayland's solid force of intellect, and his lack of subtlety, high imagination, and wide learning, are everywhere apparent in his writings. His *Elements of Political Economy* makes no claim to originality, and is strictly elementary, cogently setting forth the main principles of the orthodox school, without attempting to investigate the more complex problems of industrial life. He put more of his personality into *The Elements of Moral Science*, but even that is dry reading to-day; it presses moral law upon the conscience by solid argument, but is wholly lacking in sense for the twilight regions of the soul and quite devoid of speculative or imaginative charm. Chancellor Kent gave it its due when he wrote, "I do not know of any ethical treatise in which our duties to God, and to our fellow-men, are laid down with more precision, simplicity, clearness, energy, and truth." *The Daily Advocate*, in praising the abridged edition, unwittingly pointed out the limitations of the larger book as well: "It is metaphysics reduced to practical common sense, and made subservient to Christianity." Like all his textbooks it ignores historical development; so far as reference to thinkers before him is concerned, it might almost have been written by Adam. In the preface he does mention Paley and acknowledge indebtedness to Butler; but the following statement is far more significant: "When I commenced the undertaking, I attempted to read extensively, but soon found it so difficult to arrive at any definite results, in this manner, that the necessities of my situation obliged me to rely upon my own reflection." One of this temper never could have been a great scholar or even in any broad sense a learned man; and it must have been his educational work, not his learning, that won him a degree of LL.D. from Harvard University in 1852.

After reading Dr. Wayland's addresses on public affairs, one is at first inclined to think that he was by nature designed for political life and had in him the making of a statesman; yet even here his fundamental interest was that of the moralist and religious teacher. His addresses on the duties of an American citizen, on the panic of 1837, on the Dorr War, on obedience to the civil magistrate, all get their inspiration from the moral and religious questions involved. He wrote to a friend in 1856, "The only position the world could offer me, which I have thought I should like, is that of a judge of a court whose decisions involved grave questions of right." It was in the realm of ethics that he was greatest. His moral earnestness had in it something of the sublime, although it was too little relieved by appreciation of the lighter and more graceful things of life. His independence was at times heroic. True at once to his intellectual convictions and his conscience, he calmly stood up in a community devoted to the doctrine of a high protective tariff and year after year taught free trade to the sons of rich protectionists. His courage was shown even more by his treatise, *The Limitations of Human Responsibility*, in 1838, in which he said: "As *citizens of the United States*, we have no power whatever either to abolish slavery in the southern States; or to do any thing, of which the direct intention is to abolish it." His words about abolition societies, in the same work, required yet greater fearlessness in a Baptist minister and Northern college president at that time: "They have already become the tools of third rate politicians. They have raised a violent agitation, without presenting any definite means of constitutionally accomplishing their object. . . . They have rivetted, indefinitely, the bonds of the slave, in those very States in which they were, a few years since, falling off; and, every where throughout the South, they have rendered the servitude of the enslaved vastly more rigorous than it ever was before."

This same sturdy intellect and stern moral sense held him firmly to an unsectarian policy as president of Brown University. He was deeply attached to the principles of his denomination, which has probably never felt in closer touch with the college, in all legitimate and wholesome ways, than it did under his administration; but he never violated the catholic spirit of the college charter. In 1834 the Hon. Marcus Morton, a justice of the Massachusetts supreme court, wrote to President Wayland that he had certain objections to sending his son to Brown University, and referred to its supposed sectarianism, although denying that this was what made him hesitate. Wayland bluntly replied: "With my views of the responsibleness of a Teacher I would never advise a friend to place a son under the care of instructors who were capable of prostituting their official influence to the promotion of Sectarian views. As you have come to the conclusion that such is preeminently the character of this Institution I should therefore feel bound to dissuade you from entering your son here." When, in 1843, the Corporation requested the President to preach in the chapel every Sunday, and made the attendance of the students obligatory, they were scrupulous to add, "Excepting those who are under age whose parents or guardians by letter to the President express their desire that they should attend elsewhere, and also excepting those who are of age and express their conscientious objection so to do." Dr. Wayland was equally careful not to violate religious liberty, assuring the students on the first Sunday that "the character of the discourses would not be at all sectarian "; and in one of the later sermons he said: "In addressing you, young gentlemen, I am of no sect. Never, since I have been an instructor, . . . have I uttered a word with the conscious intention of proselyting you to the denomination of which I am a member. . . . You have all your own religious preferences, as you are connected with the different persuasions of Protestant Christianity. We would have you enjoy these preferences to the uttermost; and in this institution you have, from the beginning, enjoyed them to the uttermost, not as a favor, but as an inalienable right." His freedom from foolish narrowness also appears in an unpublished letter of January 18, 1858, referring to a proposed Baptist translation of the Bible: "A new translation may be useful, as a book of reference or otherwise. This is a different thing from pledging the whole denomination to a Baptist version. . . . I am as much opposed to a *Baptist* version as ever & as much as I would be to a *Methodist* or *Episcopalian* or any other version."

Wayland's opinions on education, as set forth in addresses before the American Institute of Instruction in 1830 and 1854, increase one's admiration for his good sense, shrewdness, and breadth of view. The earlier address shows his trend toward the utilitarian in education, which resulted later in his emphasis upon scientific and industrial training. "The object of the science of Education," he says, much in the line of Huxley's thought many years later, "is, to render mind the fittest possible instrument for discovering, applying, and obeying, the laws under which God has placed the universe." He ridicules the theory that discipline, not knowledge, is the end of education: "If you taught a boy rhetoric, and he could not write English, it has become sufficient to say that the grand object was, not to teach the structure of sentences, but to strengthen the faculties. . . .

If, after six or seven years of study of the languages, he had no more taste for the classics than for Sanscrit, and sold his books to the highest bidder, resolved never again to look into them, it was all no matter, — he had been study-ing, to strengthen his faculties, while by this very process his faculties have been enfeebled almost to annihilation.'' Yet he did not ignore the cultural aim, saying: ''I think it can be conclusively proved, that the classics could be so taught as to give additional acuteness to the discrimination, more delicate sensibility to the taste, and more overflowing rich-ness to the imagination. . . . Would not teaching them bet-ter be the sure way of silencing the clamor against them?'' Nor did he fail to insist that behind all methods must be the vitalizing power of personality: ''Let us never forget that the business of an instructer begins where the office of a book ends. It is the action of mind upon mind, exciting, awakening, showing by example the power of reasoning and the scope of generalization, and rendering it impossible that the pupil should not think; this is the noble and the enno-bling duty of an instructer.'' The later address is notable for its broad review of the progress of education in America dur-ing the preceding quarter-century. It ends with an eloquent passage on the work of the teacher, the concluding lines of which may well stand here as his own most fitting praise; for Francis Wayland will be longest remembered because of what he did to educate the young men of his day and to influence the education of the future: ''Our best efforts in behalf of our pupils are frequently those which are most rarely appreciated. But let us remember that truth is the daughter of time. The results of honest and faithful effort will, in the end, be acknowledged; but whether acknow-ledged or not, there they remain, and they can never be an-nihilated. We labor not to shape rude matter into forms of beauty or magnificence, but to cultivate the immortal mind, to invigorate the intellect, and adorn with social grace and elevate by Christian principles, the spiritual nature of man.''

CHAPTER VIII

PRESIDENT SEARS'S ADMINISTRATION

MODIFICATION OF THE NEW SYSTEM : SCHOLARSHIPS AND NEW ENDOW-
MENT : SOCIAL LIFE AND ATHLETICS : THE CIVIL WAR

AT the time of Dr. Wayland's resignation the most prominent Baptist educator in the United States, after himself, was the Rev. Barnas Sears, and consequently there was
general satisfaction when he was chosen president of Brown
University on August 21, 1855.

President Sears, the son of a farmer, was born in Sandis-
field, Massachusetts, a small village among the Berkshire
hills, on November 19, 1802. After preparatory study under
a neighboring clergyman and then in the University Grammar School, he entered Brown in the spring of 1822, and
graduated in 1825. "Of his course as a college student,"
says his biographer, Dr. Hovey, "but little is known. Yet
from a statement of later years it is certain that he made no
persistent effort to stand at the head of his class in recitation, but preferred a broader scholarship, without 'cram-
ming.'" His poverty and determination alike are seen in his
walking to Boston and back, at one time during his college
course, to borrow money. He taught school in the long
winter vacations, and in the summers laid stone walls. After
graduation he took a course in Newton Theological Institution, and became pastor of the First Baptist Church in Hart-
ford in 1827; but a bronchial affection, from which he was
henceforth never wholly free, caused him to resign in 1829
and accept the professorship of ancient languages in Hamilton Literary and Theological Institution, now Colgate University. In 1833 he went abroad for two years of study under
the great German scholars of the day,—Tholuck, Gesenius,
Bopp, Grimm, Neander, and others,—laying the founda-

[317]

tions of that learning for which he is distinguished among. the presidents of Brown University. At this time, too, he began to collect his magnificent library of some seven thousand volumes, chiefly in Latin and German. The year after his return he was called to a professorship in Newton Theological Institution, where he remained until 1848, serving also as president after 1838. In this position he gained a high reputation as a scholar and teacher; Harvard University gave him the degree of S.T.D. in 1841, and from 1841 to 1851 he was a fellow of Brown University. In 1848 he succeeded Horace Mann as secretary of the Massachusetts Board of Education, and during the next seven years he made permanent the reforms which the former had introduced, disarming opposition by his tact and geniality.

In his personality, as well as by training and reputation, Dr. Sears was peculiarly adapted to assume the guidance of Brown University when Dr. Wayland resigned it. The two men were of types so manifestly different that the merits of each could be admitted without invidious comparisons; and the new president had the combined tact and firmness needed for making certain changes in policy. His gentle nature had also a soothing effect that was most wholesome. Even in the reports of the presidents to the Executive Board it is easy to feel, in passing from the old administration to the new, that a more gracious although resolute spirit has taken the helm.

The students soon responded to the President's lovable personality. In a report of March 8, 1856, he says, "There appears to be a cordial feeling towards the Faculty, without a single demonstration of ill-will." In October of the same year he reports that, as a preventive measure, he has talked freely with the students, "as a friend, not as President," spreading before them his " views of the kind of intercourse & mode of life best adapted to the happiness & honor of the members of a literary institution; . . . what was needed was a spontaneous feeling in favor of all civilizing, ennobling & refining influences." He adds: "The students, . . . at an adjourned meeting, passed resolutions which would be an honor to any college. From that time to this the conduct of the young gentlemen has been in the highest degree commendable." On various occasions, nevertheless, President Sears was obliged to inflict punishments more or less severe, expelling several students for immorality and suspending others for "disturbing recitations" and like offenses; but he remained unruffled and sweet-tempered always, remarking philosophically after a time of unrest in 1859: "Every thing has become quiet. . . . The petty annoyances to which students sometimes resort seem to be periodical. They come & go like a flock of birds, without any very obvious reasons." The students as a whole loved and respected Dr. Sears for the graciousness of his spirit and the courtesy of his manner. "He was singularly attractive," says Dr. Hovey, his pupil in the seminary, "in his intercourse with persons younger than himself. His manner was that of undisguised friendship, not that of dignified though graceful condescension. Young men soon felt at home in his study. They were somehow made to understand that he was a brother in spirit, considerate of their feelings, their hopes, and their anxieties." "More than one wild, reckless student has been heard to say," writes a correspondent to Dr. Hovey, "that there was no fun in trying to 'get a rise' on their 'Prex.,' for he was so sincerely respectful that it made all their efforts fall flat to the ground."

His less rigid ideas of discipline also helped to relax the tension. He early urged upon the Executive Board the need of affording the students innocent forms of amusement on the college grounds, to keep them from temptations in the city. The request of the literary societies to meet in the evening, instead of the afternoon, was granted in December, 1855; thus was a long-standing cause of discontent removed, while a beneficial form of evening entertainment was encouraged. The privilege of meeting in the evening was doubtless given to the Greek-letter fraternities at the same time. Another old restraint had been removed by a recommendation of the Faculty, and a vote of the Executive Board on November 9, 1855, "that the law requiring the daily visitation of student's rooms by the officers be suspended, and that the visitation be placed at the discretion of the officers." The discreet officers have never resumed the practice. The change did not mean that all students obeyed the laws, or that the authorities thought they did, but only that this mode of securing obedience had outlived its usefulness. Nor was there at first any liberalizing of the other laws. At the same meeting of the Executive Board President Sears reported that "there are evidences that students have led & are still leading a dissolute life; that they visit billiard-saloons, eating-saloons, the theatre, & still worse places of resort; & that gambling and intoxication both in the college buildings & out of them are not without example." He asked for an interpretation of a point that had given rise to a knotty problem in morals: "There is in the law, forbidding students to go to the theatre, an indefiniteness that needs to be removed. It seems to be doubtful both to the officers & to the students whether the opera is included under that prohibition. Students have applied for an interpretation of that law, but have been dismissed without what they asked for, but with that which they did not ask for,—namely with advice to remain at their rooms, &

thus keep themselves out of the reach of blame or harm."
This expresses sympathy but not breadth, and the Executive Board promptly put themselves on record as having no doubt that opera was under the ban. The laws forbidding attendance on the theater, and requiring attendance at church twice on Sunday, were reprinted in 1856 and 1865, and the President enforced the former law by severe penalties.

In directing the educational policy of the institution President Sears had a delicate problem to handle. The New System was not working well; yet it was not easy to apply a remedy without hurting the feelings of its respected originator, who was living near by and serving as fellow. The urgent need of modifying the system is shown by the following extract from President Sears's unpublished report to the Executive Board on July 5, 1856, which frankly and fearlessly probes the wound:

It seems to be the united opinion of the Faculty that the character & reputation of the University are injuriously affected by the low standard of scholarship required for the degrees of A.M. & A.B. It is well known that the best students of preparatory schools, which would naturally direct their pupils to this college, now go elsewhere; &, in some schools, so strong is the aversion to our system of college honors, that the whole body of students, which, in the ordinary course of things, would enter this college, go now to other colleges altogether. This results chiefly from the interpretation which is generally given to our peculiar & lowered standard of degrees as an open act of underbidding other colleges, & as a scramble for an increased number of students. Even the personal relations of our professors are humiliating, so that their intercourse with the officers of other colleges is a source of mortification rather than of pleasure. No college has ever resorted to extra measures in order to facilitate the acquisition of academic honors without incurring the ridicule & contempt of other colleges. It cannot be concealed that, while, by such a public sentiment against our system of degrees, the better class of students are often turned away from us, we are flooded by a class of young men of little solidity or earnestness of character, who resort to this college not so much for the sake of sound learning as for the sake of cheap honors. We now are literally receiving the refuse of other colleges. Students who cannot go through a complete course, entitling them to the degree of A.B. in other colleges, look upon this college as a kind of convenient establishment where they can soon build up a broken-down reputation, & take a rank side by side with those with whom they could not graduate in their own college. To such an extent has this impression gone abroad, that applications are now constantly made for a degree by teachers & others proposing to study only a few weeks here for form's sake. We are in danger of becoming an institution rather for conferring degrees upon the unfortunate than for educating a sterling class of men. With reference to those who graduate here as Masters, instead of being proud of the distinction, they are generally careful to speak of themselves as graduates & not as Masters of Arts. They wish not to draw upon themselves the scorn of the graduates of other colleges, who believe that their literary honors have not been earned. Beside the meanness attributed to us in pretending to a superiority which we do not possess, there is the evil of disturbing a common system of academic honors understood & interpreted alike all over the country. If each college is to have its own private interpretation of the degrees it confers, the whole subject will loose its dignity & its utility. It was indeed contemplated that candidates for the master's degree would extend the period of study to five years, & thus afford some reason for the distinction they receive, but it is said that this expectation has not been realized in a single instance. Thus the value of that degree has depreciated sensibly, & there is not the shadow of a reason for supposing that it implies more scholarship than did the degree of A.B. before the change. Meanwhile this latter degree has become ambiguous inasmuch as one *may* obtain it, & bear the external honors of one liberally educated, & yet not be able to give the meaning of *E pluribus unum*. A liberally educated man who cannot read a sentence of Latin is a solecism in language. Every member of the Faculty is dissatisfied with our present laws in respect to degrees.

This was plain speaking, especially to men all but one of whom had helped to launch the New System; but the President took pains to say at the beginning of his report that he was not criticising the courses of study, but only the system of degrees. He carried the Executive Board and the Corporation with him; indeed, the facts on his side, then and a little later, were too strong to be withstood. Not only was the quality of the students deteriorating, but even the numbers were diminishing again. In Dr. Wayland's last year they had fallen from 283 to 252; in 1855–56 they dropped to 225, and in 1856–57 to 203. Furthermore, during the years 1854–58, when the New System was in full force, all the students then in college having entered and pursued their studies under it, only 111 received degrees after taking the four-year course; whereas during 1846–50, under the old system, when the total attendance was much smaller, the number so graduating had been 145. It was evident that, instead of drawing many persons who under the former system would not have come to college at all, the New System was acting chiefly to lessen the number of those taking the full course. Even the students in the partial course, already declining in number in President Wayland's last year, continued to decrease, there being but 53 in 1855–56, 39 in 1856–57, and 25 in 1857–58. The scientific courses were not faring well: in 1856–57 there were 23 students in "practical chemistry," and 18 in civil engineering; the next year the numbers were 17 and 6 respectively. The degree of Bachelor of Philosophy, in spite of the very easy terms on which it was offered, had also proved poor bait for attracting the masses; during the last four years of Dr. Wayland's presidency there were but 87 candidates, and of these only 14 actually took the degree.

In view of these facts it was clearly necessary to do something, but the President proceeded with caution and good judgment. He had no quarrel with the essential principles of the New System, which he had approved in advance and helped to shape. He was in favor of a certain amount of election, of courses in the practical applications of science, and even of abridged periods of study for those who had no time or inclination for more; but he saw that it was not necessary to give the degree of Master of Arts for attainments which elsewhere won only the Bachelor of Arts degree, or to lower the entrance requirements or shorten the period of collegiate study for the latter. Accordingly the Corporation voted, in September, 1857, that in the case of all students entering after that year the degree of Master of Arts should be conferred only "in course," upon those who had received the degree of Bachelor of Arts at least three years before; and that the degree of Bachelor of Arts should be given only after four years of study, including both Latin and Greek. It followed as a natural consequence that both these languages were again required for admission of those seeking that degree. The degree of Bachelor of Philosophy, however, continued to be given upon the same conditions as before, except that the candidate might, if he chose, take one or both ancient languages, having first passed the entrance examination in the language or languages which he meant to pursue in college; the elective privileges in this course also remained unchanged. For the degree of Bachelor of Arts the requirements were now substantially those for the Master of Arts degree under Wayland. Students in a partial course were still received, after examination in "the several branches of a good English education." The courses in civil engineering and in chemistry applied to the arts also continued to be given a conspicuous place in the catalogue.

As a result of these changes the Executive Board was able to say, with evident relief, in *A Sketch of the History and the Present Organization of Brown University*, published in 1861, that while "the increased opportunities for practical education are still offered," yet "in the order and the course of study, Brown University does not now differ essentially from her sister Colleges of the United States." The undergraduates also approved of the change, *The Brown Paper* saying in the issue of 1857, "Under his government the University has returned from the experiment of the last few years, towards the good old system — a change which has been hailed by the undergraduates, at least, with undivided favor." Social considerations seem to have weighed heavily with the students, however, and made them object even to the continuation of the three-year course for Bachelors of Philosophy. "Our system of three years men," said *The Brown Paper* of 1865, "mars in some degree the unity of action in the class, for it introduces among its members those who, for two years, have been with other classes, . . . and who, for the most part, (with, however, some honorable exceptions,) are too lazy to enter on a full course. . . . All regular course students will hail the day when the 'Partial Course' receives an inglorious burial."

The other changes in entrance requirements and curriculum were few and relatively unimportant. Greek composition, which had been struck out of the requirement for admission in 1854, was restored in 1857, and in 1860 four books of the *Anabasis* were added. After this year candidates for the degree of Bachelor of Philosophy had to pass entrance examinations in both Latin and Greek if they took either language in college. The curriculum in 1861–62 for the degree of Bachelor of Arts may be given as representative of the course of studies through nearly the whole of President Sears's term of office:

FRESHMAN YEAR

First Term. Greek historians, with Greek composition and the history of Greece; Livy, with Latin composition and the history of Rome; geometry.

Second Term. The *Iliad*, with Greek composition; Livy, *De Senectute*, *De Amicitia*, with Latin composition; algebra.

SOPHOMORE YEAR

First Term. Demosthenes, with Greek composition; Horace, with Latin composition; plane and spherical trigonometry; French; rhetoric, with essays.

Second Term. Demosthenes, with Greek composition; Horace, with Latin composition; French; analytical geometry, or physiology; rhetoric, with essays.

JUNIOR YEAR

First Term. Mechanics; rhetoric, with essays and declamations; chemistry; Latin; Greek.

Second Term. Astronomy; history of English literature, with essays and declamations; physiology, or two of the following: geology; political economy; Cicero or Tacitus, with Latin composition; Sophocles or Euripides, with Greek composition.

SENIOR YEAR

First Term. Intellectual philosophy; modern history; one of the following: Tacitus and Plato; German.

Second Term. Moral philosophy; English and American history, constitutional and international law; German, or two of the following: geology; political economy; Cicero; Sophocles or Euripides.

The limitations of this academic bill of fare are obvious; but it is full of highly nutritive material, which, if well cooked and well digested, could not fail to make intellectual bone and muscle. The preparation and administering of this mental diet were in the hands of an able Faculty. At the beginning of the presidency of Dr. Sears, who taught mental and moral philosophy, the Rev. Alexis Caswell, D.D., was professor of natural philosophy and astronomy; George I. Chace,

[326]

LL.D., professor of chemistry and physiology, and of chemistry applied to the arts; William Gammell, A.M., professor of history and political economy; John L. Lincoln, A.M., professor of the Latin language and literature; the Rev. Robinson P. Dunn, A.M., professor of rhetoric and English literature; James B. Angell, A.M., professor of modern languages; Samuel S. Greene, A.M., professor of mathematics and civil engineering; Albert Harkness, Ph.D., professor of the Greek language and literature; Nathaniel P. Hill, assistant to the professor of chemistry; Reuben A. Guild, A.M., librarian. Many of these men were of unusual power or charm, and most of them remained in the service of the college throughout the administration.

The first to leave was Professor Angell, who resigned to become editor of *The Providence Journal* in 1860; his subsequent career as president of the University of Vermont and the University of Michigan, as minister to China and Turkey, and as member of various international commissions, is well known. His mental clarity and grace and his genial personality made him a stimulating and popular professor. A glimpse of his work is afforded by the following entry in the student's journal before referred to, under date of March 20, 1855: "Prof. A., much to our satisfaction, dispensed with the review, etc. and proceeded with his interesting description of Germany. The subject to-day was the life of a German student. . . . Altogether my desire to try my luck at a German University was greatly increased & in company with others I spent some time after most of the class had left, asking questions & obtaining additional information." No one succeeded to Professor Angell's chair for some years, the modern languages being taught by the President or by instructors.

Professor Caswell, after thirty-six years of service, resigned his professorship in 1864; he was succeeded in the chair of natural philosophy and astronomy by Professor Greene.

Mr. Hill, who in 1859 had been promoted to be professor of chemistry applied to the arts, withdrew from the university in 1865 to engage in mining operations in Colorado, where he directed many large enterprises and was elected United States senator. By his great ability and fine character he made a deep impression on colleagues and pupils in a comparatively short term of service; and he left a permanent memorial of himself in the chemical laboratory, in the planning of which he took a leading part. After his resignation Professor Chace resumed charge of the work in chemistry, assisted by several instructors.

In 1864 Professor Gammell severed his long connection with the Faculty. He was born in Medfield, Massachusetts, on February 10, 1812, the son of a Baptist clergyman, a trustee of the college. He entered Brown University in 1827, and graduated in 1831 at the head of his class. After a year as principal of an academy, he returned to his Alma Mater as tutor; became assistant professor of belles-lettres in 1835, and professor of rhetoric in 1837, also teaching a course in history after 1843; in 1850 he was transferred to the chair of history and political economy, which he held until 1864. The remaining years of his life were filled with varied activities. Besides serving as fellow of the university from 1870 till his death, he aided in the foundation of the Rhode Island Hospital, was trustee of the Butler Hospital, and president of the Rhode Island Historical Society, the Providence Athenaeum, and the Rhode Island Bible Society. He died in Providence on April 3, 1889, leaving the college a fund of $10,000 for the purchase of books relating to the history of the United States.

Professor Gammell was one of the strongest members of the Faculty. "As a critic of college writing," says his pupil and biographer, Dean James O. Murray, of Princeton, "he was altogether admirable. He was ever ready to praise good work. . . . He could not endure flashy nor meretricious ornament. Above all, he disliked obscurity, fustian, and affectation of every sort." Dean Murray admits, however, that his teaching of rhetoric "may have tended somewhat too strongly in the direction of the coldly elegant." Professor George P. Fisher, of Yale, the historian, writes: "I have special occasion to express an indebtedness to his kind, thoughtful assistance in initiating me into historical studies. One day he invited me to his room, and showed to me several volumes of manuscript correspondence of Roger Williams, which had just been added to the collections of the Rhode Island Historical Society. He gave to me this correspondence as a theme for a composition, and let me come to his room, from time to time, to examine it, and prepare for my task." Professor J. H. Gilmore, of the University of Rochester, says: "I think I especially appreciated . . . Professor Gammell's *obiter dicta*, his incidental remarks concerning men and things of our own day. He was animated by a sturdy contempt for humbugs and shams; and, as I recall his teachings, his influence seems to have been broadening and liberalizing beyond that of most of my professors." "There was no open text-book on his desk," writes Dr. Henry S. Burrage, state historian of Maine, in a recent letter; "his own mastery of the lesson seemed complete, and his fund of illustrative material was large and always easily ready for use. I acknowledge my indebtedness to him for a silent, forceful influence, that lured me into most delightful fields of historical research." Of his personal qualities President James B. Angell says: "There was something in his bearing, in his neatness of dress, in his elegance of language, that rebuked coarseness, vulgarity, and untidiness in a manner not unsalutary to young men living by themselves in dormitories and in commons hall.''

Professor Gammell wrote the lives of Roger Williams and Samuel Ward, published in 1845 and 1846 in the Library of American Biography edited by Jared Sparks, basing both upon original investigations. In 1850 he brought out a history of American Baptist missions; the liberal spirit of the book won praise from *The North American Review*, which said: ''We look in vain for the language of bigotry, exclusiveness, or unkindness. The most generous notice is uniformly taken of the missionaries of other sects; and the ashes of buried controversy are in every instance left undisturbed.'' He read many papers before the Rhode Island Historical Society, some of which have been printed. From 1850 to 1852 he was associate editor of *The Christian Review*. He frequently contributed articles to *The Providence Journal* on a wide range of topics; and during the Civil War he wrote weekly letters for *The Examiner*, a Baptist newspaper in New York, which ''attracted wide and special attention,'' says his biographer, ''and were complimented in the warmest terms by the great war secretary, the Hon. Edwin M. Stanton.'' Such was the first professor of history in Brown University. He was succeeded by one of his pupils, the Rev. John L. Diman.

The other professors on the Faculty in 1855 served through President Sears's administration, and some of them much longer, notably those ''Great Twin Brethren'' in the classics, Professors Lincoln and Harkness, who spread the fame of the university so far, through so many years. Among the instructors who joined the teaching staff during the presidency of Dr. Sears were two destined to long and distinguished terms of service, Benjamin F. Clarke, of the department of mathematics, and John H. Appleton, of the department of chemistry, both of whom began teaching in 1863. In 1864 Mr. Elliott, who had given faithful labor as steward or registrar since 1827, yielded place to the Rev. William Douglas, of the class of 1839.

There was a considerable increase in salaries during this administration. President Sears received $1850 until 1859, when his salary was raised to $2250 and he was paid $1200 additional as back pay for four years. The professors' salaries went up to $1500 in 1858, Professor Caswell receiving $100 and Professor Chace $300 extra for additional work; the librarian was paid $900, as before, and the registrar's salary was increased to $1200; the instructor in chemistry received $500. The presidential and professorial salaries remained at these figures until 1864, in spite of the jump in prices caused by the war. The Corporation then met the situation by raising the President's salary to $2500, besides $500 for teaching German, and the professors' salaries to $1800 each; the librarian received $1200, the registrar $1500, less the rent of his living-rooms in University Hall, and the instructors from $400 to $1000. In 1866 the salaries of the President, professors, librarian, and registrar were increased by $700 each, and the two senior instructors received $1500 and $1200.

These additions to the expenses could not have been safely made without increase of endowment, for the receipts from tuition were nearly uniform. The growth in productive funds, however, had been slow. The treasurer's reports show that in September, 1856, the total was $203,050, and in 1859 only $1000 more. The report of a special committee in October, 1863, stated that the total funds were then $224,050; but expenses had exceeded the income for two or three years, and there was a debt of $30,000. The committee urged renewed vigor in the campaign already on foot to raise at least $150,000, and recommended granting more scholarships to increase the attendance, omitting the courses in civil engineering and political economy, and distributing the work in history among three other professors when the chair of history should become vacant. The course in civil engineering was given up; but instead of contracting the curriculum any further, the Corporation raised the tuition, in 1864, from $36 to $50. The attendance at once fell from 202 to 185, and in 1865–66 to 176; but the next year, the last under Dr. Sears, it rose to 190.

The subject of scholarships and of a new fund for general purposes had already received careful attention. In 1858 the University Premiums had been converted into eleven scholarships, each the income of $1000, named after Nicholas Brown, the donor of the funds from which they were derived. In 1859 the Rev. Horace T. Love was employed as a joint agent by Brown University and Waterville College to collect subscriptions for scholarships and other objects, the subscribers indicating which institution they wished to aid. This agreement terminated in 1863; but the raising of funds went on for years, and at the end of Dr. Sears's administration subscriptions to the amount of $259,000 had been received, largely through the President's individual efforts. Of the old and new friends who came to the university's aid at this time may be mentioned Robert H. Ives, Thomas P. Ives, Gardner Colby, Jefferson Borden, Governor William Sprague, William S. Slater, William H. Reynolds, Earl P. Mason, Horatio N. Slater, and John Carter Brown, son of Nicholas Brown, who subscribed sums ranging from $8000 to $30,000. A noteworthy fact is that several gave again and again during the eight years of the canvass, responding with sustained loyalty to the continued and growing needs of the college. A considerable portion of the fund was paid in rather slowly; but interest was received regularly on $64,000 of the outstanding pledges, and the treasurer's report for 1866–67 shows funds of $327,000, yielding dividends of $16,438. Under the new rates for tuition the term bills that year brought in $15,000, making an income of more than $31,000. Thirty-four scholarships had also been established, in addition to the eleven already mentioned; and although these were not directly productive, they at least helped to prevent the number of students from falling off greatly during the Civil War.

Another addition to the scholarship funds was secured by government action during this administration, although most of the money did not come into the treasury until after President Sears had retired. On July 2, 1862, Congress passed a bill giving land scrip to such states and territories as should provide colleges for the benefit of agriculture and the mechanic arts. Rhode Island's share was 120,000 acres. The legislature, at the January session of 1863, accepted the grant, and assigned the land scrip to Brown University on condition that it establish a college or department of agriculture and the mechanic arts and educate scholars "at the rate of one hundred dollars per annum, to the extent of the entire annual income" from the sale of the lands. The Executive Board, to whom the Corporation referred the matter, accepted the offer, and requested President Sears, assisted by the Rev. Horace T. Love, to select the lands. Dr. Sears and Mr. Love spent the summer vacation of 1863 in examining and choosing a part of them, and the former reported the results to the Corporation at their meeting in the autumn. It was then seen that the task was a difficult one, and a committee of five, with the President as chairman, was appointed to take charge of the whole matter. This committee, finding that the cost of locating the lands, paying taxes, negotiating sales, and defending some of the titles would be considerable, and being allowed by the Corporation only a limited sum for expenses, sold the whole to Mr. Love, on January 31, 1865, for $50,000, taking his notes, secured by United States bonds, and payable without interest at various times during the next five years. The bargain proved later to have been a bad one for the university, as the lands rose greatly in value, and the authorities were subjected to sharp criticism; but at the time the college seemed justified in selling at once, as most of the other colleges did. In 1894 the funds were transferred by the university to the state of Rhode Island, the university receiving from the state the sum of $40,000 in requital of its claim upon a fund established by Congress in 1890 for instruction in agriculture and the mechanic arts.

There were few additions to the grounds and buildings during Dr. Sears's presidency. In 1860, when Prospect Street was extended to George Street, the so-called Bowen estate, at the corner of the two streets, seventy feet by a hundred and thirty, was bought by John Carter Brown for $10,000, and given to the university on condition that it be forever kept clear of buildings.[1] In the summer of 1857 Robert H. Ives and Moses B. Ives had the walls of the chapel painted, the ceiling frescoed, and a tablet with a Latin inscription by Professor Lincoln erected to the memory of Nicholas Brown, and John Carter Brown put in stained-glass windows. The only new building in this administration was the Chemical Laboratory. The New System emphasized the value of laboratory work in chemistry, and for

[1] The Bowen house, in recent years known as the Pendleton house, was removed from this site, at the same time, to its present location, 72 Waterman Street.

some years the conviction had been growing that there was need of better facilities for it. Largely by the efforts of Professor Hill, subscriptions to the amount of $14,250 were finally obtained, Seth Padelford giving $5000; and in the spring of 1862 a committee of the Executive Board was authorized to erect a laboratory "upon the open lot East of the present college grounds, and East of, and near to, the proposed line of Brown Street." It was completed within a year, at a cost of $12,500, with some $2500 more for apparatus and fittings. The building, which was fifty feet by forty, with a projection of thirty-five feet by fifty-five on the east side, had ample accommodations for some years to come; and the interior arrangement, planned by Professor Hill and his assistant, John Peirce, was admirable.

Two records in the archives may be mentioned here for the light they throw on the condition of the college grounds at this time. The chairman of the building committee for the laboratory reported to the Executive Board on May 5, 1863, that he had made a contract the autumn before "for a path seven feet wide leading from Waterman to George Street, and also for a path six feet wide leading from the Library to the New Laboratory"; the paths were of cinders and gravel, dry in all weathers, and the first one was "constantly used by the public." The second record gives a less pleasing picture: a committee reported on December 9, 1864, that "in the absence of any regular system of drainage, or proper conveniences for the removal of dirty water from the rooms, this water is often emptied from the windows, defiling the grounds, and creating an offensive effluvia [*sic*] in the summer."

The Corporation during Dr. Sears's twelve years as president was subject to the usual changes; but half of the fellowship was the same at the end as at the beginning, and twenty-one of the trustees remained. Three treasurers held office under President Sears—Moses B. Ives, Robert H. Ives, and Marshall Woods, who handled the growing business interests of the university with shrewdness and sound judgment through the trying years just before and during the Civil War. The Executive Board, which had played so active a part since its creation in 1850, was abolished in 1865. No one can look through the records without being impressed by the energy and devotion of these men, who gave so much time and thought to the affairs of the college during some of its most critical years; most of the labor, moreover, fell upon a few, who were often reëlected and served for long periods. But the Corporation apparently violated the charter by intrusting to a specially created board the enacting and enforcement of college regulations—functions expressly reserved to the fellows—and by clothing it with general powers which the charter delegates to "the minor quorum." The Executive Board practically took over the entire immediate government of the college, determining the sites of buildings, passing on cases of discipline, attempting to influence the choice of textbooks, and even forcing the resignation of professors. In 1865 certain members, according to President Sears, tried to compel the committee on the public lands to report to the board, and this seems to have been the immediate cause of its being abolished.

The only important change ever made in the charter came about in 1863, and concerned the exemption of professors from taxation. The exemption had early provoked opposition, which found expression in a Providence town meeting in 1774. A letter of February 6, 1774, preserved in the John Carter Brown Library, indicates that the Corporation were preparing to strengthen their case by showing that other colleges had the same privileges; it is written by Henry Lloyd, of Boston, to Nicholas Brown and Company, and says that the Rev. Dr. Pemberton, an overseer of Harvard College, affirms that the president, professors, and tutors at Harvard, as well as the college lands, are exempted from all taxes by an act of the province. Two papers in the university archives prove that some members of the Corporation were willing to compromise. One paper, dated April 19, 1774, is signed by Thomas Green, a trustee, and pledges him and the other subscribers to make an effort to have the college pay town taxes, except on the college hall, the president's house and garden, and the college yard. The other paper is in the hand of David Howell, and is indorsed, "Rough Draft of what propos'd by Mr Howell Abot : payg: the Town Tax as Profeser of the College &c"; it runs as follows :

In order to put an end to a dispute at present subsisting betwixt the Corporation of the College and the Inhabitants of this Town concerning the town rates of the President & Professors of sd College the members of sd Corporation present in Town meeting do for themselves agree & consent for the sake of restoring peace & tranquillity to the town & College that sd President and Professors shall pay every town tax that is or may be assessed upon either of their private estates in the same manner as other Inhabitants of the town provided no incroachments be made upon any other of the Charter rights of sd College.

The opponents of the exemption published resolutions in *The Providence Gazette* of February 12, 1774, affirming that the legislature had no right to limit the town's levy of taxes; but nothing more seems to have come of the movement.

Nearly a century later, in 1863, the matter came up again. It was urged that in time past professors had retained a nominal connection with the college for the sake of securing large estates from taxation, and might do so again; and that by marriage to members of the Faculty the owners of great properties might escape taxation in a way quite beyond the intent of the charter. At a meeting of the Corporation on January 21, 1863, during a discussion of the proposed repeal of the exemption clause by the state legislature, a statement by the President and Faculty was read, to the effect that, so far as they were concerned, they wished to "place this whole matter in the hands of the Corporation," and would waive their rights of exemption if it were "for the advantage of the College." On February 11 it was reported to the Corporation that the legislature had that day passed an act limiting the exemption to $10,000 for each member of the Faculty, if the Corporation consented; consent was given, and the change became law.

Commencements under President Sears retained their former merit and popularity. The first one, in 1856, has some special interest because the philosophical oration was delivered by Richard Olney, a future Secretary of State, who spoke on "Patriotism in Literature." Of the speeches *The Providence Journal* said: "The themes were chosen with excellent taste, and related more than is usual to the live topics of the age. It is but justice to say that the young gentlemen acquitted themselves in a manner that . . . would have done credit to older scholars." The dinner was attended by about four hundred; Dr. Wayland was given a seat of honor, and sincere compliments passed between him and the new President. The missionary sermon of the evening before was by the Rev. Dr. Ezekiel G. Robinson, professor in Rochester Theological Seminary, and the *Journal* referred to it as " one of the best discourses of the kind to which we have for a long time been permitted to listen." In 1865, near the end of Dr. Sears's administration, the Commencement speeches by the graduating class received high praise from Governor Andrew, of Massachusetts, who (as the *Journal* reported) said at the dinner: "Having attended many Commencements, I have never heard greater maturity of thought, or greater justness and accuracy both of style and expression. The range of topics and the variety of their treatment were also remarkable." At this Commencement, for the first time in many years, the speakers did not wear academic gowns. Distinguished men from abroad delivered addresses or poems on various occasions during Commencement week throughout President Sears's administration, adding greatly to the intellectual richness of the anniversaries. Among these may be mentioned the Hon. S. S. Cox, Wendell Phillips, George William Curtis, the Rev. Dr. Peabody, editor of *The North American Review*, the Rev. Dr. Storrs, the Rev. S. F. Smith, who read a patriotic poem before the literary societies in 1861, William Winter, Professors Edwards A. Park and Charles Eliot Norton, Colonel Thomas Wentworth Higginson, and General O. O. Howard.

Commencement week of 1864 was memorable for the centennial celebration of the founding of the university. The observance was simple, probably because of the war still raging, but the exercises were interesting and impressive. On Tuesday, September 6, the day before Commencement, President Sears delivered an able "Centennial Discourse" in the First Baptist Meeting-House, reviewing the history of the institution. This was preceded by a centennial ode written by Bishop George Burgess, of the class of 1826, and set to music by Professor E. A. Kelley. A dinner followed the address, in the great tent on the college grounds, and was attended by about seven hundred. The Hon. John H. Clifford presided, and many distinguished men spoke—Dr. Wayland, Professor Goldwin Smith, of the University of

Oxford, H. G. Jones, representing a delegation from the Philadelphia Baptist Association, General Burnside, George William Curtis, Professor Caswell, and others; several poems were read, including one by John Hay. On the same day was published *Manning and Brown University*, by Librarian R. A. Guild, whose *History of Brown University* appeared three years later.

The social and festive sides of Commencement week were still attractive, and Commencement itself was yet something of a holiday. Up to 1860 *The Providence Journal* continued to announce on the first Wednesday in September, "This being Commencement day, no paper will be issued from this office to-morrow." Of the Commencement of 1859 a letter from Providence in *The Boston Journal* said: "There is a scattering display of flags, so that on the whole, the appearance of the city is gay and animated. . . . The 'Antiques and Horribles' . . . were out in numbers. . . . The great sea serpent was again attempted to be exhibited, but passed through only a few streets when it shared the fate of its predecessor." The procession to the church was nearly a quarter of a mile long, consisting of the undergraduates and about three hundred alumni. "We noticed a few of the Collegians smoking cigars, both going and returning from the church," which was "jammed, not crowded." Five hundred attended the Commencement dinner, where the tables were "adorned by bouquets of exquisite flowers, and huge water-melons erected in various parts."

But on the purely social side Commencement day came to be eclipsed by Class Day. The Faculty records of April 22, 1856, contain this entry: "A request was submitted through the President, from the graduating class, for permission to celebrate a Class Day on some day towards the close of the present term. Voted, that the request be granted, and that June 12th be fixed for the day; also that the performances be previously submitted to the Professor of Rhetoric, and that that officer be and is, hereby authorized to direct the Class-Committee in regard to the arrangements for the public proceedings of the day." *The Providence Journal* of June 13 had the following notice of the exercises:

CLASS DAY AT BROWN UNIVERSITY. — This celebration passed off yesterday in the happiest manner in the University Chapel, and was in all respects exceedingly creditable and interesting. . . . The purport of the celebration was briefly stated by Mr. George L. Stedman, the President of the day, who introduced to the audience Mr. Richard Olney, the Class Orator. This young gentleman delivered an admirable address on the importance of carrying literary culture into professional life — a theme well adapted to the occasion, and which he discussed in a manly and scholarly spirit. . . . The poem was by Mr. Francis W. White. . . . After a graceful introduction addressed to the class, the poet drew an admirable and graphic picture of the College as it was in the olden times. . . . The young gentlemen of the class dined together at the close of the day, and in the evening were entertained by President Sears.

From this simple beginning Class Day developed in a few years into essentially its present form. A Class Day program, a plain affair of four pages, was first printed by the class of 1858. It shows that the day was Thursday, June 10; the morning exercises were at 10.30 a.m., in Manning Hall, and consisted of music, prayer by Dr. Sears, an address by the class president, an oration, and a poem. Nothing was announced for the afternoon. In the evening, at nine o'clock, came the class supper. A note of instructions ends the program: "The class will form at 10.15 A.M. in front of Rhode Island Hall, and go in procession to the Chapel. At 8.45 P.M. they will meet the American Brass Band at the Chapel Steps, from whence they will be escorted to the Supper." Of the class poem, by John Hay,

The Providence Journal said: "It was marked by a fertility of conception, a depth of sensibility, and a power of poetic expression, which we have rarely heard equalled, and never surpassed, at any of our literary anniversaries." In 1859 it was announced that the other students would escort the seniors through the streets to the class supper. For the next few years no material changes were made, but in 1863 came an innovation: in the afternoon of Class Day an elm tree, "enfolded in the stars and stripes," was planted behind the Chemical Laboratory; two seniors and President Sears made addresses; the class ode was then sung, after which the seniors dispersed, while the other classes sang college songs. *The Brown Paper* of 1865 says that on Class Day of that year there was music in the evening before the class went to their supper at the City Hotel; that the supper lasted from nine o'clock until early morning, and some "fell asleep." Late hours at the supper apparently became the custom thenceforth, for *The Brown Paper* of 1868 refers to games of baseball played by the classes of 1867 and 1868 after their suppers. In 1866 the musical and social parts of the celebration were much enlarged. In the afternoon, before the planting of the class tree, there was a "promenade concert" in Rhode Island Hall, and in the evening there was a promenade on the campus. "Class-day 'spreads,'" says *The Brown Paper* of 1866, "were introduced this year at Brown." That the social exhilaration of the day reached a high point that year is apparent from this paragraph: "When the class-day of Sixty-seven shall summon the expectant fair, and shall throng the Chapel Hall with blushing visitants, may he, who has 'the honor to be the President of the Senior class of Brown University,' rise undismayed above that waving sea of bonnets. . . . May loud and cheerful strains of music again echo in Rhode

Island Hall; may bright stars, twinkling in an unclouded sky, and gentle zephyrs, sporting in the branches of the campus' lofty elms, behold a joyous Evening Promenade.'' The prayer was granted, the concert and promenade becoming permanent features of the day.

A few later steps in the development of Class Day may be anticipated here. ''The address to the undergraduates'' is first mentioned in *The Brown Paper* of 1866. A more significant innovation was dancing, in 1868, at the promenade concert in Rhode Island Hall. ''And though perhaps unexpected and sudden to some of the grave Professors,'' says *The Brown Paper*, ''this new feature gave a life and zest to the concert which it had never possessed in former years. All credit to '68 for this pleasant innovation on the old-fogy customs of past times.'' *The Brunonian's* account of Class Day in 1869 includes more new features: the music at the morning exercises was furnished by the college glee club; the President invited the seniors to lunch at his house; at the evening promenade a few Chinese lanterns were strung between the trees and on the band-stand; between the band pieces there were college songs and music by the glee club. *The Brunonian* also mentions that the custom which had obtained for ''many years,'' of marching from the south to the north end of the campus and cheering the buildings before going down the hill to the class supper, was omitted, but adds that the seniors cheered the buildings the next morning on their return. *The Brunonian* of April, 1870, refers to another custom of ''long standing''—that of students ''gathering in front of Manning Hall and passing rude criticisms on the visitors, during their arrival and after the close of the exercises,''—and asks ''whether it would not be better honored in the breach than in the observance.'' One new feature of this year recalled the tallow-candle illuminations of old days, for "Every room in Hope College and University Hall was brilliantly illuminated," says *The Brunonian* of July, which also notes that four rows of Chinese lanterns extended the whole length of the campus. From this point on the development of Class Day was chiefly a matter of details, except for the great emphasis laid in recent years on social receptions and dances by the graduating class and the fraternities.

Organized athletics date from the administration of President Sears. At the beginning of his term the chief athletic event was the annual football game between the freshmen and sophomores in September, played on what is now the middle campus, then a grassy field, and watched, says *The Brown Paper*, by "hosts of graduates, upper-class men and *scheda*" and by "many fair ladies who graced the windows of University Hall and Hope College." The struggle was evidently as much a fight as a game, and President Sears stopped it in 1862. The ban was removed in 1866, and the game, in a more healthful form, was played constantly that autumn, by members of all the classes. "The inflated ball," says *The Brown Paper* of 1866, "now raised high in air, now the centre of a swaying mass of excited players, and now driven over the goal amidst the cheers of the lookers-on, seems to possess an irresistible though inexplicable attraction for all." This proved a passing enthusiasm, however; and except for the annual game between the two lower classes, which was soon resumed, football received little attention at Brown for many years to come.

It was baseball that was first developed to some degree of scientific skill. In 1864 a baseball club, composed chiefly of members of the class of 1865, with Edward Judson as "president," won the championship of Providence by defeating the best town club, the Dexters, and as a result the club was honored by a challenge from Harvard. The following account of the game, written by the librarian of the university for one of the Providence newspapers, throws light on the state of the sport and on intercollegiate relations at that time:

Agreeably to previous announcements, the great match between the Base Ball Clubs of Harvard and Brown came off on Saturday afternoon at the Dexter Training Ground. The occasion was made a holiday by many of our citizens, who were present in large numbers to witness the contest. The delegation of Harvard students, thirty-four in number, arrived here in the middle train, and were received at the depot by members of the Brown Club, and escorted to Humphreys', where a generous collation was provided. From thence they were conducted to the College, where an hour was very agreeably spent in social intercourse, and in visiting the Library, Laboratory, and other College buildings. At half past two the two Clubs were taken in hacks to the Dexter Training Ground, where, soon after their arrival, the game commenced. The contest lasted upwards of four hours, and as was anticipated, proved highly exciting. For a long time the tallies on each side increased with even pace, and up to 6 o'clock it seemed entirely doubtful which side would win. The Brown boys did "splendid execution," but the superior muscle and the longer and more thorough training of the Harvard boys finally prevailed. They won the game by a majority of nine, the tallies counting twenty-six and seventeen. . . . The occasion was enlivened by the delightful music of the American Brass Band, and smiles and nods from countless fair ones cheered and encouraged the players. The very best feeling pervaded the Clubs, the vanquished joining with the victors in cheers at the final result. Such friendly peaceful contests do much towards uniting kindred institutions in a common bond of sympathy and love. Harvard and Brown have always sustained the happiest relations towards each other in the past years of their history, notwithstanding the somewhat different theological tendencies of the two institutions. "So mote it ever be" in the future.

The interest in baseball continued in the ensuing years. The 'varsity nines had small success; but the sport aroused general enthusiasm, which led to much miscellaneous playing and to the formation of class teams. "At almost any time during the Spring and Autumn months," said *The Brown Paper* of 1866, "the passer-by may see upon the Campus, some well-contested game in progress between two picked nines."

Boating also began to develop. Harvard and Yale had rowed their first race in 1852, their second in 1855. These contests excited great interest in other colleges, and in 1857 the students at Brown began preparations to enter a boat at the next intercollegiate race. The University Boat Club was organized in June. "On Friday, September 11th," says *The Brown Paper*, "a new boat arrived from Boston at the India Point Depot. She was there received by the club, borne to the water's edge and launched on the waves of Narragansett Bay with enthusiastic demonstrations from the assembled crowd." The boat, named "Atalanta," was a six-oared, lap-streak craft, forty-four and a half feet long. The new sport excited great enthusiasm. *The Brown Paper* of the next year contained the following: "The boating interest continues unabated. The zeal manifested by the Freshmen was as cheering as it was unexpected, and the formation of a new Club, at the opening of the season, may be considered, at least, a probability. We need only allude to the stunning appearance presented by the members of the Club, when, by presenting themselves in full uniform on the ground, they gave eclat to the Annual Foot Ball Game." The "eclat" is easily appreciated when one reads a description of the club uniform: "Blue shirts, trimmed with white; black glazed hats, inscribed 'Atalanta'; black belts, inscribed 'U. B. C.'; white pants."

In 1859 Brown entered the intercollegiate race with Harvard and Yale on Lake Quinsigamond, and was badly beaten, partly because the "Atalanta" weighed a hundred and fifty pounds more than the shells of her rivals. Enthusiasm was fired by the race in spite of defeat. *The Brown Paper* that autumn said:

Never was such a state of things known before in the old University; everybody is "training." . . . The Quickstep was purchased by members of the Freshmen Class, soon after the commencement of the present term. It was really amusing to see how delighted the little fellows were when the "lap-streak" arrived; never was a boy more tickled with his first pair of new boots, than were the Freshmen with their four-oared boat. . . . The funds for a "college shell boat" are being rapidly subscribed. . . . The "picked crew" is nearly formed, and possesses many advantages over the crew of last year. They have been practicing upon the river for the last few weeks, and have made exceedingly good time.

The freshman club adopted a uniform consisting of "red shirt, trimmed with white; tarpaulin hat; black belt, inscribed 'B. C. '63'; black pants." In this rather piratical costume, as well as in that of the 'varsity club and the dress of the crew in the race of the preceding summer—"gray check pants; salmon silk shirts; blue skull caps"—the absence of brown is noticeable. No college color had yet been adopted, nor was the question even raised until 1866, when *The Brown Paper* said that there was much debate about it: "The general opinion seems to be, that *brown* should be adopted."

The high hopes with which the college year opened were doomed to disappointment. The Brown crew entered several races in the summer of 1860, at Providence, Boston, and Lake Quinsigamond, but was defeated in all, partly through a series of mishaps. The outbreak of the Civil War soon after turned the students' thoughts in another direction, and boating languished for several years, although there were still occasional races on the Seekonk. In 1867 *The Brown*

Paper contained this dismal picture: "The swift 'Brunonia' . . . lies a shattered hulk within the forsaken boat house. The relentless tempest sweeps through the crevices of the decaying roof, and the pitiless rain descends upon the well-patched cedar of the ancient shell. The 'Atalanta,' too, . . . has departed to other waters. . . . It is not fitting that the manliest of all our sports should be neglected, and that the best rowing-stretch in New England should be without a boat."

The tendency to organization showed itself in the formation of many clubs and associations. *The Brown Paper* between 1857 and 1867 contains notices of several musical clubs, three chess clubs, and two dramatic organizations — the Thalian Dramatic Association, in 1866, and the more permanent Hammer and Tongs, formed in 1867. In addition to the Religious Society, which died in 1863, and the Society of Missionary Inquiry, both of long standing, the Bishop Seabury Association was formed in 1865, by the Episcopalian students, and prospered for many years.

The Greek-letter fraternities, increased to six by the establishment of a chapter of Chi Psi in 1860, grew more and more influential under President Sears's genial rule, and were the chief centers of social and intellectual life. Their secrecy aroused some opposition, and this led in 1860 to the formation of an open society, the Gamma Nu, which in 1868 became a chapter of the Delta Upsilon fraternity. *The Brown Paper*, a four-page annual, was published by the secret societies from 1857 to 1868, giving place in 1869 to the *Liber Brunensis*. The former contained the names of all the college societies and other organizations, with their officers and members, besides news items and editorials. The issues of 1860 and 1861 were called *The Brunonian*. In 1866 two different papers were published, because of a split in the senior class election. *The Caduceus*, one number of which was published in December, 1865, by the Gamma Nu society and non-society students, and another in December, 1868, by the Brown chapter of Delta Upsilon, was similar to *The Brown Paper*, but had less news and more literary material. It was the latter, however, which published the only verses that have survived. For the 1860 number James A. DeWolf, of the class of 1861, the editor representing the Psi Upsilon fraternity, wrote "Alma Mater," which he called "Old Brown." It was intended for a college song; and Mr. DeWolf has said that he first chose the tune, "Araby's Daughter," chiefly because of its popularity, and then wrote his words to fit the music. It attracted no attention for some years.

As the secret societies grew, the old debating societies declined. A falling off in interest had been noted as early as 1851, and was urged in that year as a reason for allowing meetings at night. In spite of the granting of this request in 1855, the societies continued to decline. After 1859 the United Brothers held few meetings except the annual initiations, and the same was true of the Philermenian Society after 1862. The initiations degenerated into a tussle for the possession of the bodies of freshmen, in the narrow entry between the doors of the rival organizations, and in 1867 even these physical debates ceased. The joint literary anniversaries of the societies, on the day before Commencement, ended in 1863 with an oration by George William Curtis and a poem by William Winter. The transfer of undergraduate interest from oratory to other forms of intellectual activity appeared also in the giving up of the senior exhibition in 1857, apparently by the concerted action of those appointed to speak. The junior exhibition lived some twenty-five years longer.

Student pranks continued to enliven if not to dignify academic routine. Junior Burials, conducted by men some of whom afterwards became pillars of church and state, yearly illuminated the streets with torches and transparencies, and helped to block the channel in Narragansett Bay by sinking textbooks in rhetoric and logic. The hazing of freshmen sometimes went to reckless extremes, sophomores visiting the same students several times, smashing doors and furniture, and in a few instances inflicting personal injury. In the autumn of 1858 nearly the whole sophomore class were suspended for a few days, although they pleaded truly in defense that their concerted action was intended to prevent the more objectionable features of individual hazing in recent years. In March, 1857, occurred the famous mock duel, which was so cunningly counterfeited that it nearly put the principals into prison and resulted in the expulsion of one of them, a Southerner, and the suspension of three other students. A less offensive though more noisy amusement, the rolling of a cannon-ball at night along the corridors of University Hall, which then ran the whole length of the building, was stopped in the summer vacation of 1860 by the building of partitions in the three upper stories. A Water Procession, the fame of which has been eclipsed by a more elaborate one in 1868, was occasioned in 1865 by the failure of the college water-supply. The rope in the well-house behind Hope College was cut one day, and the bucket removed; the registrar, wearied by the frequent repetition of this joke, did not repair the loss; whereupon "a procession of students, some sixty in number," says *The Brown Paper*, "impelled by a burning thirst, each with his bucket in hand, wended their way, to the slow and solemn time of a tin-pail drum, to the town pump, and returned rejoicing with the life-giving beverage."

In the spring of 1861 the roar of the guns at Fort Sumter

broke in upon this academic life of mingled work and play. The effect upon the college, as upon the whole country, was tremendous. "The events which have produced such an extraordinary effect upon the public mind generally," wrote President Sears in his report to the Executive Board on May 4, "have not failed to act powerfully upon the minds of the students. Some have enlisted & taken their places in the camp. Some were so excited at the first outbreak of our present national troubles that, for a few days, they nearly forgot that there was a college, & considered themselves rather as recruits than as students, till at length the Professors succeeded in reviving in them a consciousness that they still belonged to college." On April 15 came President Lincoln's call for seventy-five thousand volunteers. The whole college was at once on fire with patriotism. Fifteen students responded immediately by enlisting in the First Rhode Island Regiment then forming under Burnside at the summons of the energetic young war-governor, William Sprague; and twenty-two more entered the army during the year. The seniors held a meeting on the day of the call for troops, and asked permission of Dr. Sears to raise a flag on University Hall. There was but one dissenting voice, that of a Southern student, who courageously spoke for the Confederacy and its flag; he soon entered the Southern army, and died in its service the next year. The freshman class also held a meeting, and passed valiant resolutions upholding the national government. On April 17 the seniors raised their flag over University Hall in the presence of students, Faculty, and citizens, and music and speeches followed. Three days later the students gathered in Exchange Place, with a vast crowd of townspeople, to say good-by to the first detachment of Rhode Island infantry, which included several collegians. Bishop Clark addressed the troops and prayed, after which they embarked at Fox Point and sailed down the bay. This scene was repeated on the following Wednesday, when Dr. Wayland addressed the soldiers and marched with them to the wharf.

In May the undergraduates formed a military company, known as the University Cadets, numbering seventy-eight men. Eight of the fourteen officers, says Dr. Burrage in his *Brown University in the Civil War*, "served with distinction in the Union armies." The National Cadets allowed the company the use of their armory and muskets, the campus was an admirable training-ground, and daily drills soon made the young soldiers proficient. On Class Day they paraded through the principal streets of the city, and in the evening escorted the seniors to their class supper. In the summer of 1863 the University Cadets became a company of the Rhode Island militia, and as such spent a delightful fortnight at the entrance of Narragansett Bay, ostensibly to fortify the West Passage against the expected attack of the rebel privateer, Taconey, but really to enjoy a furlough from term examinations. Not long after, when the state militia was disbanded, the college company ceased to exist.

Even after the first outbursts of enthusiasm had subsided, the patriotism of the college and its alumni continued to burn with a steady glow. Undergraduates and graduates enlisted from time to time, 268 in all; and of these 132 came from the five classes graduating during the war, whose aggregate membership within that period was only 278. In one of the darkest hours, after the defeat of General Banks in the spring of 1862, came a call for more troops. Two days later the Tenth Rhode Island Volunteers left Providence for the field, and Company B consisted almost wholly of undergraduates from the college. The leader of the company,

Governor Elisha Dyer, has said : "The students of Brown University could brook no restraint, and, almost *en masse*, came to our recruiting rendezvous for enrollment. . . . They proved themselves worthy of their Alma Mater, and the sacred cause for which they enlisted. Always prompt, obedient, and efficient, they won for themselves an honorable record. For no delinquency, or misdemeanor, did any name of theirs ever find a place on the morning report. On the muster out of the regiment, September 1, 1862, many of these young men immediately reëntered the service, and, as commissioned officers, extended a record of which the University may well be proud."

Throughout the war the life of the college was affected by it at almost every point. At the time of the Class Day celebration in 1861, the class president was already in the army; and the secretary, the orator, and the poet all soon entered and served for several years. During the summer the war claimed its first victim among the graduates of the college, Major Sullivan Ballou, of the class of 1852, who was wounded at the battle of Bull Run and died five days later. On Commencement morning an editorial in *The Providence Journal* well expressed the general feeling :

But at this literary festival we would not, if we could, shut out from our minds thoughts of the great struggle in which the nation is engaged. Nor could we, if we would. For by the Commencement programme itself we are reminded that four of the graduating class deserve their portion of the laurels which the Rhode Island regiments won on the plains of Manassas, and that one of them wounded now lies a prisoner at Richmond. Another of them is with his regiment to-day on the banks of the Potomac, perhaps facing death in the din of the terrible contest while we sit so quietly listening to his comrades. Two of the undergraduates are also prisoners at Richmond, and others are already enrolled in the army of the Union. And all along the line from the ocean to the Rocky Mountains the graduates of

Brown are found standing up bravely in defence of those institutions without which science and letters and arts and industry and wealth are all of no avail.

The orations of the graduating class had little direct reference to the war, but at the Commencement dinner it was the chief theme. President Sears spoke warmly of the prompt response of the state to the call of the national government, and introduced with words of high praise "the brave young Governor of Rhode Island." After Governor Sprague had responded in a strain of optimistic courage, Dr. Wayland addressed the gathering with his old-time impressiveness.

On Class Day the next year the orator, home on a furlough, took for his subject, "The Alliance of Scholarship and Patriotism," and the class poem bore in part upon the war. At Commencement *The Providence Journal* remarked: "A large number of the students who gather at the anniversary to-day . . . have just returned from an arduous campaign near Washington, and wear on their cheeks the dark coloring of the fervid Virginia sun, and in their callous hands the marks of severest toil." The valedictorian, who had just enlisted for "three years or the war," spoke in the uniform of a captain of infantry; his theme was "The Scholar's Relations to Humanity." He left the Commencement stage for the field, and three months later was severely wounded at Fredericksburg. This Commencement had hardly passed before the cruelty of war was powerfully brought home to the college and the state by the death of Robert H. Ives, Jr., of the class of 1857, a descendant of one of the best Providence families, a young man of culture and fine character, who forsook all the allurements of private life to serve his country. Lieutenant Ives left Providence on September 1, as aide to General Rodman, an officer of the Ninth Corps under Major-General Burnside; seventeen days later, at the battle of Antietam, he was horribly wounded in the thigh by a cannon-ball, and although tended carefully by his faithful English servant and by relatives who reached his side in a few days, he died on September 27, in his twenty-sixth year. C. L. Kneass, of the class of 1858, was killed at the battle of Murfreesboro in December of the same year.

The oration before the undergraduate literary societies during Commencement week of 1863, by George William Curtis, was entitled "The Way of Peace," and urged pushing the war to the end as the only means of securing permanent peace. At the Commencement dinner General J. M. Thayer, of the class of 1841, fresh from the siege of Vicksburg, described the character of his chief, Ulysses S. Grant, then comparatively unknown in the East.

Even the centennial anniversary in 1864 took color from the civil strife then nearing its close. At the dinner Professor Goldwin Smith brought a message of sympathy with the North from the common people of England; Governor Salmon P. Chase, of Ohio, arraigned the British government for aiding the Confederacy; and a poem, "Centennial," by Major John Hay, was read, ending with the stanza,

> Thus bright forever may she keep
> Her fires of tolerant Freedom burning,
> Till War's red eyes are charmed to sleep
> And bells ring home the boys returning.

The end of the war excited the undergraduates hardly less than its outbreak. "When the joyful tidings of the fall of Richmond were received," says *The Brown Paper* of 1865, punning atrociously, "the Sophomoric enthusiasm . . . threw down all de*fences* of the college, and, unable to let well enough alone, set fire to the ancient curb." When the news of Lee's surrender came, the sophomores celebrated the event, according to the same chronicle, "by a mammoth bonfire, to which they generously devoted all the movable combustibles that could be borrowed in the city." More dignified festivities followed a few days later, described thus in *The Brown Paper:* "The students of all classes, aided by the generosity of the citizens, arranged a celebration more suited to the greatness of the occasion. Colored lanterns shone in all the windows and hung in festoons from the elms; rockets and Roman candles shot in every direction, to the great danger of spectators. From the chapel portico, under a canopy of flags, eloquent orators, surrounded by a *brilliant* halo from a calcium light, addressed an audience such as had never before graced our campus, while in the rear of the college, the effigy of Jefferson D. blazed in the curling flames of several hundred *tarred* barrels." The assassination of Lincoln, only two days later, changed all this rejoicing to sorrow. Dr. Wayland's speech to the citizens has already been described. The Faculty and students held a meeting in the chapel on April 17, passed appropriate resolutions, and voted to drape the chapel and wear badges of mourning for thirty days.

At the Commencement dinner, that autumn, James B. Angell, then editor of *The Providence Journal*, gave an eloquent address of welcome to the soldier sons of Brown. Brief responses were made by soldier alumni—General J. M. Thayer, General A. B. Underwood, Colonel Horatio Rogers, and Captain H. S. Burrage. On the day before the Commencement of 1866 a mural tablet in the chapel was dedicated to the memory of the twenty-one Brown men who had died in the war. The plan originated among the undergraduates, and the expense was borne chiefly by them. The inscription, by Professor Lincoln, was as follows: "IN MEMORIAM FRATRUM SUORUM QUI PRO LIBERTATE ET PRO REIPUBLICAE INTEGRITATE IN BELLO CIVILI CECIDERUNT LITERARUM STUDIOSI

IN HAC UNIVERSITATE COMMORANTES HANC TABULAM POSUERUNT. MDCCCLXVI.'' After a prayer by Professor Dunn, Professor Diman made a short address, including these words:

To the Faculty, and to the students, alike, it seemed eminently fit that such a memorial should be erected here; that here, as we gather to our daily devotions, we might be reminded of those who, only a short time since, sat with us on these benches, and joined with us in our accustomed hymns of praise; and that here those, who in years to come shall fill our places, may learn that study is not an end in itself; that liberal culture looks to larger results than are included in mere academic success; that the finest discipline becomes contemptible if not coupled with the manly virtues. Not what we learn, but the use we make of our learning is what tells the story. Surely if the instructors in this institution ever grow negligent in inculcating these high lessons, the very stone will cry out.

The names of the dead were added at a later date. A memorial to all the Brown men who served in the war was published in 1868, in the form of a handsome volume, *Brown University in the Civil War*, edited and in part written by the Rev. H. S. Burrage.

On August 28, 1867, the university sustained a sudden loss in the death of Professor Dunn. He was born in Newport, Rhode Island, on May 31, 1825, the son of an eminent physician. He entered Brown University in 1839, and took his degree four years later with the valedictory honor. During the years 1844–46 he served as assistant librarian and instructor in French. After studying in Princeton Theological Seminary, he became pastor of a Presbyterian church in Camden, New Jersey, in 1848; but in 1851 he accepted the chair of rhetoric and English literature in Brown University, and devoted himself to its duties for the rest of his life, refusing a call to a similar position in Princeton in 1860. He received the degree of D.D. from Brown University in 1864.

Professor Dunn's personality was one of almost feminine sensibility and refinement, without much robustness or breadth. He cared little for great public questions, and even in the realm of pure thought his range was limited. "His mind seemed never fascinated with the subtleties of metaphysics," said Professor Diman; "it did not grasp with ease the broad generalizations of moral and political philosophy; it found slight attraction in the physical sciences." His work as a teacher showed both the limitations and the fineness of his nature, as appears in the same colleague's words about it: "His nature had not enough enthusiasm. His quickening power was not in proportion to his other gifts. But his rare critical discernment, his exquisite taste, his appreciative love of whatever was excellent in literary works, his enthusiasm in the studies relating to his own department, rendered him a rare and eminent example of a thorough academic man." His lectures on rhetoric were skillfully adapted to the needs of the college student. "Do not labor after ornament," he said. "Let figures come unsought. Earnest feeling seldom fails to employ them, but a manifest effort to introduce them is painful and disgusting. Simplicity and precision are more pleasing and effective than show." What he taught he compelled his pupils to practice. "No one could give critical attention to the orations of Commencement day," says Professor Diman, "without seeing how successful he had been in correcting the passion for fine writing, which is at war with all moral qualities of style." His teaching of English literature, in accordance with the custom at that time, was confined to a course of lectures on the history of its earlier periods, but he read much to the class from the best authors. Of Professor Dunn's scholarship his friend and colleague, James B. Angell, said: "His critical study of our language carried him back to the Anglo-Saxon, with the structure of which he made himself familiar. The French language he had in childhood thoroughly mastered, and a considerable portion of the French literature was well known to him before he entered college. I have often questioned whether the vivacity, the brightness, the flashing but kindly wit of his conversation were not in part due to this early intimacy with the French language. . . . In the midst of his engrossing labors he found time to push his study of Italian far enough to read, with appreciation and enjoyment, the great masters of that tongue. During the last few years of his life, he added largely to his critical apparatus from the stores of German scholarship, and was a diligent student of the best German writers on Comparative Grammar, Philology, and Scriptural Exegesis.''

At the Commencement of 1867 Professor Dunn's pew was draped in black, and the salutatorian spoke of his character and work. A commemorative discourse by Professor Diman was delivered in chapel on October 16; and a memorial volume, containing this address, a biographical sketch, and selections from Professor Dunn's writings, was published in 1869. The Dunn Premium, founded in the same year by the gift of $1000 from his pupils and friends, the income to be given at the end of the junior year to the student having the highest rank in rhetorical studies, forms a permanent and fitting memorial to one who labored so long and effectively on behalf of good English.

The Commencement of 1867 was also saddened by the approaching departure of President Sears, who had resigned, partly because of his health, to become agent of the Peabody Fund for education in the South. The resignation had been regretfully accepted by the Corporation, with words of praise for ''his piety, learning and suavity ; . . . his watchfulness over the interests of the University, his general ability and his great success." Dr. Sears left for the South, thenceforth his home, a fortnight after Commencement. His hold on the affections of the undergraduates is shown by the following account of their farewell to him, taken from *The Brown Paper:*

On the morning of the 19th of September, the intelligence reached some of the students . . . that he was to leave the city in the afternoon. The tidings spread rapidly through the college, and everybody said, "Let us all be at the wharf to see him and to say our good-bye." . . . Soon all were formed in procession in the order of the classes, and passed down College street, by the President's house, Dr. Sears standing on the steps, and greeting them, as they filed by, class by class, with uncovered heads. It had been the wish of the students to escort the President to the wharf, but this was waived afterwards at his suggestion. It so happened, however, that the carriage in which he went, overtook the procession, and immediately place for it was made in the centre. . . . On arriving at the boat, Dr. Sears stood at the landing, surrounded by members of the Faculty, and the procession filed by, each student shaking hands with the President as he passed. . . . God bless him, was the word in every heart and on every lip. . . . God bless him, and make him a blessing to others, as he has been to us.

He went to a great work, which was continued almost to the hour of his death on July 6, 1880.

In reviewing the work of President Sears at Brown University it must be remembered that the central years of his administration fell in the period of the Civil War. His early labors had hardly had time to bear fruit when the war diverted much of the national energy and wealth to other than educational objects; and he resigned before recovery from the strain of the prolonged struggle had fairly begun. It is therefore not surprising that the college in his day did not grow in numbers or greatly increase in material equipment; the wonder is, rather, that it did so well in both regards. In 1861, after some shrinkage, the college seemed to have started on a period of enlargement: the number of students crept up from 189 in 1858–59 to 212 in 1859–60, and to 232 in 1860–61, when the entering class was 74, of whom only 5 were in the partial course. During the first three years of the war the average number of students was 205; the next two years, when the tuition was raised, it fell to 185 and 176, but in 1866–67 it rose to 190, with an entering class of 73. What the growth would have been if Dr. Sears had remained is only matter of conjecture, but the college at the time he left it was apparently in a way to make steady gains.

The growth in financial resources during this administration is rather remarkable, considering the disturbed state of the times. There was small increase in material equipment, but the one new building helped the work of the college at the point where help was most needed. It speaks strongly for Dr. Sears's energy and tact, and for the confidence which business men had in him, that during his term of office the productive funds increased more than $120,000, besides $36,000 for scholarships, and that reliable pledges were received for about $100,000 more. Much of the new income was wisely devoted to raising salaries and thus preserving or heightening the efficiency of the Faculty. President Sears gave ample proof of his wisdom as executive head of the institution at a gravely critical period, and fully deserved the praise given him by Dr. Hovey, that he was "a superb administrator."

His relations with the Faculty are thus described by Professor Harkness: "He was the best President to work with that I have ever had the good fortune to know. He encouraged all departments while he left all the professors free to adopt methods suited to their tastes and genius, believing that thus the best results would be reached." His views of the Faculty in relation to the university as a whole are expressed in his report as chairman of a special committee in 1863: "The strength of a university lies in its Faculty of instruction. It has become a maxim in education that a university does not consist of an assemblage of buildings, however necessary these may be, but in an assemblage of able instructors, expounding the facts & laws of science & literature to an organized body of young men eager for knowledge & discipline."

With regard to Dr. Sears as a teacher there is some difference of opinion. His profound learning no one questions. When his library was sold at auction in 1869, because his new work allowed him little opportunity to use it, the catalogue of sale described it thus: "The Library embraces the best works on doctrinal theology, Roman, Lutheran, and Reformed. It is very full in general and church history, still more in special history, ecclesiastical and civil. Biography, literary history, and history of learned institutions are each well represented, with many of the best editions of the Greek and Latin classics." Not only did he have this superb scholar's library on his shelves, but he had the contents in his head; a manuscript in the New England Baptist Library, written for the guidance of the auctioneer and indicating the peculiar merits of book after book, affords detailed proof of his familiarity with the great collection. In the class-room, furthermore, all agree that without ostentation — of which he was incapable — he gave the impression of having vast stores of learning on all the subjects that he taught. How much he made of the historical method may be seen by a statement in his annual report for 1865–66. His course in philosophy, the first term, was "followed by a critical examination of the leading systems of Grecian philosophy from the time of Thales to Plato, in the light of the principles previously laid down." The second term he took up the evidences of Christianity and Christian ethics. "In the former, there was a historical introduction containing a critique of the productions of great writers on the subject from the earliest times to the present, then a systematic outline of Evidences according to the present state of learning & science, &, in conclusion, an examination of the skeptical theories of Strauss, Renan & others. In the latter was presented in outline a complete theory of ethics on Christian principles."

He was by nature and training a historical student, and wished to present facts and theories in their development and historical relations; he was less anxious to sink into the minds of his classes the particular view which he himself held than to broaden their outlook on the world of thought, and, by showing them the successive stages through which human thinking and experience have passed, give them the means of arriving at a judicious opinion of their own. But many college seniors were not ready for this method of instruction; and it is said by some that he was too learned for his classes and shot over their heads. Others say that he had no magnetism, and failed to impress his ideas on his pupils. It is noticeable that his more mature or more scholarly pupils are the warmest in his praise. The Hon. Richard Olney, of the class of 1856, says in a recent letter: "My impressions of President Sears as a teacher are very favorable indeed. He was versed in all the latest philosophical theories and stated them with great lucidity and impressiveness. He had opinions, I am sure. If he was modest and not dogmatic in stating them, it was, I think, because he did not wish his teachings to be too glaringly in conflict with those of his famous predecessor, Dr. Wayland." The Rev. A. H. Plumb, D.D., who attended for six weeks President Sears's lectures at Brown University in 1856, wrote: 'He impressed me, as a very learned man, widely read, and profound in his philo-

sophical thinking, wonderfully rich, too, in his illustrative
comments and practical applications of principles in the
formation of correct judgments and in the guidance of conduct. . . . His replies to the questions and objections of students showed tact and power." The Rev. Dr. J. B. G. Pidge,
of the class of 1866, said: "On one occasion he remarked:
'I do not care to have you remember what I say; I am simply anxious to teach you how to think. If you learn that, you
may burn my lectures if you will.' . . . Those who sought
the class-room in order to be thoroughly drilled-into some
definite scheme of philosophy, probably went away from
Doctor Sears, grumbling that they had gotten nothing. But
some of us certainly found him the most inspiring of college
teachers."

The graciousness and poise of Dr. Sears must not be
allowed to leave the impression that he lacked force, for no
such impression was given by the man himself. The universal respect of the students for him is one proof of this.
When he was appointed agent of the Peabody Fund, the
Boston Evening Transcript said of him: "Honest, manly
and intrepid, he is still so dispassionate and unostentatious
in his conscientiousness, and so simply bent on addressing
the intellect and moral sense of those he desires to influence, that he never stings their passions into opposition to his
teachings, nor rouses their willfulness to resist the reception
of his views. He has, in short, all the reality of force, without any of its arrogance." Dr. Hovey wrote: "It is possible
to emphasize the 'sweet reasonableness' of Doctor Sears so
strongly as to obscure his indignation at wrong and even
his energy in carrying out a deliberate purpose. He was
from first to last, as every great worker must be, *tenax pro-
positi*. Clear-sighted in deliberation, he was strenuous in action." Dr. Heman Lincoln speaks of a quality in him which

is quite the reverse of amiable weakness : " No one intimate with Doctor Sears would doubt that a power of sarcasm was one of his great intellectual gifts. His intimate friends always wondered how he could hold such a power under restraint." Finally, a study of the lineaments of President Sears confirms the testimony of his friends. It is a New England face, with a touch of rusticity about it still, in spite of years of intellectual labor at home and abroad; and through its urbanity and Christian kindliness there look out Yankee shrewdness and determination. Dr. Sears was rather a wise administrator than an original thinker or great driving force in education. He was not a son of thunder, like President Wayland; but in sunshine as well as in thunder there is power.

CHAPTER IX

PRESIDENT CASWELL'S ADMINISTRATION

PROFESSOR CHACE AS TEMPORARY PRESIDENT : INCREASE IN ENDOW-
MENT : ALUMNI ASSOCIATIONS : SOCIAL LIFE OF THE
UNDERGRADUATES: BASEBALL AND BOATING

ON April 17, 1867, the same day that they accepted the resignation of Dr. Sears, the Corporation elected as his successor the Rev. Dr. Martin B. Anderson, President of the University of Rochester. His declination created a grave crisis. The Corporation could not agree on any one for the presidency, and in July appointed a committee to consider the matter. The situation caused alarm among the friends of the university, and some demand was heard that the charter be so revised as to remove the denominational restriction in the choice of president. When the Corporation met in September, the committee reported that they were awaiting an answer from the Rev. Dr. Ezekiel G. Robinson, President of Rochester Theological Seminary, who was abroad, and recommended the election of Professor Chace as president for the first term. The recommendation was adopted, and Professor Chace consented to serve as president *ad interim*. He discharged the duties of his temporary office very ably. He taught philosophy to the seniors with characteristic brilliancy; he organized a three-year course for holders of the new agricultural scholarships, under the head of "Agricultural and Scientific Department," to meet the requirements which the state had imposed five years before; and at the end of the half-year he submitted to the Corporation a vigorous and incisive report on the needs of the college, with special attention to scholarships and the Faculty.

Meanwhile Dr. Robinson had refused to accept a nomination for the presidency, and the Corporation were confronted with a difficult problem. One party strongly favored Professor Chace for permanent president; but the Corporation as a whole, although they put on record their appreciation of the "judicious faithful and successful" service of the president *ad interim*, deemed it best to recall the venerable Dr. Caswell, who was accordingly elected president on February 7, 1868. President Caswell was born January 29, 1799, in Taunton, Massachusetts, where his ancestors had lived since the settlement of the town early in the seventeenth century; through his paternal grandmother he was descended from Peregrine White, born on board the Mayflower. After a youth spent on his father's farm, he prepared for college at Taunton Academy, and entered Brown University in 1818. He graduated in 1822, at the head of his class, and for the next five years taught in Columbian College, at the same time studying theology with the president of the institution. He then became pastor of a Baptist church in Halifax, Nova Scotia, whence he returned in the summer of 1828 to be assistant pastor of the First Baptist Church in Providence. A few weeks later he was chosen professor of mathematics and natural philosophy in the university, to which he gave thirty-six years of continuous service, except for a year in Europe in 1860, resigning in 1864. He was not wholly new to executive work, for he had been acting president in 1840–41, during Dr. Wayland's visit to Europe, and regent in 1852–55. Brown University gave him the degree of D.D. in 1844, and LL.D. in 1853.

In spite of his age Dr. Caswell entered upon the presidency with the cheerful though modest confidence characteristic of him, and for four and a half years guided the affairs of the institution with sober wisdom. It was not thought best, however, to burden him with the labor of instruction, and indeed the subjects which usually fell to the president were out of his line. Professor Chace, therefore, continued to be professor of intellectual and moral philosophy. A new chancellor, the Hon. William S. Patten, had already been elected on September 5, 1867. The administrative side of the university was further strengthened at the annual meeting on September 3, 1868, by the creation of an Advisory and Executive Committee, of nine members besides the president, "to give to the President the assistance of their counsel when it is desired by him," "to act on occasions of emergency, and to suggest and prepare subjects to be considered or acted upon by the Corporation," and "to see that the Laws of the Corporation are carried into effect by the officers, and observed by the students of the University."

It was not to be expected that a man of Dr. Caswell's years and temperament would attempt innovations in educational policy or would prove a very vigorous disciplinarian. The general nature of his administration is thus described by his colleague, Professor Lincoln: "He administered the Presidential office in a spirit of manly independence, and stood firmly, at whatever cost of personal convenience and personal interest, to the responsibilities which devolved upon him. . . . In his intercourse with the students, he so tempered his official dignity with the courtesy and kindness of a friend, silently drawing all into a reciprocal relation of Christian gentlemen, that he was universally esteemed and loved."

The college made some progress under President Caswell. The funds were increased from $327,000 to $602,000, partly by the payment of pledges previously made, and partly by new donations. The tuition went up, in 1870, from $50 to $75,[1] and room rents from $9 to $20. The next

[1] Tuition at this time, or shortly before, was $150 at Harvard, $90 at Yale, $75 at Amherst, $60 at Dartmouth.

year the entrance requirements were also raised by the addition of two books of the *Anabasis* or of Homer, quadratic equations and plane geometry, and "the Analysis and Prosody of the First Act of Julius Caesar, in Craik's English of Shakspeare." In spite of all this there was some increase in number of students, the attendance rising from 186 in 1867–68 to 224 in 1871–72. This growth was doubtless due in a measure to additional aid offered. A loan fund of $11,000 was mentioned in the catalogue of 1867–68; in subsequent years, $8000. The David Howell scholarship in mathematics and natural philosophy, founded by the gift of $1000 from G. Lyman Dwight, great-grandson of Professor Howell, was announced in 1868–69. In the same year were advertised the two Carpenter premiums of $60 each, for seniors uniting in the highest degree "ability, character, and attainment"; and also the Carpenter prizes in elocution, of $60, $36, and $24, then confined to juniors. Thirty state scholarships, derived from the income of the money obtained by the sale of the Western lands, and open only to citizens of Rhode Island, were first spoken of in the catalogue of 1870–71. The Dunn Premium, established in 1869, has been mentioned in the preceding chapter.

Salaries were raised during Dr. Caswell's presidency. In 1870–71 the five older professors received $2750, and the younger ones $2500 or less; the next year these maximum professorial salaries went up to $3000, and Professor Chace was paid $500 extra for a course in geology; since 1867 Professor Lincoln had received $700 extra for teaching German. President Caswell's salary remained at $2000 throughout his term.

There were several additions to the Faculty and the curriculum. Dr. Charles W. Parsons was appointed lecturer in anatomy and physiology (including botany and zoölogy) in 1867, chiefly for the Agricultural and Scientific Department. Professor Timothy W. Bancroft succeeded Professor Dunn in 1868; and in that year instruction in civil engineering, which had been given up in 1863, was offered again, and spread over three years. In 1870 William C. Poland began his long connection with the Faculty, as instructor in Greek, and Alonzo Williams became tutor in Greek and Latin. The Hazard chair of physics, established by the gift of $40,000 from Rowland G. Hazard and Rowland Hazard, was filled in 1870 by the appointment of Eli Whitney Blake, Jr. Two years later William S. Rogers, nephew of the first student enrolled in the college, endowed the chair of chemistry by the gift of $50,000. The need of more liberal appropriations for apparatus and materials in these and other departments of science had been very great, if we may credit *The Brunonian* of April, 1870:

The chemical department needs more apparatus to enable the Professor to illustrate fully all the subjects presented. A cabinet of comparative anatomy is essential to any college. . . . Every plant and animal is an expressed thought of God, and cannot be presented through the medium of a professor. Brown has one ghastly skeleton and two or three small charts, and a few promiscuous bones! Natural Philosophy is also destitute of means for making the subject interesting, if it is possible to make it so. Juniors are edified with a clothes-line and a broken fiddle!

It must have gratified the editors to learn, two months later, that Mr. Rogers had given the department of chemistry $500 for the purchase of apparatus; and at about the same time the Corporation authorized the expenditure of $1000 for apparatus in physics. Those thoughts of God for which professors are no substitute were also soon supplied, as appears from the following statement in the catalogue of 1871–72:

During the last year several additional large cases were placed in Rhode Island Hall, for the deposit of specimens illustrating the different branches of Natural History. . . . Arrangements have now been made for adding to the Cabinet an extremely valuable collection of birds, numbering about forty-five hundred; and also such specimens in Mammalogy, Herpetology, Icthyology, Conchology and Comparative Anatomy, as will meet the wants of instruction, and of the general student in these departments. The mounting and arrangement of the specimens is entrusted to the care of Mr. J. W. P. Jenks, A.M., a well informed practical naturalist, and a most skillful Taxidermist.

One of the wisest acts of Dr. Caswell's presidency was his reviving of the almost defunct alumni association. At the end of his first half-year as president he invited the alumni to meet him in Manning Hall, on the Tuesday before Commencement, to consult on the interests of the institution. Annual meetings were held thenceforth, and a permanent organization was effected in 1872. At the suggestion of the general association local associations were also formed — in New York in 1869, in Philadelphia and Boston in 1870 — which have been centers of influence ever since, and the forerunners of many other associations all over the country. The general association showed from the first a strong desire to promote the welfare of the university, discussing the establishment of graduate scholarships, the erection of a gymnasium and a fireproof library building, and other needs. At the meeting in 1868 it was unanimously resolved, ''That in the opinion of the Alumni the interests of the University require that the whole body of graduates should be brought into some more immediate connection with it.'' Out of this there soon grew a request that the alumni be given some part in the election of trustees, which in 1875 issued in a system of nominations by the alumni for vacant positions on the board of trustees, the Corporation reserving the right to ignore the nominations if they saw fit. This quickened spirit of loyalty on the part of the alumni, together with the growing emphasis upon the social side of Commencement week, favored the custom of holding class reunions, which from about this time became more numerous and regular.

In 1870 Commencement day was changed to the last Wednesday in June. Harvard and some other universities had already set the example; and the new date was more convenient for the graduating class and for townspeople, who more and more delayed, or wished to delay, their return from seaside and mountain. In 1875 the day was moved to the third Wednesday, where it has since remained, except for a return to the fourth Wednesday in 1892 and 1893. The Commencement of 1870 was also notable for the size of the graduating class, fifty-three in number, the largest so far in the history of the university. By the close of President Caswell's administration, in 1872, the exercises of Commencement week had assumed the order which they retained, with trifling changes, for many years: Class Day came on Friday; on Saturday morning was the Carpenter contest in declamation; on Sunday afternoon the President preached a baccalaureate sermon in the First Baptist Meeting-House; the sermon before the Society of Missionary Inquiry was preached the same evening; on Tuesday occurred the annual business meeting of the Phi Beta Kappa Society, the oration before that body or the alumni, the alumni meeting in Manning Hall, and the class reunions; Wednesday was Commencement day, with the graduating exercises in the forenoon, the alumni dinner in the afternoon, and the President's reception in the evening; on Thursday the Corporation met.

The calendar for the academic year 1871–72 offers some points of interest, in comparison with both the past and the future. The year began on Friday, September 8; examinations for admission came on the same day; Thanksgiving week was a recess; no holidays are mentioned in connection with Christmas; the first term ended on January 18, and was followed by a recess of three weeks; the second term began on Friday, February 9; the junior exhibition, on April 27, was followed by a week's recess; term examinations for seniors came in the latter part of May, for the other students on June 18, 19, 20; Commencement week followed; and examinations for admission were held on June 27 and 28.

In undergraduate life during this administration social and athletic activities played an increasingly important part. Class Day grew more and more gay, although dances and receptions were still a minor feature. This growing love for the joys and graces of life made the students keenly appreciative of social attentions from members of the Faculty. Professor Chace began the practice, in 1869, of inviting the seniors in groups of four or five to tea at his home, the "Mansion House" on Benefit Street, and *The Brunonian* of January, 1871, says of one such evening:

The cheerful social character of the meeting, the interest in our personal welfare so plainly expressed both by the Professor, and also his excellent wife, the instructive conversation, the perusal of valuable books, and the examination of the costly paintings that adorn the walls of the parlors, together with the explanations of their meaning received from the lips of the Professor as we stood before them, all these and many more interesting facts connected with those meetings will be recalled with pleasure long after the memory of even Commencement Day shall have passed away.

A rather amusing passage in *The Brunonian* of May, 1872, expresses not only the undergraduates' pleasure in social intercourse, but also their sense of the need of its refining influence:

On a certain lovely evening just at the close of the half-term the members of the senior class were honored as their predecessors in that position had been. The hospitable roof of the president was made to cover the invited forms of classmates and friends of the gentler sex. . . . The dignity and affability with which Dr. and Mrs. Caswell did the honors of the evening; the brilliant assemblage and more brilliant conversation; the interchange of greetings at the instance of the ushers; the sufficient and elegant refreshments; the air of chastened pleasure which surrounded the scenes of the whole evening; — these were part of the remembrances which the class brought away. The student was led to feel by this exhibition of the good feeling of the president, that the demands of society and the cultivation of social qualities should not be overlooked. The student is himself in a certain limited sphere; but out of that very many find themselves at a loss, and the recurrence of such occasions as this but confirms the opinion, perhaps not fully formed, that relaxation is positively one of our needs.

In contrast to these cultured homes the students felt all the more keenly the unloveliness and discomfort of the dormitories. *The Brunonian* of April, 1869, says of the rooms:

Old and worn out floors ruinous to decent carpets, may be a necessity: tumble down ceilings and broken plaster, are often attendants of respectable poverty, which we believe to be the condition of Mother Brown; but broken ill fitted window sashes, through which the winter wind whistles hoarsely, and cracked doors giving unrestrained admission to lively breezes, surely these are badges of shiftless wretchedness, and admit of no excuse. These, however, are rule, not the exception, here. . . . In many of these apartments the paint and paper are old, tattered and rusty, — the furniture is broken, rickety and of many fashions, and they are lighted in the evening by the pauper method of oil lamps.

There were also loud complaints of the slovenly service of the "male chambermaids."

This regard for the attractiveness of college rooms and buildings was stimulated by the growing popularity of Class Day, when the students were hosts to mothers and

sisters and other fair guests as yet unrelated. The bare
college chapel received its share of the new aesthetic criticism; and the appearance of the grounds became an object of solicitude. "No College can boast of a finer located
campus than Brown," remarked *The Brunonian* of July,
1870. "If kept neatly shaven . . . it would add much to the
beauty of our surroundings. But when, as at present, it is
used as an adjunct of the Agricultural Department, it only
serves to practically illustrate the process of raising hay."
In the November issue the editors were able to rejoice that
one practical improvement had been made, "the muddy
paths" having given place to "numerous fine, broad concrete walks," although some dirt paths yet remained.

At least one thing in the college had a distinct aesthetic
value — the collection of portraits in Rhode Island Hall, first
mentioned in the catalogue in 1869. It had been forming
for some years. In 1857 eleven portraits (mostly copies) of
men conspicuous in the history of Rhode Island were given
to the university as the result of a movement started by the
Hon. John R. Bartlett, secretary of state; the portraits were
those of Governor William Coddington, Commodore Esek
Hopkins, Commodore Abraham Whipple, Moses Brown,
Colonel William Barton, Gilbert Stuart, Samuel Slater,
Thomas P. Ives, Tristam Burges, Henry Wheaton, and
Captain Oliver H. Perry. They were hung in the upper
room of Rhode Island Hall, and others were added from
time to time, some of which — as those of President Manning and Nicholas Brown — had been in the possession of
the university for many years. A portrait of Adoniram Judson had been given in 1846 by the First Baptist Church,
and one of President Wayland, at about the same time, by
John Carter Brown. In 1860 the friends of the Rev. Dr.
Crocker, rector of St. John's Church, presented his portrait;

and in 1863, through the efforts of Mr. Bartlett, six more historical portraits were added to the collection — General Ambrose E. Burnside, General Isaac P. Rodman, Colonel Christopher Greene, Dr. Solomon Drowne, Charles II, and Catherine his queen. The total collection in 1869 included thirty-five portraits, besides the bust of Wayland referred to in a preceding chapter; among the recent accessions was an oil painting of Dr. Sears.

Athletics at Brown made great advance for a while under President Caswell. On June 17, 1868, the sophomore baseball nine played a memorable game on the Dexter Training Ground, before an "immense crowd," defeating by a score of 22 to 19 the famous Lowell club, the champions of New England. The 'varsity nine, although composed largely of men from the '70 team, had less success. Next year it was a class team, again, that made the best showing. The freshman nine, after defeating the Harvard freshmen at Providence on July 1, set out on a week's tour — something almost unknown then in college sports, — playing freshman nines at Yale, Wesleyan, Amherst, and Dartmouth. They were beaten at Yale and Dartmouth; but the spirit shown by the nine and by the class in supporting them set a new standard in sports at Brown. Between September 26, 1870, and June 26, 1871, the 'varsity team played thirteen games and won eight. In the following year there was no 'varsity nine, and little baseball of any kind.

In 1868 had come a revival of interest in boating. The boat-club was reorganized and enlarged; the boat-house was repaired; and two crews went to practicing daily in second-hand shells. In the spring, however, the interest flagged again, and no crew was sent to the intercollegiate regatta in the summer of 1869. In the autumn of that year the system of class crews was introduced with happy results; and when winter came the crews went into training in the gymnasium — for in the spring of 1869, and during the greater part of the year 1869–70, the students had the use of a private gymnasium on Canal Street, the college bearing half the expense. In the spring of 1870 the hopes of the undergraduates centered in the freshman six-oar crew, who were taken seriously in hand by the captain of the university club, after the examinations in June, and put through a long and rigorous drill. On the day of the regatta, July 22, twenty thousand spectators lined the shores of Lake Quinsigamond. There were four freshman crews, representing Harvard, Yale, Amherst, and Brown. The course was a mile and a half to a stake, and return. Amherst took the lead, but weakened at the end of a mile, and ran into Brown's water; the two boats fouled, with the loss of Amherst's rudder, and were separated only by the coolness of the Brown bow-oar. Amherst fell out of the race, and Brown continued. Meanwhile Yale had got ten lengths ahead, and Harvard six. So steady and strong was the Brown stroke, however, that before the stake was reached Harvard had been passed and Yale had a lead of only a length. Yale turned wide; and the Brown crew, coolly using the quick turn they had practiced so often — holding the port oars deep in the water and rowing with the starboard oars, — neatly made the turn between the Yale boat and the stake, and started for the goal a length ahead. From that moment the crew never changed their steady swing, forty-four strokes to a minute, until they crossed the line in 19 minutes, 21 seconds, six lengths ahead of Yale, whose time was 24 seconds slower. Amherst claimed a foul, but the judges decided against her and awarded the prize to the Brown crew.

The victory aroused immense enthusiasm for boating among the Brown undergraduates. The next autumn four class crews took the water, and on October 15 they raced on the Seekonk, the freshman crew winning, the sophomores second. That winter practice in the gymnasium was resumed; and in the summer of 1871 a freshman crew and a 'varsity crew were sent to the intercollegiate regatta at Ingleside, near Springfield, on the Connecticut River; but both were defeated. The following summer there were class races on the Seekonk, and a freshman crew was sent to Ingleside. At the regatta at Saratoga, in 1874, Brown was again represented by an unsuccessful freshman crew. In the autumn the boat-house and all the shells were destroyed by fire; but students, Faculty, townspeople, and alumni enthusiastically combined to make good the loss, and the following summer the college sent both a 'varsity and a freshman crew to Saratoga. Continued defeat, however, at last dampened the undergraduates' ardor, and boating has since been almost wholly neglected at Brown.

A glee club representing the whole college, and giving public concerts, dates from the year 1869. On June 14 it gave a concert in the Horse Guards Armory, before a large audience; and on this occasion "Alma Mater," under its first name of "Old Brown," after sleeping unnoticed in the columns of *The Brown Paper* for nine years, was sung, and won instant favor. It was played by the band at Commencement next autumn, and two years later was sung by the glee club at the Commencement dinner. When the seniors bade Professor Chace farewell, in 1872, they sang "Alma Mater," which was then spoken of as "sweetest of college songs." The alumni, however, were not yet familiar with the words, and "Old Hundred" continued for some years to be the closing song at Commencement dinners. College musical clubs thenceforth played a conspicuous part in college life, singing at Class Day and Commencement (a cus-

tom which might well be revived), giving concerts for the
benefit of athletics, and sometimes accompanying the teams
on their trips. Dramatics also received some attention at this
time. The Hammer and Tongs revived toward the end of
the administration, and gave several successful plays. The
interest spread to the classes, juniors and seniors presenting enjoyable comedies in 1871 and 1872, for the benefit of
baseball and boating.

The literary life was not forgotten. The Sears Reading
Room Association was formed in 1868, and under different
names and in various quarters has survived to this day. In
March of the same year the college magazine, *The Brunonian*, emerged from a sleep longer than Rip Van Winkle's
and started anew on its career. For the first two years it
was a quarterly, and then was published six or seven times
a year until 1874–75, when it became a tri-weekly. The
magazine was a credit to the college from the first. The serious essays, though lacking originality, often show maturity in thought and style. Now and then appears an article
of much promise—a judicious literary criticism by W.E.
Foster; a racy, imaginative sketch by I. N. Ford, whose ini-
tials were to become so familiar at the bottom of his London letters to *The New York Tribune;* or a virile, vivid war-
sketch by E. B. Andrews. About half of each number was
filled with college news and editorial comment, and in 1871
a department of alumni notes was begun. In *The Brunonian*
and the *Liber Brunensis* the undergraduate life found a voice.
They were the effect of increasing social consciousness in
the student body, and became in turn a cause of its further
growth. Combined with the athletic and social activities of
the whole college and of classes and smaller groups, they
cultivated the sense of a common life larger than that of
the individual; and therefore it is not an accident that *The*

Brunonian soon began to invoke by name that invisible but potent deity, "college spirit," whose worship has been cultivated so ardently ever since, sometimes with zeal not according to knowledge, but on the whole with good results.

In 1872 Professor Chace withdrew from the university, in which he had been a teacher since 1831. He was born at Lancaster, Massachusetts, on February 19, 1808. After a boyhood on a farm, he studied in Lancaster Academy, and entered Brown University as a sophomore in 1827, graduating in 1830 as valedictorian. The next year he was principal of the academy in Waterville, Maine, but returned to Brown in the autumn of 1831 as tutor; his promotion was thenceforth rapid, and his versatility is shown by the diversity of subjects he taught. He became adjunct professor of mathematics and natural philosophy in 1833, professor of chemistry in 1834, and professor of chemistry, geology, and physiology in 1836; at various times thereafter he also taught chemistry applied to the arts, physical geography, and Butler's *Analogy*, and from 1867 to 1872 he was professor of mental and moral philosophy. Whatever the subject, he taught it with signal ability. The Rev. George P. Fisher, of the class of 1847, professor in Yale College, writes: "He was regarded . . . by all the students as a teacher of remarkable acuteness and logical ability, and as exacting, in the good sense of the term. . . . His order was lucid; he did not crowd the hearer's mind with minutiae; he set forth the main facts and principles of the science simply and precisely; he was fluent without being too rapid." President James B. Angell, of the class of 1849, says: "He untangled a difficult problem with such simplicity that men disinclined to mathematics learned to like them under his instruction. In illustrating scientific teaching he was very skillful as a manipulator and experimenter. He was one of the few men who could talk well while conducting an experiment." President E. B. Andrews, of the class of 1870, says: "Professor Chace had the keenest analytic power of any thinker whom I have ever heard discourse; and, what is very rare indeed, he joined with this a hardly less remarkable faculty for generalization, which enabled him, on grasping the salient notions of a philosophical system, to think his way rapidly to its remotest deductions with but a fraction of the reading which many another scholar would have required. . . . There was moral quickening as well as intellectual, continual pungent reminders of the supremacy of moral law, of the reasonableness and worth of religion. Pupils awoke to their powers and their duties."

Professor Chace had a wide reputation as a lecturer, giving lectures before the Smithsonian Institution, the Peabody Institute in Baltimore, the Andover and Newton theological seminaries, and elsewhere. His clear and vigorous style also made him a favorite contributor to periodicals: among his articles are a series on natural theology in the *Bibliotheca Sacra* in 1848–50, "The Persistence of Physical Laws," in *The North American Review*, July, 1855, and a review of Rowland G. Hazard's "Man a Creative First Cause," in *The Andover Review*, December, 1884. Although not an original investigator, he was skillful in the application of science to the useful arts, and introduced new methods in some of the manufactories of Providence; in the early sixties his advice was so much sought by prospective buyers of gold mines that he was often given leave of absence that he might visit mines in Nova Scotia, Canada, Colorado, and Central America. His executive ability was early recognized by the corporation of Waterville College, who in 1841 urged him to accept the presidency of that institution. Brown University gave him the degree of LL.D. in 1853.

Yet with all his gifts Professor Chace was not a popular man. His manner was reserved, almost to coldness, and in class he was severe and sometimes caustic, although in his later years he cultivated closer and more friendly relations with his pupils. A man of deep convictions and a lifelong member of the Baptist denomination, he yet was disliked by religious conservatives: to the zealous he seemed cold and to the rigidly orthodox dangerously rationalistic, although in his later years, like his friend Agassiz, he withheld assent from the doctrine of evolution. His supposed theological unsoundness and the fact that he was not a clergyman were the main reasons, it is said, for the opposition to him as a candidate for the presidency of his Alma Mater. But in spite of his disappointment he remained loyal to the college, and in his will left $9000 for two scholarships which bear his name.

After resigning his professorship Professor Chace traveled in Europe for a year and a half, and upon his return to Providence gave his last days to various good works of a semi-public nature. For a short time he held the office of alderman; he continued his trusteeship in Butler Hospital until 1883; he was chosen a trustee of the Rhode Island Hospital in 1875, and its president in 1877, remaining in office for the rest of his life. His greatest work, however, was done as chairman of the State Board of Charities and Corrections from 1874 to 1883: during these years the board reorganized and administered the charitable, corrective, and penal institutions at Cranston, supervising the erection of many buildings, laying out the grounds, selecting officers, and preparing measures for presentation to the legislature; and in directing these activities Professor Chace displayed not only scientific knowledge but sound judgment and rare executive ability. Failing health forced him to withdraw from most of his offices in 1883, and he died on April 29, 1885.

The presidency of Dr. Caswell could in the nature of things be only temporary; and in September, 1872, having given notice of his intention the year before, he retired. During the years 1864–67, when he was not officially connected with the college, Dr. Caswell had occupied himself with scientific and philanthropic labors and with business, being president of the National Exchange Bank and the American Screw Company. He now resumed some of these occupations and added others. He was a trustee of the college from 1873 to 1875, and a fellow from 1875 to 1877. He continued to be a trustee of the Rhode Island Hospital, which he had aided in founding, and was president of it from 1875 till his death. During his closing years he was an inspector of the state prison, and often conducted religious service there. In these serene labors he passed the Indian summer of his age, and died peacefully on January 8, 1877, when he had nearly finished his seventy-eighth year.

As a professor Dr. Caswell was of the older school. Patient and clear rather than inspiring as a teacher, and kindly in discipline, he gave his pupils sound instruction and won them by his geniality, but was not a great vitalizing force in their lives. Without the brilliancy of Professor Chace he yet could teach well a wide range of subjects, and gave instruction at various times in chemistry, natural history, ethics, Butler's *Analogy*, and constitutional law, besides his specialties, mathematics, natural philosophy, and astronomy. He served for twenty-three years on the library committee, and in all the miscellaneous work of the Faculty was exceedingly useful. He rendered valuable aid to President Wayland throughout his administration, assisting him in executive work and giving wise counsel on many difficult problems.

He was an efficient solicitor of subscriptions, and raised a considerable part of the library fund of 1831, besides aiding in similar movements later.

As a scientist Dr. Caswell was not an original investigator or a brilliant generalizer. He did not even confine himself to one science, much less to one corner of one science, although his favorite study seems to have been astronomy. But he had a broad and thorough knowledge of his subjects, and kept up with their progress. Professor Joseph Lovering, of Harvard University, says of his lectures on astronomy before the Smithsonian Institution in 1858, "They were of the highest order of popular instruction, and, on that account, were thought by Professor Henry worthy of being permanently preserved in his printed report for that year." Professor Lovering adds that, although no specialist, "he was never superficial." Dr. Caswell was elected vice-president of the American Association for the Advancement of Science at its meeting in Providence, in 1855; and when the National Academy of Sciences was established by Congress, in 1863, he was named as one of the fifty incorporators. His publications include articles in *The Christian Review* and *The North American Review*, and "Meteorological Register; Providence, R.I.," from December, 1831, to May, 1860, in the publications of the Smithsonian Institution, 1860, filling 179 pages. Dr. Caswell continued these observations to the end of 1876.

The central quality in President Caswell's character was serenity. "Dr Caswell is universally known to be a man of imperturbable good nature," wrote President Wayland, in 1852, to an irate parent. "I have known him, intimately for more than twentyfive years, and I never have heard him utter an unkind or even a hasty expression. He never told your son that he was a liar, but he did tell him, that he

[384]

found great difficulty in believeing the account which he had given.'' Yet he did not lack moral courage: in 1868 he resolutely opposed a motion in the Warren Baptist Association condemning Baptists who practiced open communion, although he himself believed in close communion as the usage of the apostles; and when attacked by a leading newspaper of the denomination, he stoutly held his ground. ''Inflexible in his own peculiar theology,'' says Professor Lovering, ''he had no taint of illiberality in his intellect or his heart. . . . There was no austerity in his goodness; hence it attracted those who could not have been driven. . . . And behold the end of such a man: it is all honor, and affection, and peace. The press, the university, the church, and the State, have borne witness to the excellence of his character and the usefulness of his life.''

CHAPTER X

PRESIDENT ROBINSON'S ADMINISTRATION

NEW BUILDINGS : GROWTH OF THE FUNDS : ENLARGEMENT OF THE
ELECTIVE SYSTEM : GRADUATE STUDY : THE PROBLEM OF ATHLETICS :
THE PRESIDENT AS DISCIPLINARIAN AND TEACHER

WHEN President Caswell resigned his office, the majority of the Corporation turned again to Ezekiel G. Robinson, and on January 24, 1872, "duly" though not unanimously elected him president of the university and professor of moral and intellectual philosophy. With some reluctance he accepted, on February 20, in a characteristic letter expressing his purpose to administer the affairs of the college "in the broad & catholic spirit of the Christian religion & of its immutable morality," and the following September he entered upon his new duties.

President Robinson was born March 23, 1815, in South Attleboro, Massachusetts, on a farm that had been held by his ancestors since it was bought of the Indians. His father, successively a farmer, innkeeper, and sheriff, died when the boy was four and a half years old; his mother returned with her family to the farm, where the outdoor life, he says, "nurtured a naturally weak constitution into a strength that has since been equal to many a year of mental strain." He had poor teaching in various schools, and entered Brown University in 1834 with inadequate preparation. He graduated in the middle of his class, delivering a philosophical discussion, one of the minor honors, on "The value of Metaphysical Speculations." "I had drifted aimlessly into college," he writes, "and drifted aimlessly through it, waking up only during the last year to see what I might and ought to have done." After a half-year of graduate study in Brown

University, he entered Newton Theological Institution in 1839, and graduated there in 1842. For the next three years he was pastor of a Baptist church in Norfolk, Virginia, serving one year as chaplain to the University of Virginia. After a year's pastorate in Cambridge, Massachusetts, he became professor of Hebrew in a theological seminary in Covington, Kentucky; a dispute over slavery broke up the institution in 1848, and he took a church in Cincinnati, where he gained fame as a preacher. In 1853 he was called to Rochester Theological Seminary as professor of biblical theology, a position which he held until 1872, serving also as president after 1860. Brown University gave him the degree of D.D. in 1853, and of LL.D. in 1872; Harvard University also conferred the latter degree on him in 1886.

When Dr. Robinson came to Providence in 1872, driving his span of spirited horses across country from Rochester, he was in his fifty-eighth year, his thin hair prematurely white, but his tall spare figure as erect and active as ever. The impatient energy of the man spoke out through his prominent features and penetrating eye, his rapid stride, and his speech and manner, brusque at times to the verge of rudeness. He was neither a man of affairs nor a scholar of wide culture. His long residence in other parts of the country had put him somewhat out of touch and a good deal out of patience with New England conservatism, and, having more force than tact, he was likely to cut against the grain. His very success in his former field, combined with certain infirmities of temper, made it harder for him to adapt himself to new conditions and conciliate where he could not command. ''The iron man'' he was called in undergraduate days, it is said; and as president he had both the strength and the flaws of that inflexible metal. Yet so keen and so true was his vision of what Brown University ought to be that his unbending will urged him forward in the right direction; he did a great work in the seventeen years of his presidency, and prepared the way for things yet greater.

In his racy and outspoken autobiography, dictated in the last year of his life, Dr. Robinson thus describes the situation when he became president: "We were stifled and cramped for lack of buildings, and I was ashamed of the narrow range of studies open to our students, particularly in the Natural Sciences and in Modern Languages. The necessity was inexorable that we should strike at once for a widened curriculum and for new buildings." At a later point he adds: "The introduction of new departments of study and of new professors made necessary a readjustment of studies and a multiplication of electives. Naturally there was a jostling of old hereditary prejudices in behalf of certain studies which from time immemorial had taken precedence of all others. But science then got a foothold in the curriculum which it is never likely to lose." These sentences mark the large outlines of his policy throughout his administration.

In connection with his plans for adding to the college buildings President Robinson was spared the consideration of a change of site. This question had been raised by President Wayland in a report at the end of his first year of office, as appears from an entry in the Corporation records of September 6, 1827, to the effect that "so much of said Report as relates to the removal of the Institution to another place" was referred to a committee. The committee seems to have practiced a masterly inactivity, for the matter does not come up in the records again until 1872, when, on July 15, the Advisory and Executive Committee adopted the following preamble and resolution: "Whereas at the late annual com-

mence[ment] dinner of Brown University the Hon Benj.
F. Thurston announced a proposition from the Hon. Wm.
Sprague for the presentation of a tract of ten acres of land
for a new site for the University in case it should elect to
change its location, Therefore Resolved that Rev. Dr Caswell President, Hon. Wm. S. Patten Chancellor and Marshall Woods AM. Treasurer, be a Committee to confer
with the Hon Wm Sprag[u]e upon the subject of that
proposition." On September 3 President Caswell reported
that Mr. Sprague "had not found time to give special attention to the subject." He also said that gentlemen in East
Providence, Cranston, and Newport had made offers of land,
and that sites on Doyle Avenue and Butler Avenue had been
suggested to him. No offers for the existing site having been
received, the committe requested President Caswell to report
to the Corporation on the morrow that "it is not expedient,
at the present time to take any action upon the subject."

The panic of 1873 made it doubly difficult to raise money
for educational purposes, and President Robinson's movement for better housing went slowly for some years. The
first building was a two-story addition to Rhode Island Hall
on the east side, chiefly to provide rooms for the department
of physics. How urgent was the need is shown by Dr. Robinson in his autobiography: "The professor of Physics had
no laboratory; the damp, dark basement rooms of Rhode Island Hall . . . could be occupied by him only at the risk of
his health and life." The work, which cost nearly $9000,
was completed shortly before the end of 1874, and the added
rooms afforded excellent quarters for the department of
physics, besides providing a well-lighted portrait gallery and
more space for the ever-growing natural history museum.

The university library had also been growing: the number of volumes was 24,000 in 1850, 29,000 in 1860, and

38,000 in 1870, besides many unbound pamphlets. Most of the special collections which now distinguish it had not then been received, but it contained many rare works, besides a good assortment of standard books for general use. The need of a new library building is stated vividly by Dr. Robinson: "The library was crowded into the dark room on the first floor of the chapel building, and was so crammed with books, two or three feet deep on the shelves, that only the librarian could find what was wanted." The need had been foreseen long before, and the feeling that something must be done had been growing stronger for years. President Wayland, in a report to the Executive Board in 1853, had said that "the erection of another Library building will soon become indispensable." A committee was appointed at the end of President Sears's first year, to report "the best plan of a Fire Proof Building for the Library" and ways and means for securing it. In 1868 President Chace declared that "the Library has quite outgrown its accommodations," and that "a suitable and fireproof building of sufficient capacity . . . is becoming every year a matter of more urgent necessity." During the academic year 1869–70 John Carter Brown paid into the treasury the sum of $15,000 toward the erection of such a building, and in 1871 the Corporation appointed a committee to take the matter into consideration.

So matters stood until 1874. In June of that year occurred the death of John Carter Brown, at the age of seventy-seven. Inheriting the spirit with the fortune of his father, he had been a lifelong friend and patron of the college, serving on its Corporation for forty-six years and contributing to it liberally of his time and his wealth. From early manhood he had taken a special interest in books; he had been forming through years the famous collection of Americana which now bears his name, and he had given thousands of volumes to the college library. It was therefore no surprise to the friends of the university when they learned that he had bequeathed to it a site for a library building, at the corner of Prospect and Waterman Streets, and $50,000 for the building itself. These gifts, in addition to his former gift of $15,000, now grown to over $20,000, made it possible to proceed at once with the erection of the building which had been so long needed. The foundations were laid in the summer of 1875, and the structure was dedicated on February 16, 1878. The total cost was $95,588, the widow of Mr. Brown paying the excess over what he had given. The building, Venetian Gothic in style, was cruciform, with very short arms, the extreme dimensions being ninety-six by eighty-six feet. The walls were brick, with stone trimmings; the roof was of iron, covered with slates; no wood was used except for shelves and other finishings. In the center was a large octagonal reading-room lighted by windows in the cupola-like roof; from this center radiated the alcoves, in three stories, with estimated shelf-capacity of one hundred and fifty thousand books. The new library was at first open from 10 to 3 every week day but Saturday, when it closed at noon; during vacations it was open only on Saturday. In 1882 the time was extended one hour a day, and so remained to the end of Dr. Robinson's administration. A card-catalogue was begun in 1878.

Although the library now had fitting quarters, it was not adequately endowed; but the only considerable addition to its funds at this period was the Stephen T. Olney bequest of $10,000, received in 1880–81, for the purchase of botanical works. In 1885–86, however, the library was enriched by a special collection of great value, the Harris Collection of American Poetry, begun by Albert G. Greene, of the class of 1820, much enlarged by C. Fiske Harris, and still further increased by the Hon. Henry B. Anthony, of the class of 1833, who in 1884 bequeathed it to the university; it contained some 6000 volumes, many of them very rare.

While the new library building was going up, better quarters for the students were also begun. Not even *The Brunonian* could condemn the condition of the dormitories more vigorously than did Dr. Robinson. Of University Hall he said, "Its battered doors, its defaced walls, the gaping flooring of its hall-ways, and the unmistakable odor of decay pervading the building, made parents who came to select rooms for their sons, turn from the premises with ill-concealed disgust." "The other dormitory," he added, "erected in 1822, had inside and out fewer marks of age, but was only a little less uninviting than the older building. The entries and stairways of the dormitories had never been lighted at night; the students groped their way up and down as best they could." The President early set his heart on renovating University Hall. But he thought it necessary to erect an additional dormitory first, and for this purpose a fund was now available. When Dr. Robinson had been weighing the question of accepting the presidency, Horatio N. Slater, the tried friend of the university for many years, had promised to give $25,000 if he would come; this money, with accumulated interest, Mr. Slater consented to have used for a new dormitory. A site was chosen, the south end of the middle campus, and in the autumn of 1877 the cellar was dug and the foundation partly laid, when suddenly protests began. The site was objected to because the view across the middle campus would be obstructed by the new building; as "A Tax-Payer" said, in a letter to *The Providence Journal* of November 17, it was a matter of surprise and regret "that grounds upon which so many are accustomed to gaze while taking their daily walks are to be disfigured by the march of events.'' A petition signed by many of the most wealthy and influential men in the city was presented to President Robinson; he poured oil on the flames by publishing an ironical rejoinder, and the furnace was heated seven times hotter. The building committee finally gave way, and erected a smaller dormitory in the rather narrow space between University Hall and Rhode Island Hall. Slater Hall, so named from the donor of the fund, was completed in the autumn of 1879; and being attractively finished in modern style, it at once became popular with students of means.

The renovation of University Hall was still delayed for lack of funds. Meanwhile other needs which President Robinson had long been pressing upon the attention of the Corporation and the public — additional and better recitation rooms, and a hall large enough to hold Commencement dinners in — were supplied by the Hon. William F. Sayles, whose purpose is expressed in a letter to President Robinson on June 14, 1878:

For a long time I have had under consideration (as you are aware from my repeated conversations with you and my friend, Professor Lincoln, upon the subject) the propriety of offering to Brown University a sum of money, for the erection of a building, as a memorial to my dear son, William Clark Sayles, who died February 13th, 1876. At the time of his death he was a member of the class of '78, now about to graduate. The thought of the project indicated has been cherished, because of the strong attachment of my dear son to the University, and his and my own appreciation of the higher education which it affords; and I have therefore concluded to propose to give to the University fifty thousand dollars for the erection of a building, containing rooms and a hall, which shall be exclusively and forever devoted to lectures and recitations, and to meetings on academic occasions. . . . I have selected this Commencement, when my dear son, if living, would have graduated, for the expression of what I hope will be regarded with favor, in order that when his classmates are conferring credit on their Alma Mater his brief life may also not be without a beneficial influence on the institution he loved so well.

Sayles Hall was begun in the summer of 1879, and completed two years later, the dedication occurring on June 4, 1881. The material was reddish granite, with trimmings of brown sandstone. "The style of the building," said Professor Lincoln at the dedication, "is, in its main features, of the Romanesque type; so judiciously treated, however, by the omission of all excessive ornament, that it impresses you with the noble simplicity and serene repose which belong to the old Roman style." On the front was carved the simple inscription, by Professor Lincoln, "FILIO PATER POSUIT." The hall, 105 feet by 50, has been invaluable for Commencement dinners and various other gatherings, and of late years for chapel exercises and examinations; the eight classrooms have also been of great use. The entire cost of the structure was borne by Mr. Sayles, and has never been made known, but it far exceeded the original estimate of $50,000.

The erection of Sayles Hall was the indirect cause of two other improvements. The portraits were transferred to its auditorium, which formed a noble gallery, and a large room in Rhode Island Hall thus became available for the growing work in natural science. Extensive alterations were also made in the grounds. "To the lasting credit of Mr. Sayles be it said," writes Dr. Robinson, "that, when the site for the Hall was selected, he foresaw the necessity of regrading the middle campus on which it was to front, and in his own mind he determined it should be done. Till then it had presented to the eye on its northern side, toward Waterman Street, an ungrassed and unsightly bank, and over the whole area its uneven surface reminded one of the recent days when it had been used as a cow-pasture. On the completion of the building, Mr. Sayles insisted that the campus should then be graded and put in order. The result was one of the most beautiful spots in the city of Providence." At the same time the grading of the front campus was improved, and the whole was seeded with lawn grass. "While in the humor of grading the middle campus," adds the President, "it occurred to some of us that, by the requisite grading and filling up of an unsightly swamp-hole, the eastern slope and terminus of the college land on Thayer Street could be transformed into much needed ball-grounds. . . . One man only in the Faculty, Professor S. S. Greene, felt interest enough in the matter to give himself and his time to raising the money and superintending the work. Quietly, and without words, he took the work in hand, and persisted in it till the task was completed."

"There still remained," says Dr. Robinson, " the old University Hall, both within and without an eyesore and a reproach. The grave question was, What should be done with it? The loud demand of many friends of the College was to level it to the ground, and to put up a modern structure in its place. A few of us were equally earnest in insisting that the old walls should stand, and the interior be entirely renewed. Minutest inspection could discover not so much as the sign of a crack in its walls." Renovation was decided upon, and the necessary sum, about $50,000, was raised by subscription. In April, 1883, the work of tearing out the interior began, the students removing to other dormitories or to private houses, and the reconstruction was completed by the autumn. The final report of the committee in charge shows the nature of the changes:

The walls, with the openings for the windows and doors, remain as of old, while everything within the walls and the roof has been actually renovated by the use of new material. The principal change in the plans of the interior is in taking away from the hallway, which of old ran the whole length of the building, one hundred and fifty feet, that portion of it which ran through the centre of the building, thirty-three feet in length, and using this space in the public rooms. . . . In the centre of the building the plan of the old chapel with its gallery is retained, widened by taking in half the old hallway. On the opposite side [the eastern] that which was of old Commons Hall . . . is changed into a room similar to the chapel, with a gallery. Both rooms are found useful for lectures and recitations, and meetings of students. . . . There are no longer apartments for a steward's family in the building. . . . The whole building is heated by steam, though in twenty-seven rooms there are also fire-places. . . . The building is lighted by gas. Water is carried through the building, with bath-rooms and closets in the basement. The stucco upon the outside walls of the building, put upon the brick nearly fifty years ago, was found so perfect that it was not removed, but again painted of a neutral olive tint, so that the building stands externally the same, except slight changes in the color and windows.

The two large rooms with galleries were designed by President Robinson to stimulate a revival of the debating societies, to whose influence he himself had owed so much as an undergraduate.

One more building, the new physics laboratory, was begun during this administration. It received the name Wilson Hall in memory of George F. Wilson, who at his death in 1883 left the university $100,000 to promote the study of natural science. The bequest was not received until 1887, and circumstances caused further delay in beginning the work of construction; but Dr. Robinson had the satisfaction of seeing the walls part way up when he resigned his office. The money for two other buildings was secured, although they were not erected until later. Daniel W. Lyman bequeathed the university $50,000 in 1887 for some building to be known as the Lyman Memorial; this gift, with other contributions, built the Lyman Gymnasium. At the Commencement dinner in 1889, Governor Herbert W.

Ladd, who sat beside the President, authorized him to announce to the alumni that he would erect an astronomical observatory at a cost of $20,000. "This ended my efforts," wrote President Robinson, "to provide the University with its necessary buildings." It was a work of which any college president might be proud, for it made possible still further extension of the work of instruction. It is only to be regretted that, although each of the new buildings was individually a fine structure, the taste of the day did not insist upon more harmony in the total effect.

The funds of the university increased under this administration from $602,000 to $1,000,000, a clear gain of almost $400,000, besides about $200,000 expended in erecting new buildings, extending or renovating old ones, and improving the college grounds.

In his second main line of policy, the enlargement of the curriculum, especially in the sciences, President Robinson was the educational successor to President Wayland, with the advantage of living in a time that was more ripe to receive and respond to his views. His first annual report contained this admirable statement of the case:

Adequate as the College may have been to the wants of the past, it manifestly is not equal to the needs of to-day. . . . That in a community like ours, which in some sense is a centre of manufactures for a population of millions if not for our whole country, liberal provision should be made for instruction in the applications of science to the mechanic arts is too evident to need discussion. . . . Unless I am misinformed, a large number of the intelligent citizens of our state are now desirous that a SCIENTIFIC SCHOOL of high order, — a School which, in addition to its more immediate aims, shall not fail to provide also for sub-schools of Design, of Drawing, of Civil Engineering, of Architecture, of the Fine Arts, etc.— may speedily be established in Rhode Island, and if possible may be established in conjunction with, and in a sense, as a part of Brown University.

He was unable to carry out this plan in its entirety, and indeed it is still unrealized; but he made some advance toward it. In addition to the enlarged laboratory facilities already described, several new professorships in the sciences were created. Dr. Charles W. Parsons, lecturer in physiology from 1867 to 1870, was appointed professor of that subject in 1874, and retained the office until 1882, when he was succeeded by Dr. Charles V. Chapin as instructor, who became professor in 1886. In 1875 the curator of the museum of natural history, J. W. P. Jenks, who had also been lecturer in agriculture, was promoted to be professor of agricultural zoölogy, and remained in that position until 1894. In 1877 William W. Bailey was appointed instructor in botany; and in 1881 he became the first holder of the professorship of natural history (including botany), which had recently been founded by the bequest of $25,000 from the estate of Stephen T. Olney. At about the same time valuable herbaria were received from the executors of Mr. Olney, and from Professor Bailey and James L. Bennett. A tract of thirteen acres in the northern part of the city, the homestead of Whiting Metcalf, was given to the university in 1884 by his widow for use as a botanical garden. In 1877 a professorship of geology was established; and in the following year Alpheus S. Packard, soon to become one of the foremost men of science in the United States, was made professor of zoölogy and geology. Upon the death of Professor Greene, in 1883, astronomy, with logic, became a separate department, and a highly trained astronomer, Winslow Upton, was appointed professor. The establishment of the new departments was justified by the demand for instruction in them; indeed, their limited facilities for laboratory work were in most cases soon outgrown, and even the chemical laboratory was taxed to its utmost capacity.

In the department of civil engineering similar conditions prevailed. As early as 1872 Professor Clarke, with the calm foresight characteristic of him, wrote in his annual report: "The public demand for the instruction in this department is greater than the college can at present supply. . . . The University then must soon decide the not unimportant question, whether its course of study shall be so enlarged as to meet this public demand or allow an institution to be planted by its side which must eventually supplant its Scientific Department." Without ample funds little could be done, however, and the department therefore made slow progress for many years. A fourth year of instruction was added in 1878, and was considerably expanded in 1885. The number of students continued to increase; forty-three were connected with the department in 1881–82, of whom fourteen were candidates for the degree of A.B., and the rest for the degree of Ph.B., as the degree of C.E. was not yet given by Brown University. The vitality of the department under adverse conditions was considerably due to the energetic labors of two younger members of the Faculty, Nathaniel F. Davis, instructor in 1874, assistant professor in 1879, and Otis E. Randall, instructor in 1885.

The needs of other departments of instruction meanwhile had not been overlooked. In his second annual report Dr. Robinson urged the strengthening of the work in modern languages, of which there had been no professor since 1860, French and German being taught by instructors or by professors of other subjects. In 1876 Alonzo Williams was appointed professor of modern languages, and began at once to develop the department. French, which since 1856 could not be taken before the sophomore year in the Bachelor of Arts course, was at once given a place among freshman studies, although two hours a week were all that could be spared for it until 1889; German, which for many years had been very ably taught by Professor Lincoln as a senior study, was opened as a junior elective in 1877; short courses in Italian and Spanish were offered to seniors in 1885. With the appointment of an instructor in 1884, the courses in French and German began to be extended, until in 1888 French could be studied through the first half of the junior year, and German through the last three years.

Himself a master of extempore speech, President Robinson naturally took a deep interest in the teaching of English. Again and again in his annual reports he urged upon the Corporation the fundamental importance of this study and the necessity of improving and widening the instruction in it by appointing additional teachers. In 1883, when the need had been accentuated by the illness of Professor Bancroft from overwork, the President recommended that "at no distant day" the duties of his department be divided between a professor of rhetoric and a professor of English literature. "Of nothing am I more thoroughly convinced," he wrote, "than that the most radical defect to-day in our American colleges is a want of due attention to rhetorical studies, understanding by these studies not only practice in the arts of composition and of speech, the patient acquisition of power to think justly, and to express one's thoughts accurately, but also the acquisition of that correctness of literary taste, that knowledge of English literature and that appreciation of its riches, without which facility and skill in the use of our tongue are never attainable." If the President had had his wish, he would thus have anticipated by some years the great development of English studies which was soon to come in all American colleges. As it was, the overburdened professor had to struggle along unaided until 1886, when an instructor was appointed who

[400]

divided his time between rhetoric and modern languages. The teaching of composition, now the Old Man of the Sea to all English departments, had not then quite the same strangling clutch; yet Professor Bancroft's reports show that he had to read and correct about one hundred and twenty-five essays and orations monthly, some of considerable length, in addition to all his class-room work in rhetoric and literature. He did his best, nevertheless, to meet the growing demand for instruction in English. When the course in English literature was extended, in 1874, from half a year to a year, he added a study of individual authors to the survey of the history of the literature; after 1880 he offered an elective in literature in the second half of the senior year; and in 1887–89 he taught a voluntary class in Old English. No man could have done more; and he, at least, ought not to have done so much.

While the curriculum was thus widening, the standards for admission and for degrees became more severe. In 1875 French grammar and English composition were added to the subjects required for admission. The requirement in French during this administration never included more than a knowledge of the grammar and a few reading lessons. The English requirement, however, passed through a period of rapid development: the study of literature was introduced in 1876, although it was then confined to one act of *Julius Caesar;* by 1881 a knowledge of four works — *Othello*, *The Vicar of Wakefield*, *The Deserted Village*, and *The Bride of Lammermoor*—was expected, and year by year the list was gradually extended. The entrance requirements in the classics for the Bachelor of Arts course were also increased. Under President Caswell in 1871, six books of the *Anabasis*, instead of four, had been required, with an option of substituting two books of Homer for two of the *Anabasis;* in

1876 another book of the *Anabasis* was added, with the same option as before, and in 1881 Greek history to the death of Alexander. The Latin requirement was raised in 1876 by a fifth book of Caesar's *Commentaries* and an eighth oration of Cicero; but seven orations, including the long one on the Manilian law, were accepted two years later; Roman history was added in 1881. Sight translation as a substitute for a part of the prescribed reading in both Latin and Greek was allowed in 1881. In mathematics the same upward tendency appeared. Plane geometry had been added in 1871; three years later the metric system was required; solid geometry was added in 1876, but was struck out the next year. The standard set in the examinations for admission seems to have been high. The time for them was extended in 1875 from two days to three. In 1876, of 78 students applying for entrance only 22 were admitted without conditions; in 1878, only 18 out of 85; in 1880, only 26 out of 94, while 9 were turned away altogether. Admission by certificate from approved schools began in 1885.

In the college course more and more proficiency was exacted. On recommendation of the Faculty in 1875, the Corporation raised the passing mark from twenty-five per cent to fifty. Holders of scholarships were warned two years later that "A scholarship is forfeited if the candidate . . . fails to secure at least *seventy-five* per cent. of the maximum mark." Additional scholarships and prizes were established from time to time. The Hartshorn premiums for excellence in the mathematics required for admission were first announced in the catalogue of 1872–73; the scholarship of the class of 1838 (President Robinson's class), the income of $3800, in 1874–75; the essay prize of the class of 1873, in 1877–78; the Foster premium in Greek, the income of a fund of $3000 bequeathed by the Hon. La Fayette S.

Foster, of the class of 1828, in 1881–82. A new system of honors for high standing in the studies of the entire course, and of departmental honors for specialization and high rank in the studies of a department, were instituted in 1886, as one consequence of the enlargement of the elective system.

The most unmistakable sign of the purpose to raise standards at this time was the treatment of the course for the degree of Bachelor of Philosophy. This inheritance from President Wayland's latter years had long been regarded with disfavor by the Faculty and most of the undergraduates. It had failed of its original purpose — to spread widely the benefits of collegiate study among young men who could not or would not prepare themselves for the classical course —for it had never been taken by many, and the numbers were now very small, only 20 out of the 204 students in 1872–73. Furthermore, certain evils attended it; the President said in his first annual report, "Of those who enter college with a view to this degree, it cannot be denied that a few do distinguish themselves in special studies; neither on the other hand can it be denied that the great majority of them come with aims and habits of mind unsuited to successful study, and so accomplish but little that is valuable to themselves, or creditable to the University." In 1875 the Corporation therefore voted that after 1875–76 the course should consist of four years instead of three. They also raised the entrance requirements by adding French for all candidates for the degree, and five books of Caesar (or an equivalent in Cicero or Virgil) for those who did not intend to study the classics in college; others took, as before, the same entrance examinations as candidates for the degree of Bachelor of Arts, except that, as formerly, if they purposed to pursue only one ancient language, they might omit the entrance

[403]

examination in the other. The effect of these changes was soon apparent in the improved quality of the men offering themselves for the degree.

These additions to the requirements for admission and to the college curriculum brought in their train a readjustment of studies, the general effect of which was an enlargement of the elective system. Since the reaction against that system shortly before the middle of the century, it had been gaining ground in the North, first at Harvard and then elsewhere. In his first annual report, after stating the difficulty caused by the conflicting claims of old and new studies, Dr. Robinson gave it as his judgment that the solution lay chiefly "in multiplying the number of elective studies, and perhaps in permitting the election to begin even at an earlier period in the course than it now does." He added: "But the liberty of election should always be rigidly restricted within certain limits; thoroughness of knowledge being always of much more importance to the student than the number of topics to which his attention may be given." This remained substantially his position to the end.

In conformity with these ideas a limited and guarded elective system was gradually worked out. The year before Dr. Robinson came, there were no electives in the Bachelor of Arts course for the first two and a half years; in the second half of the junior year the student chose two of four subjects—geology, political economy, Cicero or Tacitus, and Plato; in the first half of the senior year he had a choice between a course in Tacitus and Plato and a course in German; in the second half he chose two of four subjects again —geology, political economy, Cicero or Tacitus, and Sophocles or Euripides. It will be noticed that the senior in the second term had practically no choice at all except in Latin and Greek; for the other courses were the same offered him the previous year, and what he omitted then he must take now unless he preferred to read more of the classics. In the Bachelor of Philosophy course there was considerably more opportunity for selection.

For several years there was no change, except that in 1873, when German became a required study, the seniors had no option at all in the first half-year. In 1877, after French was required for admission, a choice between French and German was possible in the second half of the sophomore year; juniors were allowed to choose German or Latin or Greek in the first term, and six hours from eight subjects in the second; seniors had five hours of electives from eight subjects the first term, and six hours from ten subjects the second term. Little by little the electives increased in number, and crept back into the first term of the sophomore year.

In 1885, after long deliberation, the Faculty adopted a comprehensive scheme of studies, which was approved by the Corporation, and with only minor changes remained in force during the rest of President Robinson's term of office. In the course for the degree of Bachelor of Arts all the freshman subjects were required: Greek and Latin, four hours each; mathematics, six hours; French, two hours. In the first term of the sophomore year, twelve hours were required, divided equally among Greek, Latin, English, and astronomy, and four hours were elective, to be chosen from two-hour courses in mathematics, German, French, and physiology; in the second term the only changes were that astronomy gave way to mechanics among the required subjects, and physiology to botany among the elective. In the junior year, first term, twelve hours were required — four in English, three in chemistry, and five in physics — instead of fifteen as before, and four or five hours were to be elected

from Greek, Latin, mathematics, German, French, and botany; in the second term only nine hours—divided equally
among logic, history, and English—were required, and
seven or eight hours were to be elected from Greek, Latin,
mathematics, surveying, German, French, chemistry, zoölogy, and political economy. In the first term of the senior
year the only required subjects were intellectual philosophy,
four hours, and history, three hours, and from seven to nine
hours were elective, to be chosen from Greek, Latin, mathematics, German, Italian, Spanish, chemistry, geology, Roman law, and political economy; in the second term moral
philosophy, five hours, was the only required course, except
a one-hour course in agricultural zoölogy for students holding state scholarships, and electives amounting to seven,
eight, or nine hours (one hour less for holders of state
scholarships) were allowed from the history of philosophy,
Greek, Latin, mathematics, mechanics, English literature,
German, Italian, Spanish, chemistry, geology, and international law. The increase of range in electives was really
greater than appears from a bare list of subjects, because in
most cases advanced courses or different authors were now
presented in the successive terms. An interesting experiment was made by allowing juniors to take one hour more
or less as they chose, and seniors two hours. The course for
the degree of Bachelor of Philosophy had a wider range of
electives in the first two years, as other subjects, chiefly scientific, might be taken in place of Greek and Latin.

A change in the nature of the Commencement parts naturally followed the widening of the elective system. Since
the students who had second and third rank might now have
specialized in other subjects than the classics, the Latin salutatory and the classical oration had to be given up, and
with them the other honors. A new system went into effect,

therefore, in 1886; the upper three-fifths of the senior class were appointed to write orations, the best ten of which were chosen for delivery at Commencement.

A more significant consequence also attended the enriching of the curriculum: graduate study of some thoroughness was now possible, and was soon undertaken. Occasional requests for graduate instruction had already been received from time to time, and had been met in part. In 1878–79 and 1879–80 the President gave courses of lectures on philosophical subjects through the greater part of the year to a number of graduates and others; and in 1880–81 thirteen lectures by six members of the Faculty were delivered in Manning Hall to a select audience. In the following year a class of fifteen graduates met Professor Lincoln once a week for six months to study Cicero's *Tusculan Disputations*. Reading aright these signs of the times, President Robinson brought the question of graduate instruction before the fellows, who in 1883 appointed a committee to confer with the Faculty, but there the matter stopped. In 1886 the President said in his annual report: "The time, it seems to me, has now fully come for Brown University to offer a course of study to be pursued by candidates for the degree of Doctor of Philosophy. . . . The frequent and earnest requests recently made for permission to pursue a course of study that, on examination, should entitle to receive it, would seem to require on our part some provision to this end." The Board of Fellows, after receiving suggestions from the Faculty on the matter, in 1887 authorized the publication in the next catalogue of the conditions upon which the degrees of Master of Arts and Doctor of Philosophy would be conferred: the former required one year of graduate study in residence or two years in absence; the latter, two years of graduate study in residence and "a thesis giving evidence of high

scholarship and of special excellence in the studies pursued."
The first students to take graduate degrees upon these conditions were Austen K. De Blois and George G. Wilson,
each of whom received the degree of Master of Arts in 1888
and of Doctor of Philosophy in 1889. The former, a prominent Baptist clergyman, was for several years president of
Shurtleff College; the latter is professor of international law
at Harvard. The university may well be satisfied with the
first fruits of its graduate instruction.

All this progress toward higher academic ideals was due
in part to Dr. Robinson's vigorous leadership, but much of
the success of his administration was also dependent upon
the counsel and support of the Faculty, among whom were
men of mature years and long experience in college affairs.
Professor Lincoln had been connected with the Faculty since
1839, Librarian Guild since 1847, Professor Greene since
1851, and Professor Harkness since 1855. During these
years of service they had gained a knowledge of college education in general, and of Brown University in particular,
which would have been invaluable to any president and was
especially so to one coming to a new field rather late in life;
the advice of the senior professor was peculiarly helpful to
Dr. Robinson in many trying situations. Among the younger
members of the Faculty were men of unusual brilliancy,
energy, or wisdom, several of whom were to be mainstays
of the institution for many years.

The most brilliant of them, however, Professor John L.
Diman, died suddenly on February 3, 1881, in the middle
of President Robinson's administration. His death came as
a blinding blow to the college and the city, and as a great
loss to a much wider circle. Professor Diman was born on
May 1, 1831, in Bristol, Rhode Island, where his paternal
ancestors, who were of French descent, had lived for four

generations. His father, a man of strong character and intellect, became governor of the state in 1846; his mother was descended from John Alden, and was a grand-niece of Benjamin Franklin. He was prepared for college by a clergyman, entered Brown University in 1847, and graduated four years later with the third honor. His subsequent training was varied and thorough. He spent a year in the study of philosophy, theology, and the classics with a scholarly clergyman in Newport; studied for two years in Andover Theological Seminary; and then gave nearly the same period to study in Germany, devoting himself to theology, philosophy, history, and art. After graduation at Andover in 1856, he was pastor of Congregational churches in Fall River and Brookline, Massachusetts, until 1864, when he became professor of history and political economy in Brown University. The university gave him the degree of D.D. in 1870.

As a teacher Professor Diman made a brilliant success from the first, but grew in power and influence with every year. Soon discarding textbooks, he instructed wholly by lectures; and his lectures were so deep and vital in substance, so luminous, polished, and witty in manner, that he became the idol of the undergraduates in spite of his high-bred reserve. *The Brunonian* said, immediately after his death: "His manner of teaching furnished such an ineffable relief from the general tedium of college duties as to greatly enhance his popularity as a professor. His racy sketches of life and character, his humorous pictures of past times and events, his inimitable method, not only served to render complete the students' conception of History, but also continually to keep before him the perfect model of an instructor." His fame soon spread beyond the college walls. He was offered professorships at Princeton and Johns Hopkins, and thrice at Harvard; he could have had the presidency of Vermont University or the University of Wisconsin; he was in great demand as a speaker on various civic occasions and as a lecturer at other universities. One of his most brilliant series of lectures was given at Johns Hopkins University, in 1879, on the Thirty Years' War. President Gilman, after speaking of the difficulty of the subject, said: "From the beginning to the end, however, he held the attention of his hearers in the closest manner. . . . If he used any notes they were of the briefest sort. He seemed to be talking to a company of friends on a subject of great importance, which he perfectly understood, with an unhesitating command, not only of names and dates, but of the exact epithets, and discriminating sentences which he wished to employ." The following year he delivered twelve lectures on theism at the Lowell Institute. His fluency in extemporaneous speech was the more remarkable because his spoken style, like his written, was of close texture. "He satisfied the most critical at the same time that he captivated the multitude," wrote Edward J. Young, in a memorial sketch published in the *Proceedings of the Massachusetts Historical Society*. "He never resorted to any rhetorical tricks or artifices. . . . His delivery was faultless."

Professor Diman left no work that fully embodies his great gifts. His published writings consist of a few reviews in magazines, several addresses, the Lowell Institute lectures, and a group of sermons; the last named, with most of the addresses and reviews, are contained in a memorial volume, *Orations and Essays*, published in 1882. These writings reveal his quality, although they cannot exhibit the scope of his learning or the full power of his mind. His culture was remarkable for its completeness and symmetry, the spiritual, the intellectual, and the aesthetic meeting in him in satisfying harmony. His mental and spiritual breadth, his historical sense, his love of art, all united to create in him an understanding sympathy with the great historic and ritualistic churches, yet he was so modern in his outlook that he could also do justice to the most rationalistic of faiths; hence there was a basis of truth in the crude opinion, often expressed, that he was both a Roman Catholic and a Unitarian. Candor and intellectual fearlessness are conspicuous in his lectures on theism, in which he faced all difficulties with unflinching fairness. His fidelity to the truth as he saw it is shown, not only by his teaching free trade in Rhode Island, but also by his address at Providence on Roger Williams, perhaps the best example of his historical method, in which he strove to be just to colonial Massachusetts even though he shattered some illusions about the founder of Rhode Island. On every page that he wrote is the charm of a style at once intellectual and beautiful, flexible, quiet, wholly free from false ornament, dignified yet unpretending, and, like his own nature, uniting fineness and force in remarkable degree. In the death of Professor Diman Brown University and the state of Rhode Island lost a natural prince.

The courses in history and political economy were taught by temporary substitutes until 1883, when the chair was again filled by Elisha Benjamin Andrews.

Two years after the decease of Professor Diman, the university lost by death another of its most valuable teachers, Professor Samuel S. Greene, who was stricken with paralysis on January 22, 1883, while on the way to his class-room, and died two days later. Professor Greene was born on May 3, 1810, in Belchertown, Massachusetts. A farmer's son, with few early opportunities for education, he entered Brown University at the age of twenty-three, and graduated in 1837 the valedictorian of his class. His whole life thereafter was given to the cause of education. He taught in Worcester Academy (which in later years he rescued from death by poverty and started on its present prosperous career) and in the Boston schools; he was superintendent of schools in Springfield in 1840–42, the first official of this kind in Massachusetts; in 1849–51 he was agent of the Massachusetts Board of Education; in 1851–53 he was superintendent of the Providence schools, at the same time holding a professorship in the university and giving lectures to teachers, which led in 1853 to the establishment of the Rhode Island State Normal School. He served eighteen years on the Providence school committee; was president of the Rhode Island Institute of Instruction; and as president of the American Institute of Instruction and of the National Teachers' Association exerted a wide influence. By his eight books on the English language and grammar, published between 1848 and 1878, and having an average sale of fifty thousand copies a year, his name became known throughout the country. He began his connection with the Faculty of Brown University in 1851, as professor of didactics; from 1855 till his death he held a professorship variously styled of mathematics, civil engineering, natural philosophy, and astronomy, also teaching logic for some years and English for a short time. The university gave him the degree of LL.D. in 1870.

Professor Greene was deeply interested in the workings of the mind, and developed a science and art of teaching, according to the lights of his day. He was himself a skillful teacher. "His power of condensing and logically arranging all the various points, not only of mathematical problems and theorems, but of all the subjects with which he had to do, was remarkable," says his pupil and colleague, Professor Benjamin F. Clarke; who adds, "He possessed, too, a remarkable faculty of *drawing out* the pupil beyond and outside of the text, and inspiring him with the feeling that he was investigating for himself." He had also the natural teacher's keen interest in his scholars, loving their society and enjoying their sports to the end. "As an associate and an officer," writes Professor Clarke, "we found in him a wise and reliable counsellor, a man of rare wisdom and sound judgment. . . . His efforts to increase the financial resources of the University have been unceasing, and much of its material prosperity is due to his own personal influence."

Registrar Douglas was succeeded in 1879 by his son, Francis W. Douglas; the latter gave place in 1884 to Gilman P. Robinson, who retained the office until 1889. A steward of the grounds and buildings, Archibald G. Delaney, was appointed in 1884.

Four chancellors held office during Dr. Robinson's presidency. Chancellor Patten died in 1873, after a term of only six years. His successor was the Hon. Benjamin F. Thomas, of the class of 1830, who after a distinguished career in Massachusetts as lawyer, justice of the supreme court, and member of Congress, came to Providence to spend the rest of his days; he served as chancellor only four years, dying in 1878. He was followed by the Hon. Thomas Durfee, of the class of 1846, a Providence lawyer who had held many offices of trust in the state, including that of chief justice. On his retirement from the chancellorship in 1888, he was succeeded by his classmate, Colonel William Goddard, who had already been a trustee for thirty-one years, and was to serve the university as chancellor for nearly a generation. In President Robinson's third year the secretary of the Corporation, the venerable John Kingsbury, died after holding the office for twenty-one years ; he was succeeded by the Rev. Dr. Samuel L. Caldwell, professor

[413]

in Newton Theological Institution, soon to be president of Vassar College, who served through the rest of the administration. In 1882 the treasurership passed from Marshall Woods to Arnold B. Chace.

President Robinson was a stern disciplinarian, yet he favored certain relaxations in the regimen of the students. Compulsory chapel attendance on Sunday was abolished early in his first year ; and after 1877 undergraduates were no longer "required to attend public worship twice on Sunday," the President himself, according to report, informing them that "once was enough." The custom of allowing students a certain number of absences from class exercises and chapel was also introduced under President Robinson, in 1885.

A few changes in the calendar, made early in this administration, brought the college year into nearly its present form. In 1875 Commencement was put into the third week in June, the week thus lost being made up by shortening the vacation between the terms. The following year the process of reducing the midwinter vacation, which had been eight weeks long in President Messer's day, was completed by its elimination, the second term beginning the day after the semi-annual examinations closed. The academic year now opened on the third Wednesday in September, instead of the first Friday. The Thanksgiving recess was shortened from a week to three days, and a Christmas vacation of ten days was granted. The spring vacation was also lengthened to nine days. The total result of the changes was that the working time of the college year was about a week shorter.

The tax for Commencement expenses, chiefly for the dinner to the alumni, which had long been levied on the graduating class, was reduced in 1876 from $25 to $18, and abolished in 1881. Tuition, on the other hand, was raised in

1877 from $75 a year to $100. The attendance, which for the three years previous had been slightly above 250, at once fell to 231, but soon rose again, and reached high-water mark for this administration with 270 students in 1882–83. The maximum professor's salary remained at $3000, the point it had gained in 1871. The President's salary was $5000.

During the latter part of this administration the extension of the elective system and the enlarged opportunities for the study of physical science began to develop a new type of student, who, with less interest in general culture, acquired a semi-professional enthusiasm for some one line of study. Partly as a result, the interest in old forms of public speaking continued to decline. Commencement parts were more and more considered a bore; junior exhibitions languished, and after 1882 wholly ceased to be; debating and other literary practice survived, however, in many of the Greek-letter societies. *The Brunonian*, published every third Saturday after 1873–74, and fortnightly after 1878–79, became more readable with every change, containing fewer essays and more light verse, sketches, editorials, and college news; but if there was gain, there was also loss, which had to be repaired in the next administration by the founding of a college magazine.

Offensive social pranks and serious disorders more and more declined as undergraduate life became better organized and more dignified. Hazing almost wholly vanished. Junior Burials came again into favor for some years, but finally grew stale, *The Brunonian* expressing the opinion in 1881 that they gave more pleasure to "the vast crowds on the sidewalks" than to the participants. Next year the celebration was omitted, and has never been resumed in its original form.

While these phases of undergraduate life waned, two

others continued to wax. The Greek-letter fraternities flourished in spite of the open hostility of the President, numbering nine in 1889, with a membership of 172 out of 265 undergraduates. The social features of Class Day more and more overshadowed the literary. In 1878 fifteen seniors made a new departure by holding an elaborate reception in University Hall and Manning Hall, the two buildings being connected by a covered way. In 1880 a similar reception was held in University Hall and the Commencement tent directly behind it. Two years later the whole graduating class held a reception, with some dancing, in the newly completed Sayles Hall, and this became the custom thereafter. In the spring of 1885 the Boat Club gave in Sayles Hall the first ball ever given on the college grounds, exciting diverse comment. The next year the senior reception on the night of Class Day became chiefly a dance; and in the same year the receptions and "spreads" of the Greek-letter societies, held in the various college buildings, were a great feature.

The history of athletics at Brown under President Robinson is almost wholly the history of one sport. Boating languished, in spite of fitful attempts to revive it; football existed only in the form of an annual battle between the two lower classes, until near the end of the period, when the modern game began to be played; track athletics received small attention; tennis had some vogue for a time, but never excited widespread interest. Baseball, however, grew more and more into favor, and became the great rallying-point of enthusiasm for undergraduates and graduates alike. A 'varsity nine was formed in 1874 for the first time in three years; the teams henceforth increased in skill from year to year, until in 1879 Brown won the intercollegiate championship in a season ending with a memorable victory over Yale.

Since then the college has stood in the front rank in this sport.

The ever-rising standard of skill in sports and the ever-growing emphasis upon intercollegiate contests began at this period to raise problems that still engage the anxious thought of college officers. The attitude of Dr. Robinson and his colleagues was substantially that of most college Faculties now : they desired that students should enjoy as widely as possible the health and pleasure to be had from physical sports, but feared that concentration upon intercollegiate contests between a few men, with high-wrought excitement, would deprive the majority of these benefits and at the same time shift the center of their enthusiasms and ambitions to other than intellectual pursuits. President Robinson discussed the various aspects of the problem in his reports from year to year; and in 1884 he surveyed the whole ground, and outlined a program the main features of which were realized in the next administration :

As matters now stand, only a small portion of our students receive any personal benefit from our athletic sports. Those who take part in them merely to fit themselves for the match games, too often run into hurtful extremes; others, engaging in them fitfully and unintelligently, fail of the good they might otherwise receive; while the majority, content with merely looking on and applauding, get no real benefit whatever from them. The question is worth considering whether the time has not come for this University to take some decisive action toward providing itself with a Gymnasium of its own, and not merely with the hired and limited advantages of one in the city; and whether some provision ought not to be made for such instruction in hygiene and practical physical training as shall not only secure to our students a knowledge of the laws of personal health, but shall habituate them to a compliance with the conditions of a healthful physical development.

It was perhaps not an accident that at the alumni meeting, two days before this report was read to the Corporation,

Dr. W. W. Keen offered a resolution, which was adopted by a unanimous vote, "That a committee . . . be appointed by the Chair for the purpose of taking immediate steps for the erection of a first-class gymnasium for Brown University." The building which President Robinson had for years urged the need of was not to be erected during his term of office, but an organized movement to secure it was at last under way.

It is clear that, under the leadership of Dr. Robinson, Brown University made large advances in equipment and in educational policy. In his relations with the students the President was less successful.

The first impression made upon the undergraduates by his commanding presence and manifest power was very favorable. "Our president is a man," said *The Brunonian* of September, 1872. "Not merely a 'figure-head,' he is such a power as has not been felt here for years. The respect yielded to him is not that extorted by the office, but is inspired by the man who fills it." The students never lost their admiration for his ability, but he failed to win their confidence and love. Most of them thought him hard, cold, unsympathetic, and some regarded him as harsh and unjust. There was considerable basis for these impressions. Many years of contact with students of theology had made him less able than he might otherwise have been to understand and sympathize with younger and more frivolous minds. In dealing with actual or supposed delinquents he was often rough and not careful enough about making accusations on insufficient evidence. "Not unfrequently," says one of his early pupils and warm admirers, "did he lose influence, when in conference with offenders, by laying himself open to the satirical charge of knowing too many things that were not so." "And yet in truth it should be added," says the same critic, "that

[418]

he who was so stern in the public proclamation of the law was apt to become even too tender when approached with an appeal in behalf of the individual offender.'' This mode of administering justice has never won favor with either the criminal or the public. The truth is that in spite of his profound reverence for ''immutable law,'' Dr. Robinson did not have the judicial temperament, but was a man of strong emotions, which swayed him now to one extreme and now to another, his anger and his compassion alike often proving too strong for the leash of his intellect and will. This impetuous center of his nature was usually concealed by a lifelong habit of reserve, but sometimes the lava broke through the crust. Gusts of righteous wrath over infractions of discipline swept him beyond the bounds of good judgment and good taste; *Jupiter Tonans* would roll his thunders and brandish his lightnings when in truth he knew not where to strike. Yet he never lost his dignity, even in his personal encounters with culprits in those days when a college president was expected to be policeman as well as judge. ''There was something majestic, even Olympian,'' writes one of his pupils, ''in the long stride and flying silvery hair, when seen in the moonlight, and in his tight grasp on a sophomore's coat collar there was the relentless vigor of sixty years of Calvinism.'' The gentler feelings were less often displayed, commonly showing themselves only by a slight tremulousness of the lips and an almost imperceptible tremor in the voice, but at times they found freer vent. ''He talked to me like a father,'' said a notorious scapegrace after an official interview with the President, ''and I mean to do better.'' In chapel, on the morning when he had to announce the death of Professor Diman, Dr. Robinson was so moved that he could not go on with the service.

A lighter side of the President's attitude toward college

disorders, unsuspected by the students at least, is shown in his autobiography, which sometimes lets one hear the laugh of Hermes behind the frown of Zeus. After describing the almost deserted chapel one morning when a cane rush was going on outside, he continues: "But on leaving the chapel a most comical scene met the eye. Under a steadily falling rain the ground was covered with text-books, note-books, coats, hats, waistcoats, fragments of shirts and flannels, while from the lower end of the campus came two or three bareheaded, half-stripped Sophomores, bearing in triumph the offending cane." At the time, however, the President concealed his sense of the humor of such situations even more successfully than he hid his tenderness, inflicting severe penalties on ringleaders and sometimes on others. In spite of individual mistakes his discipline as a whole, aided by the improving spirit of the times, had good results. His own summary of the case is just: "Drastic measures became a necessity. In due time a healthier tone prevailed; and years before my withdrawal from office a more quiet and orderly body of students could not be desired."

Dr. Robinson was undoubtedly a great teacher. Some of his pupils at Rochester are rapturous in his praise, and even the cooler-headed portray him as a powerful stimulus to independent thought and action. He was himself a fearless thinker in theology, suspected of heresy by some, and much of his teaching was destructive. "As I listened to the lectures," writes the Rev. Dr. Behrends, "I seemed to be walking through a mass of theological ruins. . . . But the ruthless havoc was the greatest blessing of my life. It broke the chafing bonds of traditionalism; it drove me from the mud huts into God's free and boundless air." The Rev. Dr. Strong, his successor at Rochester, says: "In his class-room I found my intellectual awakening. His searching questions, and the discussions that followed, roused my thinking powers as nothing ever had before." Dr. Strong adds that his influence was widespread: "The impulse to clear and manly utterance in the pulpit, the love of exact statement, the disposition to preach truth rather than tradition, which have of late years transformed our Baptist pulpit and brought it abreast of our advancing age, have been chiefly due, under God, to the teaching and the example of Dr. Robinson."

President Robinson's work as teacher of philosophy in Brown University was not equal to his work at Rochester. By nature and attainments he was less qualified for teaching philosophy, and he came to it when he had lost some of the enthusiasm of youth. Furthermore, the minds with which he was now dealing were more immature and more indifferent; they challenged him less, and seemed less worthy of being challenged by him. Yet a distinction must be made between his earlier and his later teaching at Brown. In the earlier period he encouraged freedom of discussion and aroused thought, somewhat as he had done in the seminary. "The sparks flew," writes one of his pupils of this time, Alfred G. Langley, of the class of 1876, translator and editor of Leibnitz, "and the intellects of the students participating in the discussion were aroused and stimulated into such action as till then they had never known or even dreamed of." "More than one student," adds Mr. Langley, "owes to him all the rational faith he has." President Benjamin I. Wheeler says: "When I came under his instruction in 1874, I was in rebellion against the faith of my boyhood. The old formulas had lost their meaning for me. . . . Dr. Robinson's teaching all tended to make a man approach the problems of the religious life with an openness and fearlessness that engendered confidence and rebuked the thought of shame, and best of all led to the construction of a faith that could hold a natural and constituent place in a man's whole thought and view of the universe.'' But in the last third of his presidency, whether from increasing years or from a growing burden of official and private cares, Dr. Robinson became more stereotyped in his teaching, more dogmatic and intolerant of dissent. Sometimes still ''the sparks flew,'' but not in mental fence with even a semblance of equality; it was rather a conflict between Thor's hammer and an anvil, and the anvil was not likely to provoke a second blow.

A distinction must also be made between his instruction in metaphysics and in moral philosophy. His teaching of ethics was always animated, pungent, powerful, for here his emotional and religious nature combined with the intellectual to give weight and motion to his words. Many undergraduates, uninterested in the subtleties of psychological introspection or the history of philosophical doctrines, responded deeply to his sternly sublime teaching of the immutability of moral law as grounded in the eternal nature of God, and were the stronger for it all their lives. One of his later pupils, Professor Walter G. Everett, says: ''Already the new movements of thought which have so profoundly affected the statement of the problems of psychology, ethics, and metaphysics were beginning to take shape. Dr. Robinson's philosophy, representing as it did the traditional Scottish realism, faced the past rather than the future. Unquestionably his best constructive work is found in his chapter on 'Moral Law.' Here he showed that morality is grounded in the needs of human nature. This was admirable. It gave to many a man a new and vital interpretation of the moral order. If Dr. Robinson did not develop all the significant implications of the doctrine, he at least laid a secure foundation for them.''

[422]

Early and late, too, whatever the subject, he was powerful in the class-room by his terse, pithy statements of great
truths, with telling illustrations from varied sources. His
pupils delight to repeat the epigrams stored up in their note-
books:

Physical science will undoubtedly smash some of our crockery gods.

Deity need not send a policeman after the sinner; the sinner carries
the policeman inside.

As soon as any church says that it alone is the true church and there
is no other, take your hat.

A man's principles and emotions come out and sit on his features.

An idea is quite prevalent that moral law is a sort of scarecrow
which Deity has set up in the cornfields of this world, and which he
will take down whenever he thinks it safe to do so.

Disciplined intellect, gentlemen, asks no favor but that of God.

The same power of statement is richly illustrated in his
Lectures on Preaching, delivered at Yale in 1882 and published the next year; these lectures, spoken extempore and
printed from shorthand notes, give a far better idea of
his power as a teacher than any other of his works.[1] Sometimes he conveys a historical truth by a picture, as when he
says of the Puritans, "But long and tedious as were their
sermons, narrow as were their views, and bigoted as they
were in spirit, they yet made lines on the English face that
to-day help to give it dignity." At another time he lashes,
with a sarcasm that Carlyle would have relished, the preacher
who over-cultivates "the homiletic habit" and begins by
"striking twelve": "When he should be ripest and fullest
in his strength, he stands up to preach, but, like an old and

[1] Dr. Robinson's other works, besides numerous articles in magazines (especially *The Christian Review*, which he edited for several years, *The Baptist
Quarterly*, and *The Homiletic Review*), are *Principles and Practice of Morality*, 1888, *Christian Theology*, 1894, *Christian Evidences*, 1895, *Baccalaureate Sermons*, 1896, and his *Autobiography*, 1896.

worn-out clock, there is a muffled sound of moving machinery, a buzz and a whirr, but no stroke; he cannot strike one." Or he ridicules by a humorous misuse of a poetical quotation, as when he says of the "mild" preacher: "Another is always soft in tone and meek in spirit and gentle in word, even when denouncing the vilest of iniquities. . . . You hear him, and are reminded of the poet's —

> '—noise like a hidden brook
> In the leafy month of June,
> That to the sleeping woods, all night,
> Singeth a quiet tune.'"

His usual style was impressive by its very directness and simplicity: "If any man among men needs to be watchful over his own soul, and to strive incessantly to keep himself alive to the solemnity of the truth he handles, it is he who is always at work on the sensibilities of others." "In the final great struggle between the Christian religion and all false religions, now so close at hand, that one of them will prevail which can do the most and the best for mankind." These and like utterances came home to his hearers with the greater force because back of them was felt to be an intense, virile personality, charged with electric energy of will. His very roughness was a needed tonic for many listless souls. "What scorn he felt," writes President Faunce, "for idlers and aimless, boneless men! How caustic could he be in his allusions to week-kneed, sentimental, lachrymose piety, copious in profession but poor in deed! How he took some men by the mental coat-collar and shook them into self-realization! How he taught some to stop shambling and lounging and to stand erect in God's world!"

Dr. Robinson's work as a teacher was done partly in the pulpit, for many students heard him there who never reached his class-room. Of his method as a preacher no one is so able to speak as his present successor in the presidency, who says:

As a speaker he was logic on fire. He thought on his feet, not repeating sentences carefully conned in the study, but actually going through the thought process in the presence of his audience, and we had the same pleasure in hearing as in watching a powerful engine in resistless and serene movement. . . . Probably no man in this country possessed a finer extemporaneous English style. Like his own body, it was flexible and muscular, the perfect vehicle of his burning thought. He was absolutely simple and lucid. One might disagree: he could not misunderstand. Fogginess he hated. His style was like a morning atmosphere in which each object stands out sharp and bold. Hence he had immense power to carry conviction to an assembly. As he proceeded he kindled, until his voice grew clear and resonant, the eyes gleamed dark with scorn of falsehood and evil, the gestures grew more swift and awkward until at some critical moment his left hand was thrust into his pocket! Then came the lightning and the thunder. The hand in pocket was the unfailing sign that the preacher had been totally swept away in the torrent of his own conviction.

Dr. Robinson gave seventeen years of his life to the service of Brown University; and when he resigned in 1889, at the age of seventy-four, he had the right to say in his letter of March 20 to the Corporation: "I am now the more ready to retire, because the prospects of the University have at no time since my connection with it been so encouraging as they now are, and because it is now in a condition from which, under wise guidance and with such changes as in due course of events will necessarily come, it can rapidly advance to a measure of usefulness not hitherto attainable." His physical vigor, like his mental, was still unimpaired; yet it was felt that the time had come for him to retire, and he did so with dignity and honor.

But his work was not yet done. In spite of heavy personal misfortunes his bodily strength and the Roman hardihood of his spirit, more and more mellowed by Christian grace, carried him heroically through five years of toil. During the greater part of 1890 he supplied the pulpit of a church in Philadelphia, at the same time giving courses of lectures before the Andover, Rochester, and Crozer theological seminaries; at Crozer he also lectured in the four succeeding years. During 1891 he preached almost constantly in Philadelphia churches, and in the spring of 1892 he gave a short course of lectures at Brown University. From the autumn of that year until the spring of 1894 he was professor of ethics and apologetics in the University of Chicago. During his second year there he knew that his days were numbered, but he kept steadily at work. "Without a single omission," said President Harper, "he performed the duties of his chair, being conveyed to and from the University in a carriage on days when the weather was particularly inclement." In these last months, amid conditions much like those at Rochester, he seems to have returned to his earlier methods in the classroom. "The utmost freedom was allowed," writes Professor Goodspeed, his colleague, "and all sorts of objections, arguments, suggestions, received a fair hearing; only prolixity and irrelevancy being mercilessly choked off. My informant tells me that it was a most stimulating exercise; the Doctor was full of electricity, and the sparks and shocks were frequent."

Dr. Robinson returned to the East in April, 1894; and on the Sunday before its Commencement he preached at Vassar College, of which he had been a trustee since the founding. The exertion sapped his fast-failing strength; on arriving in Boston soon after, he was taken to the city hospital, on June 10, where three days later he passed away. The old warrior had fought the good fight to the end, and died with harness on.

CHAPTER XI

PRESIDENT ANDREWS'S ADMINISTRATION

AT a meeting of the Corporation on June 20, 1889, the
Rev. Elisha Benjamin Andrews was unanimously
chosen president of the university and professor of moral
and intellectual philosophy. President Andrews was born in
Hinsdale, New Hampshire, on January 10, 1844. His father
and grandfather were Baptist ministers of some prominence;
his brother, Charles B. Andrews, was governor of Connecticut in 1879–81. He began to prepare for college at the Connecticut Literary Institution, in Suffield, but on the outbreak
of the Civil War enlisted as a private in the First Connecticut
Heavy Artillery. He rose to be second lieutenant in two years ;
was wounded in the siege of Petersburg in 1864, losing an
eye; and was mustered out of service in the same year. Completing his preparation for college at academies in Bernards-
ton and Wilbraham, Massachusetts, he entered Brown University in 1866, and graduated in 1870 with the fourth
honor. He was principal of the academy at Suffield during
1870–72, and then studied in Newton Theological Institution, graduating there in 1874. After a year's pastorate in
Beverly, Massachusetts, he served as president of Denison
University in Granville, Ohio, from 1875 to 1879. During
the next three years he was professor of homiletics at Newton. Receiving an appointment to the chair of history and
political economy in Brown University in 1882, he spent a
year studying in Germany, and entered upon the duties of
his professorship in 1883. It was felt at once that a great

power had come into the university. His robust, magnetic personality thrilled and stimulated the students both in and out of his classes, and hero-worship became a popular cult. His reputation soon spread : Colby University gave him the degree of D.D., and the University of Nebraska the degree of LL.D., in 1884; and in 1888 he accepted a call to Cornell University as professor of political economy and finance. His loss was deeply lamented at Brown and among the alumni; and when the presidency became vacant, there was a widespread and eager demand that he be chosen to fill it.

It was soon clear that he was the man for the place. At his touch the old college leaped into new life, and began to grow at an astonishing rate. The number of male undergraduate students, which had reached 200 as long ago as 1823, and 277 in 1853, but which for the thirty-five years since had seldom gone above 250 and had often fallen much below it, now began to rise like the incoming tide. Under President Robinson the highest mark had been 270 in 1882; under President Andrews the attendance of undergraduate men rose in successive years to 276, 326, 348, 422, 490, 532, 622, and 641 — a gain of more than 140 per cent in eight years. And this was not all: the graduate students, of whom there were but three at the end of the previous administration, increased even more rapidly, until they numbered 117, in 1895; and when to these are added the undergraduate students in the Women's College, the totals have a new hundred with each succeeding year from 1892 to 1896 — 549, 660, 740, 859, and 908, a gain of almost 240 per cent.

The Faculty and the curriculum had a like enlargement. In 1888 there were fourteen professors, two assistant professors, six instructors, a librarian, an assistant librarian, a registrar, and a steward — a total of twenty-six. Eight years later there were twenty-one professors, thirteen associate professors, three assistant professors, thirty-one instructors, eleven assistants, a librarian, an assistant librarian, three cataloguers, a dean of women, a registrar, an assistant registrar, and a steward—a total of eighty-eight. During President Andrews's first year, instruction was given in seventeen departments; eight years later, in twenty-five. This did not mean, however, that eight wholly new departments had been added, for the increase was due partly to a division of old departments. Rhetoric and oratory were separated from English literature in 1891; Germanic languages from Romance languages in 1892; history from political and social science in 1892; zoölogy from comparative anatomy in 1892; and engineering was divided into drawing, civil engineering, and mechanical engineering in 1894. The new subjects introduced, either as separate departments or as subdivisions of old departments, were Semitic languages and Oriental history in 1890, styled biblical literature and history in 1895; classical archaeology in 1890, enlarged to fine arts in 1892; classical philology and Sanskrit in 1891, revived as Indo-European philology in 1895; military science in 1892; pedagogy, under philosophy, in 1893; law, under political and social science, in 1893; architecture, under fine arts, in 1894; music, under fine arts, in 1895; books and libraries in 1896. One or two departments, on the other hand, were dropped or merged with others. A far more significant thing was the great increase in the range of instruction, whether under old heads or new. In philosophy the number of hours of teaching per week, through the year, increased from $6\frac{1}{2}$ in 1889 to $21\frac{2}{3}$ in 1896; in fine arts, from $1\frac{1}{2}$ to 9; in mathematics, from 14 to 22; in English, from $9\frac{1}{2}$ to 48; in history from 3 to 20; in political science, from 3 to 8; in social science, from 0 to 7; in German, from 9 to 21; in Romance languages, from 9 to 36; in chemistry, from

19½ to 32; in physics, from 4½ to 33. The increase in the whole university was from 135 hours per week to 458⅔.

With this increase in number of courses went an extension of the elective system. In 1889 Greek and Latin became elective after the freshman year, even in the course for the degree of Bachelor of Arts, and mechanics was no longer required; the number of required hours in the sophomore year thus fell from eleven to seven, while the elective hours rose from five to nine. Smaller changes in the last two years brought down the required work in the whole course from 72 per cent to 56. After 1892–93 the studies of the senior year were wholly elective, and after 1894–95 all but four hours in the junior year. By 1896 the total number of required hours was twenty-six, of elective thirty-seven. From the first, under President Andrews, the required studies for the degree of Bachelor of Philosophy became identical, after the freshman year, with those for the degree of Bachelor of Arts.

These bare facts and figures, however, give no adequate impression of the change which had come over the institution. At best they touch but the quantitative side, and the New Brown was at bottom not quantity but quality, a spirit and a life, of which the growth in size was only a result. The primary source of this new life was the President. Other causes, indeed, coöperated from the first, and grew in strength as the movement went on. It would be false and unjust to ignore the foundation that had been laid through years of work by Corporation, presidents, professors, and students in the past; other men had labored, and the new president entered into their labors. In particular the raising of standards, and the growth in funds, buildings, and Faculty under President Robinson, had prepared the way for greater things. Conditions in the community and the nation, also, were increasingly favorable for expansion. Growth in wealth and population made it natural that more and more youth should seek a college education, and the multiplication and improvement of high schools put the means of preparing for college within the reach of an increasing number. The intellectual life of America was rising to a higher plane, chiefly under the stimulus of modern science; the scientific spirit was permeating every department of thought, and arousing multitudes to a new realization of the value of trained intellect in confronting the problems of life on all its levels. But all these conditions had existed for some time and yet Brown University still lay half dormant. Something more was needed to complete the circuit and send electric currents through the whole. President Andrews proved to be the something more. He was not only a powerful personality — strong of body, intellect, and will, racy in speech, of large outlook, great of heart, — but the avenues of influence between him and other men, particularly young men, were always open. Vitality streamed from him into them, invigorating and ennobling. The range and robustness of his thinking, his absolute fearlessness, the impression he gave of having wrestled with the toughest problems in the spiritual world and come off conqueror, inspired admiration; while his mental hospitality, which was only the intellectual phase of his broad humanity, caused the feeblest mind to feel at home in his presence and begot self-confidence. He made his pupils wish mightily to be bigger men and believe that they could be. In short, he was a great natural leader and inspirer of young men, arousing both their intellectual interests and their personal loyalty in remarkable degree, and hence he was a great teacher and a great college president.

In the presence of this personal power at its head must

be found the fundamental explanation of the impetus which the college now received, and which sent it forward, after lagging for so many years, far more rapidly than the other New England colleges during the same period. The exhilaration was for a time intense. Brown University experienced a genuine Renaissance. The consciousness of swelling life, of growing power, of a larger and more splendid future entered into professors and students alike. A contagious new life of this sort spreads in a thousand traceless ways by the touch of personality on personality; each teacher and undergraduate and alumnus became a magnet drawing others to the old college now fast growing into a new university. This is the primary and central fact. But in addition it is necessary to look more closely into some of the ways by which the President called forth and shaped the vital energies of the institution.

The new Faculty was largely of his selection, although several of the strongest members antedated his presidency by many years and formed an invaluable bond of continuity with the past. Some of these, unfortunately, did not long remain to support him in the onward march, and they should be spoken of first.

Professor Bancroft died on December 8, 1890, as a result of worry and overwork. He was born in Worcester, Massachusetts, on March 9, 1837, received an education in the public schools of that city, and graduated at Brown University in 1859; after a short experience in business life, and several years of successful teaching in high schools at Waltham and Newton, Massachusetts, he succeeded Professor Dunn in the chair of rhetoric and English literature at Brown University in 1868, retaining the office till his death. As a teacher he was practical and sensible rather than brilliant or inspiring. His pupils still remember with gratitude his plain, common-sense instruction in the art of writing, particularly in the systematic planning of a discourse. In teaching literature he was less successful, having neither wide learning nor a distinctly popular gift; yet he started many students on fruitful courses of reading, and laid the foundations for an appreciation of Chaucer, Shakespeare, and Milton. In all his work he was cruelly overburdened. His wit and courageous good-cheer made him generally liked by his colleagues and pupils, and his upright, open nature won him respect as a man. His memory is fittingly perpetuated by the Bancroft Fund, established by his widow and friends, for the purchase of books in the department he served so long and faithfully.

Dr. Guild retired from active service in 1893, enjoying the well-deserved title of librarian emeritus until his death on May 13, 1899. He was born in Dedham, Massachusetts, on May 4, 1822; graduated from Brown University in 1847; and from that time devoted his life to the service of the college as its librarian and historian, even his years of retirement being given to a revision of his books and the collection of new material. He received the degree of LL.D. from Shurtleff College in 1874. Dr. Guild served on the Providence common council and the school committee for many years; he was a member of various historical societies, and helped to found the American Library Association in 1876, acting also as its first secretary. But to the end his thoughts centered in Brown University and its library. He knew the history of the university more intimately than any other man; his interest in its present and future was equally keen; and he welcomed undergraduates and alumni to the library, as to the hearthstone of the academic family, with a fluent geniality that never tired. As a librarian his fundamental principle was that all users of the library should have free access to the shelves; the method needed supplementing in the many ways devised by modern library science, but it was the one thing most needful, and thousands of readers cherish grateful memories of Dr. Guild for allowing them the comfortable society of the books themselves without the formality of an introduction by means of cards in a catalogue. He thus encouraged the reading habit in undergraduates; modern librarians do much else, but they do nothing better.

Professor Jenks died on September 26, 1894, in his seventy-fifth year. After graduation in the class of 1838, he gave himself chiefly to teaching, and was principal of Peirce Academy, Middleborough, Massachusetts, from 1842 to 1871. From 1871 till the year of his death he was curator of the museum of natural history in Brown University, and professor of agricultural zoölogy for nearly the same period. The museum was practically his creation; he devoted to it through almost a quarter-century his rare knowledge and skill as a collector and taxidermist, often contributing liberally of his means, and it remains his best memorial.

A year later occurred the death of Professor Blake. He was a native of New Haven, Connecticut, where he was born on April 20, 1836. His father was a nephew of Eli Whitney, inventor of the cotton-gin; and his mother was descended from the Rev. James Pierpont, a founder of Yale College. After graduation at Yale in 1857, and some time spent in teaching and graduate study in this country, he went to Germany, where for three and a half years he studied chemistry and physics under Kirchhoff, Bunsen, Kolbe, Dove, and Magnus. Upon his return he held temporary professorships in physics at Vermont University and Columbia College during 1866–69, and then accepted the chair of physics and the mechanical arts in Cornell University. In

1870 he came to Brown as the first incumbent of the new Hazard professorship of physics, and held the chair twenty-five years, resigning in the spring of 1895. His health had already begun to fail, and he died on October 1 of the same year. Professor Blake was by nature an investigator, not a teacher; in required courses he was not severe enough, and lazy undergraduates easily took advantage of his guileless good nature. He was, nevertheless, a delightful man to know, even across the desk of a lecture room; and those who came away from his classes with very hazy ideas of mechanics and physics were yet the better for contact with so gentle and pure a spirit. In the conduct of small classes and in guiding laboratory work he was much more successful. But his gift was for invention and research. "The little that he had leisure to do in this direction," says the writer of the memorial sketch of him, "was of such a quality as to make his name known and esteemed in the scientific world, both in this country and abroad. His beautiful device for photographing the motion of metallic plates vibrating under human speech, merits special attention. . . . It was his great pleasure, during the winter of 1876–7, in connection with his intimate friend, Professor John Peirce, to assist Mr. Alexander Graham Bell in experiments with the telephone —then in the very early stages of its development." Professor Blake's last great service to the university was his planning and supervision of the building of Wilson Hall, the physics laboratory, to which he gave minute attention for many months.

It remains to speak of two members of the Faculty who had long labored side by side, and, next to President Wayland, had done more than any others to spread the fame of the college—Professors Lincoln and Harkness.

Professor Lincoln died on October 17, 1891. He was born

in Boston, Massachusetts, on February 23, 1817, of an old New England family. His father was a printer and publisher; his brother Heman was for twenty years professor in Newton Theological Institution. He attended the Boston Latin School and the Boston high school, entered Brown University in 1832, and graduated in 1836. He taught in Columbian College for a year and then entered Newton Theological Institution; but deciding that he was not adapted for the ministry, he became tutor in Greek at Brown University from 1839 to 1841. The next three years he spent in study abroad, the first two chiefly in Germany, the third in France and Italy, and returned to Brown as assistant professor of Latin in 1844, becoming professor the next year. In this chair he devoted the rest of his life to the service of the university, except for six months abroad in 1857 and a year abroad in 1887–88; during the years 1859–67, however, he was principal of a school for young women, although he still had charge of all the Latin courses in college and taught some of them. He published selections from Livy in 1847, the works of Horace in 1851, and selections from Ovid in 1882; the books had a total sale of about sixty-five thousand copies. He wrote essays and reviews for *The North American Review*, *The Christian Review*, and the *Bibliotheca Sacra*, besides many papers for the Friday Club, and much miscellaneous matter for the newspapers, including the Brown necrology for many years. Brown University gave him the degree of LL.D. in 1859. Colby University and Vassar College would have elected him president, but he declined to leave his professorship. At the semi-centennial of his graduation, in 1886, the alumni gave to the college a portrait of him by Herkomer; four years later a fund of $100,000, raised in his honor and named after him, was added to the endowment, the income to be used to secure him his usual salary so long as he lived, whether he was able to teach or not.

The impression made by Professor Lincoln was due chiefly to his delightful personality. He was not a nature of great power, although he had force and a cutting edge when there was need; perfect order, without undue restraint, prevailed in his class-room. It was not his force but his quick sympathy, his youthful freshness and gaiety of spirit, and the indefinable quality called charm, that drew students to him and kept his memory delightful to them through all after years. There was in him to the end something of the boy, though mellowed and chastened by study and time, and hence a rare kind of intellectual comradeship between him and his pupils was always possible. As a teacher of literature, too, his personality was the main thing. He could not be called a great scholar or a great critic, but in the class-room he was inimitable. His published essays, although they reveal him as a thoughtful interpreter of literature, cannot show what was most delightful and stimulating in the living teacher — the high response to noble sentiment, the deep content with the simple, primary values of life, the exquisite sensitiveness to felicities of word and phrase, the boyish glee over some bit of fun or happy fancy. Choice Latin was to him like a draught of old Falernian. But literary sensibility brings its penalty to a teacher; and his pupils sometimes took quiet amusement in watching the twinges of pain on his sensitive lips while some ruthless sophomore was bumping through an ode of Horace. On the other hand good work by his pupils gave him keen pleasure. "How he beamed and glowed over a happy translation!" writes President Faunce. "With what contagious gladness he expounded some *callida junctura* in Tacitus! How he radiated his own joy in the Ars Poetica! How he exploded over some venerable joke in Ter-

ence, as if it were the latest cartoon in Punch! The Latin
a dead language? No one ever said that who sat under
'Johnny Link' in 23 University Hall.'' He was in the
truest sense a teacher of the humanities; in Latin literature
he saw human life and culture, and helped his pupils to feel
its broadening and refining influence. "It was his hand,"
writes a former student in *The Providence Journal*, "that
opened for them the gates of an exceedingly pleasant land
whither, in intervals between the cares and labors of active
life, it is still the privilege of the educated man to steal away
for refreshment.''

Professor Harkness retired from teaching in 1892; but
as professor emeritus for many years he kept in close touch
with the university, besides serving on the Board of Fellows
from 1904 till his death on May 27, 1907. He was born in
Mendon, Massachusetts, on October 6, 1822. He attended
district school, and the Uxbridge high school and Worcester
Academy each for one term; after a year's study at home,
with some help from a minister, he entered Brown University in 1838, and at once took high rank; in the junior
exhibition of 1841 he was assigned the Latin oration, the
second honor, and the next year graduated as valedictorian. After teaching in the Providence high school for ten
years, also serving as principal for eight years, he studied
in Berlin, Bonn, and Göttingen during 1853–55, receiving
the degree of Ph.D. from Bonn in 1854. In 1855 he took
the chair of Greek in Brown University, and held it until
1892, but spent the academic years 1870–71 and 1883–84
in Europe on leave of absence. He received the degree of
LL.D. from Brown University in 1869. He was a founder
of the American Philological Association, and held in it the
offices of secretary, treasurer, vice-president, and president.
He was also a founder of the American School of Classical

Studies in Athens, and a member of its managing committee for many years. He early began to publish Latin textbooks, bringing out some fourteen different works between 1851 and 1905, besides revisions, and *A First Greek Book* in 1860. His Latin books include editions of Caesar, Cicero, and Sallust, and the famous *Latin Grammar*, first published in 1864; all his books had a wide sale, and the grammar for many years practically supplanted all other Latin grammars in the United States. He also published articles in the *Transactions of the American Philological Association*, the *Bibliotheca Sacra*, and elsewhere.

The facts of Professor Harkness's academic career and authorship afford a hint of the useful diversity of temperament between him and his colleague, Professor Lincoln. It was an excellent thing for Brown University that its departments of the classics had as their heads for so long a time two men of such different types although fundamentally harmonious; for each emphasized a needful side of culture without excluding the other side. The undergraduates needed the literary enthusiasm of Professor Lincoln. They also needed the insistence upon exact and accurate scholarship in which lay the peculiar strength of Professor Harkness. The latter's nature was essentially intellectual, and hence his approach to language and literature may be broadly called scientific. His joy in knowing and stating the exact truth about the lost digamma or the original cases was really one with that of a paleontologist in restoring the skeleton of a dinosaur; his insistence upon the shades of meaning conveyed by μέν and δέ had the precision of mathematics, and brought even to the thoughtless undergraduate some realization that a language, as well as a theodolite, might be an instrument of extremely nice adjustment. But all this should not be taken to mean that Professor Harkness was indifferent to literature or lacked artistic faculty. His *Latin Grammar* alone might disprove that, for it is itself a work of art in its lucidity of statement, sense of proportion, and adaptation to the minds for which it was designed. Those who had never heard him make an address, but knew him chiefly as a grammarian, were often surprised at the Attic grace and finish of his style and the justness of his thought. These qualities charmed the great audience in his address at the Commencement dinner of 1902, on the sixtieth anniversary of his graduation. In the class-room, it is true, he gave relatively little attention to the purely literary aspect of the subject-matter; but he had his characteristic reason for this, saying in his annual report of 1874–75, "It is indeed somewhat disheartening that we are able, in the brief time allowed us, to read so little, that we must leave untouched such a wide range of the choicest literary treasures, but when the alternative is between reading a small amount critically, and hurrying over a large amount superficially, I think the true educator cannot long hesitate." His manner in the class-room had its own charm of Hellenic urbanity and repose. His uniformly pleasant relations with his pupils were continued in after years, notably at the receptions to the alumni in his house and garden on Prospect Street, which became one of the most delightful features of Commencement week. His old age was one that a Greek might have envied — spent with family and friends around him, and full of peaceful labor done in health and mental clarity to the very end.

With the passing of these men went much of the strength of the old Faculty; but much remained in the persons of Professors Clarke, Appleton, Williams, Poland, Packard, Davis, Bailey, Upton, Chapin, and Instructor Randall. Most of these experienced teachers already held full professorships, and the others were soon promoted. Professor Poland was made associate professor of Greek and curator of the museum of classical archaeology in 1889, and professor of the history of art in 1892, a position for which he was peculiarly fitted by his prolonged study of classical literature and art and by his residence in Greece in 1891–92 as director of the American School of Classical Studies in Athens. Professor Davis, long a mainstay of the department of mathematics by reason of his vigor and skill as a teacher, became associate professor in 1889, and professor the next year. Mr. Randall was promoted to be assistant professor of mathematics and civil engineering in 1891, associate professor of mechanical drawing in 1892, and professor in 1896. To this Faculty President Andrews rapidly added new men; and the success of his administration was due largely to his gift for selecting colleagues full of zeal and ideas, many of them his former pupils or friends and animated by a like spirit with himself.

Two of the new teachers had been added in President Robinson's last year. John F. Jameson, A.B. (Amherst), Ph.D. (Johns Hopkins), became professor of history in 1888; he stimulated scientific historical research by his advanced pupils, besides raising the general level of historical study in the university; from 1901 to 1905 he was head of the department of history in the University of Chicago, and since then has been director of the department of historical research in the Carnegie Institution at Washington; while at Brown he became editor of *The American Historical Review*, published *The History of Historical Writing in America* and *Dictionary of United States History*, and edited the correspondence of Calhoun. Henry B. Gardner, A.B. (Brown), Ph.D. (Johns Hopkins), was appointed instructor in political economy in 1888, associate professor in 1890, and professor in 1898; he has been a vice-president of the American Economic Association and a member of its executive committee; since 1904, while retaining his professorship, he has been directing the research work in federal and state finance for the Carnegie Institution at Washington.

James Seth, A.M. (University of Edinburgh), was called to Brown University in 1892 as associate professor of natural theology, becoming professor of philosophy and natural theology in 1894; he accepted the professorship of moral philosophy in Cornell University in 1896, and since 1898 has held the same chair in the University of Edinburgh; even his brief stay at Brown was a great inspiration to philosophical study. He was succeeded by Walter G. Everett, A.B., Ph.D. (Brown), who studied in Germany in 1895–96; he was associate professor of philosophy from 1894 to 1899, when he became professor; in the absence of President Faunce during the greater part of the year 1912–13, he served as acting president. The modern study of psychology at Brown University began with the appointment of Edmund B. Delabarre, A.B. (Amherst), A.M. (Harvard), Ph.D. (Freiburg), as associate professor of psychology in 1891; he was promoted to the professorship in 1896; in 1896–97, during Professor Münsterberg's absence, he was director of the Harvard psychological laboratory. The chair of "didactics," renamed and remodeled, was again placed in the Faculty row in 1893, and filled by Walter B. Jacobs, A.B., A.M. (Brown), as instructor in pedagogy, who became associate professor in 1895 and professor of education in 1901.

Albert G. Harkness, A.B., A.M. (Brown), the son of Professor Harkness, after study in Germany in 1881–83 and a professorship in Madison University, returned to Brown as associate professor of Latin in 1889, and succeeded to the chair of Professor Lincoln in 1893; he was resident professor in the American School for Classical Studies in Rome in 1902–03. The new professor of Greek was James Irving Manatt, A.B. (Iowa), Ph.D. (Yale), LL.D. (Iowa), who, after professorships in Denison University and Marietta College, was chancellor of the University of Nebraska from 1884 to 1889, and then consul at Athens for four years, coming to Brown in 1893; in collaboration with Dr. Tsountas he brought out *The Mycenaean Age* in 1897, and has recently published *Aegean Days* at the press of John Murray, London. The department of Greek had previously been strengthened by the appointment of Charles E. Bennett, A.B. (Brown), as professor of classical philology in 1891; his resignation at the end of the year, to accept a professorship in Cornell University, left a vacancy which was filled by the appointment of Francis G. Allinson, A.B. (Haverford and Harvard), Ph.D. (Johns Hopkins), as associate professor of Greek in 1895 and as professor of classical philology in 1898; in 1910–11 he was the resident professor in the American School of Classical Studies in Athens; he published selections from Lucian in 1905, *Greek Lands and Letters* (with Mrs. Allinson) in 1909, and is now editing and translating Menander for the Loeb Classical Library.

The first teacher in the new department of Semitics, James R. Jewett, A.B. (Harvard), Ph.D. (Strasburg), after three years in the Orient and a year as instructor in Semitic languages at Harvard, came to Brown in 1890 as instructor, and was made associate professor the next year; in 1895 he resigned to take a professorship in the University of Minnesota. His successor, Charles F. Kent, A.B., Ph.D. (Yale), after two years as instructor in the University of Chicago, became associate professor of biblical literature and history at Brown in 1895, was promoted to the professorship in 1898, and resigned in 1901 to take a similar position at

Yale; while at Brown he began his career as a prolific author by publishing seven books.

Before the death of Professor Bancroft the department of English had been enlarged by the addition of Lorenzo Sears, A.B. (Yale), recently professor of English in the University of Vermont; he was made associate professor of rhetoric at Brown in 1890, and associate professor of American literature in 1895, retiring in 1906; he is the author of books on oratory, literary criticism, American literature, and American public men. John M. Manly, A.B. (Furman), Ph.D. (Harvard), was appointed associate professor of the English language in 1891, becoming professor the next year; in 1898 he went to the University of Chicago as head of the English department; he first brought to Brown the modern methods of teaching English philology, and while here published two of the works which have brought him international reputation as an English scholar. Walter C. Bronson, A.B. (Brown), A.M. (Cornell), Litt.D. (Colby), after two years as professor of English at De Pauw University, returned to Brown as associate professor of English literature in 1892, becoming professor in 1895; he is the author of a short history of American literature, and the editor of several volumes of English and American verse and prose. Hammond Lamont, A.B. (Harvard), instructor in English at Harvard in 1892–95, came to Brown as associate professor of rhetoric in 1895, and was made professor in 1898; in 1900 he left the university to become managing editor of the New York *Evening Post;* at his death in 1909 he was editor of *The Nation;* under his rigorous and stimulating discipline, modern methods of teaching English composition became a strong factor in the Brown curriculum.

Wilfred H. Munro, A.B., A.M. (Brown), president of De Veaux College from 1881 to 1889, and historical student in the United States and Germany in 1889–91, became associate professor of history in 1891 and professor of European history in 1899, retiring as professor emeritus in 1911; he edited Prescott's works in 1905–06. George G. Wilson, A.B., Ph.D. (Brown), after study in Berlin, Paris, and Oxford, was appointed associate professor of social and political science in 1891, professor in 1894; in 1910 he accepted the chair of international law in Harvard University; in 1908 he was a representative of the United States at the Conference of London; he is the author of several books and encyclopaedia articles on international law. James Q. Dealey, A.B., Ph.D. (Brown), became assistant professor in the same department in 1895, associate professor in 1898, professor in 1905; he has published several books on sociology.

Instruction in the Germanic languages was extended by the appointment of Asa C. Crowell, A.B., Ph.D. (Brown), as instructor in 1892, assistant professor in 1894, associate professor in 1901; and of Adrian Scott, A.B., Ph.D. (Brown), as instructor in 1891, associate professor of Germanic philology and Scandinavian during 1894–96. The head of the new department of Romance languages, Courtney Langdon, A.B. (Brown, honorary, 1891), after three years of study in Harvard and six years as instructor in Cornell University, became assistant professor at Brown in 1890, associate professor in 1892, and professor in 1899; he is now publishing at the Harvard University Press a translation of Dante.

The department of mathematics was strengthened by the appointment of Henry P. Manning, A.B. (Brown), Ph.D. (Johns Hopkins), as instructor in 1891, assistant professor in 1895, and associate professor in 1906; he is the author of several books on the higher mathematics. John E. Hill,

B.S. (Rutgers), M.C.E. (Cornell), instructor in Cornell for four years, was appointed instructor in civil engineering at Brown in 1894, associate professor in 1895, professor in 1898.

Professor Blake's successor was Carl Barus, Ph.D. (Wurzburg), physicist in the United States geological survey for twelve years, and in the Smithsonian Institution for two years, whence he came to Brown as professor of physics in 1895; he is the author of numberless scientific publications, was awarded the Rumford medal in 1900 for his researches in heat, was president of the American Physical Society in 1904, and is an honorary member of the Royal Institution of Great Britain. His colleague, Albert DeF. Palmer, Ph.B., Ph.D. (Brown), graduate student at Johns Hopkins in 1891–93, was appointed instructor in 1893 and associate professor in 1896.

Hermon C. Bumpus, Ph.B. (Brown), Ph.D. (Clark), became assistant professor of zoölogy in 1890, associate professor in 1891, and professor of comparative anatomy in 1892; in 1902 he resigned to be director of the American Museum of Natural History in New York. From 1893 to 1896 he was assisted by George W. Field, A.B. (Brown), Ph.D. (Johns Hopkins), an associate professor of cellular biology; and from 1895 to 1901 by Albert D. Mead, A.B. (Middlebury), Ph.D. (Chicago), who became instructor in comparative anatomy in 1895, associate professor of embryology and neurology in 1896, and succeeded to the professorship of comparative anatomy in 1901.

The successor of Dr. Guild as librarian was Harry L. Koopman, A.B. (Colby), A.M. (Harvard), Litt. D. (Colby), trained in modern library methods in the Astor Library and at Cornell and Columbia.

In the department of military drill, established in 1892

in belated fulfillment of the terms of the Morrill land-grant fund in 1863, the university had the services of three United States Army officers as professors of military tactics: Lieutenant William C. Pardee, 1892–95; Lieutenant John Baxter, 1895–96; and Captain Cunliffe H. Murray, 1896–98.

The office of registrar was held from 1889 to 1891 by the Rev. Dr. John C. Stockbridge, A.B., A.M. (Brown); he was succeeded by Frederick T. Guild, Ph.B., A.M. (Brown), who still fills the position.

The infusion of all this new blood into the veins of the old college was a source of immense vigor. The Faculty was now not only larger, but contained a far greater proportion of highly trained specialists, men of varying types of mind and coming from different universities and different sections of the country. The range and depth of instruction offered had never been approached before in the history of the institution; and it is no wonder that increasing numbers of students came, and that more and more remained for graduate study. The work that the Faculty were doing, furthermore, was now set forth to greater advantage in the pages of the catalogue, which also had been touched and revivified by the shaping hand of the President. The courses were grouped by departments as well as by years, and the extent to which study could be pursued along any one line was now patent at a glance. Various other changes in the substance and form of the catalogue helped to make it more attractive than formerly.

Three phases of the expansion of the work of the university call for special notice. The first two were realizations on a larger scale of ideals cherished by President Wayland. The third he dreamed not of.

The course in civil engineering, established as a part of the New System in 1850, had never been given up except for a short time under President Sears, while in the next two administrations it had some growth; under President Andrews it was greatly expanded. A course leading to the degree of Civil Engineer was opened in 1891, and one leading to the degree of Mechanical Engineer in 1892. The entrance requirements for these courses were rather low, consisting of the mathematics, English, French, and Greek and Roman history required for admission to the Bachelor of Arts course. Each engineering course covered four years, and included both theoretical and practical work, although the latter was limited for some years because of insufficient apparatus and laboratory facilities. A course for the degree of Bachelor of Science was also opened in 1891, and the degree was first granted in 1897.

University Extension, though not by that name, had been one of President Wayland's democratic plans; but he had been unable to carry it out on any large scale. A few years before the beginning of President Andrews's administration a carefully organized movement for bringing some of the benefits of university study to outside circles gained great headway in England, and soon spread to this country, where it was first taken up by the University of Pennsylvania. Brown University entered the field in 1890–91, giving four courses in the winter and spring of that year. Professor Munro was then appointed director, and organized thirty-five courses for 1891–92, which were attended by about fifteen hundred persons in sixteen towns and cities. The courses were self-supporting, admission fees paying for the lectures and other expenses. One of the Providence courses, on practical physics, attended by workmen from the Browne and Sharpe Manufacturing Company, recalls the days of Professor Chace's lectures to metal-workers in 1853. "Its sessions," says Professor Munro, "were held in the great lecture room in Wilson Hall. They were very largely attended, and excited so much interest that a second class, in Electricity, was organized by the same men." In 1892–93 thirty-eight courses were given, with an attendance of some two thousand. This was the high tide of the movement at Brown University. Financial depression during the next few years, and a waning of interest on the part of lecturers and classes as the novelty wore off, resulted in a steady decline; in 1898–99 no courses were given, and at the end of the year Professor Munro resigned his directorship. A somewhat similar series of lectures had been started in 1888–89, by the Brown University Historical and Economic Association (after 1892 called the Brown University Lecture Association), organized by Professor Jameson and comprising citizens of Providence, resident graduates, and members of the senior class. Lectures on a wide range of subjects were given each winter for several years, in Manning or Sayles Hall, by the professors of the university and scholars from a distance, and were attended by large numbers of students and townspeople.

One of the most interesting phases of the recent development of Brown University is the origin and growth of the Women's College. In this movement President Andrews had a leading part, but the beginnings of it lie farther back. For the first hundred years, it is true, no one in authority seems to have given a thought to opening the university to women, although the seniors in their Commencement parts sometimes approached the subject, as in "A Dissertation in Favor of Female Education" in 1796, or presented thoughts having a collateral bearing on the subject, as in a dissertation in 1812 on "The rank of the Fair Sex in the scale of being." Credit for squarely facing the problem belongs, however, to the college branch of the Philandrian Society, who at their first meeting, in 1800, debated the question, "Would it be good policy to allow females in the United States an Education equal to the males?" But the centenary of the founding of the college had hardly passed before the question of higher education for women in Rhode Island began to be discussed, the establishment of women's colleges in the East and the spread of co-education in the West forcing the matter on the attention of thoughtful men and women.

The problem seems to have first come before the university in a semi-official way at the alumni meeting in 1869, when a committee submitted the following as one of their "most important recommendations": "In these days it may not be premature to inquire, whether a college which justly prides itself in the possession of an eminently liberal charter, should not open its doors to the admission of women, so that students of both sexes might within its halls, share together all its advantages of education." At Commencement in 1870 President James B. Angell, of the University of Vermont, in his address before the alumni touched on the question, saying that it must "receive much fuller discussion at the east than it has yet received." The next year the matter came directly before the governing board of the university. "The President informed the Corporation," run the minutes of September 6, 1871, "that there had been three applications for young women to enter college and pursue the studies usually allotted to young men. After some little discussion of the subject it was Voted to lay it on the table." In the spring of 1874 a young woman boldly claimed for the "fair sex" a high "rank in the scale of being" by applying for admission to Brown University; in reply the Advisory and Executive Committee resolved, at a meeting on April 10, that they were "not prepared to recommend the opening of the College for the admission of young women as students," and the Corporation approved the resolution at their meeting in June.

The revival of the subject seven years later seems to have been due to the Quaker members of the Corporation. The poet Whittier, a trustee, wrote to a Providence lady in the summer of 1881, "I shall be glad to do all in my power to open the doors of Brown University to women." In an inclosed note for Richard Atwater, another Quaker trustee, he said: "I hope the time is not far distant when Brown University will be open to woman. The traditions of the noble old institution are all in favor of broad liberality and equality of rights and privileges. . . . Brown University cannot afford to hesitate much longer in a matter, like this, of simple justice." Meanwhile various organizations of Rhode Island women helped in quiet ways to keep the matter before the college; and in June, 1885, the Corporation took their first favorable action, appointing a committee to consider and report "what, if any, facilities should be offered by this University for the higher education of women." The committee reported at the September meeting, recommending "that the Faculty allow the attendance of women at the regular entrance and term examinations of the University, and that certificates of standing in each examination be issued to the applicants." The report was recommitted for further consideration.

The situation as it lay in the minds of the majority of the Corporation and Faculty at this time is fairly stated by President Robinson in his report in June, 1886. He first gives reasons against co-education at Brown: the buildings "are not so constructed as to furnish the requisite accommodations for young women, and cannot without great expense be so changed as to fit them for use by both sexes"; many persons in the community object to co-education on moral and intellectual grounds, thinking that the sexes had better be educated apart at "the inflammable age," and that women need a different training from that of men. He then states the other side with equal fairness and force: Rhode Island has an increasing number of young women, graduates of high schools, who wish to fit themselves for the higher positions as teachers or for the largest usefulness in society; by experience in the schools they are prepared to meet the dangers of co-education in college; many of them cannot afford to go away from home, and therefore they expect Brown University, as the only Rhode Island college, to admit them to equal privileges with their brothers. President Robinson adds, "The plea thus presented is not a weak one." He then offers a compromise plan, somewhat like that finally adopted, as follows:

I would recommend . . . that the following experimental provision be attempted: That young women be admitted by us on the same conditions as young men; that instruction be given them separately, during their first year in college, in the afternoon, and in the recitation rooms of Sayles Hall, which during the afternoon shall be given up to their exclusive use; that instruction shall be given them by such members of the Faculty as shall be willing to undertake the service, and that the compensation for this service shall be derived from, and consist of, a *pro rata* distribution of the tuition received from the members of the class. . . . As to what should be done in future years, all might safely, it seems to me, be left to be determined by the results of a first year's experiment. . . . My own present impressions are in favor of a distinct but appended college, some of whose professors should be women of the highest culture, and members of whose higher classes should be admitted to the higher elective classes of the University.

At the meeting of the Corporation in September, 1886, this plan was first approved by the Corporation, and then postponed for further consideration. The next year Dr. Robinson reported that four young women had sent him a letter asking if Brown University would admit them to its courses of study, and renewed his recommendation. Thereupon, at the September meeting of the Corporation, a committee was appointed to consider the problem and report later. This committee, through the chairman, Professor Gammell, at the September meeting in 1888, presented a very able report. "In the nature of things," they said, "there is no substantial reason why the higher intellectual training of young women should be essentially different from that of young men. . . . The noticeable fact is that whenever provisions of any kind have been made for the higher training of young women by means of College studies, the results have been uniformly advantageous. The young women have always gained & the young men have not lost, by what has been done. The time probably is not distant when the whole question will cease to be a matter of discussion, since the higher education of women will, as a matter of course, no longer be different from that given to young men at our best schools of learning of every name." Nevertheless the committee advised against opening Brown University to women at that time, because the demand seemed insufficient, the college buildings were not adapted for co-educational classes, and the Faculty were lukewarm on the subject. They did recommend, however, that as a preliminary step the Faculty be asked to prepare a scheme by which women might be admitted to college examinations and receive certificates of proficiency. The Corporation approved, and here the matter rested for a time.

Soon after the election of President Andrews, who was known to be a warm friend to the higher education of women, a committee of Rhode Island women consulted with him on the situation, and by his advice an attempt was made to raise at least a small fund; little came of it, but the Rhode

Island Women's Club voted to found a scholarship for women as soon as they should be admitted to the university.
On February 11, 1890, the Faculty adopted for submission
to the Corporation, in response to their vote of 1888, a plan
regarding examinations for women; and this was presented
to that body in the autumn. It admitted women to entrance
examinations at the same times and places as men; specified that they might take college examinations at the college, the examinations to be identical with those for men or
closely similar; and provided for certificates of attainment.
The report ended with a statement that if the Corporation
adopted the plan, the Faculty would "cordially execute the
same to the best of their ability," but that in their judgment
it gave undue prominence to examinations in the system
of college education. The Corporation approved the plan
a year later, on September 2, 1891; in the following June
the Board of Fellows recognized women as candidates for
all degrees, and the Corporation admitted women graduate
students to the university class-rooms.

The barriers once removed, the young women of the state
soon gave proof that there was demand enough for the higher
education of women in Rhode Island. The women undergraduates increased from 7 in 1891–92 to 157 in 1896–97;
while the graduate women students in the latter year numbered 31, of whom 21 held degrees from other colleges.
The problem was not to get students but to provide quarters and instruction for them. During the first term of the
first year the classes met in the University Grammar School,
in the early afternoon, and, as there were no lights in the
school, in President Andrews's office in University Hall when
the darkness fell; during the second and third terms the
Normal School building on Benefit Street was courteously
opened to them. The instruction was given by members of

the Brown Faculty, but was paid for wholly by fees. The classes had no official relation to the university, which had as yet merely opened its examinations to women; formally the class-room work was private "coaching" for the examinations, but in reality it was identical with the instruction given to men in the same courses.

From 1892 to 1897 the classes met in a small wooden building on Benefit Street, near the corner of College Street, which had been the home of a high school for girls from 1828 to 1877, Professor Lincoln being its principal during the years 1859–67. These quarters were soon outgrown, and the students swarmed in the hallways and even on the stairs, the latter being the only seats available for some during study hours. But in these cramped rooms much excellent work was done. The average standing of the women students was regularly higher than that of the men in corresponding classes, and some of them showed marked ability for independent, original work. The report of the new professor of physics for 1895–96 is especially significant on this point. "I wish in particular," he wrote, "to bear testimony to the uniformly admirable work done by the women. I began the course of lectures to the Women's College with diffidence, believing that the mind of woman is not, as a rule, of a kind to be willingly tethered by exact considerations of the material universe. But I found neither lack of aptitude nor of grasp."

Two women graduated in 1894: Anne T. Weeden, who took the degree of Master of Arts four years later, studied in Germany, and has long held an honored place among the teachers in the Providence high schools, besides contributing in other ways to the intellectual culture of the city; and Mary E. Woolley, who proceeded to the Master of Arts degree the next year, became instructor and professor in

Wellesley College, and since 1900 has been president of
Mount Holyoke College. Of the other women graduates in
these early years, nearly all have filled positions in schools,
libraries, or other institutions of high responsibility and
influence—including the home.

The success of the movement during these years of experiment was due first of all to President Andrews, the strong
prop and inspiring soul of the whole. He found an efficient
helper in Louis F. Snow, a recent graduate of Brown and
Harvard, and instructor in elocution in the university from
1890 to 1892, who was appointed dean of the Women's College in 1892, and by his business ability, tact, and unfailing courtesy did much to make straight and smooth the path
of the institution along its untried way. The members of
the Faculty also proved to be less indifferent than had been
supposed, many of them readily undertaking the additional labor and receiving the additional compensation. The
number of courses given increased with the growth in
attendance, until in 1896–97 they numbered thirty-one
year-courses, taught by seventeen professors and eight instructors, and representing fifteen of the twenty-five departments in the university.

Such life as this was sure to get for itself means of subsistence. "So important and so interesting is this cause,"
wrote President Andrews in his report for 1891–92, "I cannot think that the half million dollars needed to erect as part
of Brown University a thoroughly equipped Woman's College will be long withheld." His robust optimism outran
the facts, but a beginning was soon made. During the next
year the Rhode Island Women's Club provided an annual
scholarship of $50; and the pupils of Miss Sarah E. Doyle
—a teacher in the Providence schools from 1846, in the high
school from 1859, and principal of the girls' department

of the latter from 1878 to 1892—gave to the university a scholarship fund of $1000 bearing her name. It was not until 1895, however, that a movement was set on foot to raise funds for the erection of a college building. At the suggestion of Dr. Andrews a large committee was then organized, with Miss Doyle as chairman, and in spite of financial depression a considerable sum was soon subscribed, Andrew Comstock and Jesse Metcalf being among the chief donors. The committee was incorporated, on September 14, 1896, as the Rhode Island Society for the Collegiate Education of Women, with Miss Doyle as president, and took charge of the erection of the new building, which was situated on land owned by the Corporation on Meeting Street, a few rods north of the university grounds. The Corporation at their June meeting had meanwhile voted to establish "a department of the University to be known as the Women's College in Brown University," under the general direction of the president and the immediate charge of a dean, further providing that the instruction should be given by the university professors and instructors; at graduation its students were, as before, to receive their degrees from the university. Thus was realized the ideal which President Andrews had set forth in his report of 1892–93, in which he said: "No mere 'annex' is desired or intended. The College must be part and parcel of the University, giving women students the full university status." The votes of the Corporation were not to go into effect until the building then contemplated had been finished and given to the university. This was done in 1897, when Pembroke Hall, named after the college in Cambridge University founded by the Countess of Pembroke and attended by Roger Williams, was dedicated on November 22, with appropriate exercises, including addresses by Miss Doyle, Dean Emily J. Smith, of Barnard College, and

President Andrews. The building, which cost $38,000, was of red brick with stone and terra-cotta trimmings, in the English university style of the sixteenth century; besides recitation rooms, a library (beautifully finished through the generosity of Miss Amelia S. Knight), and a large assembly room, it contained offices for the dean, a lunch room, a rest room, lockers, etc., being skillfully planned for the various purposes, intellectual and social, to which it was to be put. In this building the Women's College found a suitable home, where the students could have their separate social life and receive instruction in separate classes, and yet be in and of the university. This scheme of an affiliated, not an appended, college, which is expressed in the name "The Women's College in Brown University," has proved most satisfactory, and has since been adopted for other institutions in various parts of the country.

Undergraduate life among the men students soon showed new energy in various ways. A monthly periodical, *The Brown Magazine*, was established in April, 1890; *The Brunonian* became a weekly in September of the same year; and on December 2, 1891, appeared the first issue of *The Brown Daily Herald*. *The Brunonian*, thus exposed to double competition, had a hard struggle for existence, and in 1898 united with the magazine, which took the name of the former. Greek-letter societies increased in numbers, until in 1898 there were twelve, with a membership of 272. The social features of fraternity life were increasingly emphasized, a tendency that was hastened by the erection, in 1892, of the beautiful chapter house of Psi Upsilon on Thayer Street. Athletic sports, which found an enthusiastic advocate in President Andrews, got more and more attention from undergraduates, alumni, and Faculty. The Athletic Association was formed in 1890, and a Faculty committee on athletics was appointed in 1893. A new and larger athletic field, situated about a mile to the north of the campus, was laid out in 1899, and named Andrews Field in honor of the President.

. The rapid growth of the university brought serious problems, which were not easily solved. The need of more buildings and of equipment of all kinds soon became acute. A few new buildings were indeed erected early in President Andrews's administration, with funds which had been received wholly or chiefly under his predecessor. Wilson Hall, constructed and fitted up according to the latest ideals for work in physics, at a cost of $99,000, was partly occupied early in 1891, and formally opened in June of that year. For aid in planning and furnishing it Professor Blake was deeply indebted to Professor John Peirce, who had been for years the good genius of the department, and by whose death in 1897 the whole university lost one of its most intelligent friends. Ladd Observatory, with a twelve-inch telescope, situated on high ground about a mile to the north of the campus, was finished in the autumn of 1891, at an expense of some $25,000. The Lyman Gymnasium, costing with its equipment nearly $66,000, was opened for use in November, 1891, and made possible a system of instruction in various forms of athletic drill, which was for some years required of all classes in the winter months. In the summer of the same year Hope College, which was much out of repair — the north wall cracked, timbers rotting, and the whole interior worn and dingy — was thoroughly renovated under the vigilant eye of Marshall Woods, chairman of the real estate committee, at a cost of $35,000; a cellar was dug, weak parts were strengthened, and the interior was completely refinished in far better style than before. At the same time the heating station, begun in 1890 to heat Sayles Hall and

Wilson Hall, was extended so as to heat all the buildings on the campus.

But here building operations stopped for lack of funds, although there was crying need for larger accommodations of all kinds. "The Chapel is outgrown," wrote President Andrews in his report in June, 1892. "It can no longer be made to hold all our students. . . . The dormitories are outgrown. Every room in Hope, in Slater, in University is at this moment rented for a year. . . . The Chemical Laboratory is outgrown. New tables are to be introduced this summer, enabling us to work at some rate all the students electing chemical courses for a year or two; but they will be much too crowded for best results, and even this device will not serve us long. . . . The Botanical Laboratory is totally outgrown. It is ludicrously inadequate to our requirements. . . . Except the two largest, all the recitation rooms in Sayles Hall are outgrown. They can at best be used only for elective classes, and the fullest of these crowd them almost to suffocation. . . . Surprising as it may seem, our Library Building, new as it is, and inadequate as are our funds for stocking it with books, is, if not outgrown, on the point of becoming so." But he adds, "Desperately restricted as are the accommodations for much of our work, we cannot spare a dollar of our invested funds or current income to enlarge them."

During the next few years the situation was much the same. The pressure for dormitories and class-rooms was somewhat relieved by the building of Maxcy Hall in 1894–95, which cost with its furnishings about $48,500; this sum was taken out of the funds, and the investment proved a profitable one. But in 1897, when students and Faculty had multiplied more than threefold, the endowment was practically what it had been eight years before. If it be asked how, then, all this expansion had been possible, a glance at the treasurer's reports will answer. In 1888–89 the total income for general use was $53,105; in 1896–97, it was $140,906. Of this gain of $87,801, over $77,000 was due to increase in receipts from students for tuition, room rent, etc., chiefly on account of the great growth in numbers, the charges having been but slightly advanced; in 1888–89 the receipts from this source were $30,343; in 1896–97 they were $107,779. This money in hand had provided for the enlargement of the Faculty, although it had not raised the scale of salaries: the total amount paid in salaries out of the Common Fund in 1888–89 was $43,775; in 1896–97, $83,222. Other expenses also increased as the institution grew larger; and in several years there were deficits ranging from $2646 to $34,537. These deficits, although wholly or partly met by a guarantee fund, naturally caused grave concern to the Corporation, who finally decided that retrenchment was imperative. "That we have to interrupt our progress, and to take, in this way, even a considerable step backward, is a cruel fate, which must evoke protest from every true friend of the University." So wrote President Andrews in his report at the end of the year 1896, when, with broken health, he was about to seek rest in a year's absence abroad. Before his return the Corporation, in their anxiety to improve the finances, had taken action which led to his resignation and stirred up a controversy of deep significance for university education in America.

In his report for 1891–92 President Andrews had said that Brown University needed three million dollars, "A MILLION DOLLARS within a year, and TWO MILLION MORE in ten years," if she were not to "fail of her proper privilege and destiny." When, a few years later, the first million had not been received, various reasons were assigned. Some found the cause in the financial depression under which the country still suffered after the panic of 1893 ; others thought that the natural patrons of the institution had not yet caught the modern habit of making large gifts to education ; but still others said that the President's political views stood between the university and an ample endowment. Dr. Andrews believed in free trade and in international bi-metallism. On the first subject he had expressed himself freely while a professor in the university, but had been reticent since his election to the presidency. On international bi-metallism, which was not a party issue, he had uttered his views orally and in print, both before and after becoming president, and in 1892 had been a delegate to the international monetary conference at Brussels. Early in the summer of 1896 the public learned, by two or three letters of his which were published, that he had taken a new position in regard to bi-metallism, holding that the United States should begin the free coinage of silver at the ratio of sixteen ounces of silver to one ounce of gold, without waiting for the coöperation of other nations. There followed the heated presidential campaign of 1896, in which the free coinage of silver by the United States alone was the leading issue; President Andrews was in Europe, but his views as expressed in these letters were widely quoted.

At the Corporation meeting in June, 1897, Dr. Andrews's views on free silver came up for discussion, and a resolution was passed appointing a committee "to confer with the president in regard to the interests of the University." The committee met with him on July 16, and at his request presented a written statement, of which the following is the essential part:

The resolution was passed after remarks from several members of the corporation, showing more specifically the reason for it. . . . They signified a wish for a change in only one particular, having reference to his [*i.e.*, the President's] views upon a question which constituted a leading issue in the recent Presidential election and which is still predominant in National politics—namely, that of the free coinage of silver as legal tender at a ratio of sixteen ounces of silver to one of gold. They considered that the views of the President, as made public by him from time to time, favored a resumption of such coinage, and expressed the belief that these views were so contrary to the views generally held by the friends of the University that the University had already lost gifts and legacies which would otherwise have come or have been assured to it, and that without a change it would in the future fail to receive the pecuniary support which is requisite to enable it to prosecute with success the grand work on which it has entered. The change hoped for by them, they proceeded to explain, is not a renunciation of these views, as honestly entertained by him, but a forbearance, out of regard for the interests of the University, to promulgate them, especially when to promulgate them will appeal most strongly to the passions and prejudices of the public.

The next day President Andrews resigned, on the ground that he could not meet the wishes of the Corporation, as he understood them, "without surrendering that reasonable liberty of utterance . . . in the absence of which the most ample endowment for an educational institution would have but little worth."

There ensued a discussion throughout the country, attended with much froth and fury, but also evoking much thoughtful argument. It was urged that the head of a public institution should voluntarily limit his freedom of speech, in order not to hurt the institution or use its influence in support of partisan views, and that, if he failed to do so, it was the right and duty of the governing board to check him. On the other side it was said that the action of the Corporation had struck a blow at academic freedom, and that freedom, not money, is the life-blood of a university. It was also brought out that President Andrews had published nothing on free coinage of silver by the United States alone, but that letters written in reply to questions put to him by friends had been published without his consent and in one case without his knowledge. Twenty-four Brown professors addressed an open letter to the Corporation, arguing the academic question involved and requesting them not to accept the President's resignation, on the ground that to do so "would stamp this institution, in the eyes of the country, as one in which freedom of thought and expression is not permitted when it runs counter to the views generally accepted in the community or held by those from whom the University hopes to obtain financial support." A petition signed by some six hundred alumni was sent to the Corporation, asking that they "take that action upon the resignation of President Andrews which will effectually refute the charge that reasonable liberty of utterance was, or ever is to be denied to any teacher of Brown University." Forty-four of the forty-nine alumnae also sent a petition. More than a hundred college presidents, professors, authors, and other public men united in sending to the Corporation their opinion that "the future influence of the American Universities and the interests of free thought and free speech under a just sense of accountability would be promoted by such action on the part of the Corporation as might naturally lead to the withdrawal of the resignation of President Andrews."

At the meeting of the Corporation in September the committee of conference made a written report, embodying the statement given to the President, and speaking of the friendly tone of the conference on both sides. A statement by Dr. Andrews was read, in which he said:

The studied effort visible during the summer to produce estrangement between the Corporation and myself I deeply deplore. On my side it has had no effect. . . . I have sought only peace, feeling that if the

Corporation and myself could no longer coöperate amicably, we could at least separate amicably. . . . In any movement by our country to restore silver to its ancient monetary character, I still desiderate the coöperation of other nations no less than I did previously to 1896, as earnestly as any man who voted for the St. Louis platform. I have simply changed to the belief that United States initiative is the surest if not the only way to secure such coöperation. But this changed belief, I had, in June, never publicly advocated by so much as a single word. . . . But for a few personal communications last summer, made at a time when no one could have anticipated the ferocity which the campaign developed, probably not a soul in this country outside of my family would at this moment know that my view had altered. . . . In respect to this as in respect to the tariff, I have been reticent and careful to the very verge of self-respectability. That, touching any of these delicate questions, I have been loud, a declaimer, parading my views, ambitiously or otherwise, I emphatically deny. Unfortunate I have been: indiscreet, I believe, I have not been.

Here was ground for reconsideration on both sides. The Corporation, after full deliberation, unanimously adopted the following address, five members not voting:

To the President of Brown University, —

The Corporation of Brown University has this day received, with the greatest regret, yóur resignation as President. It most earnestly desires that you will withdraw it. It conceives that it was written without full knowledge of the position of the Corporation. With the earnest hope that a statement by it, bearing the formal sanction and approval of the governing body of the University as a whole, may bring us again into hearty accord, the Corporation desires to assure you that it in no way sought or desired the severance of our official relations, which, so far as it knows, have been most cordial from the time of your acceptance of the Presidency of the University.

The only vote and only expression hitherto made by the Corporation bearing upon the question at issue was at the last June meeting and consisted of the appointment of a committee to "*confer* with you as to the interests of the University." The extent of authority thus given its committee was that of *conference*, which it fully believes you would unhesitatingly admit was a legitimate and friendly exercise of its privileges, relating, in the terms of the vote, to "the interests of the University" which you and the Corporation have closely at heart.

It is perfectly true that the vote in question was occasioned by the differing views entertained on the one hand by you and on the other by most and probably all of the members of the Corporation as to the free and unlimited coinage of silver by the United States as far at least as affecting "the interests of the University," and the fear that your views with reference to it, publicly known or expressed, might perhaps in some degree be assumed to be representative and not merely individual.

It was not in our minds to prescribe the path in which you should tread, or to administer to you any official rebuke, or to restrain your freedom of opinion, or "reasonable liberty of utterance," but simply to intimate that it would be the part of wisdom for you to take a less active part in exciting partisan discussions and apply your energies more exclusively to the affairs of the college.

Having, as it believes, removed the misapprehension that your individual views on this question represent those of the Corporation and the University, for which misapprehension you are not responsible and which it knows you too would seek to dispel, the Corporation, affirming its rightful authority to conserve "the interests of the University" at all times by every honorable means and especially desiring to avoid, in the conduct of the University, the imputation even of the consideration of party questions or of the dominance of any class, and that in the language of its charter "in this liberal and catholic Institution . . . all members hereof shall forever enjoy full, free, absolute and uninterrupted liberty of conscience" (which includes freedom of thought and expression), cannot feel that the divergence of views between you and the members of the Corporation upon the "silver question" and its effect upon the University is an adequate cause of separation between us, for the Corporation is profoundly appreciative of the great services you have rendered the University and of your sacrifice and love for it. It therefore renews its assurances of highest respect for you and expresses the confident hope that you will withdraw your resignation.

Dr. Andrews thereupon withdrew his resignation, writing to the committee of conference, "The action referred to [*i.e.*, that of the Corporation] entirely does away with the scruple which led to my resignation.''

The year that followed was a successful one, in spite of some necessary retrenchments, which reduced expenses by $3170; unfortunately there had been a falling off in attendance, and the income also decreased by $9154, but the deficit of nearly $6000 was covered by the guarantee fund. The endowment of the institution at this time was $1,125,685. The assessed value of the university lands was $599,173; the estimated value of the buildings, $578,793; a total of $1,177,966. The President's comprehensive survey at the end of the year showed that a large amount of good and varied work had been done; and also that a movement recently started by the Boston Alumni Association, for the purpose of raising a fund of $2,000,000, afforded ground for hope that the resources of the university would before long be enlarged.

On July 15, 1898, Dr. Andrews resigned, to accept the superintendency of the Chicago public schools. The Corporation, at their meeting in September, adopted this minute of appreciation:

In accepting the resignation of Elisha Benjamin Andrews DD. LL.D. as President of Brown University the members of the corporation desire to place on record their high appreciation of the valuable service which he has rendered to the university during the nine years in which he has held the office of President. His administration has been both vigorous and conservative; his method that of extending as widely as possible the influence and help of liberal education; his relation to students, faculty and officers such as to bind them to him in sincere respect and personal regard. His success as an educator is shown in the remarkable growth of the University during his term of office and in the enthusiasm which he has inspired in those who have been under him. The record which he leaves of his labors here is one in which he may well take an honest pride and one which marks an epoch in the history of Brown. In parting with Dr. Andrews we assure him of our best wishes for success in the new field to which he is called and of our gratitude for the generous, manly and able service which he has given here. The Secretary will enter this minute upon the records and forward a copy of it to Dr. Andrews.

Dr. Andrews served as superintendent of the Chicago schools for two years, and then became chancellor of the University of Nebraska, which during his term of office increased greatly in numbers and reputation. On account of his health he resigned in 1908, receiving the newly created title of chancellor emeritus. In spite of failing strength he has continued to add to the list of his writings, which now include the following books, besides many magazine articles: *Institutes of Constitutional History, English and American*, 1884; *Institutes of General History*, 1885, 1895; *Institutes of Economics*, 1889, 1900; *An Honest Dollar*, 1894; *Wealth and Moral Law*, 1894; *History of the United States*, 1894, 1902; *History of the Last Quarter Century in the United States*, 1896; *History of the United States in Our Own Times*, 1904; *The Call of the Land*, 1913. In 1904 a portrait of Dr. Andrews, by W. M. Chase, was presented to the university by the class of 1893.

CHAPTER XII

PRESIDENT FAUNCE'S ADMINISTRATION

UPON the resignation of Dr. Andrews, Professor Benjamin F. Clarke, who had acted as president *pro tempore* in 1896–97, was appointed president *ad interim*. On June 3, 1899, the Corporation elected the Rev. William H. P. Faunce president of the university and professor of moral and intellectual philosophy. President Faunce, the son of a Baptist clergyman and author, was born in Worcester, Massachusetts, on January 15, 1859. He graduated from Brown University in 1880 with the third honor, was instructor in mathematics for a year, attended Newton Theological Institution, and then served as pastor of Baptist churches in Springfield and New York. He studied in the University of Jena in 1895, and received the degree of D.D. from Brown in 1897; he has since been given the degree of D.D. by Yale, of S.T.D. by Harvard, and of LL.D by Baylor University, the University of Alabama, Dartmouth College, Wesleyan University, and Denison University. Before election to the presidency he had been a trustee of Brown University and Rochester University, a lecturer in the University of Chicago, and resident preacher at Harvard.

The time has not yet come to write the history of President Faunce's administration, but the leading features of it thus far may be briefly sketched.

While there has been some numerical growth, the students increasing to nearly a thousand and the Faculty from ninety to one hundred and seven, the chief work of the administration has not been expansion but upbuilding. Three endowment funds of $1,000,000 each have been raised, the first in 1900, the second in 1902, and the last in 1912. In 1902 the university fell heir to more than $500,000, the largest single gift in its history, by the death of George L. Littlefield, who became interested in the institution through his warm friendship for President Andrews. In 1911 a legacy of about $85,000 was received from the estate of Dr. Oliver H. Arnold. These gifts, with many others, have raised the endowment to $4,466,243.

The last fifteen years have also been the greatest building era in the history of the university. A handsome brick house for the president was built in 1901, at the corner of Hope and Manning Streets. Memorial gates at the College Street entrance to the campus, and an Administration Building on the site of the University Grammar School, were erected in 1901 and 1902, with a bequest of $45,000 from Augustus Van Wickle. The beautiful gates shamed the old wooden fence and brought about its replacement by an iron one with brick posts; the fence was completed in 1905, at a cost of $21,912, forty-four of the fifty-one sections being paid for by classes or by individuals in memory of classes, and gates at minor entrances were erected by the classes of 1872, 1884, and 1887. A marble swimming-pool, named for the donor, Colgate Hoyt, was opened for use in 1904. Caswell Hall, a dormitory costing $88,000, was erected by the university on the back campus in 1904. Rockefeller Hall, at the north end of the middle campus, built for the use of the Christian Association and the Brown Union, was completed in the same year: the cost of the building and its furnishings, $107,358, was met by John D. Rockefeller; an endowment of $25,000, raised by undergraduates and alumni, was increased to $50,000 in 1909 by a gift from

John D. Rockefeller, Jr. The departments of civil and mechanical engineering, which had labored for many years without adequate facilities, were given a modern building on the back campus in 1903; the cost of the building and equipment was $59,737, which was paid from the university funds supplemented by gifts from Henry K. Porter and others.

In 1904 the trustees of the estate of John Nicholas Brown transferred to Brown University the famous John Carter Brown Library, endowed it with $500,000, and spent $150,000 to erect a building. This structure, of classic design and exquisite proportions, made of Indiana limestone without and largely of marble within, was dedicated on May 17, 1904. On the same day the John Nicholas Brown Gate, the gift of Mrs. Brown, at the southeast corner of the middle campus and near the library, was opened for the first time. The John Carter Brown Library now consists of about thirty thousand volumes. Some of these were purchased before the Revolution by Nicholas Brown, Sr.; but the real founder of the library as a great collection of early books relating to North and South America was his grandson, John Carter Brown, who spared no effort or expense to make it unrivaled in its special field. It contains books and manuscripts of great rarity, some of them unique, and during the last three generations it has been invaluable to many scholars in America and Europe.

The university library had outgrown its building, which was crammed with books from cellar to roof. In 1906 Andrew Carnegie offered $150,000 for a new building in memory of John Hay, and his condition that a like sum be added was soon met by a few graduates and friends of the university. The site chosen was that of the old president's house, at the head of College Street, increased by the purchase of land to the north.[1] The corner-stone was laid on April 30, 1909, and the building was dedicated on November 11, 1910, when addresses were made by President James B. Angell and the Hon. Elihu Root. The John Hay Library covers about seventeen thousand square feet of ground, is made of marble (except the stacks, which are brick), and is of fireproof construction throughout. The style is English Renaissance. In the vestibule stands a bronze bust of Mr. Hay by Saint-Gaudens, and on the wall is this inscription: "IN MEMORY OF JOHN HAY OF THE CLASS OF 1858 POET HISTORIAN DIPLOMATIST STATESMAN WHO MAINTAINED THE OPEN DOOR AND THE GOLDEN RULE THIS BUILDING HAS BEEN ERECTED BY HIS FRIENDS AND FELLOW-ALUMNI." The great reading-room, with tables for nearly two hundred readers, is lined with shelves containing several thousand books of reference; the stacks open directly off it, and the stack on the same floor is given up to a students' library of seventeen thousand selected books, to which undergraduates have free access. The stacks have a capacity of two hundred and fifty thousand volumes, and can be readily enlarged. The main library now consists of about one hundred and eighty thousand volumes. Rooms have also been provided for the special collections in which the library is so rich: the Harris Collection of American Poetry, now grown to more than thirteen thousand volumes; the Rider Collection of manuscripts, books, and pamphlets relating to the history of Rhode Island, formed by Sidney S. Rider and given to the university in 1903 by Marsden J. Perry; the Wheaton Collection of International Law, consisting of more than sixteen hundred volumes, presented at various times by William V. Kellen; the Hammond Lamont Library of twenty-seven hundred volumes of English litera-

---

[1] This land was included in the gift of Nicholas Brown in 1839, but was sold by the university in 1868.

ture, presented in 1910 by the classes of 1899 and 1900; the George Earl Church Collection, the bequest of Colonel Church in 1911, comprising thirty-five hundred volumes on South America; the Corthell Engineering Library of seven thousand books and pamphlets, given in 1912 by Elmer G. Corthell, with an endowment of $5000; the Chambers Dante Collection, containing eleven hundred volumes besides many rare pamphlets, the gift of Henry D. Sharpe in 1912; the sociological and scientific library of the late Professor Lester F. Ward, of one thousand volumes, presented in 1913 by his family; and the linguistic library of the late Dr. Adrian Scott, consisting of one thousand volumes, given by the class of 1872.

A structure unique among the buildings of American colleges, a campanile and clock-tower in one, costing $32,000, was erected in 1904 at the northwest corner of the front campus, by Paul Bajnotti, of Italy, in memory of his wife, Carrie Mathilde Brown Bajnotti. In 1905 the exterior of University Hall was restored to its original appearance by removing the cement which had hidden its brickwork since 1834, putting in windows of colonial style, rebuilding the old chimneys, and remodeling the belfry on the lines of the first one; the cost of the work was borne by Marsden J. Perry. A bronze copy of the marble statue of Caesar Augustus in the Vatican was set up in front of Rhode Island Hall in 1906, and a replica of the equestrian statue of Marcus Aurelius on the Capitoline Hill was erected behind Sayles Hall in 1908; both were gifts from Moses B. I. Goddard. In 1910 the Goddard gates on George Street were presented by Mrs. C. Oliver Iselin in memory of her father, Chancellor William Goddard. A field house was erected on Andrews Field in 1907, at a cost of about $13,000, by Edgar L. Marston. A biological laboratory is now going up at the corner of Thayer and Waterman Streets; the cost, some $76,000, will be met chiefly by the legacy of Dr. Oliver H. Arnold.

During this period of material enrichment it has not been forgotten that buildings and equipment are but tools for the use of Faculty and students. While the number of departments has remained the same, the Faculty has grown larger by nearly twenty per cent; and still more significant is the fact that teachers of professorial rank have increased from thirty-six to fifty-five, while instructors have decreased from thirty-two to nineteen. The amount paid from the common fund in salaries has risen from $87,638 in 1897–98 to $157,628 in 1913–14. In accordance with the recommendation of the President, the Corporation established pensions for members of the Faculty in 1904; they were inadequate, however, and in 1913 $225,000 of the new endowment fund was set apart to provide for a pension system practically the same as that of the Carnegie Foundation. The interpretation of these facts may be read in the words of President Faunce in his report for 1907–08: "It can never be said that Brown University has expended its resources for brick and stone rather than for teaching. . . . We still value men more than materials."

The personnel of the Corporation and the Faculty has undergone the usual changes. Eight fellows and twenty trustees have resigned or died; among them William Goddard, trustee since 1857, chancellor since 1888, whose death occurred in 1907. Arnold B. Chace, who had resigned the treasurership in 1900 and been succeeded by Cornelius S. Sweetland, was elected chancellor. The Rev. Thomas D. Anderson still retains the position of secretary, to which he was appointed in 1890. Of the ninety members of the Faculty at the end of Dr. Andrews's presidency only twenty-nine remain, but the loss has been chiefly among instructors and assistants, twenty-one of the thirty-six teachers of professorial rank being the same.

Professor Alonzo Williams died in 1901. He was born in Foster, Rhode Island, in 1842, a descendant of Roger Williams; he served through the Civil War, graduated from Brown in 1870, taught in the Friends' School, and became professor of modern languages at Brown in 1876. He was a spirited teacher, and the department grew rapidly under his energetic management; he also built up a valuable seminary library, and secured the funds for the Grand Army Fellowship of $10,000. His abounding vitality overflowed into public life: he was an effective political speaker, state commander of the Grand Army of the Republic, and supervisor of the Rhode Island census of 1890.

Alpheus S. Packard died in 1905. He was born in Brunswick, Maine, in 1839, graduated from Bowdoin and the Maine Medical School, studied under Agassiz, and was state entomologist in Massachusetts before coming to Brown as professor of zoölogy and geology in 1878. While performing faithfully the duties of his professorship for more than a quarter-century, he carried on original researches of remarkable range and depth, publishing some three hundred and fifty papers in entomology alone. His monographs and books brought him international reputation, and he was honored with membership in many learned societies — the American Academy of Science, the Société des Sciences de Liége, the Linnean Society of London, and entomological societies in Paris, St. Petersburg, Brussels, and Stockholm. Yet withal his spirit was as that of a little child.

Professor Benjamin F. Clarke became professor emeritus in 1905, and died in 1908. He was born in Newport, Maine, in 1831, graduated from Brown in 1863, and from then until his retirement was a teacher in the departments of mathematics and engineering, besides being twice president *pro tempore* and serving as a member of the Corporation from 1906 till his death; the university gave him the degree of Sc.D. in 1897. A true picture of the man was drawn by the President in his report for 1908–09: "He was obviously at peace within. There was about his outer seeming a sort of patriarchal gentleness, of apostolic dignity, in the presence of which the base, or even the trivial, seemed impossible. . . . By nature reverent, conservative, and self-contained, he was yet hospitable to new ideas and methods. When called to administrative position, he showed a judicial temper not easily surpassed, and an attention to detail that brought genuine success. In a period when educational ideals are swiftly changing, a man like Professor Clarke gives to an institution continuity of policy and tradition."

One of the most faithful servants of the university, Assistant Librarian John M. Burnham, died in 1909. He was born in Manchester, New Hampshire, in 1847, graduated from Brown in 1874, and after some experience in business and teaching became Dr. Guild's assistant in 1881; he remained in this position for almost the whole period during which the old library building was in use, dying shortly before the new one was finished.

Professor Lester F. Ward died in 1913. He was born in Joliet, Illinois, in 1841, served in the Civil War, graduated from Columbian University, and became geologist to the United States geological survey; in later years he gave himself chiefly to the study of sociology, and came to Brown as professor of that subject in 1906. His many books won him international recognition as one of the foremost sociologists of the age.

Professor Thurston M. Phetteplace died in 1913. He was

born in Providence in 1877, graduated from Brown in 1899, and was at once appointed instructor in mechanical engineering, becoming assistant professor in 1906; he took the degree of A.M. at Columbia in 1908. His ability as a teacher and his genial nature made him greatly respected and liked by his colleagues and pupils.

Professor Winslow Upton died in 1914. He was born in Salem, Massachusetts, in 1853, graduated from Brown as valedictorian in 1875, received the degree of A.M. at the University of Cincinnati in 1877, was assistant in the Harvard astronomical observatory for two years, and then served for five years in the United States lake survey, naval observatory, and signal office. In 1884 he became professor of astronomy at Brown, also teaching mathematics and logic for some years; he was dean in 1900–01; the university conferred on him the degree of Sc.D. in 1906. He was the author of numerous astronomical papers, and went on several expeditions for the observation of solar eclipses. He had the gift of remarkable lucidity in exposition, and, although tenacious of his opinions, was singularly reasonable and sweet-tempered in argument. A clearer-headed or better-poised man was never in the service of Brown University.

Professor William W. Bailey, who became professor emeritus in 1906, died in 1914. He was born at West Point, where his father was professor, in 1843; he entered Brown with the class of 1864, but did not receive his degree until 1873; after serving as assistant in chemistry at Brown and the Massachusetts Institute of Technology, he devoted himself to botany, studying at Harvard and Columbia, and was appointed botanist to the United States geological exploration of the fortieth parallel in 1867–68. He became instructor in botany at Brown in 1877, and professor in 1881; the University of New Brunswick gave him the degree of

LL.D. in 1900. He was an enthusiastic instructor, combining the scientist's interest in nature with that of the poet; he published several botanical books and a volume of poems. Through years of almost constant pain his cheerfulness and wit made him a delightful teacher and friend.

After completing more than half a century of continuous service — a record unequaled in the history of the university — Professor John H. Appleton retired in 1914 as professor emeritus. He became assistant in chemistry in 1863, instructor in 1865, and professor in 1868; under his direction the department of chemistry has had steady development, and has kept in close touch with the manufacturing industries of the state. Professor Appleton is vice-president of the American Chemical Society, and is the author of numerous books on chemistry.

In the midst of all changes the Corporation and Faculty have maintained or bettered the ancient ideals of the university. Religious intolerance is still a stranger on College Hill. Throughout a recent agitation over proposed changes in the charter, there was no hint of sectarianism in the administration or the teaching. "During recent years," wrote President Faunce in his report for 1908–09, "we have constantly had at our chapel service Protestants and Roman Catholics, Hebrews, Confucianists and Buddhists, and I have yet to hear of any one of them who complained that the service was an invasion of his religious conviction. They have all realized that our worship is so broad in its method and content that conscientious objection to it would betray a sectarian mind." The Hon. James H. Higgins, of the class of 1898, a Roman Catholic, said at an alumni dinner in 1907: "What pleases the student greatly in his four years at Brown is the fairness and equality which seem to pervade the very atmosphere on College Hill. Nominally a

Baptist institution, it is really a stronghold of liberality, broad-mindedness, and toleration.''

Scholarship among Faculty and students was never higher than now. The former have had healthful diversity of training: fifty-four per cent of the teachers of professorial rank hold first degrees from colleges other than Brown, and sixty-five per cent have studied at two or more institutions; fifty-six per cent are Doctors of Philosophy. The students are held to stricter requirements than ever before. The entrance requirements for the degree of Ph.B. were raised in 1903 to practical equality with those for the degree of A.B.; those for engineering courses were raised in 1902 and in 1906. The entrance requirements for the degree of A.B. were broadened in 1902 by allowing substitutes for one of the two ancient languages, and again in 1913 by widening the range of choice among other subjects. Brown University, in common with other colleges, has benefited by the formation in 1903 of the New England College Certificate Board, which has lessened the evils incident to the certificate system of admission.

In the courses leading to the degrees of A.B. and Ph.B., changes intended to check the abuse of the elective system have been made. Since 1902 candidates for the former degree have been required to take courses in an ancient language, a modern language, mathematics, English, history, physical or natural science, economics, social and political science, and philosophy, the total amount being thirty-four year-hours (an increase of eight) out of the sixty-three necessary for graduation. In 1911 the amount of required work for the degree of Ph.B. was made substantially the same; and concentration in one department or indicated group of departments, to the extent of four year-courses, was required. Thoughtfulness in the selection of subjects and con-

[479]

tinuity in the pursuit of them are encouraged by the regulation, adopted in 1905, that each student must elect his courses
for the entire year. A return to the semester system, in 1911,
works to the same end, and favors broader views and more
thorough preparation for examination. Second examinations
in case of failure were abolished at the end of the present
academic year. New incentives to high and broad scholarship have been created. Since 1904 Commencement appointments have been made on the basis of scholarship, ability to write, and ability to speak; and final departmental
honors have been awarded to students who attain high rank.
Several endowed scholarships, some yielding considerable
sums, and honor scholarships without stipend have been
established. Elections to Phi Beta Kappa receive more pub-
licity and honor; and the Sigma Xi Society, a chapter of
which was founded at Brown in 1900, stimulates undergraduates and graduate students to do original work in
science. Since 1903 students who show more than average
ability and industry have been allowed to take additional
courses, and thus obtain their first degree in three years or
a bachelor's degree and a master's degree together at the
end of four years.

The curriculum has been enriched, not by adding new
departments, but by widening and deepening the instruction in departments already established. The number of
hours of instruction offered per week has increased from
458⅔ in 1897–98 to 620½ in 1913–14, the increase being
greatest in the departments of biology, chemistry, mathematics, physics (including electrical engineering), civil and
mechanical engineering, economics, political and social science, education, and philosophy. Many of the new courses
are of an advanced nature, and consequently there has been
considerable increase in the number of graduate degrees

taken: during the period, beginning in 1888, in which master's and doctor's degrees have been given after examination, 627 of the former and 63 of the latter have been granted; 467 and 43 of these, respectively, have been given since 1899. Twenty-five candidates received the degree of Master of Science, which was first given at Brown in 1905. Laboratory and seminary methods have become general; nearly all the departments now have their laboratories or seminary rooms, with departmental libraries, where advanced work is done by graduate students and upper classmen. Especially worthy of note are the quarters of the department of economics, on the ground floor of the old library building, with a special library of more than fifteen thousand volumes; and the pathological laboratory of the United States bureau of forestry, established in 1912, in connection with the department of botany.

The greater efficiency of the university is due partly to better organization. The office of dean was created in 1900, and was filled very ably for one year by Professor Winslow Upton. His successor, Professor Alexander Meiklejohn, did invaluable service for eleven years, in his relations to both the Faculty and the students. Upon his retirement, in 1912, to take the presidency of Amherst College, he was succeeded by Professor Otis E. Randall. A reduction in the number of Faculty committees, with concentration of power in one committee, has resulted in more consistent policy and greater dispatch in the routine business of the Faculty. Something has been done toward bringing the departments into closer touch with one another, to avoid duplication of courses and secure unity of view in presenting subjects. The graduate work has been effectively reorganized since the appointment of Professor Carl Barus, in 1903, as dean of the graduate department.

Coöperation on a wider scale has been a conspicuous achievement of the present administration. The university has been brought into closer relations with other educational institutions, with the community as a whole, and with the alumni and other educated men throughout the country. Some courses in the Rhode Island School of Design count toward a degree in the university, and students of the school are admitted to any university classes for which they are prepared. Newton Theological Institution accepts toward its degree certain university courses amounting to nearly a year's work. The state of Rhode Island appropriates $5000 annually for graduate courses in education and for scholarships to graduate students of education. The city of Providence appoints several student-teachers yearly from graduates of the university who have taken courses in education, and a similar arrangement has recently been made with the city of Fall River. Men of prominence in the community and elsewhere are members of the visiting committees which annually hold conferences with the various departments. The community in general has shared in the life of the university by attending public lectures and vesper sermons. Recitals upon the great organ in Sayles Hall, the gift of Lucian Sharpe in 1903, have drawn thousands on Sunday afternoons to the college grounds. University extension was revived in a new form, in 1906, by courses of lectures given in the college buildings. The alumni have been brought into closer touch with the university and with one another. The Brown University Teachers' Association, formed in 1903, assembles hundreds of Brown graduates, with other teachers, at the university each year, to discuss problems of interest to school and college alike. *The Brown Alumni Monthly*, started in 1900, keeps thousands of graduates informed of what is doing on the campus. Some fifteen new alumni associations, making twenty-seven in all, have been formed in widely separated sections of the country and the world. As a result of all this the alumni have more influence upon the life and policy of the university than ever before.

In undergraduate life the notable tendencies are toward more careful supervision by Faculty and alumni, an increased number of organizations, and some degree of self-government.

Since 1900 there has been an attempt to make plainer the way of the freshmen by designating members of the Faculty as their advisers. A Faculty supervisor of athletics was appointed in 1906, and a Faculty supervisor of non-athletic organizations in 1913. The Christian Association has had a graduate secretary and advisory committee for several years, and the Brown Union a graduate treasurer and board of management since its formation in 1904.

Student organizations are legion. The Greek-letter societies have increased to twenty, with a membership of about two-thirds of all the undergraduate men. Chapter houses are either owned or rented by ten of the societies, and other societies are assigned groups of rooms or entire sections in the college dormitories. The Christian Association now gives itself chiefly to social service, aiding freshmen to get started, securing work for many students through its employment bureau, and coöperating with religious and charitable organizations in the city. The membership of the Brown Union includes most of the undergraduates besides many alumni and members of the Faculty, and in its rooms students, graduates, and Faculty meet on familiar terms. There are three musical clubs. The Sock and Buskin gives a play yearly, during "Junior Week"; and Pi Kappa, a junior society, presents an original farce at the same time. Intercollegiate debating has given rise to the Debating Union. The

Sphinx exists for the discussion of philosophical and other problems. The Wastebasket Club is a group of students and professors interested in creative writing. The engineering students and teachers have a society for the consideration of engineering questions.

All these organizations give training in self-government. But through two others the students as a whole exercise a degree of self-government on a wider scale. The Cammarian Club, consisting of twelve seniors, men of recognized leadership and force of character, who are chosen by popular vote from nominees by the club, has come to exert a strong influence on college sentiment and action, and the President and Dean have placed more and more responsibility upon it. In 1906 the Faculty voted to grant the students a large measure of self-government in the management of athletic sports, for the reason that the attempt of college authorities to enforce unpopular rules had served only to foster deceit among undergraduates. The vote laid down the following principle: "The Faculty . . . should determine under what rules as to scholarship and attendance participation in athletics should be allowed. . . . To students should be entrusted the choice of regulations concerning organization, rules of play and eligibility, apart from matters of scholarship and attendance; and of them must be demanded that they conduct their games and affairs honestly and fairly." The students, acting through the Athletic Association, promptly abolished the rule that forbade playing for money on "summer nines," but still debarred from college teams men who had played on professional league teams. As to the results of this experiment in student self-government during the last eight years, the chairman of the Faculty committee on athletic organizations has recently said: "There is no longer any evasion or concealment, no reason to feel uncertain as to the real status of the teams. . . . The rules meet with practically universal support on the part of students, faculty, and alumni. . . . We never before had such an atmosphere of clean sport and fair conduct as that which now prevails in our athletics.''

The development of the Women's College has in general been parallel to that of the university as a whole. There has been some gain in number of students, which has increased to over two hundred; but the chief progress has been in material and intellectual resources and in social life. At the beginning of Dr. Faunce's administration the endowment of the Women's College was $60,000; it is now $280,453. In 1899 Pembroke Hall was the only building. In 1900 Mrs. Horatio N. Slater gave the fine old family mansion at 66 Benefit Street as a dormitory, a purpose which it served admirably for several years. In 1906 an urgent need was met by the erection of Sayles Gymnasium in the rear of Pembroke Hall, at a cost of $50,000, the gift of Frank A. Sayles; and an endowment of $25,000 has since been secured. With the growth in number of students, an increasing proportion of whom came from a distance, the need for a larger dormitory became pressing; and in 1910 Miller Hall was built on Cushing Street, near the gymnasium, on land given by a member of the Corporation. The greater part of the cost, about $75,000, was met by the bequest of Dr. and Mrs. Horace G. Miller; the rest was given by a few friends of the college. The building is colonial in style, beautiful in its lines and beautifully furnished; it has forty-eight single rooms for students, besides reception rooms and a dining-room, and forms a social center for all the women students. Land to the east of Pembroke Hall and Sayles Gymnasium has been laid out in an attractive campus. On its northern side a handsome iron gate, with brick posts, was erected in 1913 by the class of 1900 in memory of their classmate, Josephine M. Scholfield.

Dean Snow retired in 1900, and was succeeded by Annie Crosby Emery, Ph.D., Litt.D., a graduate of Bryn Mawr, and for several years dean of women in the University of Wisconsin. By her union of scholarship with social charm she raised the college to a higher level of intellectuality and culture. She resigned in 1905, to become the wife of Professor Francis G. Allinson, of the Brown Faculty, but still has an official connection with the Women's College as a member of its Advisory Council. Her successor is Lida Shaw King, Litt.D., LL.D., a graduate of Vassar and Brown, formerly a student of archaeology in Greece and head of the classical department in Packer Collegiate Institute. Under her leadership the Women's College has continued to develop rapidly. The college was brought into closer administrative relation with the university in 1903 by the creation of an Executive Committee consisting of the president of the university, the dean of the Women's College, and three members of the Corporation. The Advisory Council, a bond between the college and the Rhode Island Society for the Collegiate Education of Women, was increased to seven members in 1906, the two additional members being chosen by the Corporation from alumnae nominated by the Alumnae Association.

The curriculum of the Women's College has been much enlarged. In 1897–98 courses aggregating $84\frac{1}{3}$ hours of instruction per week were given; they represented sixteen of the twenty-five departments of the university, and were conducted by sixteen professors and ten instructors. In 1913–14 thirty-eight professors and eight instructors or assistants gave courses representing twenty-one departments and occupying 148 hours weekly. Undergraduate women

[486]

students are also admitted, on recommendation of the dean, to certain university courses; and all have the use of the John Hay Library and the special libraries, on the same terms as the undergraduate men. There are ten endowed scholarships for women, and four prizes for essays and stories; the prize examinations of the university are also open to women, the winners receiving collateral prizes of equal value with those established for men. The scholarship of the women students remains high, and they earn more than their share of final honors. A surprisingly large number have won advanced degrees: of the 672 graduated between 1894 and 1913, inclusive, 111 have taken the degree of A.M. and 5 the degree of Ph.D. The students of the Women's College were first elected to membership in Phi Beta Kappa in 1900; in 1914 a separate section of the Brown chapter, called the Women's College Section of the Rhode Island Alpha of the Phi Beta Kappa Society, was established. Women are also elected to membership in the Sigma Xi Society.

The Student Government Association, organized in Dean Emery's first year and intrusted with "the regulation of all matters pertaining to the social life of the students and of certain academic matters involving conduct," has proved very successful in outward results and as training in self-government. Greek-letter societies prospered for several years, but in 1911 they were suppressed as not beneficial to the social life of the students as a whole. Athletic, musical, and dramatic organizations thrive, however; a Christian Association does work similar to that of the men's association; and two publications are supported, *The Sepiad*, a magazine, and the *Brún Mæl*, an annual corresponding to the *Liber Brunensis*. The women candidates receive their degrees with the men at Commencement, but have an Ivy Day of their own, corresponding to Class Day.

The alumnae have shown much active loyalty to the college and the university. The Andrews Association, formed in 1900 by some of the alumnae, worked zealously for several years "to promote the interests of the Women's College,"supplying the reading-room with periodicals and raising money for a gymnasium fund. In 1906 was organized the Alumnae Association of Brown University, including all the alumnae, and the next year the Andrews Association merged itself in the new organization. The Alumnae Association has aided the college in many ways. It has cultivated the social life of the undergraduates by teas, receptions, lectures, and plays; it has contributed to the gymnasium fund; for several years it bore the whole expense of one course in the college; and it is now raising money for a graduate fellowship. The annual meeting, on the Saturday before Commencement, has combined business with intellectual and social features. A mid-winter banquet, on alternate years, is attended by many alumnae and undergraduates and by members of the Faculty and Corporation. Local alumnae associations have been formed in Boston and New York.

What position does Brown University hold to-day among the colleges of New England? After seven years of service on the Brown Faculty, a graduate of another and venerable American university wrote thus in 1908: "It would appear that there is, in New England, no other institution just like Brown, and it is doubtful whether her exact counterpart can be found outside of New England. . . . In the size of her graduate school and the spirit and method of her liberal courses of undergraduate study, she appears sharply distinguished from other American colleges. Shall we, then, style her a small university? . . . This title may obscure the fact that she is, in reality and in present aim, predominantly an undergraduate institution. . . . Brown, on the other hand, strives to introduce undergraduates into scientific methods of work. She has developed the seminar method to a remarkable degree. Into the seminars she admits, with graduates, all undergraduates who show any aptitude for training in investigation. . . . The problem that lies before all the stronger institutions is to mingle, in due proportion, the best from the old English-American college with the best from the modern German university. To me, it is evident that no other New England institution, and no other that I know outside of New England, has gone so far in solving this problem as Brown. Through its relatively small size, its democratic traditions, its whole history, in fact, and the Rhode Island air which it breathes, this has been possible. . . . Young men who are fitted to profit by the spirit of intellectual freedom and who desire, with this, the close contacts of an American college should not be left ignorant of Brown, the *university college*."

For a century and a half Brown University has shown a principle of life that could adapt itself to changing human needs. From a small colonial college with a narrow curriculum, designed chiefly to fit youth for the ministry, she has grown with the growth of the country and the times, until her courses of study cover the modern world of thought and prepare her sons and daughters for the varied activities of the present age. The graduates and friends of the university may therefore feel sure, as they close the record of her past, that in the centuries to come, amid conditions that can be but dimly guessed, she will continue her beneficent work for the spirits of men.

APPENDIX

APPENDIX A

THE CHARTER

I

PETITIONS FOR A CHARTER

I N the archives of the university is the following petition, with autograph signatures:

Colony of
Rhode Island $\Big\}$ Ls

> To the Hon'ble the General Assembly of his Majesty's
> Colony of Rhode Island to be held at Newport on the
> first Monday of August AD 1763, by Adjournment.

The Petition of diverse of the Inhabitants of said Colony.

WHEREAS Institutions for liberal Education are highly beneficial to Society by forming the rising Generation to Virtue Knowledge and usefull
Literature and thus preserving in a Community a Succession of Men
qualified for discharging the offices of Life with Usefullness and Reputation They have always merited and receivd the Publick Attention & Encouragement of every wise Polite and well regulated State AND whereas
a Publick School or Seminary erected for this Purpose within this Colony
to which the Youth may freely resort for Education in the vernacular and
learned Languages and Instruction in the liberal Arts and Sciences woud be
for the general Advantage and Honour of this Government And whereas
there is a confess'd Absence of Polite & usefull Learning in this Colony
Your Petitioners affected with a deep Sense thereof and prompted alone
by Motives drawn from the Publick Good and desirous as far as in them
lies to subserve the Political Interests of this his Majesty's Colony and solicitous for cultivating the Moralls and improving the Knowledge of the
rising Generation upon which Foundation the Harmony good Order and
Reputation of Society depend HUMBLY shew that for the good Intents
and Purposes above mentioned they have concerted and plann'd the Charter herewith presented and the same having carefully considered and revised do propose and submit to the Consideration of this hon'ble Assembly
requesting your Honours that out of your great Regard for usefull Literature and the good Moralls of the Youth of this Colony and others that
may resort to the same for the Advantage of Education woud give your
Assent to and grant and confirm the aforesd. Charter with all it's Powers
Priviledges & Immunities as amply and fully as in said Charter is specified and express'd. And your Petitioners as in Duty bound will ever Pray &c

Nicho. Tillinghast	Sam. Ward	J Gardner
Charles Wickham	Job Bennet	Jos: Sanford
Silas Cook	Joshua Clarke	John Tillinghast
Peter Mumford	Gardner Thurston	Nicholas Easton

APPENDIX

Sam. Fowler
Jos Clarke
Thos: Rodman Doctr
Thos. Wickham Jr.
Benjn: Mason
Thomas Rodman
Henry Ward
John Bowrs
Oliver Arnold
Willm: Burroughs
Standft Wyatt
Wm. Taggart

Josias Lyndon
John Wheaton
William Ellery junr
Jona. Willson
Gideon Cornell
Martin Howard
Israel Brayton
Paul Coffin
Charles Bardin
John Treby
Benj Sherburne
Silvester Child
Caleb Gardner
Jonathan Nichols
Shubael Barr
Naphly (?) Hart Junr
Jona Easton
Jonat. Otis

Joshua Saunders
James Tanner
John Tanner
Robt Stevins
Saml Greene
Joseph G Wanton
David Moore
Saml. Lyndon
Elnathan Hammond
Nathan Rice
Jas: Gardner
Clarke Brown
Benjn. Hall
Ezekl Burroughs
Jos. Rodman
Jonathan Rogers
Cromel Child
Robt Potter
Wm Vernon
Wm: Rogers

This petition referred to the charter drafted by Ezra Stiles. At the October session of the Assembly a petition for the charter as amended by the Baptists was presented and rejected. It contained the words, "And whereas a Plan for a Charter for erecting a publick School or Seminary within this Colony now lies before the General Assembly wherein are divers Things contained tending to frustrate the good Design which the Generality of ye. Petitioners in ye former Petition had in view." The petitioners were all Baptists — Elisha Reynolds, Thomas Eyres, Thomas Potter, Jr., Gideon Hoxsey, John Holmes, Daniel Jenckes, James Barker, Jr., Josias Lyndon, John Waterman, Ezekiel Gardner, Nicholas Gardiner, and Nicholas Tillinghast.

A similar petition was prepared for presentation at the session in January, 1764, but on account of pressure of business it was not taken up.

At the February session four petitions, which had circulated in various parts of the state and bore two hundred and twenty-one names, were presented, and resulted in the granting of the charter which Brown University now holds. The petitions were all worded alike, and contained this passage: "And whereas a Plan or Charter for erecting a Publick School or Seminary of Learning within this Colony was presented to the General Assembly at their Session at Newport in August last, which Plan upon a Review and Examination was found to be different from the Original Design and Intent thereof and contrary to what many of the Petitioners had in view." [1]

II
THE STILES CHARTER

In the archives of the university is a copy of Dr. Ezra Stiles's draft of a charter for a college in Rhode Island. The hand is apparently that of Dr. Stiles. Dr. Reuben A. Guild, former librarian of the university, has prefixed the following statement, dated May 4, 1864, about the finding of the manuscript: "The present document was found some thirty years ago, among the old files and papers of the church in Newport, over which Dr. Stiles was Pastor. . . . The Rev. A. H. Dumont, into whose hands, as Pastor of the church, the document naturally fell, kept it for some time, and then gave it to the Rev. Dr. William B. Sprague of Albany, as an addition to his autograph collection. The Librarian, having ascertained this fact, entered into a correspondence with Dr. Sprague which resulted in placing it in the College Library."

Whether this was the copy submitted to the Assembly and then lost, is very doubtful; more probably it is Dr. Stiles's private copy. Except for spelling, capitalization, punctuation, and minor verbal differences, it is for the most part identical with the charter granted in 1764. There are, however, several essential differences, the more important of which are as follows:

The initiatory address shows that the charter was to come up for consideration at the "General Assembly held at Newport . . . on the first monday of August Anno Domini One Thousand seven hundred & sixty three."

Of the forty-six men named as petitioners, all but eleven are different from those in the charter of 1764; nineteen of the trustees and four of the fellows are the same in the two documents.

The Stiles charter provided for thirty-five trustees, instead of thirty-six. Nineteen were to be Baptists, seven Congregationalists or Presbyterians, five Quakers, and four Episcopalians. The charter of 1764 made the number of Baptists twenty-two, Episcopalians five, and Congregationalists four.

---

[1] The October, January, and February petitions are in the Rhode Island Statehouse.

APPENDIX

In the Stiles charter eight of the twelve fellows were to be Congregationalists; in the charter of 1764 eight are Baptists. In the former charter eight fellows were necessary to a quorum; in the latter, five.

According to the Stiles charter the president might be of any Protestant denomination; the charter of 1764 specifies that he shall be a Baptist.

The Stiles charter provided that a trustee or fellow who removed out of the colony thereby vacated his place on the Corporation. The effect of this provision would have been to make the college more exclusively a Rhode Island institution and to bar from its governing board the Baptist leaders in the Philadelphia Association. If the Corporation neglected for more than a year to fill vacancies, each branch might fill its own.

In view of the Baptist majority in one branch and the Congregationalist in the other, the division of power between the two in the Stiles charter is of special significance: "There shall be, in the Exercise of their respective separate & distinct powers, the joynt concurrence of the Trustees & Fellows by their respective Majorities, EXCEPT, in adjudging & conferring the academical Degrees, which shall forever belong exclusively to the *Fellowship* as a *learned Faculty;* and the Election of a *President*, which shall forever belong exclusively to the *Trustees*, they the said Trustees consulting advising with & taking the opinion of the learned Faculty previous to their Choice and Appointment of such a learned and important Officer. And furthermore it is constituted that the Instruction, immediate Government of the College, Nomination of all Officers, except the President, together with the Origination preparing and enacting all Laws, shall forever be & vest in the President & Fellows or Fellowship: and that the Election of the President and Confirmation of all Officers & Laws shall forever be & vest in the Trustees." "And still more clearly to define & ascertain the respective Powers of the two Branches on making & enacting Laws it is further ordained & declared that the Fellowship & shall have power and they are hereby impowered from Time to Time & at all Times hereafter to make enact & publish all such Laws Statutes Regulations & ordinances . . . ; and the same Laws Statutes & ordinances to repeal:—which Laws & the Repeals thereof shall be laid before the Trustees, and with their Approbation shall be of Force & Validity, but not otherwise." The charter of 1764 put the election of the president and professors into the hands of the whole Corporation, and took away from the fellows the right of nominating professors.

The provisions regarding religious liberty are fuller in the Stiles draft. After the passage beginning, "into this Liberal & catholic Institution shall never be admitted any religious Tests," and ending with "the Laws & Statutes thereof," comes this passage: "And that to all the purposes of this Corporation Persons of different Sects shall be sufficiently distinguished & known by their free profession or declaration & by their general Attendance on the public Worship of their respective Denominations. And it is hereby ordained & declared that in this College shall no undue Methods or Arts be practised to allure and proselite one another, or to insinuate the peculiar principles of any one or other of the Denom. into the youth in general; which as well as the Monopoly of Offices might discourage the sending of Students to this College, involve unhappy Controversies among the Instructors & defeat this good Design: and it is thereupon agreed declared constituted & established that every Thing of this Nature shall be accounted a Misdemeanor, mutually avoided as much as possible, and by all the Denominations generously disdained and discountenanced as beneath the Dignity & foreign from the true Intention of this Confederacy: that accordingly the public Teaching shall in general respect the Sciences, and that the Sectarian Differences of Opinion and Controversies on the peculiarities of Principle shall not make any part of the public & classical Instruction."

The words after the last colon are in the charter of 1764 also, with the exception of "accordingly" and "and Controversies on the peculiarities of Principle." The word "accordingly" makes it plain that the much discussed phrase in the charter of 1764, "the Public teaching shall in general Respect the Sciences," was originally put in to bar sectarian teaching and not to secure instruction in physical science. "Sciences" was evidently used in its common sense at that time, meaning sure truths, in whatever field, and the whole may be paraphrased as follows: Instruction in the class-rooms shall be confined to those broad fields of human knowledge that the learned world holds in common, instead of dealing with doubtful sectarian disputes.

After making the concession, as the charter of 1764 does, that "all religious Controversies may be studied freely examined & explained by the President, Professors & Tutors in a personal separate & distinct Manner to the youth of any & each Denomination," the Stiles charter adds the safeguarding phrase, underscored in the manuscript, "*they or their parents requesting the same.*" There immediately follows this passage: "And that in this the President Professors & Tutors shall treat the Religion of each Denom. with peculiar Tenderness Charity & Respect; so that neither Denomination shall be alarmed with Jealousies or Apprehensions of any illiberal & disingenuous Attempts upon one another, but on the contrary an open free undesigning & generous Harmony & a mutual honorable Respect shall be recommended & endeavored, in order to exhibit an Example in which Literature may be advanced on protestant Harmony & the most perfect religious Liberty:—yet nevertheless shall be publickly taught & explained to all the youth the *Existence Character & Dominion of the supreme Being*, the general *Evidences of natural & revealed Religion*, and the *Principles of Moral Philosophy*." In a memorandum written on the last page, in the same hand, is the statement, "And the whole Paragraph for securing the Freedom of Education with Respect to Religion [is] so mutilated [*i.e.*, in the charter of 1764], as effectually to enable & empower the Baptists to practice the Arts of Insinuation & proselyting upon the youth, by private Instruction without the Request of the Parents." The memorandum says further: "Instead of Eight or a Majority of Congreg. in the Branch of the Fellowship, according to the original Agreement, they have inserted Eight Baptists; thus Assuming a Majority of about Two Thirds in both Branches hereby absorbing the whole Power & Govt of the College & thus by the Immutability of the Numbers establishing it a Party College more explicitly & effectually than any College upon the Continent." In the lower corner of the last page is written, still in the same hand, "For the Revd Dr. Cha. Chauncy Boston," which seems to indicate that the memorandum was for his benefit.

The university has three other copies of the Stiles charter, two in the archives and one in the John Carter Brown Library. In general they agree with the Stiles draft, but a comparative study reveals some interesting differences. One of the copies in the archives and the copy in the John Carter Brown Library are full of clerical errors and illiterate mistakes (such as "decorum" for "quorum" and "avoidable" for "available"), and seem to have been very hastily made. The second copy in the archives is written in a small but clear and beautiful hand, and is much more correct in punctuation, spelling, and use of words. The names of the petitioners, trustees, and fellows are the same and in the same order, in all three, except for two or three obvious clerical mistakes in the library copy. The Stiles draft, on the other hand, contains twelve names of petitioners not found in the other three copies, omits two of the names in the latter, and gives several others a different place in the list. In the list of trustees the Stiles draft has one new name, and omits two of the names in the other lists. These facts show that the three copies were not made from the Stiles draft but from some other original. It is probable that copies circulating in different sections of the colony would contain varying lists of persons desired for petitioners and members of the Corporation, in order to interest local leaders in the "valuable Design." The two copies in the archives have a very significant variation from either of the others: in the clause authorizing the Corporation to erect college buildings "in such place within this Colony as they shall think Convenient," are inserted after "place" the words "on Rhode Island," which would confine the college to Newport or its vicinity; it would seem that these copies were meant for circulation in "Rhode Island" and not in "Providence Plantations." The Stiles draft says, "in such place within this Colony as they shall think convenient." The copy in the John Carter Brown Library tries to please both sections by the phrase, "on Rhode Island or within the colony." This copy is also unique in excluding the Baptists altogether from the board of trustees; but this is clearly due to the omission of a line by the copyist, who made a similar omission in the passage about religious freedom, resulting in a confused jumble of two separate provisions.

In the archives is an unfinished draft of a charter intended for presentation at the session of the legislature in October, 1763. The language is in the main that of the Stiles draft; but it affirms that the college is desired by persons "particularly of ye. Baptist Denomination" (although this phrase is marked to be omitted), and provides that eight of the fellows shall be Baptists, two Friends, one Congregationalist, and one Episcopalian, Ezra Stiles being named as the Congregationalist fellow. It is clearly an early (very likely the first) attempt of the Baptist committee to reshape the Stiles charter, and forms an interesting link between that and the charter finally secured.

APPENDIX

III
THE CHARTER OF 1764

THERE are two manuscript copies of the charter finally granted, in 1764. The original is at the statehouse; it is written on fourteen pages, in two hands, and is signed by the clerk of the lower house and the secretary of the upper house but not by the governor, nor is the colony's seal attached. The other copy, engrossed on a parchment of four pages, is in the archives of the university; it differs from the statehouse copy in capitalization, punctuation, etc., and in being signed by the governor and having the seal affixed. The copy in the statehouse is as follows:

> At the General Assembly of the Governor and Company of the English Colony of Rhode Island and Providence-Plantations in New England in America, begun and held at East Greenwich within & for said Colony by adjournment upon the last Monday of Febr:, one Thousand Seven Hundred and Sixty-four, and in the fourth Year of the Reign of His Most Sacred Majesty George the Third, by the Grace of God, King of Great Britain, and so forth

WHEREAS Institutions for liberal Education are highly beneficial to Society, by forming the rising Generation to Virtue Knowledge & useful Literature & thus preserving in the Community a Succession of Men duly qualify'd for discharging the Offices of Life with usefulness & reputation they have therefore justly merited & received the attention & Encouragement of every wise and well regulated State, and whereas a Public School or Seminary erected for that purpose within this Colony, to which the Youth may freely resort for Education in the Vernacular & Learned Languages & in the liberal Arts & Sciences, would be for the general Advantage & Honor of the Government, and whereas

Mr. Gideon Hoxsey	Mr. Ezekiel Gardner	Daniel Jenckes Esqr.
		Nicholas Tillinghast Esqr.
Mr. Thomas Eyres	Mr. John Waterman	
		Nicholas Gardiner Esqr.
Mr. Thomas Potter Junr.	Mr. James Barker Junr	Col. Josias Lyndon
Mr. Peleg Barker	Mr. John Holmes	Col. Elisha Reynolds
Mr. Edwd. Thurston	Solomon Drown Esqr.	
Mr. Wm Redwood	Mr. Saml Windsor	Peleg Thurston Esqr
		Simon Pease Esqr.
Joseph Clarke Esqr.	Mr. Joseph Sheldon	

APPENDIX

Mr. John G Wanton

Mr. Thos. Robinson

Charles Rhodes Esqre.

Mr Nicholas Brown
Col. Barzilla Richmond
Mr John Brown

John Tillinghast Esqr.
George Haszard Esqr.
Col Job Bennet
Nicholas Easton Esqr.
Arthur Fenner Esqr.

with many other Persons appear as undertakers in the valuable design, & thereupon a Petition has been prefer'd to this Assembly praying that full Liberty and Power may be granted unto[1] such of them with others[2] as are hereafter mentioned to found endow, order & govern a College or University within this Colony & that for the more effectual execution of this design they may be incorporated into one Body Politic to be known in the Law with the powers priviledges & franchises necessary for the purpose aforesaid —

Now, therefore know ye that being willing to encourage and patronize such an honorable and useful Institution, we the said Governor & Company in General Assembly convened do for ourselves and our Successors in and by virtue of the Power and Authority within the Jurisdiction of this Colony to us by the Royal Charter granted & committed enact grant constitute ordain & declare & it is hereby enacted granted constituted ordained and declared that the

Revd. James Manning
Revd. Russel Mason
Colo. Elisha Reynolds
Colo. Josias Lyndon
Colo. Job Bennet
Mr. Ephraim Bowen
Joshua Clarke Esqre:
Capt. Jona Slade
John Taylor Esqre:
Mr: Robert Strettell Jones
Azariah Dunham Esqre:
Mr. Edward Thurston Jr.
Mr. Thomas Eyres
Mr. Thomas Haszard
Mr. Peleg Barker

Joshua Babcock Esqre:
Mr: John G Wanton
Revd: Edward Upham
Revd: Jeremiah Condy
Revd: Marmaduke Brown.
Revd: Gardner Thurston.
Revd: Ezra Stiles
Revd: John Greaves
Revd: John Maxson
Revd: Saml: Winsor
Revd: John Gano
Revd: Morgan Edwards.
Revd: Isaac Eaton
Revd: Saml: Stillman
Revd: Saml: Jones

Hon'ble Stephen Hopkins Esqre:
Hon'ble Joseph Wanton Junr Esqr:[3]

Hon'ble Samuel Ward Esqre:
Hon'ble William Ellery Esqr:
"   John Tillinghast Esqr:
"   Simon Pease Esqre:
"   James Honyman Esqre:
"   Nicholas Easton Esqre:
"   Nicholas Tillinghast Esqre:
"   Darius Sessions Esqre:
"   Joseph Harris Esqre:
"   Francis Willet Esqre:
        Wm: Logan Esqr:
"   Daniel Jencks Esqre:
        George Hazard Esqre.
        Nicholas Brown Esqr.
"   Jeremiah Niles Esqre:

or such or so many of them as shall within twelve Months from the date hereof, accept of this trust and qualify themselves as herein after directed, and their Successors shall be for ever hereafter one Body Corporate & Politic in Fact and Name to be known in Law by the Name of Trustees, and Fellows of the College or University in the English Colony

---

[1] The next two words are an interlineation.

[2] The next four words are an interlineation.

[3] "Hon'ble John Gardner Esqre:" followed but was crossed out.

[501]

APPENDIX

of Rhode Island and Providence Plantations in New England in America the Trustees and Fellows at any Time hereafter giving such more particular Name to the College in Honor of the greatest & most distinguished Benefactor or otherwise as they shall think proper which Name so given shall in all Acts, Instruments and Doings of said Body Politic be superadded to their corporate Name aforesaid, and become a part of their legal Appellation, by which it shall be for ever known and distinguished, and that by the same Name, they and their Successors chosen by themselves as hereafter prescribed shall and may have perpetual Succession, and shall & may be Persons able and capable in the Law to Sue, & to be Sued to Plead and to be impleaded to Answer, and to be Answered unto, to defend and to be defended in all and singular Suits Causes Matters Actions and Doings of what kind so ever & also to have take possess purchase acquire or otherwise receive & hold Lands Tenements Hereditaments, Goods Chattles or other Estates of all which they may and shall stand and be seized notwithstanding any Misnomer of the College or the Corporation hereof and by what ever Name or however imperfectly the same shall be described in Gift, Bequests and Assignments provided the true intent of the Assigner or Benefactor be evident. Also the same to grant demise alien lease use manage and improve according to the Tenor of the Donations, and to the Purposes Trusts & Uses to which they shall be seized there of and full Liberty Power & Authority is hereby granted unto the said Trustees & Fellows and their Successors to found a College or University within this Colony for promoting the Liberal Arts and Universal Literature, and with the Monies Estates & Revenues of which they shall from time to time become legally Seized as aforesaid to Endow the same and erect the necessary Buildings & Edifices thereof on such Place within this Colony as they shall think Convenient : And Generally to regulate Order & Govern the same Appoint Officers & make Laws as herein after prescribed & hold use & enjoy all the Liberties Priviliges exemptions, Dignities & Immunities enjoy'd by any College or University whatever, And furthermore that the sd. Trustees & fellows & their Successors shall and may forever hereafter have a public Seal to use for all Causes matters & affairs whatever of them and their Successors and the same Seal to alter Break & make anew from time to time at their Will and Pleasure which Seal shall always be deposited with the President or Senior fellow and furthermore by the Authority afforesaid it is hereby enacted Ordained & declared that it is now and at all Times hereafter shall continue to be the unalterable Constitution of this College or University that the Corporation thereof shall consist of two Branches Vizt : that of the Trustees & that of the fellowship with distinct seperate & respective powers, and that the Number of the Trustees shall and may be thirty six [1] of which twenty two shall forever be Elected of the Denomination called Baptists or Antipedobaptis Five shall for ever be elected of the

---

[1] "Five" was first written and then crossed out.

APPENDIX

Denomination called Friends or Quakers, four shall for ever be elected of the Denomination called Congregationalists, & Five[1] shall for ever be elected of the Denomination called Episcopalians & that the Succession in this Branch shall be for ever chosen & filled up from the respective Denominations in this proportion and according to these Numbers which are hereby fixt & shall remain to perpetuity imutably the same and that the said

Revd. Isaac Eaton [2]	" Francis Willet Esq.	Hon'ble Stephen Hopkins Esqre.
Revd. Saml. Stillman	" Daniel Jencks Esq.	Hon'ble Joseph Wanton Jun Esqr.[3]
Revd. Russel Mason	George Haszard Esqr.	
Colo. Elisha Reynolds	Nicholas Brown Esqr.	Hon'ble Samuel Ward Esqr
Colo. Josias Lyndon	" Jeremiah Niles Esq.	Hon'ble William Ellery Esqre
Colo. Job Bennet	Mr. John G Wanton	" John Tillinghast Esq.
Mr. Ephraim Bowen	" Joshua Clark Esqr.	" Simon Pease Esqre
John Taylor Esqre.	" Revd. Gardner Thurston	" James Honyman Esqre.
Capt. Jona. Slade	" Revd. John Greaves	" Nicholas Easton Esqre.
Mr. Robert Strettell Jones	" Revd. John Maxson	" Nicholas Tillinghast Esq.
Azariah Dunham Esqre.	" Revd. John Gano	" Darius Sessions Esqre.
Mr. Edward Thurston Junr.	" Revd. Saml. Winsor	" Joseph Harris Esq.
Mr. Peleg Barker		

or such or so many of them as shall qualify themselves as aforesaid shall be and they are hereby declared and established the first and present Trustees.— And that the Number of the Fellows inclusive of the President who shall always be a Fellow, shall and may be Twelve of which eight shall be for ever elected of the Denomination called Baptists or Antipædobaptists, and the rest indifferently of any or all Denominations and that the

Joshua Babcock Esq.	Revd. Ezra Stiles	Revd. Edward Upham
Mr. Thomas Eyres	Revd. Saml: Jones	Revd. Jeremiah Condy
Mr. Thomas Haszard	Revd. James Manning	Revd. Marmaduke Brown
	Wm. Logan Esqr.	Revd. Morgan Edwards

or such or so many of them as shall qualify themselves as aforesaid shall be, and they are hereby declared the first and present Fellows and Fellowship to whom the President when hereafter elected[4] who shall forever be of the Denomination called Baptist or Antepedo Baptist shall be Joined to compleat the Number. AND furthermore it is declared and ordained that the Succession in both Branches shall at all times hereafter be filled up and supplied according to these Numbers and this established and invariable Proportion from the respective Denominations by

[1] " Four" was first written and then crossed out.

[2] Opposite this name is written, "N.B take out the Titles."

[3] "Hon'ble John Gardner Esqr." followed but was crossed out.

[4] The twelve words that follow, through "Antepedo Baptist," are an interlineation.

the seperate Election of both Branches of this Corporation which shall at all Times sett and Act by seperate and distinct Powers, and in general in order to the validity and consummation of all Acts there shall be in the Exercise of their respective seperate and distinct Powers, the Joint concurrence of the Trustees and the Fellows by their respective Majorities except in adjudging and conferring the Academical Degrees which shall for ever belong exclusively to the Fellowship as a Learned Faculty And further it is constituted that the Instruction and immediate Government of the College shall for ever be and Rest in the President and Fellows or Fellowship—And furthermore it is ordained that there shall be a General Meeting of the Corporation on the first Wednesday of September Annually within the College Edifice, and untill the same be Built at such Place as they shall appoint to consult Advise and transact the Affairs of the College or University at which or at any other time the Public Commencement may be held and Celebrated and that on any special Emergencies the President with any two of the Fellows[1] or any Three of the Fellows exclusive of the President may convoke and they are hereby impowered to convoke an Assembly of the Corporation on twenty Days Notice and that in all Meetings the Major Vote of those Present of the two Branches respectively shall be deemed their respective Majorities aforesaid, provided that not less than twelve of the Trustees & five of the Fellows be a Quorum of their Respective Branches— That the President or in his Absence the Senior Fellow present shall always be Moderator of the Fellows, that the Corporation at their Annual Meetings once in three Years or oftner in Case of Death or Removal shall and may chose a Chancellor of the University and Treasurer from among the Trustees, and a Secretary from among the Fellows, that the Nomination of the Chancellor shall be in the Trustees whose Office shall be only to Preside as a Moderator of the Trustees and that in his Absence the Trustees shall choose a Moderator for the time being by the Name of Vice Chancellor and at any of their Meetings duly formed as aforesaid shall and may be elected a Trustee or Fellow, or Trustees or Fellows in the Room of those Nominated in this Charter who may refuse to accept or in the Room of those who may Die, Resign or be Removed—And furthermore it is enacted ordained and declared that this Corporation at any of their Meetings regularly convened as aforesaid shall and may Elect and appoint the President and Professors of Languages and the several Parts of Literature, and upon the demise of him or them or either of them their Resignation or Removal from his or their Office for Misdemeanor Incapacity or Unfaithfulness, for which he or they are hereby declared removeable by this Corporation others to Elect and Appoint in their Room and Stead, & at such meeting upon the Nomination of the Fellows to Elect and Appoint Tutors Stewards Butlers and all such other Officers usually appointed in Colleges or Universities as they shall find

---

[1] The ten words that follow, through " President," are an interlineation.

necessary and think fitt to appoint for the promoting Liberal Education and the well ordering the Affairs of this College and them or any of them at their discretion to remove and substitute others in their Places, and in Case any President Trustee or Fellow shall see Cause to change his Religious Denomination the Corporation is hereby impowered to declare his or their Place or Places Vacant, and may proceed to fill up it or them accordingly as before directed otherwise each Trustee and Fellow not an Officer of Instruction shall continue in his Office, during Life or untill Resignation and further in Case either of the Religious denominations shou'd decline taking a Part in this Catholic Comprehensive and liberal Institution the Trustees and Fellows shall and may compleat their Number by electing from their Respective Denominations always preserving their Respective Proportions, herein before prescribed and determined, and all Elections shall be by Ballot, or written Suffrage, and that a Quorum of four Trustees & three Fellows may transact any Business excepting placing the College Edifice, Election of Trustees, President, Fellows and Professors that is to say so that their Acts shall be of Force and Validity until the next Annual Meeting and no longer ————

AND it is further Enacted and Ordained by the Authority aforesaid that each Trustee and Fellow as well those Nominated in this Charter as all that shall hereafter be duly Elected shall previous to their Acting in a corporate Capacity take the Engagment of Allegiance prescribed by the Law of this Colony to his Majesty King George the third, His Heirs and Rightful Successors to the Crown of Great Britain which Engagement shall be Administered to the present Trustees and Fellows by the Governor or Deputy Governor of this Colony and to them from time to time hereafter Elected by their Respective Moderators who are hereby impowered to Administer the same, ————

AND still the more clearly to define and Asscertain the Respective Powers of the two Branches on making and enacting Laws, it is further Ordained and Declared that the Fellowship, shall have Power and are hereby impowered from time to time and all times hereafter to make Enact and Publish all such Laws Statutes Regulations and Ordinances with Penalties as to them shall seem meet for the successful Instruction and Government of said College or University not contrary to the Spirit Extent, true Meaning and Intention of the Acts of the British Parliament or the Laws of this Colony, and the same Laws, Statutes and Ordinances to Repeal, which Laws and the Repeals thereof, shall be laid before the Trustees, and with their Approbation shall be of Force and Validity but not otherwise, and further the Trustees and Fellows at their Meetings aforesaid shall asscertain the Salaries of the Respective Officers and Order the Monies assessed on the Students, for Tuition Fines and Incidental Expences to be collected by the Steward or such other Officer as they shall appoint to Collect the same, and the same with their Revenues and other College Estates in the Hands of the Treasurer to appropriate, in discharging Salaries and other College Debts and the College Accounts shall be Annually Audited and Adjusted in the Meeting of the Corporation and furthermore it is hereby enacted and declared that into this Liberal & Catholic Institution shall never be admitted any Religious Tests but on the Contrary all the Members hereof shall for ever enjoy full free Absolute and uninterrupted Liberty of Conscience and that the Places of Professors, Tutors and all other Officers[1] the President alone excepted shall be free and open for all denominations of Protestants and that Youths of all Religious Denominations shall and may be freely admitted to the Equal Advantages Emoluments & Honors of the College or University and shall Receive a like fair generous & equal Treatment, during their Residence therein, they conducting themselves peaceably and conforming to the Laws and Statutes thereof: And that the Public teaching shall in general Respect the Sciences and that the Sectarian differences of opinions, shall not make any Part of the Public and Classical Instruction, altho' all Religious Controversies may be studied freely examined and explained by the President Professors and Tutors in a personal seperate and distinct manner, to the Youth of any or each Denomination and above all a constant Regard be paid to and effectual Care taken of the Morals of the College and furthermore for the honour & encouragement of Literature we constitute and declare the fellowship aforesaid a learned faculty and do hereby give grant unto and invest them & their Successors with full Power & Authority, and they are hereby Authoriz'd & impowered by their President & in his Absence by the Senior Fellow or one of the Fellows appointed by themselves at the Anniversary Commencements or at any other times and at all Times hereafter to Admit to & Conferr any & all the Learned Degrees which can or ought to be *given and conferred in any of the Colleges & Universities in America*[2] or any such other Degrees of Literary Honor as they shall devise upon any and all such Candidates and Persons as the President and Fellows or Fellowship shall Judge worthy of the Academical Honors, which Power of conferring Degrees is hereby restricted to the Learned Faculty, who shall or may Issue Diplomas or Certificates of such Degrees or conferr Degrees by Diplomas and Authenticate them with the Public Seal of the Corporation, and the Hands of the President and Secretary, and of all the Professors as Witnesses and deliver them to the Graduates as Honorable and Perpetual Testimonies, and furthemore for the greater Encouragement of this Seminary of Learning and that the same may be amply endow'd and enfranchised with the same priveledges Dignities and Immunities, enjoy'd by the American Colleges and European Universities, we do grant enact Ordain and Declare and it is hereby granted Enacted Ordained and Declared that the College Estate, the Estates Persons and Families of the President and Professors for the Time being lying and being within the

[1] The next four words are an interlineation.

[2] "Europe & particularly in the University in Cambridge & Edinbourgh in Great Britain" followed but was crossed out.

APPENDIX

Colony with the Persons of the Tutors[1] and Students during their Residence at the College shall be freed and exempted from all Taxes, serving on Juries and Menial Services, and that the Persons aforesaid shall be exempted from bearing Arms Impresses and Military Services except in Case of an Invasion And furthermore for establishing the perpetuity of this Corporation and in case that at any time hereafter through oversight or otherwise through misapprehensions and mistaken Constructions of the Powers Liberties and Franchises herein contained any Laws should be enacted or any matters done and transacted by this Corporation contrary to the tenor of this Charter it is hereby enacted ordained and declared that all such Laws Acts and Doings shall be in themselves null and void : yet nevertheless the same shall not in any Courts of Law or by the Genrle. Assembly be deemed taken interpreted or adjudged into an avoidance, defeazance or forfeiture of this Charter but that the same shall be and remain unhurt inviolate and entire unto the said Corporation in perpetual Succession, which Corporation may at all times and forever hereafter proceed & continue to Act; and all their Acts conformable to the Powers, tenor, true intent and meaning of the Charter shall be and remain in full force and validity, the nullity and avoidance of any such illegal Acts to the Contrary in any wise notwithstanding—and lastly, We the Governor and Company aforesaid, do for Ourselves and our Successors, forever hereby enact, Grant & confirm unto the said Trustees and Fellows and to their Successors that this Charter of Incorporation and every part thereof shall be good and available in all things in the Law according to our true Intent and meaning, and shall be construed, reputed & adjudged in all cases most favorably on the behalf and for the best benefit and behoof of the said Trustees and Fellows and their Successors so as most effectually to answer the valuable Ends of this usefull Institution——
In full Testimony of which Grant and of all the Articles and Matters therein contained, the said Governor & Company do hereby order that this Act shall be Signed by the Governor and Secretary and Sealed with the publick Seal of this Colony and Registred in the Colonys Records and that the same or an exemplification thereof shall be a sufficient Warrant to the said Corporation to hold, use and exercise all the Powers, Franchises, and Immunities herein contained————

March 2d : 1764

To the House of Magsts——

Gent. Resolvd that the aforewritten Pass as an Act of this Assembly

Voted & passd Nemine Contradicente
Pr Ordr. Josias Lyndon Cler

In the Upper House

Read (on the Third) and concurred Nemine Contradicente

By Ord. Henry Ward Secr'y

[1] "Graduates" followed but was crossed out. The context shows that it referred to graduate students only.

EARLY LAWS OF THE COLLEGE

I

THE LAWS

OF THE COLLEGE IN PROVIDENCE IN THE STATE OF RHODE ISLAND,
ENACTED BY THE FELLOWSHIP AND APPROVED BY THE TRUSTEES
OF SD. COLLEGE

[*From the Corporation Records of* 1783]

CHAPTER. 1ST.

Concerning admission—

1. No PERSON may expect to be admitted into this College, unless, upon examination by the President and Tutors, he shall be found able to read accurately construe and parse *Tully* and the Greek Testament, and Virgil; and shall be able to write true Latin in prose, and hath learned the rules of Prosody and Vulgar Arithmatic; and shall bring suitable Testimony of a blameless life & conversation—

2. No PERSON shall be admitted under-Graduate into this College until his father or Guardian or some other person of property shall have given to the Steward a sufficient bond for the payment of his quarter Bills, approved of by the Authority of the College from time to time, so long as he shall continue to be a member of College, which bond the Steward shall keep until the said Scholar shall have taken his second Degree, unless it should be given up sooner by the order of the President. And the Steward is obliged to produce and transmit to his father or guardian, a general state or account of the several sums or dues to be charged in the quarter bill.—

3. No student shall be admitted into this College until he shall have written out a correct copy of the Laws of the College, or have otherwise obtained them, and had them signed by the President, & one, or more of the Tutors, as the Evidence of his admission, which copy he shall keep by him during his residence in College—

4. EVERY scholar, thus admitted, whether he be present or absent, shall be obliged to pay all College dues, except for victualling, until he shall be regularly dismissed ; or at least, until he shall, by the advice of his parents or guardians, if under age, ask a dismission of the President—

5. AFTER admission, every Student shall reside in the College Edefice, and there pursue his Studies, lodge & board in Commons, except the Inhabitants of the town and its vicinity, who are permitted to victual at home; also such indigent Scholars to whom the Faculty may grant any indulgence; and also such young Gentlemen as the President may think proper to receive into his his own family as boarders—

APPENDIX

CHAPTER. 2D.

Concerning scholastic exercises—

1. THE hours of study betwen the fall & spring vacations shall be from morning prayers one hour before breakfast, and, from 9 OClock A.M. until 12 OClock; —from 2. OClock P.M. until sunset; and from 7. until 9 OClock in the Evening; —And between the Spring and Fall vacations, one hour after morning prayers; from 8 OClock A.M. until 12; from 2 OClock P.M until 6. OClok; and no Student shall be out of his Chamber after 9 OClock in the Evening

2. BOTH before and afternoon, and after 9 OClock in the Evening the Tutors in their turns shall duly visit the rooms of the Students, to observe whether they be within and pursuing their Studies; and shall punish all those who are absent without liberty, or necessity—

3. THE President and Tutors, according to their judments, shall teach and instruct the several Classes in the learned Languages and in the liberal Arts and Sciences, together with the vernacular Tongus—
The following are the clasics appointed for the first year, in Latin, Virgil, Cicero's Orations and Horace, all in usum Delphini. In Greek, the new Testament, Lucians Dialogues & Zenophon's Cyropaedia; —For the second year, in Latin, Cicero de Oratore & Caesars Commentaries; —In Greek Homer's Iliad & Longinus on the Sublime, together with Lowth's vernacular Grammar, Rhetoric, Wards Oratory, Sheridan's Lectures on Elocution, Guthrie's Geography, Kaims Elements of Criticism, Watts's and Duncan's Logic.—For the third year, Hutchinsons moral Philosophy, Dodridges Lectures, Fennings Arithmatic, Hammonds Algebra, Stones Euclid, Martins Trigonometry, Loves Surveying, Wilsons Navigation, Martins Philosophia Britannica, & Ferguson's Astronomy, with Martin on the Globes.—In the last year Locke on the Understanding, Kennedy's Chronology and Bollingbroke on History, and the Languages, Arts & Sciences, studied in the foregoing years, to be accurately reveiwed.

4. DURING the two first years, such Latin Exercises shall be exhibited as shall be directed by their respective Teachers; and, throughout the two last years weekly disputations shall be held on such subjects as shall be previously assigned them, both in the forensic and syllogistick way, as shall be judged most conducive to their improvement—

5. Two of the Students, in rotation, shall every Evening, after prayers, pronounce a piece upon the Stage; and all the members of the College shall meet every Wednesday afternoon in the Hall, at the ringing of the Bell at 2 OClock, to pronounce before the President & Tutors, pieces well committed to memory, that they may receive such corrections in their manner, as shall be judged necessary—

6th. ON the last wednesday in every month, every Student in College shall pronounce publikly on the Stage, memoriter, such an Oration or piece as shall be previously approved by the President, on which occasion the two upper classes shall make use of their own compositions —

APPENDIX

7. No student may read any book in the hours of study, excepting the Classics, or such as tend to illustrate the subject matter of his recitation, for the time being—

8. No. one may enter anothers Chamber without knocking and obtaining liberty; nor shall he even do this in study hours, except to do an errand, in which he shall be speedy—

9. EACH student shall be duly prepared for, and duly attend on recitations, at such times and places as their Instructors shall appoint, during which no one shall suggest any thing to his Class-Mates, or by any means interrupt their Attention—

10. IT is not permitted any one, in the hours of study to speak to another, except in Latin, either in the College, or College Yard—

11. THE Senior Class shall attend recitations, and other public exercises, until the second Wednesday in July, on which they shall appear in the Hall to be examined by the President, Fellows, Tutors, or any other Gentlemen of liberal Education, touching their knowledge and proficiency in the learned Languages, the liberal Arts and Sciences, and other qualifications requisite for the Degree of Bachellor in the Arts; and upon approbation they shall not leave the College before they have compleated their necessary preparations for the public Commencement; nor then without the Liberty of the President—

12. ON the last Wednesday in every quarter there shall be a public examination of the three lower classes on the studies they shall have pursued during that quarter; and if it shall appear that any one has neglected his business, so as not to have made such proficiency in them as his opportunity and abilities would admit of, the President and Tutors may put him upon a conditional standing with his Class, which shall continue to the end of the Year (unless by his better conduct he shall merit an exemption therefrom at a future examination) and then if there appear no hopeful signs of reformation, they may degrade him to a lower class—

CHAPTER 3D.

Concerning a religious, moral & decent conduct—

1. ON ringing of the Bell for morning and evening prayers, all the members of the College shall immediately, without unnecessary noise repair to the hall, and behave with decency, during the time of the exercises—

2. THE senior class, when required, shall read a chapter out of the Greek Testament into english before morning prayers, the President or Tutors calling on whom they think proper of the class to perform this duty—

3. EVERY student shall attend public worship every first day of the week, where he, his parents or Guardians shall think proper; provided that any who do not attend with any officer of instruction, produce vouchers, when demanded, of his steady and orderly attendance—

N.B. Such as regularly and stately observe the seventh day as a

APPENDIX

Sabbath, are exempted from this Law; and are only required to abstain from secular employments, which would interrupt their fellow Students —

4. WHEN any student attends public worship at any religious Society whatever, he shall behave with suitable gravity and decency —

5 No student, boarding in commons, is permitted on the first day of the week to go out of the College Yard, unless to public worship; nor those who board in Town except to public worship and to meals; but the whole of the day is to be observed by abstaining from all secular concerns, recreation and diversion. —

6. AGREEABLY to the Charter of this College, which enacts that Christians of every denomination, shall, without the least molestation, in the peculiarities of their religious principles, enjoy free Liberty, &c.

It is ordered that if any Student of this College shall deny the being of a God, the existence of Virtue & Vice; or that the books of the old and New Testament are of divine authority, or suggest any scruples of that nature, or circulate books of such pernicious tendency; or frequent the company of those who are known to favour such fatal errors; or harrass and disquiet the minds of his fellow Students, respecting any of the peculiarities of their christian faith, by ridicule, sneers, scoffing, Infidel Suggestions, or in any other way; and shall continue obstinate therein after the first & second admonition, he shall be expelled from the College —

Young Gentlemen of the Hebrew Nation are to be exempted from this Law, so far as it relates to the New Testament and its authenticity —

7 IF any scholar shall be guilty of Blasphemy, Robbery, fornication, Forgery, or any such attrocious crime he shall be forthwith expelled —

8. EVERY scholar is strictly forbidden to play at cards, or any unlawful Games; — to swear, lye, steal, get drunk, or use obscene or idle words, strike his fellow Students or others; or keep company with persons of a known bad Character; or attend at places of idle or vain Sports —

9. THE conduct of the students with respect to morality and good manners, in the times of Vacation, shall be cognizable equally as when present at the College —

10. EVERY scholar is required to shew all due honour & reverence, both in words & behaviour, to all his superiors, viz, to Parents, Magistrates, Ministers; and, especially to the Trustees, Fellows, President & Tutors of this College; nor shall in any case use any reproachful, reviling, disrespectful or contumacious language; but shall show them all proper tokens of reverence and obedience —

11. No student, excepting those who statedly attend the Friends Meeting, is permitted to wear his hat within the College walls; nor when speaking to, or spoken to by, or is in company with an officer of instruction, unless he be permitted by them to put it on —

12. ALL due respect shall be paid, by inferiors, to those of a superior standing, by giving them the precedence and choice of seats —

13. EVERY student is required to treat the Inhabitants of the Town and all others with whom they converse with civility and good manners —

APPENDIX

14. No student shall refuse to open the door when he shall hear the stamp of the foot or staff at his door in the entry, which shall be a token that an officer of instruction desires admission, which token every student is forbid to counterfiet, or imitate under any pretence whatever—

15. No one is permitted to make any stay in any room or meddle with any thing in it belonging to the occupant in his absence—

16. No one is permitted to make a practice of receiving company in his room in study hours; or keep spirituous Liquors in his room without liberty obtained of the President—

17. No student may at any time make any unnecessary noise or tumult either in his room or in the Entries; but each one shall endeavour to preserve tranquility and decency in words & actions—

18. No one when in anothers room shall meddle with or examine his books and writings—

19. No one is permitted to be absent from collegiate exercises without first rendering his excuse to his instructor, or go out of the College yard, in the time of study without Liberty—

20. If any student shall do damage to the College edefice, or the Goods of others, he shall repair the same; nor shall any attempt to throw anything over or against the College

21. No student is permitted to make use of any boards, timber, or any other materials, belonging to the College Edefice, for any purpose whatever, without first obtaining Liberty of the Committee for the finishing, or repairs of the Edefice—

22. Every student in College shall take a particular care of fire, not carrying it needlessly out of his room in pipes or otherwise; and shall carefully cover or quench his fire when retireing to bed or leaving his room.

23. The chimney of every inhabited room shall be swept at the expence of the occupants, once every year—

24. The senior Class are authorized to detain in the Hall, after evening prayers, such of the under classes as they shall observe violating any of the Laws of College, and there admonish them for such offences; as well as to correct and instruct them in their general Deportment; correcting their manners in such minute particulars of a geenteel carriage and good breeding as does not come within any express written Law of the College, which corrections, &c. are to be strictly observed

Chapter. 4.

Concerning the Library—

1. The oldest Tutor, in case of no other Appointment, shall be the Librarian, who shall open the Library once a week, at an hour appointed and attend and deliver out such books as shall be called for by such of the students as are permitted the use of them—

APPENDIX

2. ALL students, except the members of the freshman Class shall be permitted the use of the Library —

3. THE following conditions of taking out books shall be strictly regarded; — Each one shall sign a receipt for every book he shall take out, engaging to return it in the like good order with in the time he is permitted the use of it, which shall be four weeks for a Folio; three weeks for a Quarto; two weeks for an Octavo; & one week for a Duodecimo. —

4. IN case any book, so taken out, shall be lost, or unnecessarily damaged, the delinquent shall replace it by a new one, within three months, or pay the Librarian double the price which it cost, the Librarian being the judge, in the Case —

5 No student shall lend a book which he has taken out unto another; nor take out more than one book at a time, except Duodecimos, of which he may take two. —

6. EVERY new, or neatly bound book, shall be covered, so as to defend the binding from injury, during the time of using it —

7. No person shall be allowed to take any book out of the Library with out the knowledge of the Librarian, and the Librarian shall enter, in the receipt the title and size of the book taken out, & the time when taken & returned. —

8. FOR every book not returned, agreeably to his receipt, the delinquent shall pay for one month, for a Folio, one Shilling, and so in proportion for a longer or shorter time; — Two thirds as much for a Quarto; — half as much for an Octavo, and one quarter the sum for a Duodecimo —

CHAPTER 5TH.

Concerning the rooms in College

1. THE senior class shall always have the choice of rooms; — The junior next, & the Sophimore next, except where a student of the lower Classes shall have been at the expence of painting & papering a room; or shall offer to do so, in that case such scholar shall have the preference; and be not only permitted to reside in it during his stay at College; but on leaving the same, shall have the Liberty of disposing of his property therin to any member of the senior or junior classes, who shall thereby become possessed of the same right —

2. IF any scholar shall be absent from College beyond the time allowed him; or shall be guilty of any great misdemeanour, the President at discretion may take away the chamber assgned him, and may dispose of it to another —

3. WHEN a Chamber shall be assigned to a student he shall immediately certify the Steward of all the Damages already done, who shall enter the same in a Book and carry it to the President, in order that he who lived last therin, or did the damages, may be obliged to make restitution. And during the time that any room shall stand assigned to any one, he (whether present or absent) shall be accountable for all the damages done

therin, unless he shall prove that it was done in such a manner, as implies no carelessness of his own—

4. WHEN any Glass shall be broken in the hall, Entry, in any public room, or in any room not inhabited, the expence of mending the same shall be born equally by all the Scholars.—

5. No student when permitted to be absent from College; or when he leaves the same, shall carry away the Keys of his doors; but shall fasten a piece of wood to each key, with his name, and the number of his door theron, and deposit it in the hands of the President or Steward.

CHAPTER. 6TH.

Concerning the Steward and Commons

1. THE Steward shall cause all the rooms, inhabited by the Students, who board in commons, together with the Entries, to be swept once pr day; and cause all the beds, in said rooms, to be decently made every forenoon—

2. THE Steward shall furnish three good meals of victuals pr: day, sufficient for those who board in Commons, agreeably, or nearly so, to the following prescriptions—

For Dinners every week, two meals of salt Beef & Pork, with Peas, Beans, Greens, Roots, &c.—For drink good small Beer or Cyder.—Two meals of fresh meat roasted, baked, broiled or fried with proper Sauce or Vegetables.—One meal of Soup & Fragments.—One meal of boiled fresh meat, with proper vegetables & broth.—One meal of salt or fresh Fish, with brown bread for dinner.—

For Breakfast, Tea, Coffee, Chocolate, or milk; with Tea or Coffee white Bread, with Butter; with Chocolate or Milk, white Bread without Butter. With Tea Coffee, Chocolate, brown Sugar—

For Supper, milk with hasty Pudding, Rice, Samp, with bread, &c. or Milk, Tea, Coffee, Chocolate, as for Breakfast—

3. THE several Articles and provisions abovementioned, especially dinners, are to be diversified & changed, as to their Succession throughout the week, as much as may be convenient & agreeable—

4. ALL the articles of Provision shall be good, genuine and unadulterated—

5. THE meals shall be appointed at stated times; and, the Cookery well, neatly, and decently executed—

6. THE Steward shall sit at meals with the Students, unless prevented by company or Business, and exercise the same authority as is customary or needful for the head of a family at his Table—

7. THE Steward shall be exemplary in his moral Conduct, and not fail to give Information to the Authority of College against any of the Students who shall transgress any of the College orders and regulations; and for this purpose he, as well as every other Officer of College, shall constantly keep by him a copy of the College Laws—

APPENDIX

8. THE Students who board in Commons, shall observe order in going into & coming out of the dining room, as of the Hall; and at Table each Class shall sit together in alphabetical order, and while there, shall behave decently, making no unnecessary noise or disturbance, by either abusing the Table Furniture, or ungenerously complaining of the Provisions, &c. Notwithstanding which, should any be dissatisfied, they may mention it decently to the Steward in private, and, if he does not redress any supposed grievances, they may then apply to the President —

9. THOSE who neglect to attend at the stated Mealtimes, shall forfeit such meals, unless sufficient reasons of absence appear to the Steward, who shall be judge in that case —

10. No allowance shall be made to any Student for absence from Commons for any Term under a week —

11. WHOEVER shall stay beyond the limitted term of Vacation, or the expiration of the term for which he had liberty to be absent, shall pay his commons Bill to the Steward, in the same manner as though present, unless he shall bring a certificate from some reputable Physician, that his state of health would not permit him to prosecute his Studies; or shall assign such just reasons of his detention as shall be deemed sufficient by, at least, three of the Fellowship & four of the Trustees —

12 THE scholars shall all treat the Steward as an officer of College, & his family with all due respect —

13. No scholar shall be permitted to rise to a higher standing, or be admitted to the Honours of the College, who shall have neglected to pay the Bills against him, to the Satisfaction of the Steward.

The Steward shall be permitted to sell to the Students, in the times allowed for Recreation, Cyder, Strong Beer, Small Beer, Candles, Bread, Butter, Sugar, Milk, Tea, Cheese, Coffee, Chocolate & Apples; and any other necessaries which the Students are allowed the use of in the Hours of play, — provided he has the Permission of their Parents or Guardians for so doing; and that they be sold at a reasonable profit, and not in such quantities as may lead them to neglect their Studies. —

14. As as a Compensation to the Steward, it is agreed that he be allowed the use of three rooms on the lower Floor, and one, in an upper Story rent free; and while the whole of the rooms are not occupied by the Students, more if he needs them, he paying the rent, which shall be eight Dollars pr: year for each Room. He shall also have the use of both the Cellar-Kitchens, together with sufficient room in the cellar, free from Rent. He shall be permitted the use of the Garden at the South west part of the College Lot, and the Stable at the South East part of it —

15. EVERY student shall pay for his board in Commons, making his Bed & sweeping his room, pr: week such Sum, or sums as the Corporation shall from time to time direct the Steward to take; also, each scholar shall pay to the Steward four Dollars pr: Quarter Tuition Money —

16. EACH student shall pay 6 / pr: Quarter Room rent, for the use of one half a Chamber —

APPENDIX

17. THE Steward at the close of each quarter, shall make out a regular bill, containing the several quarterly Sums, payable by each Student, with a duplicate thereof; in which shall be charged Fines, the Sums for broken Glass & all other Damages; and shall show both these Bills to the President, which, being by him approved, and one of the Tutors, shall be signed by the President; one of which the President shall deliver to the Steward, and keep the other himself, together with a Bond signed by the Steward, acknowledging the receipt of the other Bill; and engaging himself to be accountable to the President & Faculty, for the whole Sum contained therein; And the Steward shall collect all the money contained in the quarter Bills, and pay out the whole Sum (except for Commons & the Butlers Bill, according to orders given by the President and Faculty —

CHAPTER. 7.

Of monitors & the duties of the Freshman Class —

1. A weekly bill shall be kept in rotation, beginning and proceding alphabetically, by all except the senior Class, in which shall be noted, nonattendance at prayers, unbecoming conduct when there, or any breach of the Laws of the College, of which the monitor shall take strict notice —

2. THERE shall be a quarterly monitor appointed, who shall take the weekly bills, after they are examined; & shall take a particular account of all the transgressions which shall not be excused, & of all the fines which shall be imposed; which bill shall be produced at the quarterly examination before the gentlemen who may attend the same as matter of conviction of those who shall be tardy or deficient; he shall also collect the money for fines & deliver it to the Steward; of which, if not paid, he shall, at the end of his quarter, put the Accompt into the hands of the Steward —

3 ALL the money ariseing from fines, shall be converted into Premiums, to be awarded to those who shall excel at the public examinations, always observing that the Premiums of each Class shall be made up of the fines of that Class —

4. IN order to perpetuate the infamy of the transgressions of the Laws, all the punishments, excepting pecuniory, publickly inflicted on any delinquent, shall be registered in a book for that purpose, together with an account of the crime for which it was inflicted; and, every Student who shall be recorded therin, as a transgressor, shall be excluded from being chosen by the President, or his Class, to any of the orations at Commencement: however, in consequence of extraordinary & continued reformation, the Authority may erase such cencures before the time of choosing Orators —

5. THE Freshman Class shall, in rotation, ring the bell (beginning, and proceeding through the Class, in alphabetical order) at all the

APPENDIX

seasons of ringing it, except for meals, & the recitation of the upper Classes —

6. In the same order the Freshman Class shall kindle a fire seasonably before morning prayers in the room where they may be attended, during the winter season —

CHAPTER: 8TH:

Of Commencements, Degrees and Vacations —

1. All scholars who have been regularly admitted into College, and have diligently attended their Studies, & performed the duties prescribed them in the Laws, and made good proficiency in the several branches of Learning pursued in this College; and after they have given proof of this at the public examination, on the second Wednesday in July, may expect to be honoured with the Degree of Bachelor in the Arts.—

2. All such as shall have applied themselves to their Studies, or any honourable profession in Life for the space of three years from the time of their taking their first Degree, and have been guilty of no gross crime, may expect to receive the honour of a second degree, provided they apply for it one week before Commencement —

3. Every Candidate shall pay the President four Dollars for every degree conferred on him —

4. No Scholar shall have his Degree unless the Steward on the morning of Commencement, or before, shall certify the President that he has paid all his College dues. This Law is to be read publickly in in the hall in the beginning of the Month of July, and on monday before the public Commencement —

5. No student shall presume to exhibit anything at the public Commencement, which has not been previously approved by the President —

6. The times of Vacation shall be from Septr: 6th: to October 20th; — From December 24th: to January 10th; — and from April 21st: to June 1st: —

7. No scholar shall presume to leave College at the time of Vacation, before the Vacation be publicly notified in the Hall; nor at any other time leave the College, without previously obtaining Liberty from the President —

CHAPTER. 9TH.

Concerning the Authority of College —

1. The legislative Authority of this College is, by the Charter, vested in the President & Fellowship, who have Authority to make & give Sanction to all such Statutes, Laws, Rules & Orders (not repugnant to the Laws of this Government) which they shall think proper for the well ordering the College, which shall also be approved by the Trustees of the College —

2. The executive Authority is vested principally in the President, who,

in concurrence with the advice of the Professors & Tutors hath power to rule govern & direct the College, and all matters relating thereto —

3. THE penalties annexed to the foregoing Laws, where not expressed, shall be proportioned to the Nature, circumstances, & Agravations, attending the several offences — After private admonition, pecuniary Penalties shall be from two Pence Lawful money, to three Shillings. The highest, & last, excepting absence from College, shall be six Shillings or a Dollar; — after which they shall be publicly admonished before the College & Corporation, which proving ineffectual, the offenders shall be rusticated, or suspended from all connection with the College; after which degraded if judged necessary; — for the last & concluding punishment, they shall be totally & forever expelled from the College —

4. AND whereas the Statutes are few & general, there must necessarily be lodged with the President & Tutors a discretional, or parental Authority; & therefore, where no Statute is particularly & expressly provided for a case that may occur, they are to exercise this discretionary authority according to the known customs of similar institutions, & the plain, general rules of the moral Law. And, in general the penalties are to be of the more humane kind, such as are at once expressive of compassion to the offender, & indignation at the offence. Such as are adapted to work upon the nobler principles of humanity, & to move the more honourable Springs of good Order and submission to Government —

5. AND in case any person or persons shall judge themselves injured by any heavy punishment inflicted by the President & Tutors, such as expulsion dismission or Rustication for a year, they have Liberty to bring a Petition to the Corporation for relief therin, setting forth the grounds & reasons of their petition, provided the persons apprehending themselves to be injured, their Parents or Guardians shall previously have desired, a rehearing before the President & Tutors —

Finis Legum

II

EXTRACTS FROM THE

SUPPLEMENT TO THE LAWS OF RHODE-ISLAND COLLEGE

[*Enacted in* 1793. *From a Printed Copy of that Year.*]

1. No member of an under class may go into the chapel, dining-hall, or other room, where different classes may meet — or come out of them, before any member of any class above him.

2. No member of an under class may go into the chapel or dining-hall, without stopping at the door, and looking round to observe whether any of the classes above him are coming from any part of the College; and it shall be the duty of all the students, in passing gates or doors, to stop and observe whether any of their superiors are coming towards them,

and to wait for them, unless permitted to go forward by a wave of the hand from the superior; and in walking together, the member of an under class shall give the right hand side to the member of an upper class.

3. ANY student passing by one of a class above him, shall take off his hat in a respectful and decent manner.

4. THE seniors may call up, by billets decently written, any of the under classes, for violation of any of the foregoing laws, as far as they respect the attention to be paid to seniors. The juniors may do the same to any of the classes below them who violate or neglect the laws respecting the attention to be paid to juniors. If any sophomore is neglected or insulted by a freshman, he may call up the freshman, by obtaining liberty of a senior.

5. No billets shall be sent in the hours of study; but when they are sent in hours of recreation, the students to whom they are sent shall immediately repair to the room specified in said billets; and all students billetted shall be treated politely, and shall treat those so who billet them.

6. WHEN any member of an upper class calls up one of an under class, he shall suffer none to be in his room except one of his classmates.

7. IF any number of students of an under class, or the whole class, shall offer an insult to any member or members of an upper class, or the whole of an upper class, the member or class thus insulted may call up all the offenders, whose duty it shall be to make satisfaction, by acknowledging their fault, and promising reformation; and it shall be the duty of all who shall be called up for the violation of these laws, to make satisfaction in the same way. If any student shall refuse to make satisfaction as the law requires, or shall refuse to go to the room of the student who billets him, he shall be immediately cited before the authority, and be punished by admonition, fine or rustication, as they shall judge necessary.

8. IT shall be the duty of the freshmen to carry the above mentioned billets, and all others ordered by the authority of College, to such persons as they are directed; and it shall be the duty of the freshmen to wait on the Corporation when they meet, and also to attend the Librarian on the days on which the library shall be opened.

9. No student is allowed to wear his hat within the walls of the College; and all the students are required to take off their hats respectfully when passing by any of the Fellows, Trustees, Officers, and Steward of the College. Every student who shall neglect to comply with this law, shall be punished for every offence one shilling, or be admonished, if the offence is repeated. . . .

11. ALL the students shall rise respectfully from their seats, when any officer of College shall enter the room where they are convened — except when the students have begun their meals in the dining-hall. The students also are required to rise, when addressed by an officer of College; and no student is permitted to have his hat on, when speaking to any officer of College.

THE COLLEGE SEALS

In 1765, at the second annual meeting, the Corporation voted that a seal for the college should be procured immediately (see page 35). The records show that this first seal, which was of silver and was made in Boston, cost £10 13ˢ sterling; it was a fine piece of workmanship. After the Revolution, a committee was appointed "to break the old Seal of the College" (see page 76). The last reference to this seal is

in the inventory of things handed over to the Corporation by Mrs. Manning after the death of the President, in 1791; what became of the seal itself is unknown. The university now possesses, however, a beautiful reproduction of the first seal, made from an impression of the original in the Rhode Island Historical Society, and given to the

Corporation in 1910 by the Rhode Island Chapter of the Society of Colonial Dames. From this copy was taken the accompanying imprint.

The committee appointed to break the old seal was also authorized to "agree upon a new Seal," but seems to have done nothing. On September 4, 1783, a new committee was appointed "to devise, & get a new Seal engraved for the College as soon as may be." On January 9, 1784, President Manning, chairman of the committee, wrote to William Rogers, of Philadelphia: "Inclosed you have the Device of the College Seal, which you are requested to procure engraved in the best Manner, & at the lowest Price, by the famous Engraver, who executes for the Public their curious Devices. . . . It is to be cut in Silver, & executed with with all convenient Speed, that it may be forwarded by the first good Conveyance in your Power. . . . The Treas-

urer has put a Note of 20 Dollars in my Hands, which I herewith inclose, to pay for the Execution &c. With his Promise to immediately remit the Remainder, should there be a Deficiency. But as you know the Poverty of the College we rely on you to obtain it on the best Terms; & as it is to seal your great Commission [see page 79] we de-

pend on your having it executed in the best manner." Rogers replied, on April 2, 1784: "The Seal, with suitable Directions, I have got Josey Anthony to procure, he has an Intimate Acquaintance with the best Engraver & does the silver Work himself." The second seal is inferior to the first in workmanship and design, as may be seen from the imprint.

When the name of the institution was changed to Brown University, in 1804, no one seems to have thought of the desirability of changing the seal. On September 3, 1833, President Wayland in his report to the Corporation called attention to this strange oversight, and asked for authority to have a new seal made. A committee was accordingly appointed; and at the annual meeting a year later  it recommended the device for the present seal, which was thereupon ordered to be engraved.

APPENDIX D

BIBLIOGRAPHY

A LIST OF THE CHIEF SOURCES USED IN THE PREPARATION OF THIS BOOK,
FORMING A PARTIAL BIBLIOGRAPHY OF THE HISTORY OF
BROWN UNIVERSITY[1]

GENERAL

Miscellaneous Papers, 1763–1804. (An invaluable collection of documents, including a petition for a college charter, copies of the Stiles charter, the original minutes of the Corporation meetings, letters, etc.)

Records of the Corporation of Brown University, 1764–1914.

Corporation Papers, 1827–1914. (Reports of committees, etc.)

Annual Reports of the Treasurers of Brown University: manuscript, 1775–1868; printed, 1869–1913.

Annual Reports of the Presidents to the Corporation of Brown University: manuscript, 1831–68; printed, 1829, 1830, 1869–1913.

Records of the Faculty of Brown University, 1829–1914.

Records of the Executive Board of the Corporation of Brown University, 1850–65.

Records of the Advisory and Executive Committee of the Corporation of Brown University, 1868–1914.

Annual Catalogues of Brown University: broadsides, 1800, 1805 (April 1 and May 1), 1806, 1807, 1808 (April and October), 1809–20, 1822, 1823; pamphlets, 1821–26, 1827–1914.

Commencement Theses: broadsides, 1769–74, 1786, 1788–92, 1794–1800, 1802–05, 1808–11; pamphlets, 1812–17 (in Brown University Exercises and Theses).

Commencement Programs: 1789–96 (in Rippon's Baptist Annual Register, 2 vols., London, 1790–97); original leaflets, 1794–1914.

Valedictory Addresses, 1774–1806. Boston and Providence.

Programs of Junior and Senior Exhibitions, 1798–1879.

Class Day Programs, 1858–1914.

The Brunonian, 1868–1914.

---

[1] The works are in the archives or library of Brown University, unless another place is indicated. The titles are often abridged.

APPENDIX

Liber Brunensis, 1869–1914.

Manning and Brown University; or, Life, Times and Correspondence of James Manning, and the Early History of Brown University. By R. A. Guild. Boston, 1864. (Revised as Brown University and Manning, etc.; Providence, 1897.)

History of Brown University, with Illustrative Documents. By R. A. Guild. Providence, 1867.

Celebration of the One Hundredth Anniversary of the Founding of Brown University. Providence, 1865. (Contains a historical discourse by President Sears, etc.)

Memories of Brown. Edited by R. P. Brown, H. R. Palmer, H. L. Koopman, and C. S. Brigham. Providence, 1909.

Historical Catalogue of Brown University, 1764–1914. Providence, 1914.

Preface to the Catalogue of the Library of Brown University, with the Laws of the Library. By C. C. Jewett. Providence, 1843. (Contains a sketch of the history of the library. In Brown University Historical Documents, vol. 1.)

The Providence Journal, 1829–1914. (In the cabinet of the Rhode Island Historical Society.)

Record of Deeds in the City Hall, Providence. (Transfers of land to Brown University are recorded in Book 19, pp. 106, 108; Book 38, p. 198; Book 45, p. 153; Book 73, p. 346; Book 77, p. 152; Book 78, p. 18; Book 154, p. 320.)

Rhode Island. By I. B. Richman. Boston and New York, 1905.

Annals of the Town of Providence. By W. R. Staples. Providence, 1843.

Brown University Bibliography, 1756–1898. Issued by the Library. Providence, 1898.

CHAPTER I. THE FOUNDING

Records of the Philadelphia Baptist Association, 1756.

Materials for a History of the Baptists in Rhode Island. By Morgan Edwards. 1771. (The MS. is in the cabinet of the Rhode Island Historical Society. It is published in Rhode Island Historical Collections, vol. 6.)

A History of New-England, with particular Reference to the Denomination of Christians called Baptists. Vol. 1. By Isaac Backus. Boston, 1777. Vol. 2 (Providence, 1784) and Vol. 3 (Boston, 1796) are

APPENDIX

entitled A Church History of New-England. Second edition, with Notes, by David Weston. 2 vols. Newton, Mass., 1871.

MSS. and Library of Isaac Backus. (In New England Baptist Library, Boston.)

A Fish Caught in his Own Net. By Isaac Backus. Boston, 1768.

A General History of the Baptist Denomination in America. By David Benedict. 2 vols. Boston, 1813.

A History of the Baptist Churches in the United States. By A. H. Newman. New York, 1894.

Discourse on Christian Union, 1760. By Ezra Stiles. Brookfield, Mass., 1799. (In the cabinet of the Rhode Island Historical Society.)

The Literary Diary of Ezra Stiles, 1769–95. Edited by F. B. Dexter. 3 vols. New York, 1901.

Petitions for a charter for a college in Rhode Island, 1763–64. (In Petitions to the Rhode Island General Assembly, 1762–65. In the Rhode Island Statehouse.)

Draft of a charter for a college in Rhode Island, 1763. By Ezra Stiles.

Charter of Rhode Island College, 1764. (Original document in Rhode Island Statehouse, in Acts and Resolves of the Rhode Island General Assembly, 1762–65; contemporary official copy, in Brown University archives.)

Notes on College Charters. By members of the Corporation of Brown University. Providence, 1910.

A History of Harvard University. By Benjamin Peirce. Cambridge, 1833.

The History of Harvard University. By Josiah Quincy. 2 vols. Cambridge, 1840.

Statuta of Yale College. Novo-Portu, MDCCLIX. (In Yale University Library.)

The Laws of Yale College, 1745. (MS. in Ezra Stiles's hand. In Yale University Library.)

The Annals or History of Yale-College. By Thomas Clap. New-Haven, 1766.

Sketch of the History of Yale University. By F. B. Dexter. New York, 1887.

Charter of the Trustees of the College of New Jersey, 1748. (In Reprint of Educational Charts. Princeton, 1900.)

APPENDIX

Laws and Customs of New Jersey College, 1764. (Typewritten copy of a MS. copy by an undergraduate. In Princeton University Library.)

An Account of the College of New Jersey. Published by order of the Trustees. Woodbridge, N. J., 1764. (In Princeton University Library.)

History of the College of New Jersey, 1746–1854. By John Maclean. 2 vols. Philadelphia, 1877.

Charter of King's College, 1754. (Contemporary printed copy. In the archives of Columbia University.)

The Additional Charter, 1755. (Contemporary printed copy. In the archives of Columbia University.)

Laws and Orders of King's College, 1755. (Contemporary printed copy. In the archives of Columbia University.)

Statutes of Columbia College, 1785. (Contemporary printed copy. In the archives of Columbia University.)

The Charter of the University of Pennsylvania. Philadelphia, 1755.

Early History of the University of Pennsylvania. By G. B. Wood, with Supplementary Chapters by F. D. Stone. Philadelphia, 1896.

A History of the University of Pennsylvania, from its Foundation to 1770. By T. H. Montgomery. Philadelphia, 1900.

CHAPTERS II AND III
PRESIDENT MANNING'S ADMINISTRATION

Correspondence of James Manning, 1759–91.

Letters of James Manning, Morgan Edwards, and others, to Samuel Jones, 1778–87. (In the library of Mr. George Henderson, of Philadelphia.)

Letter of James Manning to Moses Brown, March 25, 1779. (In the cabinet of the Rhode Island Historical Society.)

James Manning's Diary of his Journey from Providence to Philadelphia and back, April 29 to September 26, 1779.

A Charge from the President to the Graduates at the Commencement at Providence, September 2, 1789. By James Manning. Boston, 1806. (Another copy in Brown University Miscellanies.)

A Sermon Occasioned by the Death of the Rev. James Manning. By Peres Fobes. Providence, 1791. (In Brown University Miscellanies.)

APPENDIX

A Funeral Sermon Occasioned by the Death of the Rev. James Manning. By Jonathan Maxcy. Providence, 1791.

A Biographical Sketch of the Rev. James Manning. By John Howland, in the Rhode Island Literary Repository, January, 1815. (In Brown University Historical Documents, vol. 1.)

Life and Recollections of John Howland. By E. M. Stone. Providence, 1857.

Memoir of the Rev. James Manning. By W. G. Goddard. Boston, 1839. (In Brown University Historical Documents, vol. 1.)

Subscription Book of Morgan Edwards, 1767–68.

Guild Papers. (President Manning's salutatory at New Jersey College, the MS. of the valedictory and a copy of the debate at the first Commencement of Rhode Island College, Solomon Drowne's college notebook and extracts from his diary, and other valuable documents, collected by R. A. Guild.)

Laws of Rhode Island College. (MS. copy by Enoch Pond in 1774. In Brown University Charters and Laws.)

Laws of Rhode Island College, 1783. (In the Corporation Records. A copy in Manning's hand is in Brown University Charters and Laws.)

Records of the Warren First Baptist Church, 1764–70. (In the archives of the church.)

Records of the Providence First Baptist Church, 1774–91. (In the archives of the church.)

Records of the Providence First Baptist Charitable Society, 1774–91. (In the archives of the society.)

Correspondence and Accounts of Nicholas Brown and Company. (In the John Carter Brown Library.)

The Providence Gazette, 1762–91. (In the cabinet of the Rhode Island Historical Society.)

The Newport Mercury, 1767–70. (In the Redwood Library, Newport, the cabinet of the Rhode Island Historical Society, and the John Carter Brown Library.)

Brown's Record in the Revolution. By C. S. Brigham. The Brunonian, November, 1898.

Early Rhode Island. By W. B. Weeden. New York, 1910.

Providence in Colonial Times. By Gertrude S. Kimball. Boston, 1912.

APPENDIX

History of Rhode Island, 1636–1790. By S. G. Arnold. 2 vols. New York and London, 1859–60.

Maps of Providence in 1770 and 1798. By Henry R. Chace. Providence, 1914.

CHAPTER IV. PRESIDENT MAXCY'S ADMINISTRATION

A Poem on the Prospects of America. By Jonathan Maxcy. Providence, 1789(?). (In Brown University Miscellanies. Several pages of the poem are missing.)

An Address, delivered by the Rev. Jonathan Maxcy to the Graduates at the Commencement, September 3, 1794. Providence, 1794. (Another copy in Brown University Miscellanies.)

An Address, delivered to the Graduates, September 5, 1798. By Jonathan Maxcy. Providence, 1798.

An Address, delivered to the Candidates for the Baccalaureate in Rhode-Island College, at the Anniversary Commencement, September 2, 1801. By Jonathan Maxcy. Wrentham, 1801.

Baccalaureate Addresses, by Jonathan Maxcy, in 1798, 1800, 1801, 1802. (In Brown University Baccalaureate Addresses.)

Orations and Sermons, by Jonathan Maxcy, in 1795–97, 1799–1803, 1812. (In Brown University Pamphlet Publications, Maxcy and Messer.)

The Literary Remains of the Rev. Jonathan Maxcy, with a Memoir of his Life, by Romeo Elton. New York, 1844.

The Laws of Rhode-Island College. Providence, 1793. (In Brown University Charters and Laws.)

Supplement to the Laws of Rhode-Island College. Providence, 1793. (In Brown University Charters and Laws, and in Brown University Miscellanies.)

Records of the College Library, 1787–1800.

Records of the Philandrian Society, 1799–1810.

Records of the Philermenian Society, 1804–66.

The Cause of Man; an Oration: together with the Valedictory Addresses, Pronounced at the Commencement of Rhode Island College, September 7, 1796. By Tristam Burges. Providence, 1796. (Another copy in Brown University Miscellanies.)

APPENDIX

Memoir of Tristam Burges; with Selections from his Speeches and Occasional Writings. By Henry L. Bowen. Providence, 1835.

Addresses before the Federal Adelphi. Providence, 1798, 1799, 1800, 1805, 1831. (In Brown University Orations, Federal Adelphi.)

Correspondence of the Green Family, 1795–1800. (Printed in Memories of Brown, from copies in the library of Mr. T. F. Green.)

CHAPTER V. PRESIDENT MESSER'S ADMINISTRATION

Letter-Books of Asa Messer, 1811–36. 6 vols.

Addresses to the Graduating Class, by Asa Messer, in 1799, 1803, 1810, 1811. (In The Literary Remains of the Rev. Jonathan Maxcy. All but the last are also in Brown University Baccalaureate Addresses.)

Orations and Sermons, by Asa Messer, in 1803, 1812. (In Brown University Pamphlet Publications, Maxcy and Messer.)

A True and Candid Statement of Facts, relative to the Late Affairs and Proceedings of the Government of Brown University. New Haven, January, 1826. (In Brown University Historical Documents, vol. 1.)

An Exposition of certain Newspaper Publications relative to the Management of the Affairs of Brown University. Providence (?), August, 1826. (In Brown University Historical Documents, vol. 1.)

Brown University under the Presidency of Asa Messer. By an Alumnus. Boston, 1867.

Asa Messer. The Brunonian, July, 1871.

Life and Labors of Rev. Stephen Gano. By H. M. King. Providence, 1903.

The Laws of Rhode-Island College. Providence, 1803. (In Brown University Laws and Rules, 1803–1901, and in Brown University Charters and Laws.)

Supplement to the Laws of Rhode-Island College. Providence, 1803. (In Brown University Charters and Laws.)

The Laws of Brown University. Providence, 1823. (In Brown University Laws and Rules, 1803–1901, and in Brown University Charters and Laws.)

A Letter to the Corporation of Brown University, suggesting certain Improvements in its Academical System. By Alumnus Brunensis. Providence (?), 1815.

APPENDIX

Catalogue of Books in the Library of Brown University. Providence, 1826.

Records of the United Brothers Society, 1810–53.

Records of the Philendean Society, 1815–48.

The Medical School formerly existing in Brown University. By C. W. Parsons, M.D. Providence, 1881. (In Rhode Island Historical Tracts, No. 12.)

Letters and Journals of Samuel Gridley Howe. Edited by his Daughter, Laura E. Richards. 2 vols. Boston, 1906–09.

CHAPTERS VI AND VII
PRESIDENT WAYLAND'S ADMINISTRATION

Letter-Book of Francis Wayland, 1831–52. (Copies by the registrar, L. H. Elliott.)

Correspondence of Francis Wayland on university affairs. (In the Corporation Papers.)

Reports of Francis Wayland to the Executive Board. (In the Corporation Papers.)

Discourse on Education: delivered in Boston, before the American Institute of Instruction, 1830. By Francis Wayland. (In Occasional Discourses. Boston, 1833.)

The Elements of Moral Science. By Francis Wayland. Boston, 1835.

The Elements of Political Economy. By Francis Wayland. Boston, 1837.

The Limitations of Human Responsibility. By Francis Wayland. Boston, 1838.

Thoughts on the Present Collegiate System in the United States. By Francis Wayland. Boston, 1842.

Domestic Slavery, Considered in a Correspondence between the Rev. Richard Fuller and the Rev. Francis Wayland. New York and Boston, 1845.

University Sermons. By Francis Wayland. Boston, 1848.

Report to the Corporation of Brown University on Changes in the System of Collegiate Education, Read March 28, 1850. By Francis Wayland. Providence, 1850. (In Brown University Pamphlets.)

APPENDIX

The Education Demanded by the People of the United States. By Francis Wayland. Boston, 1855. (In the Metcalf Collection, vol. 6.)

Addresses and Sermons by Francis Wayland, 1823–57. (In Brown University Pamphlet Publications, Wayland, vols. 1 and 2.)

Proceedings of the Corporation and of the Alumni of Brown University in reference to the Resignation of President Wayland and the Induction of President Sears. Providence, 1856. (Another copy in Brown University Miscellaneous Pamphlets.)

Death of Rev. Dr. Francis Wayland. By J. B. Angell. The Providence Journal, October 2, 1865.

A Discourse Commemorative of Francis Wayland. By George I. Chace. Providence, 1866. (In Metcalf Collection, vol. 157. Reprinted in George Ide Chace, LL.D.: a Memorial.)

The Late President Wayland. By G. P. Fisher. The New Englander, January, 1866.

A Memoir of the Life and Labors of Francis Wayland. By his Sons, Francis Wayland and H. L. Wayland. 2 vols. New York, 1867.

The Late President Wayland. By J. L. Diman. The Atlantic Monthly, January, 1868.

How I Was Educated. By E. G. Robinson. The Forum, December, 1886.

Francis Wayland. By J. O. Murray. Boston and New York, 1891.

The Laws of Brown University. Providence, 1827. (In Brown University Laws and Rules, 1803–1901, and in Brown University Charters and Laws.)

The Laws of Brown University. Providence, 1850. (In Brown University Laws and Rules, 1803–1901, and in Brown University Charters and Laws.)

Thomas Jefferson and the University of Virginia. By H. B. Adams. Washington, 1888. (Published by the United States Bureau of Education.)

Annual Reports of the President and Treasurer of Harvard College, 1883–84. Cambridge, 1885. (Contains a history of the elective system at Harvard, by President Eliot.)

Circular letter of W. A. Norton and J. A. Porter, in regard to the causes of their resignation from the Faculty of Brown University. Providence, 1852.

A Discourse in Commemoration of the Life and Character of the Hon.

APPENDIX

Nicholas Brown. By Francis Wayland. Boston, 1841. (In Brown University Historical Documents, vol. 1, and in Brown University Pamphlet Publications, Wayland, vol. 2.)

The Late Nicholas Brown. By W. G. Goddard. Providence, 1841. (In Brown University Historical Documents, vol. 1, and in Goddard's Political and Miscellaneous Writings, vol. 1.)

Sketch of the Educational and Other Benefactions of the Late Nicholas Brown. By William Gammell. (Reprinted from Barnard's American Journal of Education, June, 1857.)

The Political and Miscellaneous Writings of W. G. Goddard. Edited by F. W. Goddard. 2 vols. Providence, 1870.

A Discourse in Commemoration of the Life and Services of W. G. Goddard. By Francis Wayland. Providence, 1846. (In Brown University Pamphlet Publications, Wayland, vol. 2.)

The Diary of Williams Latham, 1823–27. (Mr. Latham was a student in Brown University in 1823–27.)

Praeterita. Journal of Acts and Thoughts, 1854–55. By W. G. Dearth. (Mr. Dearth was a student in Brown University in 1851–55.)

The Brunonian. Providence, 1829–31.

Prize Essays by Brown University Students, 1843–52.

Records of the Class of 1841.

Reading Room Record, 1843.

Triennial Catalogue of the Members of the Philermenian Society. Providence, 1849. (Contains a sketch of the history of the society.)

Catalogue of the Library and Members of the United Brothers Society. Providence, 1853.

Reminiscences of a Journalist. By C. T. Congdon. Boston, 1880.

CHAPTER VIII. PRESIDENT SEARS'S ADMINISTRATION

Reports of Barnas Sears to the Executive Board. (In the Corporation Papers.)

Barnas Sears. By Alvah Hovey. New York, Boston, Chicago, 1902.

Lectures on Rhetoric. By R. P. Dunn. (In a note-book in the library of the late W. W. Bailey.)

In Memoriam: Robinson Potter Dunn. Cambridge, 1869. (Contains a

APPENDIX

biographical sketch by S. L. Caldwell, a commemorative discourse by J. L. Diman, and selections from Professor Dunn's writings.)

William Gammell. A Biographical Sketch, with Selections from his writings. Edited by J. O. Murray. Cambridge, 1890.

The Brown Paper, 1857–68.

A Sketch of the History and the Present Organization of Brown University. Published by the Executive Board. Providence, 1861. (In Brown University Pamphlets.)

Brown University in the Civil War. By H. S. Burrage and others. Providence, 1868.

CHAPTER IX. PRESIDENT CASWELL'S ADMINISTRATION

Address before the American Association for the Advancement of Science. By Alexis Caswell. Cambridge, 1859.

Lectures on Astronomy. Washington, 1858. (In appendix to the report of the director of the Smithsonian Institution, 1858.)

A Discourse Commemorative of the Life and Services of Rev. Alexis Caswell. By J. L. Lincoln. Providence, 1877.

Memorial of Alexis Caswell. (Contains a memoir by William Gammell, reprinted from the New England Historical and Genealogical Register, July, 1877; a memorial by Joseph Lovering, reprinted from the Proceedings of the American Academy of Arts and Sciences; the discourse by J. L. Lincoln; a notice of the funeral services; and tributes from various sources.)

A Discourse delivered before the Porter Rhetorical Society of Andover Theological Seminary. By G. I. Chace. Boston, 1854.

George Ide Chace: a Memorial. Edited by J. O. Murray. Cambridge, 1886. (Contains a biographical sketch by the editor, and selections from Professor Chace's writings.)

CHAPTER X. PRESIDENT ROBINSON'S ADMINISTRATION

Lectures on Preaching. By E. G. Robinson. New York, 1883.

Principles and Practice of Morality. By E. G. Robinson. Boston, 1888.

Christian Theology. By E. G. Robinson. Rochester, 1894.

Baccalaureate Sermons. By E. G. Robinson. New York, Boston, Chicago, 1896.

APPENDIX

E. G. Robinson: an Autobiography. With a Supplement by H. L. Wayland, and Critical Estimates. New York, Boston, Chicago, 1896.

Memorial Address on Ezekiel Gilman Robinson. By T. D. Anderson.
Providence, 1894.

Ezekiel Gilman Robinson: a Memorial Address. By W. H. P. Faunce.
Boston, 1895.

The Theistic Argument as Affected by Recent Theories. By J. L. Diman. Boston, 1882.

Orations and Essays. By J. L. Diman. Boston, 1882.

Professor J. Lewis Diman: a Memorial Tribute. By E. J. Young. Cambridge, 1881. (Reprinted from the Proceedings of the Massachusetts
Historical Society.)

Memoirs of the Rev. J. Lewis Diman. By Caroline Hazard. Boston and
New York, 1888.

A Commemorative Discourse on the Life, Character and Services of Professor Samuel Stillman Greene. By Professor B. F. Clarke. Providence, 1883.

Final Report of the Library Building Committee, with the Exercises
at the Dedication of the Fire Proof Library Building. Providence,
1878.

Sayles Memorial Hall: Opening Exercises. Providence, 1882.

CHAPTER XI. PRESIDENT ANDREWS'S ADMINISTRATION

An Address in Memory of Timothy Whiting Bancroft. By Lorenzo Sears.
Providence, 1891.

In Memoriam: John Larkin Lincoln. By W. E. Lincoln. Boston and
New York, 1894. (Contains a memorial address by G. P. Fisher, a
biographical sketch by W. C. Poland, and selections from Professor
Lincoln's diaries, lectures, and magazine articles.)

In Memoriam: Eli Whitney Blake. Providence, 1895.

An Open Letter Addressed to the Corporation of Brown University by
Members of the Faculty of That Institution. Providence, 1897.

APPENDIX

CHAPTER XII. PRESIDENT FAUNCE'S ADMINISTRATION

Brown a University College. By H. T. Fowler. The Brown Alumni Monthly, June, 1908.

Albert Harkness. Liber Brunensis, 1889. (An authoritative biographical sketch.)

Memorial Exercises in Honor of Professor Albert Harkness, with Addresses by W. H. P. Faunce, T. D. Seymour, and W. G. Everett. Providence, 1907.

Exercises Commemorating the Restoration of University Hall, with Addresses by W. H. P. Faunce, G. H. Utter, and William Macdonald. Providence, 1905.

Alumnae Record. By E. S. Bronson. Providence, 1910.

The Women's College in Brown University: its Origin and Development. By Anne T. Weeden. Providence, 1912.

Brún-Mæl, 1909–14.

The Brown Alumni Monthly, 1900–14.

INDEX

INDEX

A<small>DAMS</small>, Jasper, 166, 201.

Administration and policy, 98-101, 199-200, 206, 211-17, 230, 258-86, 294-97, 313-14, 321-25, 361-62, 368, 387-88, 428-32, 441, 467, 478, 484.

Administration Building, 470.

Advisory and Executive Committee, 368.

Advisory Council of the Women's College, 486.

Agricultural and Scientific Department, 333-34, 366, 370.

Agriculture, 286, 287, 288, 289, 333-34, 366, 370.

Allen, Paul, 148, 154.

Allinson, Francis G., 443; Mrs. F. G., 486.

"Alma Mater," 349, 378.

Alumnae associations, 486, 488.

Alumni associations, 237-39, 371, 372, 467, 483; *see also* Federal Adelphi.

American Museum of Natural History, 446.

American School in Athens, 438, 441, 443.

American School in Rome, 443.

Ames, Samuel, 203.

Amherst College, 259, 368, 376, 377, 481.

Anatomy ; *see* Biology.

Anderson, Thomas D., 474.

Andover Theological Seminary, 426.

Andrews Association, 488.

Andrews, E. Benjamin, 379, 411, 427-28, 430-32, 461-68, 470; resignation of, in 1897, 461-67.

Andrews Field, 459.

Angell, James B., 240, 288, 327, 356, 472.

Anthony, Henry B., 392.

Apparatus, 81, 106-8, 145-46, 163, 220-21, 222-23, 335, 370, 459.

Appleton, John H., 331, 440, 478.

Arnold, Oliver H., 470, 474.

Arnold, Thomas, 101.

Athletic Association, 458, 484.

Athletics, 245-47, 344-48, 376-78, 416-17, 458-59, 483, 484-85, 487.

B<small>ABCOCK</small>, Joshua, 34, 501, 503.

Babcock, Rufus, 201.

Bachelor of Arts, 41, 273, 279-84, 290, 291, 321-22, 324, 325, 404-6, 430, 479.

Bachelor of Philosophy, 273, 279, 281, 283-84, 290, 291, 299, 323-25, 403, 405-6, 430, 479.

Bachelor of Science, 448, 479.

Backus, Isaac, 6, 8, 26, 94, 95, 170.

Bailey, William W., 398, 440, 477-78.

Bajnotti, Paul, 473.

Ballou, Sullivan, 353.

Bancroft Fund, 433.

Bancroft, Timothy W., 370, 400-1, 432-33.

Baptist academy at Hopewell, N.J., 7, 36.

INDEX

Baptist college, plan for, 7-9, 15.

Baptists, 1-10, 13, 15-27, 33, 49, 50, 92, 94-95, 100, 101, 157, 494.

Bartlett, Elisha, 164-65.

Bartlett, John R., 375.

Barus, Carl, 446, 481.

Baseball, 245, 344-46, 376, 416.

Baxter, John, 447.

Beecher, Henry Ward, 300.

Bell, 173.

Benedict, David, 202.

Bennet, Job, 15, 18, 20, 25, 27, 34, 101, 493, 501, 503.

Bennett, Charles E., 443.

Berkeley, Dean, 12-13.

Bibliography, 522-34.

Bi-metallism, 462-66.

Biological Laboratory, 474.

Biology, 145, 159, 163, 223, 286, 369, 370-71, 474.

Blake, Eli W., 370, 434-35.

Boating, 246, 346-48, 376-78, 416.

Borden, Jefferson, 332.

Botany, 159, 165, 166, 369, 391, 398, 460.

Bowen, Horatio G., 170, 212, 229.

Bowen, Jabez, 41, 101, 158.

Bowen, John, 220.

Bowen, William C., 159, 161.

Bridgham, Samuel W., 228.

Bronson, Walter C., 444.

Brown Alumni Monthly, 482.

Brown and Ives, 171.

Brown Daily Herald, 458.

Brown, John, 52-56, 63, 72, 81, 84, 101, 107, 156, 501.

Brown, John Carter, 171, 182, 203, 278, 332, 334, 375, 390-91, 471.

Brown, John Nicholas, 471.

Brown, Joseph, 53, 73-74, 81, 107, 108.

Brown Magazine, 458.

Brown, Moses, 45, 46, 47-49, 53, 55, 69, 109, 375.

Brown, Moses, Jr., 88.

Brown, Nicholas, 34, 53, 73-74, 89, 471, 501, 503.

Brown, Nicholas, and Company, 56.

Brown, Nicholas, Jr., 85, 128, 144, 156-57, 158, 170, 171-73, 218, 220, 222, 223-24, 225-28, 332, 334, 375, 472.

Brown Paper, 348-49.

Brown Union, 470, 483.

Brown University, 155-57.

Brown University Medical Association, 163-64.

Brown University Teachers' Association, 482.

Brún Mǽl, 487.

Brunonian, 242-43, 348, 379, 415, 458.

Bumpus, Hermon C., 446.

Burges, Tristam, 133, 137, 139, 148, 149, 154, 166, 168, 213-15, 233, 375.

Burgess, George, 202, 339.

Burnham, John M., 475.

Burning of compositions, 244-45.

Burrage, Henry S., 329, 356, 357.

Butler Hospital, 227, 304, 328, 382.

INDEX

INDEX

INDEX

Museum of Natural History, 145, 371, 434.

Musical clubs, 244, 348, 378, 483, 487.

Naming the college, 78, 144, 155-57.

Natural History; *see* Biology.

Nebraska, University of, 428, 443, 468.

New Jersey, College of; *see* Princeton University.

Newport, 5, 9, 10, 11-14, 15, 18, 21, 24, 25, 34, 35, 36, 37, 44-50.

New System, 260-94, 301, 321-25.

Newton Theological Institution, 318, 427, 482.

Norton, Charles Eliot, 339.

Norton, William A., 286, 296-97.

Olney, Richard, 338, 341, 363.

Olney, Stephen T., 391, 398.

Oratory and Belles-Lettres, 104-5, 122-27, 132, 136-39, 156, 166, 168-69, 237-38.

Organ recitals, 482.

Packard, Alpheus S., 398, 440, 475.

Packer Collegiate Institute, 486.

Padelford, Seth, 335.

Palmer, Albert DeF., 446.

Pardee, William C., 447.

Park, Calvin, 159, 165, 189.

Park, Edwards A., 182, 202, 299, 339.

Parsons, Charles W., 369, 398.

Parsons, Usher, 162, 212.

Partial Course, 268-69, 323, 324, 325.

Patten, William S., 368, 413.

Peck, Solomon, 202, 229.

Peirce, John, 335, 459.

Pembroke Hall, 457-58.

Pennsylvania, University of, 3, 4, 30, 32, 92, 448.

Pension system, 474.

Perry, Marsden J., 472, 473.

Petitions for charter, 15-18, 24, 26, 493-95.

Phetteplace, Thurston M., 477.

Phi Beta Kappa, 213, 236, 239, 241, 299, 372, 480, 487.

Philadelphia Baptist Association, 6, 7, 8, 13, 16, 18, 24, 94, 340.

Philandrian Society, 147-48, 449.

Philermenian Society, 147, 173, 180-81, 233, 236, 239-40, 349.

Phillips, Wendell, 339.

Physical training, 417, 459; *see also* Gymnasium.

Physics, 223, 370, 389, 459; *see also* Apparatus *and* Curriculum.

Physiology; *see* Biology.

Poland, William C., 370, 440, 441.

Porter, Henry K., 471.

Porter, John A., 286, 296-97.

Portraits, 375-76, 394.

Prentice, George D., 202.

Presbyterians, 3, 32; *see also* Congregationalists.

Presidency of the college, 17, 22-24, 188, 366.

President's house, 55, 57, 223-24, 470.

INDEX

Princeton University (College of New Jersey), 3, 4, 8, 28, 29, 30, 32, 36, 38, 55, 59, 101, 104, 112, 113, 120, 409.

Prizes and premiums, 218-20, 237-38, 292, 359, 369, 402-3, 487.

Providence, 5, 10, 25, 37, 44-54, 63, 69, 95, 255, 289, 304, 412, 433, 482.

Providence Athenaeum, 227, 255, 328.

Quakers, 10, 22, 24, 32, 50, 451.

Randall, Otis, E., 399, 440, 441, 481.

Reading-Room Association, 243, 379.

Recitations, 112, 207-11, 284-85, 293.

Redwood Library, 12, 13, 14, 19.

Reed, David, 202.

Reformed Dutch Church, 3.

Religious freedom, 1, 8, 10-11, 29-31, 98-101, 187-88, 313-14, 478.

Religious tests, 4, 29, 30-31.

Revolutionary War, 63-75.

Reynolds, William H., 332.

Rhode Island, 1, 5, 8, 9-11, 12, 14, 37, 50, 64, 68-69, 94, 157, 200, 252-54, 256, 289-90, 304, 333-34, 369, 382, 482.

Rhode Island Chapter of the Society of Colonial Dames, 520.

Rhode Island College, 9, 155, 157.

Rhode Island Hall, 223-24, 236, 287, 371, 375, 389, 394.

Rhode Island Historical Society, 255, 328, 329, 520.

Rhode Island Hospital, 304, 328, 382, 383.

Rhode Island School of Design, 482.

Rhode Island Society for the Collegiate Education of Women, 457, 486.

Rhode Island State Normal School, 412.

Rhode Island Women's Club, 454, 456.

Richards, William, 170.

Rider Collection, 472.

Rider, Sidney S., 472.

Robbins, Ashur, 77, 91, 97, 108, 148, 239.

Robinson, Ezekiel G., 240, 301, 338, 366, 386-88, 418-26.

Robinson, Gilman P., 413.

Rochester Theological Seminary, 387, 426.

Rockefeller Hall, 470.

Rockefeller, John D., 470.

Rockefeller, John D., Jr., 471.

Rogers, William, 36, 40, 41, 79, 127, 237, 520.

Rogers, William S., 370.

Root, Elihu, 472.

Rutgers College, 3.

Salaries, 38, 58, 71, 143, 159, 177, 231-32, 259, 265, 284, 293-94, 331, 361, 369, 415, 461, 474.

Sayles, Frank A., 485.

Sayles Gymnasium, 485.

Sayles Hall, 393-94.

Sayles, William F., 393-94.

INDEX

AMERICAN EDUCATION:
ITS MEN, IDEAS, AND INSTITUTIONS
An Arno Press/New York Times Collection

Series I

Adams, Francis. **The Free School System of the United States.** 1875.

Alcott, William A. **Confessions of a School Master.** 1839.

American Unitarian Association. **From Servitude to Service.** 1905.

Bagley, William C. **Determinism in Education.** 1925.

Barnard, Henry, editor. **Memoirs of Teachers, Educators, and Promoters and Benefactors of Education, Literature, and Science.** 1861.

Bell, Sadie. **The Church, the State, and Education in Virginia.** 1930.

Belting, Paul Everett. **The Development of the Free Public High School in Illinois to 1860.** 1919.

Berkson, Isaac B. **Theories of Americanization: A Critical Study.** 1920.

Blauch, Lloyd E. **Federal Cooperation in Agricultural Extension Work, Vocational Education, and Vocational Rehabilitation.** 1935.

Bloomfield, Meyer. **Vocational Guidance of Youth.** 1911.

Brewer, Clifton Hartwell. **A History of Religious Education in the Episcopal Church to 1835.** 1924.

Brown, Elmer Ellsworth. **The Making of Our Middle Schools.** 1902.

Brumbaugh, M. G. **Life and Works of Christopher Dock.** 1908.

Burns, Reverend J. A. **The Catholic School System in the United States.** 1908.

Burns, Reverend J. A. **The Growth and Development of the Catholic School System in the United States.** 1912.

Burton, Warren. **The District School as It Was.** 1850.

Butler, Nicholas Murray, editor. **Education in the United States.** 1900.

Butler, Vera M. **Education as Revealed By New England Newspapers prior to 1850.** 1935.

Campbell, Thomas Monroe. **The Movable School Goes to the Negro Farmer.** 1936.

Carter, James G. **Essays upon Popular Education.** 1826.

Carter, James G. **Letters to the Hon. William Prescott, LL.D., on the Free Schools of New England.** 1824.

Channing, William Ellery. **Self-Culture.** 1842.

Coe, George A. **A Social Theory of Religious Education.** 1917.

Committee on Secondary School Studies. **Report of the Committee on Secondary School Studies, Appointed at the Meeting of the National Education Association.** 1893.

Counts, George S. **Dare the School Build a New Social Order?** 1932.

Counts, George S. **The Selective Character of American Secondary Education.** 1922.

Counts, George S. **The Social Composition of Boards of Education.** 1927.

Culver, Raymond B. **Horace Mann and Religion in the Massachusetts Public Schools.** 1929.

Curoe, Philip R. V. **Educational Attitudes and Policies of Organized Labor in the United States.** 1926.

Dabney, Charles William. **Universal Education in the South.** 1936.

Dearborn, Ned Harland. **The Oswego Movement in American Education.** 1925.

De Lima, Agnes. **Our Enemy the Child.** 1926.

Dewey, John. **The Educational Situation.** 1902.

Dexter, Franklin B., editor. **Documentary History of Yale University.** 1916.

Eliot, Charles William. **Educational Reform: Essays and Addresses.** 1898.

Ensign, Forest Chester. **Compulsory School Attendance and Child Labor.** 1921.

Fitzpatrick, Edward Augustus. **The Educational Views and Influence of De Witt Clinton.** 1911.

Fleming, Sanford. **Children & Puritanism.** 1933.

Flexner, Abraham. **The American College: A Criticism.** 1908.

Foerster, Norman. **The Future of the Liberal College.** 1938.

Gilman, Daniel Coit. **University Problems in the United States.** 1898.

Hall, Samuel R. **Lectures on School-Keeping.** 1829.

Hall, Stanley G. **Adolescence: Its Psychology and Its Relations to Physiology, Anthropology, Sociology, Sex, Crime, Religion, and Education.** 1905. 2 vols.

Hansen, Allen Oscar. **Early Educational Leadership in the Ohio Valley.** 1923.

Harris, William T. **Psychologic Foundations of Education.** 1899.

Harris, William T. **Report of the Committee of Fifteen on the Elementary School.** 1895.

Harveson, Mae Elizabeth. **Catharine Esther Beecher: Pioneer Educator.** 1932.

Jackson, George Leroy. **The Development of School Support in Colonial Massachusetts.** 1909.

Kandel, I. L., editor. **Twenty-five Years of American Education.** 1924.

Kemp, William Webb. **The Support of Schools in Colonial New York by the Society for the Propagation of the Gospel in Foreign Parts.** 1913.

Kilpatrick, William Heard. **The Dutch Schools of New Netherland and Colonial New York.** 1912.

Kilpatrick, William Heard. **The Educational Frontier.** 1933.

Knight, Edgar Wallace. **The Influence of Reconstruction on Education in the South.** 1913.

Le Duc, Thomas. **Piety and Intellect at Amherst College, 1865-1912.** 1946.

Maclean, John. **History of the College of New Jersey from Its Origin in 1746 to the Commencement of 1854.** 1877.

Maddox, William Arthur. **The Free School Idea in Virginia before the Civil War.** 1918.

Mann, Horace. **Lectures on Education.** 1855.

McCadden, Joseph J. **Education in Pennsylvania, 1801-1835, and Its Debt to Roberts Vaux.** 1855.

McCallum, James Dow. **Eleazar Wheelock.** 1939.

McCuskey, Dorothy. **Bronson Alcott, Teacher.** 1940.

Meiklejohn, Alexander. **The Liberal College.** 1920.

Miller, Edward Alanson. **The History of Educational Legislation in Ohio from 1803 to 1850.** 1918.

Miller, George Frederick. **The Academy System of the State of New York.** 1922.

Monroe, Will S. **History of the Pestalozzian Movement in the United States.** 1907.

Mosely Education Commission. **Reports of the Mosely Education Commission to the United States of America October-December, 1903.** 1904.

Mowry, William A. **Recollections of a New England Educator.** 1908.

Mulhern, James. **A History of Secondary Education in Pennsylvania.** 1933.

National Herbart Society. **National Herbart Society Yearbooks 1-5, 1895-1899.** 1895-1899.

Nearing, Scott. **The New Education: A Review of Progressive Educational Movements of the Day.** 1915.

Neef, Joseph. **Sketches of a Plan and Method of Education.** 1808.

Nock, Albert Jay. **The Theory of Education in the United States.** 1932.

Norton, A. O., editor. **The First State Normal School in America: The Journals of Cyrus Pierce and Mary Swift.** 1926.

Oviatt, Edwin. **The Beginnings of Yale, 1701-1726.** 1916.

Packard, Frederic Adolphus. **The Daily Public School in the United States.** 1866.

Page, David P. **Theory and Practice of Teaching.** 1848.

Parker, Francis W. **Talks on Pedagogics: An Outline of the Theory of Concentration.** 1894.

Peabody, Elizabeth Palmer. **Record of a School.** 1835.

Porter, Noah. **The American Colleges and the American Public.** 1870.

Reigart, John Franklin. **The Lancasterian System of Instruction in the Schools of New York City.** 1916.

Reilly, Daniel F. **The School Controversy (1891-1893).** 1943.

Rice, Dr. J. M. **The Public-School System of the United States.** 1893.

Rice, Dr. J. M. **Scientific Management in Education.** 1912.

Ross, Early D. **Democracy's College: The Land-Grant Movement in the Formative Stage.** 1942.

Rugg, Harold, et al. **Curriculum-Making: Past and Present.** 1926.

Rugg, Harold, et al. **The Foundations of Curriculum-Making.** 1926.

Rugg, Harold and Shumaker, Ann. **The Child-Centered School.** 1928.

Seybolt, Robert Francis. **Apprenticeship and Apprenticeship Education in Colonial New England and New York.** 1917.

Seybolt, Robert Francis. **The Private Schools of Colonial Boston.** 1935.

Seybolt, Robert Francis. **The Public Schools of Colonial Boston.** 1935.

Sheldon, Henry D. **Student Life and Customs.** 1901.

Sherrill, Lewis Joseph. **Presbyterian Parochial Schools, 1846-1870.** 1932 .

Siljestrom, P. A. **Educational Institutions of the United States.** 1853.

Small, Walter Herbert. **Early New England Schools.** 1914.

Soltes, Mordecai. **The Yiddish Press: An Americanizing Agency.** 1925.

Stewart, George, Jr. **A History of Religious Education in Connecticut to the Middle of the Nineteenth Century.** 1924.

Storr, Richard J. **The Beginnings of Graduate Education in America.** 1953.

Stout, John Elbert. **The Development of High-School Curricula in the North Central States from 1860 to 1918.** 1921.

Suzzallo, Henry. **The Rise of Local School Supervision in Massachusetts.** 1906.

Swett, John. **Public Education in California.** 1911.

Tappan, Henry P. **University Education.** 1851.

Taylor, Howard Cromwell. **The Educational Significance of the Early Federal Land Ordinances.** 1921.

Taylor, J. Orville. **The District School.** 1834.

Tewksbury, Donald G. **The Founding of American Colleges and Universities before the Civil War.** 1932.

Thorndike, Edward L. **Educational Psychology.** 1913-1914.

True, Alfred Charles. **A History of Agricultural Education in the United States, 1785-1925.** 1929.

True, Alfred Charles. **A History of Agricultural Extension Work in the United States, 1785-1923.** 1928.

Updegraff, Harlan. **The Origin of the Moving School in Massachusetts.** 1908.

Wayland, Francis. **Thoughts on the Present Collegiate System in the United States.** 1842.

Weber, Samuel Edwin. **The Charity School Movement in Colonial Pennsylvania.** 1905.

Wells, Guy Fred. **Parish Education in Colonial Virginia.** 1923.

Wickersham, J. P. **The History of Education in Pennsylvania.** 1885.

Woodward, Calvin M. **The Manual Training School.** 1887.

Woody, Thomas. **Early Quaker Education in Pennsylvania.** 1920.

Woody, Thomas. **Quaker Education in the Colony and State of New Jersey.** 1923.

Wroth, Lawrence C. **An American Bookshelf, 1755.** 1934.

Series II

Adams, Evelyn C. **American Indian Education.** 1946.

Bailey, Joseph Cannon. **Seaman A. Knapp: Schoolmaster of American Agriculture.** 1945.

Beecher, Catharine and Harriet Beecher Stowe. **The American Woman's Home.** 1869.

Benezet, Louis T. **General Education in the Progressive College.** 1943.

Boas, Louise Schutz. **Woman's Education Begins.** 1935.

Bobbitt, Franklin. **The Curriculum.** 1918.

Bode, Boyd H. **Progressive Education at the Crossroads.** 1938.

Bourne, William Oland. **History of the Public School Society of the City of New York.** 1870.

Bronson, Walter C. **The History of Brown University, 1764-1914.** 1914.

Burstall, Sara A. **The Education of Girls in the United States.** 1894.

Butts, R. Freeman. **The College Charts Its Course.** 1939.

Caldwell, Otis W. and Stuart A. Courtis. **Then & Now in Education, 1845-1923.** 1923.

Calverton, V. F. & Samuel D. Schmalhausen, editors. **The New Generation: The Intimate Problems of Modern Parents and Children.** 1930.

Charters, W. W. **Curriculum Construction.** 1923.

Childs, John L. **Education and Morals.** 1950.

Childs, John L. **Education and the Philosophy of Experimentalism.** 1931.

Clapp, Elsie Ripley. **Community Schools in Action.** 1939.

Counts, George S. **The American Road to Culture: A Social Interpretation of Education in the United States.** 1930.

Counts, George S. **School and Society in Chicago.** 1928.

Finegan, Thomas E. **Free Schools.** 1921.

Fletcher, Robert Samuel. **A History of Oberlin College.** 1943.

Grattan, C. Hartley. **In Quest of Knowledge: A Historical Perspective on Adult Education.** 1955.

Hartman, Gertrude & Ann Shumaker, editors. **Creative Expression.** 1932.

Kandel, I. L. **The Cult of Uncertainty.** 1943.

Kandel, I. L. **Examinations and Their Substitutes in the United States.** 1936.

Kilpatrick, William Heard. **Education for a Changing Civilization.** 1926.

Kilpatrick, William Heard. **Foundations of Method.** 1925.

Kilpatrick, William Heard. **The Montessori System Examined.** 1914.

Lang, Ossian H., editor. **Educational Creeds of the Nineteenth Century.** 1898.

Learned, William S. **The Quality of the Educational Process in the United States and in Europe.** 1927.

Meiklejohn, Alexander. **The Experimental College.** 1932.

Middlekauff, Robert. **Ancients and Axioms: Secondary Education in Eighteenth-Century New England.** 1963.

Norwood, William Frederick. **Medical Education in the United States Before the Civil War.** 1944.

Parsons, Elsie W. Clews. **Educational Legislation and Administration of the Colonial Governments.** 1899.

Perry, Charles M. **Henry Philip Tappan: Philosopher and University President.** 1933.

Pierce, Bessie Louise. **Civic Attitudes in American School Textbooks.** 1930.

Rice, Edwin Wilbur. **The Sunday-School Movement (1780-1917) and the American Sunday-School Union (1817-1917).** 1917.

Robinson, James Harvey. **The Humanizing of Knowledge.** 1924.

Ryan, W. Carson. **Studies in Early Graduate Education.** 1939.

Seybolt, Robert Francis. **The Evening School in Colonial America.** 1925.

Seybolt, Robert Francis. **Source Studies in American Colonial Education.** 1925.

Todd, Lewis Paul. **Wartime Relations of the Federal Government and the Public Schools, 1917-1918.** 1945.

Vandewalker, Nina C. **The Kindergarten in American Education.** 1908.

Ward, Florence Elizabeth. **The Montessori Method and the American School.** 1913.

West, Andrew Fleming. **Short Papers on American Liberal Education.** 1907.

Wright, Marion M. Thompson. **The Education of Negroes in New Jersey.** 1941.

Supplement

The Social Frontier (Frontiers of Democracy). Vols. 1-10, 1934-1943.

DUE

Randall Library – UNCW
LD638 .B7 1971   NXWW
Bronson / The history of Brown University, 1764–19

304900144566%